The Aga Khan
Historic Cities Programme

STRATEGIES FOR
URBAN REGENERATION

The Aga Khan Historic Cities Programme

STRATEGIES FOR URBAN REGENERATION

Edited by Philip Jodidio

PRESTEL

Munich · London · New York

Contents

Introduction

Approach and Methodology

Case Studies

Protecting the Past, Inspiring the Future

HIS HIGHNESS THE AGA KHAN

More than fifty years ago, when I became the Imam of the Ismaili Muslim community, I discovered that ignorance or indifference about other cultures, the drive to standardize cultures through imposed external models, or sometimes open aggression, together with the desire to 'modernize' the built environment, had resulted in the irreparable loss of important cultural characteristics in developing countries, particularly those in the Muslim world. The highly distinctive cultural features of those societies and countries were being eroded and new environments created which were dysfunctional. The situation required a broad-based response that would find support amongst the communities and nations concerned. Culture, far from being a luxury, needed to be recognized as an essential factor for any society to prosper.

With so many social and economic needs still unmet around the world, why is culture so important? Conventional thinking suggests that there is a sequence that must be followed in every instance – first addressing humanitarian and social needs, then economic challenges and finally, perhaps, culture. We have found, however, that the equation is not so simple. Culture itself can be the catalyst for social and economic development.

The notion of cultural heritage as an asset rather than a drain on resources remains a new one in many parts of the world. The sad result is that many important buildings and monuments – the physical patrimony of mankind – have already succumbed or are in a precarious state. This is especially true in the Muslim world. A third of the world's heritage sites are in the Muslim world, and many of them are suffering from serious decay. Budgets for maintenance and repair of cultural heritage have declined or have been cut drastically. Traditional settlements have been abandoned in favour of modern construction, bringing its own economic and social problems.

Improving the Quality of Life

When I created the Aga Khan Award for Architecture, I discovered that the cultural dimension of the Islamic world was an extraordinarily powerful trampoline for development. It became apparent that by developing patrimonial sites one could improve the quality of life of the people who live in and near them. The populations of these historic areas are often the poorest in the countries concerned. Here, by acting in the realm of culture, it was actually possible to improve the quality of life for the poorest of the poor. By giving its true value back to culture, new forms of productivity, a new form of socio-economic development, come into being.

My effort to defend the value of culture, through the Aga Khan Development Network, and specifically through its dedicated agency, the Aga Khan Trust for Culture, focuses its activities in four main areas: the Aga Khan Historic Cities Programme; the Aga Khan Award for Architecture; the Aga Khan Music Initiative; and Museum Projects. These activities, which are themselves subdivided into a number of subsidiary programmes in many countries, obey four key principles. Firstly, they seek to increase the beneficiaries' independence, to involve local communities, and to secure the support of public and private partners. Secondly, they are carried out in poor environments where there are considerable centrifugal, sometimes even conflicting, forces at play. Thirdly, they are designed to have maximum beneficial impact on the economies of the populations involved and their quality of life in the broadest sense of the term. Finally, they are planned in the long term, over a period of up to twenty-five years, enabling them to become self-sufficient both financially as well as in terms of human resources.

The residents of historic cities and districts know a great deal about their own cultures, but in many ways these remain at the periphery of general knowledge elsewhere. Through initiatives such as the Aga Khan Award for Architecture and the Historic Cities Programme, we have also sought to disseminate the knowledge that these cultures had developed their own traditions of architecture and that these were worthy of continuity. The fact that we have been able to rebuild pride in these cultures, which are not only cultures of the past, but of today and tomorrow as well, brings a totally different psychological attitude to the processes of change.

His Highness the Aga Khan tours the
rubbish-strewn site of the future Azhar Park
in Cairo in the early 1990s, before the
Historic Wall was uncovered and before
monument restoration work was begun in
the adjacent district of Darb al-Ahmar.

Developing Resources for Sustainability

One way that revitalized historic areas can become economically self-sustained is, of
course, through the development of tourism. In places like Cairo, Aleppo and Lahore,
tourists spend days viewing cultural monuments. Many such tourists would be attracted
by the combination of a well-maintained cultural heritage and a natural environment that
astounds even the most jaded traveller. These visitors are the kind most favoured by
tourism development organizations around the world – engaged travellers who want to
experience culture first hand rather than be aloof from it. They do not need a single
world-famous monument like the Pyramids to attract them; they are equally delighted by
the existence of a vibrant local culture. What is important is a density of well-maintained
landmark buildings and the infrastructure to accommodate and transport visitors. In an
era of mass tourism, these visitors are not searching for the package tour, but for a
unique and authentic cultural experience. We must plan carefully for the reuse of restored
or conserved buildings. A well-executed conservation plan transcends mere physical
restoration to address long-term productive reuse and sustainability. We must get this
equation right at the start.

A clear emphasis has been placed by our planners on sustainability. It has always
been clear that a strong financial base must be created in order to maintain the accomplishments of today. A project must be compatible with the long-term welfare of its
neighbourhood and community. For any important work of restoration to survive and to

thrive into the longer range future, it must contribute to the well-being of those who live in its presence – so that they in turn will have reason to safeguard its enduring viability. For this reason, the Historic Cities Programme is not only concerned with saving buildings or historic districts for future generations. It seeks to go beyond restoration and to create mechanisms that contribute to real, measurable improvement in the quality of life in rural and urban areas, also enabling their inhabitants thereby to look after their cultural assets. This is the goal of the multi-programme capacity-building strategies which the Aga Khan Development Network deploys to help the residents of historic cities or areas, whether this be the Silk Road, or Kabul and Herat in Afghanistan, Aleppo in Syria, Mopti in Mali, or Zanzibar, or Cairo, the city that my forefathers, the Fatimid Imam-Caliphs of Egypt, founded more than a thousand years ago. In all such places, rehabilitation of cultural heritage is supported by the work of the Aga Khan Development Network agencies specializing in micro-finance, health, education, water and sanitation, and promotion of economic enterprise.

Our experience in situations as diverse as remote parts of northern Pakistan, to Delhi, Zanzibar and Central Cairo, is that the restoration of historic communities and important cultural assets provides a catalyst for economic development. The restoration activity is a source of direct employment for workers and skilled craftsmen, many of whom live in adjacent neighbourhoods. The refurbished facilities themselves often become an attraction for tourists as well as fulfilling their role as community centres, generating more opportunity. And as the residents of surrounding areas find themselves with new sources of income, they spend some of it improving their own homes and neighbourhoods. These are the pragmatic reasons for revitalizing a nation's cultural assets. But equally, and perhaps more importantly, these activities restore and preserve the historic identity of Muslim societies, whose rich pluralist heritage has suffered extraordinary stresses in recent decades. It is also a heritage for the world to cherish.

The underpinning objective is to replace the risk of economic and social collapse with a new capacity, built on informed consent and knowledge capable of sustaining and guiding the transition from poverty to an improved quality of life based on choice and opportunity. Another important step in the process is to promote awareness and understanding of appropriate technologies and solutions. The Muslim world is multicultural, diverse in geography, terrain and climate and it exhibits extremes of wealth and poverty. This diversity requires us to be sensitive not only to local needs, but to local capacity and resources available to meet those needs.

The Heritage of Respect

Contrary to the image sometimes given in the press, the Qur'anic ideal is one of a vibrant humanity, rich in pluralism, and yet constituting a single human community. This heritage of respect for differences attaches value to diversity, pluralism and positive and productive relationships between different segments of society. The Holy Qur'an teaches us that mankind holds Allah's creation of the world in trust, with the duty to leave the physical environment better than they found it.

In Islam, the Holy Qur'an offers explicit direction to share resources beyond one's requirements, and to care for the poor and those in need. The injunction to service is the ethical underpinning of the work of the Aga Khan Development

Network. It drives its efforts to build the intellectual capital and institutions needed to address the problems of our world today. Indeed, the Qur'an, the Hadith, the sayings of Hazrat Ali, and many scholarly sources also make references to the forms and purposes of philanthropy. Human dignity – restoring it, and sustaining it – is a central theme. Enabling individuals to recover and maintain their dignity as befitting their status as Allah's greatest creation is one of the main reasons for charitable action.

There is dignity in the individual's ability to manage his or her destiny. That being the case, the best of charity, in Islamic terms, can go beyond material support alone. It can take the form of human or professional support, such as the provision of education for those otherwise unable to obtain it, or the sharing of knowledge to help marginalized individuals build different and better futures for themselves. Thus conceived, charity is not limited to a one-time material gift, but can be seen as a continuum of support in a time-frame that can extend to years. This means that multi-year support for institutions that enable individuals to achieve dignity by becoming self-sustainable holds a special place amongst the many forms of charity in the eyes of Islam.

A Vision of a Pluralistic Society

In the troubled times in which we live, it is important to remember, and honour, a vision of a pluralistic society. Tolerance, openness and understanding towards other peoples' cultures, social structures, values and faiths are now essential to the very survival of an interdependent world. Pluralism is no longer simply an asset or a prerequisite for progress and development, it is vital to our existence. Never perhaps more so than at the present time must we renew with vigour our creative engagement in revitalizing shared heritage through collaborative ventures.

The same view as the previous photograph. Now, in 2011, the Park has matured into one of Cairo's major attractions, the Historic Wall has undergone thorough conservation, monuments in Darb al-Ahmar have been restored and socio-economic programmes are in place.

The Future of Historic Cities

LUIS MONREAL

Haussmann's modernization programme
in Paris began in 1852 and involved
the destruction of many narrow medieval
streets in favour of broad boulevards.

Most historic cities in the Muslim world are witness to the ravages of human misery. They are often the first stop for transient populations making the leap from rural habitats to urban life. They have a rich cultural heritage but house communities that live in poverty.

What can be done to reverse such situations without making historic cities into museums, or subjecting them to a gentrification process that leads to the replacement of existing populations and activities? What new strategies can be applied to ensure a future for historic cities? What new methodologies, means and resources are required?

This is what this book is about. It intends to provide answers to some of these questions – answers based on the experience gained by the Historic Cities Programme (HCP) of the Aga Khan Trust for Culture (AKTC) during the past ten years.

The first premise for the survival of historic cities as we know them today is to give their inhabitants a real chance to improve their living standards and to break free from the constraints of poverty. The gradual development of a middle class, able to play a role in the collective effort to maintain a city's assets, its domestic and monumental architecture, infrastructure and public services, is key to this strategy. Traditional approaches to the conservation of a city's cultural heritage that do not address the social and economic dimensions of the problem are insufficient to ensure the survival of historic settlements that are irreplaceable witnesses to the development of human civilization.

At present, 242 cities are registered on the UNESCO World Heritage List. These historic cities naturally evolved over time according to specific geographic and socio-economic conditions. As the Getty Conservation Institute has made clear: "There is little question that exponential growth and uncontrolled changes put the integrity and authenticity of historic cities and urban settlements, and the values that are embedded in them, at risk. At a time of rapid urbanization and globalization, the conservation of historic cities is an urgent and difficult challenge." According to the Getty Conservation Institute, the task at hand extends beyond the conservation of architecture and the landscape. It requires the careful management of change through the adaptation of historic buildings and urban fabric to new forms of living, the creation of income and training opportunities, and real consideration for the intangible heritage that contributes to the city's cultural significance.[1]

Urban planning, as such, existed in the distant past in the Indus Valley, China and the Roman Empire, but such concepts of order gave way to organic growth in medieval Europe, for instance. It was not until the eighteenth century and the thought espoused in Denis Diderot's *Encyclopédie* (1751–72) that urban planning in a modern sense emerged. A more rational order could be imposed by demolishing large swathes of the cities that had evolved by accretion over the centuries, or so it was thought. The most stunning example of this approach is George-Eugène Haussmann's modernization of Paris, which began in 1852. Many of the narrow medieval streets of Paris were swept away in favour of

large boulevards for reasons of hygiene, traffic flow and, perhaps above all, security. A corollary of the broad 'modernization' of cities such as Paris was that districts unaffected by these major public works programmes were more obviously the subject of conservation efforts. The idea that the historic city could and should coexist with the modernity imposed by urban planning came to the fore, at least where some old structures were left standing.

New Delhi was the idea of the British, whose intention was to impose imperial control. The Rajpath, above, is the ceremonial boulevard in the design undertaken by talented architect Edwin Lutyens.

Colonial Rule and the Stamp of Authority

The use of urban planning to impose authority is, in fact, an essential element in the development of numerous cities under colonial rule. Thus, in both India and Morocco, colonial authorities decided to create their own capitals, leaving old cities outside the economic mainstream. Subsequent to the French invasion of Morocco in 1912, for example, General Hubert Lyautey decided to move the country's capital from Fez to Rabat, because of the rebellious population in Fez, and, beginning in 1913, the architect Henri Prost designed Rabat's new district, the Ville Nouvelle. Although King Mohammed V decided in 1956 to keep the capital in Rabat, strong forces obviously played on these cities as a result of colonial intervention. New Delhi, with its wide boulevards, was the idea of the English occupiers and the work of the talented architect Edwin Lutyens. Designed and built between 1912 and 1931, New Delhi replaced Calcutta as the capital of India. New Delhi was built to the south of the Old City. The point here was to impose British control through the creation of a new city and, above all, through what the architectural historian Henry-Russell Hitchcock has called a resort to a "Roman scale".[2] The British again intervened in a historic city in Pakistan, where AKTC has ongoing projects. The twenty-hectare Lahore Fort is set in the north-western corner of the Walled City of

Lahore. Though it was essentially built during the reign of the Mughal emperor Akbar (1556–1605), the origins of the Fort go back far before the sixteenth century. The English occupied the city in 1846 and turned over the Fort to the local Department of Archaeology in 1927, but not before they had accomplished one symbolic act that speaks volumes about the impact of colonialism on the heritage of historic cities. The occupiers demolished the southern section of the walls, creating a stepped structure that effectively obviated the walled nature of Lahore itself, the fruit of centuries of development and civilization. These wounds, in an almost literal sense, allowed historic cities to be drained of part of their substance, a scenario that in the worst cases leads to the creation of ghettos of a different sort than those in the new world.

The Historic Cities Programme (HCP)

AKTC, through its Historic Cities Programme, seeks to confront the very real and substantial problems faced by historic cities, in particular in the Muslim world. Although European countries, for example, have also faced these issues in the twentieth century, the process of decolonization and urbanization in the Muslim world has made many problems more acute in the period since World War II. Various multilateral initiatives have been aimed at ameliorating the situation of historic cities, beyond the efforts of individual governments or municipalities, but, until the programmes of AKTC came to their maturity in recent years, few have attempted to deal with the root causes of difficulties. The restoration of monuments, which in itself has proven to be of limited value in terms of sustainability, is but one part of the approach of AKTC. The goal is to create a global approach, which can be used with appropriate variations in many parts of the world.

International Organizations Come to the Fore

Interest in architectural heritage, particularly in historic cities, was not a matter of national concern until the twentieth century. Many European countries took national initiatives to protect their own monuments beginning in the late nineteenth century, and associations with such goals also came forward. In the developing world and former colonial areas, the need to build on national traditions to form a new identity also encouraged drives to preserve and restore historic monuments and districts.[3] A more international approach did not develop until after World War I with the League of Nations and more significantly after World War II with the United Nations and UNESCO. The idea that cultural heritage is not just the property of one nation but of all of humanity emerged.

Questions have been raised for some time about the structures and policies developed by UNESCO. The Dutch sociologist Emanuel de Kadt wrote:

"Since 1970 a series of UNESCO-sponsored Intergovernmental Conferences on Cultural Policies has stressed the importance of cultural development as an essential component of the general development of countries. Even so, the cultural and non-material aspects of development are still often neglected by those responsible for making the crucial policy decisions both nationally and internationally. Growth alone may not suffice to overcome poverty within a reasonable time, and the distribution of the material benefits of development among the poorest countries and the poorest population groups within individual countries requires special attention. From arguments about the general effects of different development strategies on distribution of income, attention has come to rest on the staggering number of people, more than 900 million of them, living in absolute poverty. More than ever before, the development community is searching for means that will enable the poor to provide for their basic needs through more productive work, more widely available social services, and increased participation in political decision making. It needs to be considered whether the deliberate and large-scale development of tourism, conceived as a major net earner of foreign exchange, leads to results."[4]

Coming to the Aid of the Ultra Poor

Having created the Aga Khan Award for Architecture in the late 1970s, His Highness the Aga Khan became increasingly preoccupied by the state of historic cities in the Muslim world, a concern that he expressed publicly in his opening speech at the Ninth Seminar in the series 'Architectural Transformations in the Islamic Word' of the Aga Khan Award for Architecture. On 11 November 1984, he stated: "When the World Heritage Convention listed 136 sites as being of major importance to the heritage of mankind, no less than one third were monuments of Islamic culture." For the Aga Khan, it was clear that this remarkable concentration of cultural history was not receiving the sort of economic, social and academic support it deserved. The historic cities of the Islamic world, and no doubt others, were noted to be a concentration most often of the ultra poor in urban environments and, because of this, there was not only a social problem that had to be addressed, but also these ultra poor, due to their poverty, were further degrading these historic cities. He concluded that it was necessary for the Islamic world to try to harness new resources to protect these historic cities, and to bring relief to the marginalized people living within them at a time when there was no agency that was committed to these goals.

Once work had begun on Azhar Park in Cairo, HCP turned its focus on Darb al-Ahmar, the impoverished neighbouring district. On Darb Shoughlan, urban decay and lack of efficient refuse collection services are evident.

Top, an aerial view of Azhar Park in Cairo and the paved promenade along the Historic Wall.

Middle, an early 19th-century lithograph by David Roberts showing what is now the southern boundary of Azhar Park in Cairo.

Bottom, the Historic Wall on the edge of Azhar Park and Darb al-Ahmar, now visible following excavation and restoration.

AKTC's involvement in Egypt began with the Aga Khan's decision to donate a park to the citizens of Cairo, subsequent to an Aga Khan Award for Architecture international seminar entitled 'The Expanding Metropolis' in Cairo in 1984. Soon thereafter a thirty-hectare site on al-Darassa was selected, because of its enormous potential as a 'lung' at the very centre of the historic agglomeration. This hilly site is surrounded by the most significant historic districts of Islamic Cairo, all of which are major destinations for visitors to the city. The topography of the site, formed by debris accumulated over centuries, now provides elevated viewpoints dominating the city and offers a spectacular 360° panorama over the townscape of Historic Cairo.

Having begun the project with the clear intention of creating a new park for Cairo (today's Azhar Park), the Aga Khan and his organizations became increasingly involved in the surrounding district. The work can be said to have developed in a pragmatic way, progressing from the idea of the Park to the discovery of the rather well preserved remains of the Historic Wall of the Old City and going quite naturally from there into the neighbouring district of Darb al-Ahmar. Although it was not originally part of AKTC's scheme for Azhar Park, it became apparent during the course of the work that an effort to excavate and renovate at least part of the fortified walls would make good sense. A length of approximately 1500 metres from Bab al-Wazir to al-Azhar Street, forming the boundary between the Darb al-Ahmar district and the Park, was thus completely unearthed and restored.

A substantial effort has been made to reintegrate monuments as complex as the long-buried Historic Wall into the life of the community. This was done not only by opening connections into the new Azhar Park, but also by renewing housing and monuments that abut the Wall or even sit partially on top of it at one point. And rather than seeking to move residents and local workshops to some distant new location, this project has taken on the training of local craftsmen in the traditional arts of carpentry and stonework that they no longer fully master. Rather than being considered as a barrier between Darb al-Ahmar and the new Park, the Historic Wall has been reintegrated as a living part of the city, and a true sense of historic continuity has been created between Islamic Cairo's past and its future.

In his introduction to the book *Cairo: Revitalising a Historic Metropolis*, published in 2004 on the occasion of the opening of Azhar Park, His Highness the Aga Khan wrote:

"We stand today confronted with starkly different visions of the future of historic cities. At a time when our heritage, the anchor of our identity and source of inspiration, is being threatened with destruction, by war and environmental degradation, by the inexorable demographic and economic pressures of exploding urban growth, or by simple neglect, there can be no doubt that it is time to act. Will we allow the wealth that is the past to be swept away, or will we assume our responsibility to defend what remains of the irreplaceable fabric of history? My answer is clear. One of our most urgent priorities must be to value and protect what is greatest in our common heritage. Breathing new life into the legacy of the past demands a creativity, tolerance, and understanding beyond the ordinary."[5]

The generous impulse of His Highness the Aga Khan to donate a Park to the city of Cairo, which at the time had very little green space, has led in some unexpected ways to the creation of the model now being employed by HCP to intervene in historic cities. Once the idea of the Park was on the table, the Aga Khan quite naturally asked himself how this new facility could be maintained. It also became apparent that giving a Park located near one of the poorest areas in Cairo would not be enough: something had to be done for the Darb al-Ahmar district. The step into the socio-economic situation of the neighbourhood became evident.

Azhar Park has become a highly popular destination for Cairenes. Here, the neighbourhood of Darb al-Ahmar provides a backdrop for a gathering of young people.

Improving Standards of Living

An ongoing analysis of the situation in Darb al-Ahmar demonstrates the impact of AKTC's intervention. Declared household incomes doubled between 2003 and 2009.[6] Although high levels of inflation nullified most of the gains that were made, there was still a substantial net increase in income during this period. This was manifested, amongst other elements, in reduced expenditure on food items as a percentage of the household budget. In late 2003 fifty-six per cent of the households surveyed reported using more than half of their income for the procurement of food items, which is an important indicator of poverty. Five years later, in early 2009, when the same households were again surveyed, fifty-one per cent reported spending more than half of their income on food. This five per cent gain was made in spite of the dramatic 2008 price increases of basic food commodities, following the removal of most subsidies. During the same period of 2003 to 2009, home ownership of those interviewed in HCP's project area increased from four to eleven per cent, while crowding (expressed as the number of people in the household divided by the total number of rooms) was reduced from 2.75 to 1.73.

It should be noted that from the first year of its operation in 2005, the Park generated an operating surplus, which grew to $1.3 million in 2009, and a total of two million visitors in that year.[7] In six years of operation, over ten million people have visited the Park. Taking into account its personnel and maintenance, the Park generates a financial surplus every year. The share of the surplus that is earned by AKTC is directly reinvested in Darb al-Ahmar.

Applying Lessons Learned in Cairo

Overpopulation, poverty and the physical decay of historic cities remain very much a part of the present in the Muslim world and beyond. Aggravated by urbanization or rampant speculative construction, these remnants of culture and civilization are threatened today as they never have been before. Despite the significant efforts of such organizations as

Left, commercial encroachments needed
to be cleared away during the restoration
by AKTC of the Chahar Suq Cistern in
Herat, seen here in the background of
a busy street scene.

Middle, a view at dusk along the central
axis and water channel to Humayun's Tomb
in Delhi.

Right, the restored facade of the
Old Customs House on the Zanzibar
seafront.

UNESCO, neither lists of worthy monuments nor a reliance on foreign visitors are sufficient
to tackle these problems at the root and to provide a sustainable alternative. Beginning
with a pragmatic series of decisions taken in part in the context of the development of
Azhar Park, AKTC and its Historic Cities Programme have developed a methodology and
an expertise that is being put to use in other projects. The work in Cairo clearly underpins
the methodology and approach of AKTC in other locations, but each set of circumstances
calls for a different approach. The work of the Trust is forward-looking and dwells little on
implicit critique of other systems. The methodology developed in the course of AKTC's
projects in Cairo, although somewhat pragmatic in its origin, points the way to a more
efficient and sustainable approach to the historic city than any practiced before. Indeed,
the process was launched again, and the lessons learned in Cairo were applied, in cities
such as Aleppo, Kabul, Herat, Lahore, Delhi and Stone Town (Zanzibar).

Essential Partnerships

It is in the unique context of Cairo that HCP first developed the use of a 'Public-Private
Partnership Agreement' (PPP), as the juridical basis for a complex project involving multiple
inputs and partners. The PPP is a useful tool to foster collaboration between stakeholders.
It allows the coordination of various competencies and inputs to a project, and helps to
structure the post-construction management and operations. In this scenario, the public
sector can offer regulatory oversight, administrative support and investment in infrastructure. The private sector can offer project management, coordination of the multiple stakeholders involved and mechanisms to bring in third-party funding through grant-making
bodies or loans. In the case of multi-input projects where HCP partners with sister agencies of the Aga Khan Development Network (AKDN), such as the Aga Khan Foundation
(AKF) and the Aga Khan Agency for Microfinance (AKAM) in the realm of health, education
and poverty alleviation, the PPP is essential for a long-term vision of development. In the
case of HCP, the mandate is to create financially self-sustainable projects in the realm of
parks that are income-generating endeavours in which surpluses are reinvested in the
project. In order to facilitate these enterprises, a legal framework with government partners
and donors, such as the World Monuments Fund or the World Bank, are essential for
AKTC, which is a non-profit entity.

The PPP system, which has emerged from the engagement of HCP in numerous projects, is one aspect of an overall commitment to create confidence in communities, where the often marginalized, poor inhabitants are initially not prepared to believe that something positive can occur in their lives. Their confidence may be won by implementing projects as quickly as possible, and offering some basic infrastructure improvements that will have an immediate positive impact on the daily lives of inhabitants. Some of these actions are the creation of associations of groups of common interest and empowering them; the establishment of vocational training and employment programmes; the development of opportunities for micro-finance to small merchants to spur economic opportunities; and providing technical assistance to populations in the form of housing, water and sanitation programmes.

The idea of the 'Public-Private Partnership' agreement is not yet common in the cultural sector; it is often not part of the existing legal framework in many countries, and it remains difficult to involve authorities in a project while still seeking to manage work in an autonomous manner. Where HCP has utilized the PPP model for cultural projects, in places like Egypt, India and Syria, a legal precedent has been set that could open the door for future investment in cultural assets by international organizations. However, it is clear that the public sector alone cannot regulate, legislate, establish norms and provide infrastructure, all of which are necessary for Area Development Projects (ADPs). The Historic Cities Programme has also partnered in a meaningful way with other organizations. Though essential to gaining the critical mass necessary in some instances, such partnerships may give rise to increased difficulties related to shifting political priorities, or complex

Above, Azhar Park in Cairo looks over the district of Darb al-Ahmar, where AKTC's intervention is having a significant impact through socio-economic activities and historic monument restoration.

Below, residents used all available spaces for rubbish. AKTC is forming partnerships in the community and with waste-disposal organizations to deal with rubbish removal.

Khorog City Park in Tajikistan, located in
a bend of the Gunt River in the heart of the
steep and barren mountain range of the
Pamirs, provides an enhanced recreational
facility for the entire city.

reporting and grant management structures. On the whole however, HCP has created a system where local populations, public authorities and other like-minded organizations have been shown to be able to work together for the common good. Close collaboration with local authorities, often rendered operative through a PPP agreement, technical expertise with presence on the ground and, above all, a broad-based approach with reference to economic sustainability and socio-economic input characterize HCP initiatives.

Influencing Urban Development

In Khorog (Tajikistan), AKTC and HCP have been called on to work on the urban planning of the city, acting as a technical agency in collaboration with the government. The truth is that many administrations in the developing world still view historic cities as a necessary evil, and are tempted to deal with them much like Haussmann did in Paris in the nineteenth century, only now using bulldozers. HCP's interventions seek to demonstrate that urban planning is particularly necessary in historic cities in order to enhance existing assets and to improve environmental quality. They are not closed to the value of modern urbanism, quite the contrary. If there is a new direction that the Programme may take, it is in terms of trying to influence the larger scale of urban planning in historic cities. By carrying out a few demonstrative projects in an approach that might be likened to acupuncture, HCP can establish the feasibility of its approach and attract the larger resources of organizations such as the World Bank or the European Community, for example.

The Best Way to Honour the Past Is to Seize the Future

What are the future prospects of HCP's approach to the rehabilitation, in material and social terms, of historic cities? The current work of the Programme gives some hint of a response. In 2007, AKTC joined the Government of the Punjab and the World Bank in support of a project for the regeneration, renewal and conservation of Lahore's Walled City. Here, all of the tools developed by HCP are being brought to bear: the involvement of the public sector, association with other competent organizations and, above all, the sense that local populations will be actively involved in the ongoing work for the sake of the improvement of their lives. In Lahore, there is a kind of poetic justice in this initiative, a sign that historic cities in the Muslim world have come a long way since colonial powers did their utmost to stamp these unique sites with their own cultural, economic and political imprint. This and other projects are explored in detail in this volume, together with the methodology and resources employed to develop a new vision of the future of historic cities.

This is by no means an exercise of self-satisfaction or a declaration of victory. The forces at work in the movement of populations and the almost inexorable degradation of historic areas associated with the onslaught of a certain vision of modernity are stronger than ever, and not likely to reverse in the foreseeable future. Rather, more modestly, HCP's initiatives seek to offer tools and examples that others can seize on, and to affirm

the ongoing value of what has come before, even in a thoroughly modern context. These efforts advance in the spirit instilled in the Programme by His Highness the Aga Khan, "remembering always the Qur'anic commandment that humankind must take responsibility for shaping and reshaping our earthly environment, employing Allah's gifts of time and talent as good stewards of His Creation."[8] There is an urgent need to combine a heightened respect for the traditions of the past with an understanding of what exists and what may come. "The best way to honour the past," states His Highness the Aga Khan, "is to seize the future."[9]

In the Delhi Gate bazaar of the Walled City of Lahore, a whirl of activity at the Chitta Gate, the entrance to the Wazir Khan Chowk.

1   'Historic Cities and Urban Settlements Initiative Project Objectives', at http://www.getty.edu/conservation/field_projects/ historic/ accessed on 26 November 2010.
2   Henry-Russell Hitchcock, *Architecture: Nineteenth and Twentieth Centuries*, Penguin Books, Baltimore, 1958: "Not since L'Enfant laid out Washington had a fiat city of such amplitude and grandeur been conceived, much less even partly executed. The Viceroy's House, finally finished in 1931, is official residence, centre of administration, and focus of the whole scheme – a *tour de force* for which, from the Queen Anne, the Neo-Georgian, and the Palladian, Lutyens lifted his sights to a Roman scale. The result is grand and broad, adapted to the climate, and even reminiscent of the Indian architectural past in some of its forms and features."
3   Luis Monreal, *Estrategias Internacionales para la Conservación del Patrimonio Cultural, 1945-1995*, Reial Acadèmia Catalana de Belles Arts de Sant Jordi, Barcelona, 1996.
4   Emanuel de Kadt, quoted in an abridged version of his introduction to *Tourism: Passport to Development?* (Oxford University Press, 1979), *The UNESCO Courier*, February 1981.
5   His Highness the Aga Khan, in *Cairo: Revitalising a Historic Metropolis*, edited by Stefano Bianca and Philip Jodidio, AKTC, Umberto Allemandi & C., Turin, 2004.
6   Data from the '2003 Darb al-Ahmar Baseline Survey' and the '2009 Post-Implementation Survey'. Both surveys were carried out by Dr Dina K. Shehayeb, of the Institute of Architecture and Housing of the Housing and Building National Research Centre (HBRC) in Cairo, Egypt.
7   Data collected by Aga Khan Cultural Services-Egypt (AKCS-E):

	2005	2006	2007	2008	2009
Total park visitors	807,000	1,073000	1,315,000	1,820,000	2,000,000
Foreign visitors	24,900 (3%)	54,730 (5%)	104,000 (7%)	147,000 (8%)	160,000 (8%)
Total sales (USD)	$2.7 million	$3.8 million	$4.8 million	$5.2 million	$5.7 million
Surplus (USD)	$0.4 million	$0.6 million	$1.1 million	$1.2 million	$1.3 million

8   His Highness the Aga Khan, Aga Khan Award for Architecture, Doha, Qatar, 24 November 2010.
9   Ibid.

APPROACH AND METHODOLOGY

Urban Regeneration

CAMERON RASHTI

Urban planning has given rise in the recent past to the concept of urban regeneration as a process of change. It has become clear that there are hidden assets in historic cities. Defining physical action zones in historic cities, determining the needs of historic settlements and sites, and setting the role of municipalities, planners, communities and investors are all keys to the urban and physical rehabilitation choices that are being made today.

Overview

An overview of urban rehabilitation, in the manner in which the Historic Cities Programme (HCP) engages in this broad-based initiative to enhance the inherited urban environment in historic settlements, requires a brief summary of factors that have been influential during the last decades. Urban development worldwide has followed an irregular trajectory that has included disdain for the past in the early twentieth century, coupled with an almost unrestricted faith in industrialization and modernity. Dense cities (particularly districts with organic layouts) were not in favour,[1] and leading planners of the time[2] proposed that urban growth be based on a quasi-suburban model, often based on the model of the garden city. Bipolar decisions grounded on solutions either replicating the known past or sheer novelty in confronting the unknown future have given rise to urban environments that are difficult to read visually and, more critically, difficult to reside in.

Urban planning entered a period characterized by the abandonment or neglect of historic cities and their cores and the development of abstract, often radial central plans, with utopian underpinnings. In the first half of the twentieth century, regional planning[3] enlarged the area of inquiry, bringing with it critical thinking on the topics of scale, hierarchy, access and environmental systems. In the process, fascination with regional scale prepared the ground for new towns that sometimes bypassed existing settlements altogether. The legacies of this movement have been numerous. Planners in the 1950s and 1960s were mesmerized by the new city movement (cities such as Brasilia, Canberra, Islamabad and Chandigarh being prime examples) with frequent reliance on the Corbusian super-block and open squares dominated by the automobile as regulating elements.[4]

In the second half of the twentieth century, in contrast to this brave new world of urban planning, a new awareness of finite resources began to make itself felt. It became apparent that a pattern of expanding environmental abuse and intensive land development or transformation, coupled with the pressure of increasing urban density, had undermined the equilibriums so highly valued in sustainable historic settlements.

More recently, while urban expansion in both controlled and uncontrolled form has continued at a rapid pace in many emerging economies, in the industrialized 'North' the cumulative inventory of urban fabric and infrastructure have been increasingly seen to

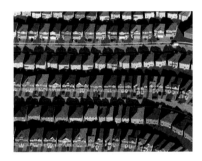

Urban development worldwide had been dominated by a disdain for the past in favour of formal quasi-suburban models, illustrated here in a housing development.

Opposite page:
By contrast, the Khayrbek complex in Cairo, restored by AKTC, is located in a busy and diverse, dense urban fabric.

Left, AKTC undertook a five-year restoration and rehabilitation effort in historic Mostar, Bosnia-Herzegovina.

Right, since 2008, as a result of building restoration and social interventions, student enrolment at the Municipal Corporation of Delhi School in Nizamuddin Basti has increased by more than one third and broadened to include various socio-economic groups.

represent a collective asset. Even when under private ownership, such assets have been understood to be extremely valuable, costly to remove and historically redolent with cultural and anthropological meaning. Existing cities have had to 'make do' with whole new districts[5] created on their edges while emerging economies plotted new central business districts, typically endowed with mid- and high-rise blocks. In the last quarter of the twentieth century, reassessment of planning practices became commonplace. It dawned on many urban planning and design professionals that what they could point to as good practice was modest in comparison to the many problem areas of urban reality that they could neither confidently handle nor readily address. The discourse shifted in the process from urban planning to urban regeneration or redevelopment.[6]

The simultaneity of urban development and decay, in all its phases across the globe, highlighted starkly by modern communications and travel, has created a confusing situation for urban planners and redevelopment specialists. When facing an urban district or area in decline, what are the appropriate responses and remedial actions? There are a variety of considered approaches, amongst them: wholesale demolition and reconstruction; abandonment and construction of new centres elsewhere (mono-industrial business centres, suburbs, edge cities, etc.); replacement of low-rise with high-rise (higher-value and multi-use buildings); and re-densification, preservation and selective reconstruction within carefully prescribed guidelines. Inaction and combinations of these different strategies are found in practice.

The Historic Cities Programme Approach: Urban Regeneration and Urban Rehabilitation

What are the benefits of the more patient process of preservation and selective reconstruction, coupled with physical and environmental improvements, adaptive reuse and community development? Unlike certain other past and present approaches, the multidisciplinary urban regeneration approach does not aim to reward a particular economic group, but tends to generate benefits across the range of stakeholders. Under this approach, externalities are not wished or abstracted away, but are taken into account in a

The Centre for Earthen Architecture in
Mopti, Mali, houses a permanent exhibition
and also serves as a small museum,
generating income for the maintenance of
the local water and sanitation system.

neutral way in major decisions. Relentless expansion is not a choice in historic districts. The remaining options are to reduce density, intensify with new open civic spaces, or to adjust density levels with new cores and buffer zones.

Urban rehabilitation, a variant of urban regeneration, seeks to practice in a mode that is inclined to spare existing buildings and community spaces wherever feasible. In so doing, it represents a summing up of the methodologies that HCP deploys in its initiatives in historic settlements. These activities and methodologies comprise: urban physical rehabilitation; conservation of historic buildings and monuments; community development; parks and environmental action and planning; adaptive reuse of existing building stock; and the development of museums and cultural centres. While this publication provides data on each of the processes employed in the urban rehabilitation of historic districts and cities, it is not the intention of the Programme to imply that any one process can be completely isolated from other valuable tools in the broad agenda of urban regeneration.

In many cases, the net effect of an initiative is boosted by the application of additional tools, in a 'multiplier effect'. Efforts by partner development agencies, municipalities, NGOs and private investors, when orchestrated within an adopted planning and conservation framework, add to this multiplier effect. It is these change processes and their physical, visual and socio-economic benefits that ultimately validate the planning investment of all concerned agents. HCP thus endorses urban rehabilitation as a proactive approach to realizing improvements in the physical and socio-economic environment of historic cities and settlements. An entity partaking in urban regeneration must assume that change is possible while avoiding the historicist notion of accommodating an evolutionary path of 'impending change' or predictive trends. History cannot be predicted but it is possible to make reasoned contributions to a better future. Ultimately, the key resources for urban regeneration are ideas and imagination.

HCP's projects seek out strong anchor communities that are tied historically to the urban terrain involved. More precisely, these communities are the best guarantee that the proposed redevelopment will remain relevant beyond the initial phase. The districts of Darb al-Ahmar in Cairo, the Old Cities of Kabul and Herat, the Nizamuddin Basti in Delhi and the Walled City of Lahore are examples of such project types.

Top, monument restoration is integral to
the revitalization of Darb al-Ahmar in Cairo.
Middle, the seawall at Forodhani Park in
Zanzibar being stabilized and restored.
Bottom, in Herat, physical rehabilitation
includes street paving.

The Importance of Local Phenomena

While attentive to the global debate on the built environment, HCP's focus is on the local
rather than the global aspect inasmuch as material, tangible heritage is local and
space-specific, reflecting each site's local genius. Within the Programme physical rehabilitation is based on intensive field research aimed at identifying urban areas that exhibit
physical or environmental distress. In addition to the relatively low percentage of urban
environments meeting the definition of sustainable physical environments or micro-
environments, the problems of improving stressed environmental, infrastructural, or
general urban building stock are of such dimension that both governmental programmes based on funding from taxes and private entities funded by entrepreneurial
investors are easily overstretched.

Historic urban or rural settlements, especially when populated by low-income communities, are typically the last areas to receive funding. Governmental agencies may
propose a rehabilitation project, but poor prospects for a future surplus of community
funds will often create the risk that useful improvements will be reversed due to lack of
maintenance. The private sector often avoids low-income areas, because these are seen as
involving a high degree of risk of project non-completion. This situation has often resulted
in the demolition of older, dilapidated urban and rural fabric, followed by reconstruction.
This has evolved into a perverse system that squeezes out low-income families, obliterating
heritage in many cases, and offering opportunities for even more unsustainable development to take place.

The preservation movement that emerged in many instances during the twentieth
century across much of the developed world was a response to this lack of an empow-
ered base within historic areas that would be able to champion the value (real or potential)
of its own heritage. In more recent decades, this movement has gained further adherents
in arguing that buildings of historic value represent captured resources and energy that
it would be foolish to discard in the new age of awareness of finite energy and resources.
The preservation movement has thus been joined by the environmental movement in
certain cases.

Heritage at Peril

The Programme, since its inception, has faced the dilemma of a profound imbalance
between the number of historic sites and settlements that are in need of rescue and rehabilitation, and the number of sites and settlements in which it can meaningfully intervene at any one time, due to the required resources. The selection of projects has been
further qualified by approaching the physical rehabilitation of historic areas not solely as
a concern for 'matter' but also for the community that resides within or around historic
sites. Physical rehabilitation in HCP's mode often involves a combined strategy of physical
rehabilitation of heritage sites and areas, and preservation-based community redevelopment. Improvements to the physical state of heritage sites and areas are linked to improvements in the quality of life of the community. The potential for success implies that
both the historic area and its associated community must be carefully defined, both
spatially and demographically.

The Organic Development of Historic Settlements and Newer Patterns of Growth

Historic cities – unlike the vast metropolises of the automobile age, which often veer between collage and chaos – have tended to develop organically, sometimes as formal nodes and often as smaller micro-settlements with a nucleus of supportive public and community activities. While these smaller units have frequently fused into larger settlements or districts, it is often possible to identify the earlier constituents, which are sub-districts, and find these still functioning as small communities with a wide array of economic functions located within a compact, densely populated area. Community development initiatives tap into the energies of proximity, involvement within a community, trust, and incentive to engage in special programmes even when no private gain is involved. The organic integrity of such settlements is not guaranteed, but often requires repair or reconstruction in harmony with the overall pattern in order to endure. HCP often encounters cases where this reality has been ignored to the detriment of the original fabric.

An aerial view of Lahore, Pakistan, demonstrates how historic cities have tended to grow organically. Functioning and unique sub-districts can be found within the larger organization of the city.

An Integrated Approach

In responding to the physical rehabilitation needs of historic settlements, the Programme has found it advantageous to employ a wide array of tools, such as surveying, planning, research, conservation, open-space improvements and community-focused support services. This is done in conjunction with its sister agencies, extending micro-credit to coherent historic districts which have monuments or significant material heritage within their boundaries. Projects such as Darb al-Ahmar in Cairo, Asheqan wa Arefan in Old Kabul,

the Nizamuddin Basti in Delhi, the Seafront Area District in the Stone Town, Zanzibar, and the Shahi Guzargah district in the Walled City of Lahore are examples of such a district or Area Development Project approach. These projects are described in other parts of this publication by theme and often as case studies in their own right.

District Rehabilitation

The Area Development Project (ADP) approach presented in this publication relies on singular historic monuments, sites or complexes as focal points to mobilize international and governmental interest in reversing decades, if not centuries, of neglect. HCP's most frequent partners in the heritage dimension are national and state level conservation authorities, whose agreement for intervention is mandatory. Municipal agencies are approached for support and collaboration on the issues of infrastructure, such as water supply, wastewater and solid waste, and community health and educational services. In efforts to assist the concerned communities to attain higher household income, vocational training, small- and medium-business enterprises, micro-credit, heritage-supporting tourism and inward investment are emphasized. When viewed in its totality, physical rehabilitation is not a goal but a method aimed at reviving the nuclei of built heritage and surrounding communities.

Rehabilitated districts have been known to revert to abandoned or distressed areas as a result of larger shifts in urban and regional development, massive economic transformations or prolonged periods of economic recession. Urban systems do tend to decline and disorder to increase over time without appropriate intervention. Overcoming municipal entropy calls for local planning capacity.

Master plans, conservation plans, development control and strategic plans are different but related tools used to generate a set of guidelines for steady state conservation and managed growth or transformation. Carried out at the level of coherent districts with popular community support, planning tends to be more responsive to needs. This suggests that "micro-planning" is sometimes more relevant than "master planning" within the historic urban domain. In some cases, "piecemeal engineering" with incremental improvement is to be preferred to an ambitious, holistic approach which can be assimilated to "utopian engineering".[7] Hence, what is 'local' is of critical importance. Without change, society would be less prone to value and preserve the past. Without preservation and the rehabilitation of our physical heritage as intermediating and stabilizing processes, change would become intolerably narrow and meaningless.

Today sufficient consensus exists regarding the value of urban rehabilitation, and both the public and private sectors have signed on to urban regeneration in the mode of Area Development Projects. Even in relatively large conurbations, space is limited and the ability to upgrade and reutilize existing building stock is usually less costly than expanding metropolitan areas and services. This has led to inspiring examples of the revitalization of inner urban environments and open spaces, and the adaptive reuse of buildings and districts with historic value. The lessons of many of the examples cited in this book have theoretical implications in terms of urban planning – but it would be more correct to state that these case studies show the power of pragmatic planning within a well-defined area and with creative attention to an area's needs and potential.

Drainage upgrading has been carried out in District 7 of Kabul, part of a wider programme of community-managed measures implemented between 2004 and 2008 in neighbourhoods close to Bagh-e Babur.

1 Cities at the time witnessed the increase of slum areas as land prices, transport and laissez-faire policies interacted with the meteoric growth of industrialization and rural to urban migration.
2 Raymond Unwin (1863–1940) and Ebenezer Howard (1850–1928) are leading examples, the latter in the 'city beautiful' movement.
3 Initiated by Patrick Geddes (1854–1932) and taken up by other professionals.
4 New Delhi, created in the early twentieth century, is seen as a different species of new town or capital as it is a restrained neo-classical composition that reflects the imperial values and self-image of the late Victorian age. Like many of its previous 'new cities', Delhi has since successfully assimilated this relatively recent urban intervention with its accumulated layers of earlier urban development.
5 Examples being La Défense (Paris), Crystal City (Arlington, Virginia), Canary Wharf (London), Diagonal del Mar (Barcelona), and so on.
6 The work of sociologists such as Jane Jacobs (1916–2006) revealed the faults in much urban planning at the time and refocused attention on the community scale.
7 See Karl Popper, The Poverty of Historicism (Boston, 1957), for arguments of each approach.

Monument Conservation

CHRISTOPHE BOULEAU

The wealth of material and tangible heritage, including monuments and their adjacent areas, is taken into account by the methods of the Historic Cities Programme (HCP) and techniques of documentation, collaboration and execution are all part of a well-defined process of conservation.

Many preservation action groups and agencies commenced their activity as a response to the threat of destruction or of damage to a specific monument of local or greater importance. Many of these struggles were successful and vindicated the investments of time, effort and expense required; others were not. The number of endangered monuments, sites and districts has increased with urbanization, with the extension of listings to new categories of landmarks, often accelerated by war or conflict, and with projects that developed without an appropriate vision. Ironically, over time, the work of conservators and preservationists has not diminished but increased. In the case of conserved projects, concern has also led to developments in the management of conservation sites.

Specialized agencies and NGOs have arisen to meet these challenges. Within the Aga Khan Development Network (AKDN), the Aga Khan Trust for Culture's Historic Cities Programme has placed monument conservation as a high priority within a preservation-based community redevelopment approach to historic settlements.

Unlike other agencies that restrict themselves for internal reasons to the site of a specific monument, the Aga Khan Trust for Culture (AKTC) intervenes not only on a monument and its site but also with its associated community or district wherever possible. This is done purposefully on the assumption that monuments without inhabitants adjacent to them are in reality barren archaeological sites. This holistic approach to conservation is based on the principles of 'Living Heritage'. Preservation of tangible heritage thus goes hand-in-hand with community development. While archaeological sites have featured in a number of AKTC's projects (the Syrian citadels, as an example), more often than not these sites are found in historic settlements (for example, Aleppo, Masyaf). At the same time, while carrying out Area Development Projects (ADPs) around key monuments, HCP has been keen to avoid the creation of districts that are actually outdoor museums, where activities are orchestrated for the visiting public but which, by the same token, lose their own intrinsic local rationale. Apart from World Heritage Sites, a maximum effort is made to develop a conservation strategy and approach that puts emphasis on a number of well-studied points, outlined below.

Research, Surveys and Planning

Architectural documentation is essential to HCP's efforts. This is the process of data collection and critical interpretation of information dealing with sources such as archives,

A north-east view of the Shrine of Abdullah Ansari in Guzargah, near Herat, reveals the extensive roof repairs that were part of the restoration process.

Opposite page:
The 14th-century Umm al-Sultan Shaaban Mosque and minaret restoration project featured stabilization of the roof and reconstruction of the top pavilion of the minaret, as well as repair of damage caused by the 1992 earthquake.

Left, the eastern facade, courtyard and wall of the Great Mosque of Mopti, after restoration.

Right, houses that had encroached on the approach to the Citadel of Masyaf, Syria, were removed.

archaeological excavations and analysis, material science, architectural and structural surveys, drawings and photographs. This process is based on a multidisciplinary approach allowing for appropriate analysis. HCP has developed up-to-date documentation of sites that had never been documented before, such as the mud mosques in Mali. Methods employed include survey techniques from manually collected data, topographic measurements with optical and electronic total stations, Global Positioning Systems, photogrammetry and three-dimensional scanning.

Project documentation is instrumental in developing damage assessments and a conservation programme of work. Throughout the entire duration of a conservation project, surveys and documentation material are collected to form a source of valuable information on the building condition before work starts, the nature and areas of conservation interventions to be implemented and, finally, a set of documents describing the building in its restored status. Such technical information is provided to local archives in soft and hard formats and is being made available on a central web-accessible data bank.

Coordination with Local and International Agencies

A majority of historic cities in which the Programme is active (Cairo, Damascus, Aleppo, the Stone Town of Zanzibar) are on the UNESCO World Heritage List, as are HCP projects involving single monuments (from Humayun's Tomb in Delhi, to the Timbuktu Mosque in Mali). Local government stakeholders usually have prime jurisdiction over the historic monuments. HCP provides technical support to the authorities dealing with monument preservation and establishes references for quality of work to be replicated elsewhere. Critical to post-construction management and maintenance is ensuring the use of vacated buildings by establishing adaptive reuse plans and empowering local citizens' committees to maintain their asset. Institutional partnerships related to monument conservation also include privately funded organizations, such as the World Monuments Fund, or the American Research Center in Egypt, that have collaborated with AKTC on multi-year projects.

Conservation Strategy

In many countries, conservation activities still involve only the restoration and replication of the given historical fabric using traditional building crafts. But an increasing number of problems affecting historic buildings requires the introduction of new reinforcement techniques, calling for meticulous damage assessment and planning. From Afghanistan to Mali, the Programme has introduced a methodological approach to conservation, involving multidisciplinary strategy and inputs.

Pilot Projects

The value of experimentation in the field via pilot projects to test remedial solutions on a small scale, and to subject them to accelerated weathering process, in order to better develop suitable conservation techniques has been successfully verified in various countries. Associated with preliminary studies and damage assessment, the implementation of small-scale prototypes has proven critical in defining adequate solutions.

Left, Aslam Mosque in Cairo has been in constant use since its 14th-century construction and has recently undergone thorough restoration.

Right, the intricate incised plasterwork decoration on the domed ceiling of Lakkarwala Burj at Sunder Nursery in Delhi being carefully cleaned while missing portions are reinstated using traditional materials and craft techniques.

Calligraphic inscriptions being restored on an interior wall of Sunder Burj, a Mughal monument in Sunder Nursery in Delhi.

In Herat, the interior of Chahar Suq Cistern is criss-crossed with scaffolding during its restoration.

Local Professionals and International Specialists

Building the capacity of technical staff in the field is a key factor in achieving quality work and ensuring sustainability. In many countries, the field of conservation is new and local professionals need exposure to international specialists to develop their own practice. When starting a new initiative, AKTC ensures that a transfer of knowledge can ensue between international specialists and local professionals.

Site Supervision

In most locations, contractors have no qualifications or previous experience in conservation. In such cases, AKTC creates its own local team, ensures training with international experts, and builds internal services associating implementation specialists, management and back-office support, in the aim to guarantee close quality control.

Post-Conservation Maintenance

Assistance to local government agencies or community leaders includes post-conservation plans. This comprises the creation of technical maintenance guidelines manuals, training of local maintenance teams and the formation of governing bodies for cultural heritage; and it also involves the preparation of financial projections to assist in identifying solutions for sustainability.

Final Project Documentation

AKTC's mandate of preserving and promoting the local cultural expression in its material heritage finds one of its best applications in the role played by monuments to boost cultural tourism and local development. Developing visitor circuits linking restored monuments to the most important areas of interest of a historic city has a dual impact. They not only bring visibility and accessibility to neglected parts of a city but also boost the community's economy and opportunities. Permitting adaptive reuse and visitation of monuments makes education and interpretation of cultural heritage possible for a wide range of students, from school pupils to university graduates.

Due to their geographic spread, HCP's conservation projects now span numerous types of buildings and technologies, including earthen architecture; coral limestone block; heavy medieval masonry with vaults and domes; brick vaulted and domed structures adorned with decorative glazed ceramic tile; low-rise stone rubble construction with timber cribbage, and so on. No single agency can master all the requisite technologies and sub-techniques involved in the conservation of such buildings and AKTC has solicited external specialist consultants and other partner agencies in many of these projects.

The tall Ayyubid bridge, still serving as the only official entrance to the Citadel of Aleppo in Syria, leads to the fortified entrance complex, certainly one of the most spectacular examples of Islamic military architecture.

Social and Economic Development

JURJEN VAN DER TAS

Physical rehabilitation is a key, but certainly not solitary, feature of the approach used by the Historic Cities Programme (HCP) in its sites of interest. The sustainability of such interventions has been understood to depend on community involvement and development, targeted to permit financially viable solutions and the ongoing preservation and adaptive reuse of historic areas.

Once conceptualized, Area Development Projects (ADPs) attain their form through a process of multidisciplinary planning and a process of organic development during the initial phase of implementation. Analysis of qualitative and quantitative data enables HCP to make choices with regard to the depth and reach of proposed core socio-economic development activities. In generic terms, this means that activities aimed at improving the quality of life of residents focus on fulfilment of basic needs, provision of the means for social welfare and on creating a secure social and physical environment. Thematically these activities nearly always include better housing conditions, higher levels of employment, stimulation of income-generating activities, better education and better health (see the table below). Once activities have been defined and targets have been set, they are implemented in phases – starting with a first or pilot phase of limited extent (geographically, as well as in terms of time and the number of beneficiaries involved). Organic growth that is permitted in the early stages of the project is recognition of the fact that the process of delivery is part of the process and that this carries as much importance as the final product.

Outside the walls of the Great Mosque of Djenné, Mali, workers construct a pit for the preparation of *banco* – a manually mixed construction material made of clay soil, sand and various straw and organic additives – on the construction site.

Opposite page:
In the urban village of Nizamuddin Basti in Delhi a vibrant community is centred around the *dargah* of the 14th-century Sufi saint, Hazrat Nizamuddin Auliya.

Development activities by theme	Cairo	Kabul	Mopti	Aleppo	Lahore	Delhi
Housing improvement	●	●			●	
Open space development and public buildings	●	●	●	●	●	●
Infrastructural improvement	●	●	●		●	●
Education programme (including TVET)	●	●	●	●	●	●
Health programme	●	●				
Micro-credit programme	●	●	●	●		

HCP's socio-economic development activities by theme in seven different Area Development Projects (ADPs).

The instruments for appreciating improvements in the quality of life, such as those that have been tested within the network of Aga Khan agencies between 2005 and 2010, can partially help to answer the question how relevant achievements are in view of overall improvements.

Achievements are measured in qualitative as well as in quantitative terms. The overall outcome is reviewed in relation to domains of asset creation that the Aga Khan Development

Network (AKDN) has defined. These are Economy, Health, Education, Social Life, Built and Natural Environments, Voice and Influence, and Local Perceptions of the overall Quality of Life. In order to fully appreciate qualitative improvements from an HCP perspective, improvements in the physical environment (housing, open space, solid waste collection), restoration or instilment of dignity (skills development and employment) and personal recognition (as happens through adult education and improved health) are taken into account.

Holistic Planning and Identification of Needs

When planning socio-economic interventions, available information concerning the size of the project area, its population and basic socio-economic data are collected and analysed. Key players are identified at both governmental and private level (including local Civil Society Organizations) and local leaders are contacted. Once an assessment is made of the desirable location for an ADP, suitable boundaries of the area are decided. These can be formal administrative boundaries (used in Cairo and Aleppo), informal boundaries recognized at local levels, such as *mohallas* or neighbourhoods in Lahore and in Kabul, watersheds (Mopti, Lahore and Kabul), mountain crests and rivers (northern Pakistan), as well as man-made boundaries such as major thoroughfares and perimeter walls (the Nizamuddin Basti).

Methods for Gathering Information

Project formulation in terms of the selection of development sectors, description of activities and budgeting is preceded by the execution of baseline surveys: a process of extensive fact-finding and orientation during which qualitative and quantitative information from within the targeted area is collected. These baseline surveys include variables that are generally difficult to assess in a straightforward manner, but that are nevertheless of great importance in the urban context. Household income and household expenditure, for

instance, are notoriously difficult to measure and therefore need to be approached from various angles in order to arrive at acceptable estimates. Neighbourhood walks with knowledgeable individuals, focus group meetings, interviews with key informants and other sources of information, such as rejected loan applications for micro-credit, provide important additional information. By applying such methods in Cairo and Aleppo, it was possible to arrive at estimates of average household income and expenditure of the population that seemed plausible. In contrast, this was not possible in Zanzibar, in spite of persistent efforts. Zanzibari income levels appear to be substantially lower than household expenditure. Very telling for all household budgets is the percentage of income spent on food. Without exception, it was found that the urban poor that live on an income of less than $1 per day (the UN definition of poor) tend to spend more than fifty per cent of their income on food. Zanzibar did not appear any different in that respect.

Although HCP collects a great deal of data (a typical baseline survey may produce 500 or more variables), the information sought still reflects a bias for the sectors of intervention that are close to HCP's mission. The development proposal for the revitalization of an urban area that eventually emerges, therefore, nearly always includes one or two major focal points of historical value that are the subject of physical rehabilitation. When used as a strategic 'entering wedge' into the community, such interventions effectively replace better-known strategies used by other agencies, such as productive investments, productive improved infrastructure, lending through micro-credit initiatives or arranging participatory social mapping exercises.

Analysis and Prioritization of Core Development Sectors

Once objectives are set and a strategy is in place, and all necessary background information and data concerning the project area have been collected and analysed, project activities for the major intervention sectors are planned. Although such activities may differ substantially from one ADP to the next, the seven domains of development by which their successes and failures are measured are nearly always represented.

Left, the first stage of housing improvements on the east side of Atfet Asaad, a small residential cul-de-sac abutting the Historic Wall in Cairo.

Right, the work after completion.

Left, upgrading work has improved living conditions for some 15,000 residents of the Old City of Kabul in the neighbourhoods of Asheqan wa Arefan.

Right, people being entertained inside the entrance to Azhar Park in Cairo.

Landscaping and newly created pedestrian zones in front of the Citadel of Aleppo in Syria are part of a wider perimeter project.

1. Housing and public buildings

This sector is at the core of HCP's Programme, although in a majority of cases public buildings are central to the initiative rather than houses. The reason for this is that the costs to redo houses in historically sensitive areas are often prohibitively high and occupants generally do not have the means to make a substantial financial contribution.

Public buildings are present in all of HCP's Area Development initiatives. The choice of building is dependent on its historic significance for the neighbourhood and its accessibility. Even the Historic Wall in Cairo, which AKTC restored over a ten-year period, has been given a new function: in a departure from its original purpose, it is now attracting visitors rather than keeping them out. The Great Mosque in Mopti (Mali), which HCP restored, has a religious function, but also draws visitors from abroad. The completion of the conservation work in Aleppo's Old City by HCP marks the start of community activities aimed at bringing benefits from tourism to the inhabitants who live around the Citadel. In all of these cases, the public buildings have proven to be a suitable entry wedge for access to the community in order to start development activities.

2. Open space

Many poor historic centres where HCP is active have high population densities. Better use of limited public open space and the creation of additional areas where the public has free access are, therefore, of great importance. In places such as Aleppo's Old City, previous work by other development agencies in public open-space development would make HCP's involvement in this field less of a necessity. However, HCP's involvement in the development of a green zone on a sixteen-hectare vacant lot just outside the project area would provide substantial benefits for all inhabitants of the Old City. A similar situation existed in the historic District 1 of Kabul, where a four-hectare heavily encroached and polluted former park was rehabilitated as a city park. City parks, as green public spaces par excellence, are nowadays part and parcel of nearly all of HCP's interventions and are considered a core component in socio-economic development.

Squares, streets and even alleys can be put to multiple uses. In Cairo's Darb al-Ahmar quarter, a small but centrally located square, which is dominated by the thirteenth-century Aslam Mosque, was identified as a key public space and as a result was developed with multiple uses in mind. Furthermore, HCP was also involved in the development of a master plan for the reuse of public space in the entire district. Of equal importance is the creation of public space around recently rehabilitated buildings. Not only does this contribute to better visibility and access to the building, but it also helps to prevent encroachment and damage, ensuring longer lasting benefits to the public.

3. Education and vocational training

Levels of education in most, if not all, of HCP's intervention areas are generally low to very low at the start of launching development activities. Literacy levels, in particular for women, reach only seventy per cent in Cairo and in Aleppo, but are as low as twenty-five per cent in Kabul and only around thirty per cent in Mali and Zanzibar. Many children do not complete primary school, as parents often do not see the need for further education in the absence of career prospects.

In a number of cases HCP has started literacy classes for adults, either directly or in collaboration with experienced local NGOs. In addition to this, attempts are being made to increase the level of involvement of parents in the education of their children. The libraries for children and adults that were set up in Cairo have become a focal point for interaction with parents and children, as have after-school activities that are aimed at stimulating creativity and emphasizing the need for continued education. A similar library will now also be set up in Aleppo.

HCP is not involved in secondary and higher education for local communities, but instead focuses on vocational and administrative training. The assumption is that the vast majority of people in the poor areas where HCP intervenes would be best served with knowledge of a particular skill or trade that could be marketable, thus adding to the family income.

The AKDN school improvement initiative in Nizamuddin Basti in Delhi has created a pleasing school environment, and the renovated Municipal Corporation of Delhi School compares with the best in the city.

As part of an overall strategy to improve the life of residents, a class, organized by HCP's Health Programme, under way in the medical clinic in Darb al-Ahmar in Cairo.

4. Health

HCP does not see a role for itself as a major provider of health care. Still, information collected at source from the target group in the intervention areas nearly always points to the lack of available health services or to their high costs – placing proper health care out of reach for most households. As a result, many suffer from poor health conditions that could easily have been avoided. Since most surveys indicate mothers, mothers-to-be and children as the groups that are most at risk, efforts have been, and continue to be, made to focus on these groups. Preventive rather than curative health care is HCP's main principle. This means that the majority of health-related activities consist in awareness-raising.

5. Water, sanitation and disposal of solid waste

Providing populations with access to proper sources of water goes hand-in-hand with improved sanitation. Nearly all intervention areas where AKTC is active suffer from a lack of both. Where drinking water and sanitation facilities are available, the focus may be on increasing accessibility. HCP would generally only be working at the secondary level (the individual street) or even more likely at the tertiary level (individual houses) when providing access to water. Primary water supply is considered a government responsibility for which other agencies are better equipped. In Zanzibar, additional taps and toilets were built in buildings that could house up to a hundred people. In the Komoguel quarter of Mopti, Mali, access to public water taps in the open street was identified as an issue of high importance. The issue has since been addressed, not just by creating more public taps, but also by creating a system of proper drainage of waste water and sewage below street level.

HCP sees a role for itself in starting up and helping to sustain community-based initiatives for waste collection and maintenance of a clean and healthy environment. On a permanent basis, however, it is believed that solid waste removal is a community and municipal responsibility. HCP can initially act as a broker between the different parties involved, and it has kick-started periodic cleaning campaigns with volunteers, in order to help clean rooftops or vacant lots where rubbish has been allowed to accumulate.

6. Employment and vocational training

HCP's involvement in employment is mainly a consequence of its engagement in vocational and administrative training, as well as its involvement in stimulating the development of income-generating activities. The basic principle is that HCP, or any of its local development agencies, is not a job provider, nor an agent that acts as a broker between employees and employers. It does promote vocational training.

Technical, Vocational and Educational Training (TVET) is the one education component that can be found in almost all HCP's interventions. The reason for this is that physical rehabilitation of monuments requires able craftsmen from start to finish. More often than not, however, such able craftsmen are not locally available and need to be trained on the job. As a result, nearly all intervention programmes include crafts training –

A new pump supplies water in District 1 in Kabul Old City, part of a range of upgrading measures that include paving alleyways and selected streets, along with the construction of drains and the improvement of water supplies.

Above, in Komoguel, Mopti, street paving work is being carried out using 'stones' made of recycled plastic bags.

Below, work being done in the interior of the Sufi shrine at the centre of the Asheqan wa Arefan area of old Kabul.

in particular construction-related crafts such as masonry, carpentry and fine woodwork, plumbing and electrical engineering. Training in administration has proven particularly attractive to women who seek to improve their skills and move up in the labour market. Local crafts development through training in quality improvement is another element that is part of the TVET approach.

7. Urban planning

Nearly all cities where HCP is engaged in urban revitalization have master plans for urban development. Many of these plans, however, have not been adjusted to the realities on the ground and have therefore lost their relevance. In order to deal with the realities on the ground, HCP has in a number of cases taken on some planning tasks that are generally associated with governmental, municipal or district units.

Meticulous plot-by-plot investigative work carried out over a number of years in all of the historic cities concerned has yielded a wealth of information. Based on this, changes can now be proposed that will have a significant impact, not just in terms of retaining physical assets within the built environment, but equally in social and cultural terms. In Cairo it led to a decision in 2006 not to demolish a core part of Darb al-Ahmar as was originally foreseen in the 1973 Master Plan. The recreation of Qazi Bagh, a four-hectare green open space in the heart of Old Kabul, is another example of a reversal of potentially harmful urban development (in this case it was the absence of any planning that had caused complete encroachment of green open space).

Sustaining Development Initiatives after Project Completion

Continuation of HCP-initiated socio-economic development activities beyond the lifetime of its projects depends on the character of the intervention, the implementing capacity of local counterparts and availability of funding. Integrated development projects, which contain a multitude of thematic elements, are generally split into several manageable components before being handed over, while some parts are considered to have been completed. Continuation of the vocational training packages beyond the project's lifetime is secured through a number of arrangements with private and governmental training institutes, whereby HCP aims at preserving the curriculum that was prepared and the quality of the training that was provided.

Physical rehabilitation usually comes to an end when the project is completed. The newly created built environment, however, requires continuous upkeep. In order to ensure that buildings and public works are properly maintained by the local entities that carry on after HCP has left, income-generating activities have been devised whereby funding comes from the public paying entry fees (for example to the Baltit Trust which manages Baltit Fort in Hunza, northern Pakistan), rent (by leasing restored public buildings to other organizations, for example the Old Dispensary in Zanzibar) or by organizing events. The Komoguel Project in Mopti is an exception, whereby physical rehabilitation of water and sanitation during the course of a number of phases will be handed over to a local counterpart that will continue similar interventions in Mopti and elsewhere.

Monitoring, Research and Evaluation

In the monitoring, research and evaluation of its projects, HCP follows the same hierarchical sequence it applies when designing projects, but it addresses these in reverse order. Project descriptions of the 'what' (goals and objectives), 'how' (strategy) and 'which' (activities) are monitored and evaluated by looking first at the results (which reflect the direct outcome of activities), then at the effectiveness (which measures the strategy) and finally at the impact (defined as lasting and durable change). There are compelling arguments for maintaining this hierarchical order in project design and in project monitoring and evaluation. Not only does it provide insight at which level outputs are directly attributable to inputs, but it can also help to trace and rank the less tangible, often indirect outputs. Development of important cross-cutting themes for HCP, such as environment, gender, and organizational and institutional development of Civil Society Organizations, are also evaluated in terms of their impact.

Top, a planning meeting with municipal officials and community planners in the Garden Pavilion of Bagh-e Babur in Kabul. Middle, restored Baltit Fort looks out over Hunza Valley in northern Pakistan. Bottom, an evening view of the restored Old Dispensary in Zanzibar.

Parks and Gardens

CAMERON RASHTI

The parks and gardens portfolio of the Historic Cities Programme has broadened in response to the dire shortage of quality open space for communities in historic districts. These projects, however recent in creation or rehabilitation, draw attention to some almost lost traditions of environmental works in historic settlements, whether mobilized by royal patrons, municipalities or local communities, which demonstrate the value of proper stewardship of our public spaces. This endeavour, linking urban and rural settlements in a common goal, indicates the vital need for people to shape their physical environment in a responsible, hospitable and sustainable manner.

The Project Portfolio

A major environmental rehabilitation project in the heart of Old Cairo, the site of the present Azhar Park, was a major impetus to the further engagement of the Aga Khan Trust for Culture (AKTC) in demonstrating the vital role of public open spaces in the rehabilitation and enhancement of historic districts. The size and diversity of AKTC's parks portfolio by the end of 2011 is, in large part, a reflection of the results of this project type, first in Cairo and then in other locations illustrated in this publication, evidencing the positive change processes these environmental projects can and have set in motion. It is useful to briefly summarize the contents of this portfolio prior to explaining the rationale behind a family of unique yet related projects.

At present, the park projects portfolio includes three gardens that are located within heritage sites: Humayun's Tomb and Garden in Delhi; Forodhani Park in the Stone Town, Zanzibar; and Babur's Garden in Kabul. The first two are within World Heritage Sites, while the latter has an application underway for such designation. Three park projects (Azhar Park, Cairo; the National Park of Mali, Bamako; and Khorog City Park, Tajikistan) are in central city sites that have cultural significance. Two more such park projects are underway: Sunder Nursery in Delhi and Bab Qinessrine Park in Aleppo. The Historic Cities Programme (HCP) has recently begun work on two further park spaces within largely natural settings covering even more expansive areas of land: Nairobi City Park in Kenya and Phase II of the National Park of Mali.

Urban Regeneration and Community Development

A number of factors unite these projects despite their diverse locations, while other elements differentiate them. The point here is not to dissect each project from a topological and morphological perspective. In a broader context, HCP is interested in questions such as what role do parks such as these play in urban regeneration and community redevelopment? Do park projects such as these transcend environmental rehabilitation

Top and middle, water is a fundamental feature in HCP park creation, as seen here at Azhar Park in Cairo. Bottom, the new Sports Centre at Bamako's National Park of Mali.

Opposite page:
A view from the elevated walkway of the Caravanserai of Bagh-e Babur in Kabul shows visitors to the garden walking up the central axis towards the Garden Pavilion.

The image of the garden in its wider connections to spirituality and mysticism is depicted in the frontispiece from the *Diwan of Sultan Ibrahim Mirza, Qazvin,* Iran, 1852. Aga Khan Museum Collection.

in the sense of a restricted physical undertaking? What impact can such parks have on urban planning and design as a practice? How does a municipality ensure that a large park facility remains maintained and sustainable in the long run? In the course of conceptualizing, implementing and then operating these diverse projects, HCP has acquired encouraging feedback from these very 'real world' prototype situations that affirm the vital importance of such initiatives, not only in general urban environments but even more so in historic urban settings. It is beneficial to consider briefly the origin of many of the formal parks and gardens showcased in this publication.

The Role of Patrons in the Historic Development of Parks

The role of royal patrons in the creation of historically important pleasure gardens in many parts of the world is well documented. In the Islamic world this involvement may have reached its apex in the series of gardens created by the Mughals, starting with Babur and extended by Humayun and his descendents, two legacies with which AKTC has become engaged and that are described in the Case Studies (pp. 78–85, 168–179).

Historians of these gardens make reference to the importance of patterns and geometry and the presence of water features in setting the scene of visual and micro-climatic relief from a hostile exterior world. Such gardens are typically enclosed with high walls for protection and isolation, creating an inner oasis in contrast to the outer world. In this manner, the garden serves as a larger manifestation of the courtyard, a domestic analogy. As described by Jonas Lehrman:

"The Islamic garden performs many functions. Whether under customary private ownership or for occasional public use, it is enclosed and protected, and affords privacy. Throughout most of the Islamic world, it offers relief from the stress of intense heat, while its beauty enhances the quality of living. Terraces, canals and tanks meet the demands of horticulture and irrigation, while the water also serves a desire for display and sound. Fruit trees shade planting on the ground, while flowers provide fragrance and colour."[1]

In such domains, gardens have allowed the display of the state of the art at the time of horticulture, with multiple species being employed for maximum effect. Typically, terrains with multiple terraces were artfully laid out between zones punctuated with canals and viewing platforms. It would not be far-fetched to consider these complex gardens as outdoor exhibitions or 'museums' of plant life. Many historic accounts confirm that gardens provided inner solace and inspired poetry. Parks and gardens have historically embodied a meaning and significance in many of the areas in which they were introduced – often in a struggle with a hostile terrain, where rich green spaces did not occur naturally.

In some cases, gardens created backdrops for impressive architectural monuments, such as the Mausoleum of Emperor Humayun in Delhi (see p. 174). Gardens occasionally became parts of larger semi-urban complexes, as in Fatehpur Sikri. Here, hydraulic systems were critical to the success and survival of gardens, with altered river courses and unsteady rainfall occasionally presenting post-construction risks.

At times, there was a lively interaction between different centres of garden design and creation, due to trade across vast territories, centralized administration of kingdoms and the mobility of craftsmen. Mughal gardens are a case in point, with many traits borrowed and fused from diverse locations. Archaeological site research has confirmed in some projects presented in this volume that the exchange of ideas, motifs and designs occurred across important sites.

Gardens in Historic Islamic Settlements

Parks and gardens in many of the regions where AKTC has been active are intact and coherent sets of landscape design. They usually stem from the vision of a patron or landowner and were developed through the use of skilled local artisans employing 'hardscape' and 'softscape' materials. Careful research and surveying provides fuller understanding not only of the final expression of the composition but also, over time, of the incremental development of large works.

Environmental design was an active field practiced in all of the areas concerned. Programme work has witnessed that these interventions included hillside retention systems and terracing, and the development of elaborate water conduits, as well as large man-made lakes. Environmental design, as seen in historic cases, has occasionally been concerned with astronomical observations and assemblies were laid out with precise measurement techniques, often involving the carefully calculated control of slopes for water flow. Well-known layouts in historic gardens, such as the *chahar-bagh*, demonstrate a facility for combining aesthetic and practical design aspects in a balanced mode. Forms that vary from the prevalent geometric and romantic gardens of the Western world reveal strong differences in the relative role of reason and nature in design.[2]

Historic Areas and Their Environmental Context

Environmental design can be seen as playing an influential role in the contexts of historic districts and monuments in the Islamic world.[3] Monuments are often found in the midst of open space and these spaces sometimes have afforded critical buffer zones between historic fabric and the expansive urban area beyond.

People stroll along the main axis of Azhar Park in Cairo, with the Citadel in the background.

Left, children ride the wooden horses in the play area in Khorog City Park, Tajikistan.

Right, the restoration of Forodhani Park, on the seafront in Zanzibar and one of the last open spaces in this densely populated World Heritage Site, has been completed.

Bait Nizam is one of the most significant courtyard residences constructed during the classical Ottoman period in Damascus and is one of three palaces being preserved and restored.

While not formally categorized as 'landscape', the many instances of ancient walls surrounding historic old cities, such as Cairo, Herat and Lahore, represent massive acts of environmental design, enclosing whole cities or districts, creating walled compounds within a larger walled territory. AKTC's projects in such areas have concerned archaeological investigation, conservation and the development of circuits for public visits. The largest of these projects, the Historic Wall of Old Cairo in the vicinity of Azhar Park, exceeds one kilometre in length and includes a major promenade and landscaped hillside. Azhar Park, thirty hectares in surface area, became the focal point not only of a major environmental rehabilitation in Old Cairo, but also the precursor to an Area Development Project (ADP). Thus, environmental design and urban rehabilitation of historic districts in AKTC's portfolio are very much intertwined.

In the case of waterside settlements and retreats, such as the Stone Town of Zanzibar and Khorog City, the cities' water edge has critical importance from the viewpoint of aesthetics as well as an early role in riverine or marine defence systems. In Zanzibar, AKTC conserved and restored sections of the historic seawall along Forodhani Park fronting the sea over an eighteen-month period. This 400-metre stretch of seawall became an important sub-project of the overall rehabilitation effort for this major urban park site, which itself is part of the Stone Town's World Heritage Site area. In this case, environmental rehabilitation and garden conservation became linked objectives. In the case of Khorog, the City Park shares a major perimeter edge with the fast-running Gunt River. The river wall became the focus of a large masonry retaining wall engineering system combined with protected footpaths for promenades.

Large urban spaces often served historically as gathering places associated with architectural complexes or shrines. Some of their rich variations can be seen through HCP projects in the cases of Guzargah, Herat and the Nizamuddin Basti. Examples of urban courtyard spaces are well illustrated in the historic beits in Damascus, while more three-dimensional examples can be found in the inner courts of remote mountain sites, such as Baltit Fort in northern Pakistan.

The Concept of 'Social Commons'

Reference should be made to the importance of public open spaces in many of the historic cities in which the Programme is active, including large squares or *maidans*. These may be partly parks, or partly open multi-purpose spaces. They can be areas in and around bazaars; graveyards (Cairo's City of the Dead; Kabul's cemeteries and

shrines within Asheqan wa Arefan; Herat's Guzargah complex; and Delhi's Nizamuddin shrine complex); caravanserai; and polo grounds (in Karimabad, northern Pakistan, and Faisabad, northern Afghanistan).

The concept of public goods or 'social commons' has lately received increasing attention in publications on subjects ranging from history and political-economy to ethics, and the environment, although this analysis dates in part back to the early twentieth century. The notion of the oceans or the atmosphere as being common goods or part of the commonwealth of mankind is often evoked in such works. A central concept is that "non-rival" and "non-excludable" services are public goods and are critical in the avoidance of the predicament of "private affluence, public squalor".[4] The term is often discussed with reference to examples from the Western world with the implication that cases in other regions are scarce or non-existent. It is hoped that HCP projects will provide evidence, to the contrary, of a range of such common goods created for wide social benefit in the regions concerned. The question is not so much about the existence of historic precedents but, rather, why such rich examples are being ignored in the further development of the urban environment in these areas.

Urban Landscape: Recovering Marginalized Tracts of Land

With the increase in urban population pressures and land speculation, land, even in marginal city areas, has become commoditized, resulting in remaining open space and parkland being encroached on or redeveloped. The lack of well-formulated planning instruments in some areas has led to insufficient land-use control, with open space suffering as a result. While land-use controls for private use usually do not lack support, the protection of key public open spaces is often left to well-intending but poorly funded civil society groups. The introduction of new infrastructure, particularly transportation systems,

Above, the garden is laid out in a geometric pattern at Lakkarwala Burj in Sunder Nursery in Delhi.

Below, at the Abdullah Ansari Shrine in Guzargah, near Herat, extensive documentary research has been carried out on the historic graves in the courtyard.

The National Park of Mali seeks to provide a much-needed public green space in Bamako. It features an interactive cultural core zone of 49 hectares and an outer, more passive ecological buffer zone of 54 hectares.

has sometimes led to the absorption of open space for needed easements or rights of way in the name of the larger public good. The lack of a reliable local tax base has resulted in park and public spaces in some areas falling into neglect. This can be overcome, through the use of modest entry fees and 'capturing' some revenues on site through public amenities while protecting the otherwise natural aspects of the site. Rehabilitating or creating significant public parks or areas around monuments typically requires large investments and collaboration with public agencies and the communities involved.

This is a process that takes time, means and perseverance. While private funding and support for large private developments are not lacking in most areas, this is not the case for large public developments. More recently, advancements are being seen aided in part by the introduction of 'Public-Private Partnership' (PPP) arrangements and similar forms of collaboration in addition to traditional public funding or grants.

While semi-agricultural and pastoral activities continue, often within a short distance of some metropolitan centres, these are vestiges that are gradually disappearing. It is important that smaller and sometimes informal, low-income communities residing in and around historic districts have some allocation of proper open space. The traditional modes of tipping rubbish on the edges of cities (as was previously the case with Azhar Park's site) need correction without wholesale removal of the existence of open space per se. These problems come at a time when modern metropolises are suffering from the syndrome of "de-centredness".[5]

The improvement of environmental conditions in historic areas is a key concern of HCP. Better field research and sensitive strategic planning can, with the support of the municipal authorities, lead to proper land-use controls for zones of each district. It is important, too, to avoid inappropriate industrial practices adjacent to residential areas. Modern transportation systems are known for their marginalization of urban areas below and adjacent to major new lines.

Good practice, coupled with successful prototypes in environmental design in the many historic districts and settlements the Programme has engaged in, are viewed as

important contributions but ones that will need replication and continuous investment by municipal authorities in the coming years if environmental degradation is to be reversed in the longer term.

AKTC's park projects typically include the development of detailed operational plans for the maintenance of the rehabilitated or new park spaces once projects are completed. The park maintenance teams often benefit from personnel trained during the plantation phase of project implementation. Turning the management and operation of restored park and open spaces into a subject worthy of planning, organizational development and proper budgeting has been a major step forward to safeguarding these local environments for the benefit of their users.

Completed parks are carefully monitored across a number of factors including park visitation levels, local jobs created, linkages to the surrounding neighbourhoods through circuits and signage, quality of maintenance, and financial performance. In the case of surplus operational funds, these are reinvested, in accordance with the relevant project agreement, in the further enhancement of the districts surrounding the park space and their communities. In 2010, five of AKTC's park projects were under operation in metropolitan centres serving a combined population of twenty-five million people, from Cairo to Khorog City. Visitation of these parks crossed the three million mark that same year, a figure equivalent to twelve per cent of the total population figure for the cities involved, proof of a firm continuing demand for public parks thus far in the twenty-first century.

The terrain in the western half of Azhar Park in Cairo consists predominantly of steep and continuous slopes, running from the summit of the hill to the foot of the uncovered and restored Historic Wall.

Revenue-generating facilities like the Balasoko restaurant will help keep the National Park of Mali from becoming a financial burden on the municipality.

1   See Jonas Lehrman's classic treatise on the Islamic garden in *Earthly Paradise: Garden and Courtyard in Islam*, University of California Press, Berkeley and Los Angeles, 1980, p.31.
2   Ibid., p.225.
3   See D. Fairchild Ruggles, *Islamic Gardens and Landscape*, University of Pennsylvania Press, Philadelphia, 2008, for a more current anthology of Islamic gardens, historic and contemporary.
4   John Cassidy, *How Markets Fail*, Farrar, Straus & Giroux, New York, 2009, p.34.
5   N. Ellin, *Postmodern Urbanism*, Cambridge, MA/Blackwell, Oxford, 1996.

Adaptive Reuse

FRANCESCO SIRAVO AND
JOLYON LESLIE

The restoration of historic sites and monuments and their adaptation for community and cultural uses can be seen as a keystone to the successful urban rehabilitation of historic settlements. Steps in this process are the definition of stakeholder needs, the interface between conservation and sustainable community reuse, and the training requisite to carry out the programmes. Perspectives on these issues, written by members of the Historic Cities Programme (HCP) team, are presented here.

BRINGING TANGIBLE HERITAGE BACK TO LIFE

Operating as a sub-domain or area of engagement, adaptive reuse projects within the Historic Cities Programme (HCP) are consequential acts following decisions to undertake an Area Development Project (ADP). Adaptive reuse of historic sites or buildings can be categorized according to their status as monuments or listed buildings or simply sites representative of a past era. In accordance with existing preservation law, statutes, or conventions, national or international, acceptable uses of monuments and listed buildings are restrictive in nature and meant to safeguard rare examples of heritage or fragile sites. Period architecture and districts require protection to ensure their survival as identifiable, coherent and authentic examples of the past but otherwise can often permit new uses, public or private, and, indeed, often such new uses are the principle means of safeguarding these elements of the urban fabric by allowing for self-sustainable forms of occupancy and maintenance.

Monuments and Listed Buildings

HCP is accustomed to working closely with international agencies and national authorities in the determination of the proper levels of access and usage of monuments by the public.

While monuments until recently have long been considered restrictive in terms of their use following preservation, these restrictions are increasingly being worn down by changing public awareness of the advantages of unique settings for leisure, residential, community functions or tourism. At the minimum, increased public visitation to preserved monuments along carefully selected routes can both protect the monument while lifting the revenue stream so critical for proper maintenance. The often surprising benefit of the attention devoted to given monuments or buildings is the vastly increased level of interest on the part of the local and regional community in what was previously an overlooked relic. This reaction is in fact critical to building an important base of civil society support and appetite for further projects of this nature.

Rehabilitation of the former Darb Shouglan School, seen here in its early stages, offered an opportunity to introduce a community centre into a context that sorely lacked public facilities.

Opposite page:
The former Darb Shouglan School, located at the edge of the Aslam neighbourhood and close to the Historic Wall in Cairo, functions today after its restoration and conversion as the Darb Shouglan Community Centre.

A number of hotels have been developed or are planned through the adaptive reuse of existing buildings. Clockwise from top left: a telecommunications building in Zanzibar; a *hammam* in Aleppo; an old palace in Damascus; and a fort in Shigar, northern Pakistan.

Several of the ADPs that the Programme has been associated with are in a number of World Heritage Sites which have called for special treatment: Humayun's Tomb complex in Delhi, Babur's Garden in Kabul, the Stone Town in Zanzibar, Darb al-Ahmar in Historic Cairo, and the Walled City in Lahore.

Non-Listed Sites and Buildings

In many of the Programme's ADPs the overwhelming percentage of building stock, protected by statute or not, is non-listed and therefore affords more forms of adaptive reuse. Reuse at its minimal level can involve the insertion of modern services in housing and other buildings to support current activities and improve the quality of life. While maintaining the authenticity of the original design or features, the site or building value is enhanced by making it reusable as a part of private or community life. Much of the building stock in Darb al-Ahmar (Cairo), Nizamuddin Basti (Delhi), Lahore Walled City, Old Kabul and Herat, and the Stone Town (Zanzibar) falls into this category. As a group of (mostly) uniform and coherent building morphology, once rehabilitated and brought up to date in terms of building services and their associated public spaces, this stock can be reused if vacant and its usage extended if occupied with much improved standards of living.

ADPs with important adaptive reuse components create a call on funds that are typically not available in the community. In many of the ADPs of the Aga Khan Trust for Culture (AKTC), the per capita household income does not exceed $2 per day. These neighbourhoods are all too frequently overlooked by banks, considered ineligible for loans due to low income, uncertain property ownership or tenancy, and lack of collateral. While micro-credit combined with house-owner investments and grants have succeeded at a certain level (Darb al-Ahmar in Cairo is an example), the number of eligible buildings still represents a minority of the cases.

Adaptive reuse occurs when the original building fabric remains intact with only structural repairs or improvements to consolidate the envelope. Too often opposing market forces are at work. A building owner may wish to see his building decay and be demolished so that the site can be sold or redeveloped in an inappropriate way to yield a capital gain. Determining what is appropriate or inappropriate is a labour-intensive process usually requiring public hearings, involvement of civil society groups, and development of building planning and design guidelines. The latter are intended to prevent new developments that represent unacceptable or overly intensive commercial or other uses or introduce building scale or stylistic signatures which are alien to an otherwise harmonious urban environment. Whether highly urban or rural in setting, the same principles and risks are faced by any community that is subjected to change without proper controls and safeguards.

REDEFINING FUNCTION AND SYMBOL

The 'adaptive reuse' of buildings, a term coined by architects in recent periods to demonstrate a design choice, in fact describes a process of which there is evidence in the earliest human settlements. Long after the original function or symbolism of a building may be forgotten, the material investment in construction can serve succeeding generations, rather than razing it. In most cases, this process of reuse is born of necessity. In the modern sense of the term, however, 'adaptive reuse' describes a conscious choice to retain a building of intrinsic value and to give it a new life, usually through a function that differs from that imagined by its builders.

The Dangers of Construction

While the beauty attributed to certain historic buildings is subjective, and not always a value shared across a society or community, a degree of understanding of collective history is common in most nations. In Afghanistan, as in other conflict-prone countries, the disruption of systems of formal education over decades has meant that many have been denied the opportunity to learn about their own history. One of the most visible manifestations of this situation since 2002 has been the transformation of urban centres, where concrete and glass buildings now surround the surviving historic fabric. The rapid inflow of population and external resources has increased demand for urban property, which has soared in value, prompting speculative building on an unprecedented scale. This construction boom, driven in part by external aid, is arguably causing more extensive damage to both the built heritage and archaeology of Afghanistan than decades of neglect or conflict. This process of transformation is one that many historic cities have witnessed, but the speed with which destruction is being wrought in Afghanistan, particularly at a time of relative peace and prosperity, is disturbing and now poses the single greatest

Above, a guest room in Shigar Fort Residence in northern Pakistan, a unique heritage conservation project that offers guests the opportunity to experience the restored original architecture of a 17th-century raja's fort-palace.

Below, the Yu Aw is one of four synagogues in the Old City of Herat which, after decades of abandonment and neglect, has been restored to provide a much-needed space for an infant school.

challenge to urban conservation initiatives, such as those being implemented by the Historic Cities Programme (HCP) in the cities of Kabul and Herat.

A Demonstrative Approach

Working within communities that may be ambivalent about the intrinsic value of their environment, with officials unwilling to enforce even the most basic form of legal control, it has been vital for the Programme to build confidence in the notion of conservation by showing results. By inviting community leaders to witness at first hand craftsmen at work on mosques and shrines that held special religious or social significance, it has been possible over time to rally residents behind a process from which they benefit directly, in terms of improved public facilities or living conditions. Such initiatives also instil a sense of collective identity and pride. Media attention on the conservation process has also contributed to building public awareness of the value and sheer beauty of what survives, and thereby helped to shift the public debate beyond a stage where the demolition of such buildings or areas might be admissible. As well as creating awareness, this 'demonstrative' approach is driven by the need to create a new reality on the ground. The fact that scaffolding is in place and teams of workmen engaged around a historic public building is a useful deterrent against those who might wish to 'modernize' it. So, too, investments in upgrading can effectively obstruct ill-conceived intrusions into the historic fabric, such as the widening of streets in Kabul or the demolition of covered passages in Herat.

Framework Agreements

In a context where a historic building may be close to collapse, or pressure is building for its 'redevelopment', there may be little time to negotiate the eventual use of a public building in advance with officials who may not be in a position to define the eventual programme. Working within the confines of framework agreements signed with central or local authorities, the initial conservation of public buildings has taken place in parallel with consultations with custodians or community representatives as to the eventual functions of a building. While clearly unorthodox, this 'exploratory' approach to the adaptive reuse of historic property has enabled the Programme to maintain momentum, while responding to the fast-changing economic and institutional environment that prevails in Afghanistan. Certain aspects of this approach are outlined in the three examples that follow.

Chahar Suq Cistern

Once the major source of domestic water for inhabitants of the Old City of Herat, the Chahar Suq Cistern became redundant with the introduction of piped water in the 1980s. The Cistern soon began to fill with waste from the surrounding bazaars and, by the time that it was surveyed in 2004, it was clear that what had been an important public facility only twenty years previously had been forgotten. Largely invisible due to encroachments, the central domed space, which measures twenty metres across, seemed at that time to have potential for a range of public functions. Rather than trying to define these in any detail, however, the priority was to stabilize the structure, parts of which were in a precarious state.

As it its name implies, the restored Chahar Suq Cistern in the centre of the Old City of Herat lies at the intersection of four bazaars. It is now used for events such as photography exhibitions and musical performances.

In a setting where conservation works on this scale are unusual, there were many visitors to the city-centre site over a period of three years, during which time it was possible to explore a range of uses for a facility that seemed to belong to everyone, and to no one. It was not until the internal scaffolding was dismantled, lights were installed and an impromptu public meeting was held in late 2008 in the space that had once served as a reservoir that the true potential of the venue became clear to local officials. After years of negotiations with municipal officials and a spirited campaign in the local media, this event opened the way for the relocation of dozens of shops that had been built in front of the main entrance of the Cistern. With the reclamation of a small urban square on the land that was previously occupied by these shops, new possibilities have opened up for the use of the Cistern and adjoining bazaars, which have also been restored. Pending the finalization of an operational agreement, the Chahar Suq Cistern is in regular use for exhibitions, seminars and receptions, which generate income now used to meet the costs of upkeep of the complex.

After conservation (left) of the Timur Shah Mausoleum in Kabul, the monument and its park is now used for cultural events.

Timur Shah Mausoleum

Although a very different type of building, the conservation of Timur Shah's Mausoleum in Kabul (see p. 86) between 2003 and 2007 provides a further example of this 'demonstrative' approach towards reuse. Built in the late eighteenth century within a formal garden originally laid out in Mughal times on the banks of the Kabul River, the massive brick Mausoleum remains one of the largest built landmarks in Kabul. Historic photos indicate that the Mausoleum underwent a series of repairs and 'improvements' in the nineteenth and twentieth centuries, before the uppermost of its two domes was damaged during factional fighting in 1993–94. The partial collapse of this brick dome posed an immediate threat to the integrity of the Mausoleum. The priority from the start was to stabilize the structure. Given the religious and historic significance of the building, there was at this early stage no discussion as to possible adaptive reuse. It was not until the closing stages of the conservation work that the main domed space of the Mausoleum, which served at this time as a carpentry workshop, came to be used for occasional lectures for students of architecture. This led to a discussion about formalizing the use of the building and the park (reclaimed after hundreds of informal traders had been relocated) for appropriate cultural events.

Left, the Queen's Palace in Bagh-e Babur in Kabul was looted and burned during inter-factional fighting in 1992 and only the ruined walls were left standing.

Right, now the Palace is fully restored and its courtyard often serves as the venue for musical and theatrical performances.

The crypt, in which the grave of Timur Shah and others lie, remains accessible for visitors who wish to pay their respects, while the main space above has, since 2007, been used for a regular series of public lectures, as well as for occasional seminars and exhibitions. Without a *waqf* (an elaborate system of endowments) to contribute to the cost of upkeep of the Mausoleum, resources could be raised through the use of its magnificent central space, as well as the newly landscaped park, for appropriate public events. Although this is an unfamiliar concept in the Afghan context, a draft agreement for the complex to be operated as a cultural venue is under discussion with the relevant authorities.

Queen's Palace

A more deterministic approach towards adaptive reuse was employed in the restoration of the Queen's Palace in Bagh-e Babur, Kabul (see p. 78). Built in the late nineteenth century as a residence for members of the royal household inside a Mughal garden, the complex was destroyed during factional fighting in the early 1990s. At the design stage, a balance had to be found between respect for the form and surviving details of this important historic monument, and the needs of future users of the Palace. It proved necessary to allay the fears of Afghan officials with limited experience of adaptive reuse, who urged that the building be faithfully restored to its original form and converted into a 'museum'. In the end, a compromise was reached whereby modern services were introduced to the Palace with the least possible intrusion. Collapsed sections were rebuilt, and the major reception areas restored in a manner that retains the proportions and details of the original, enabling them to serve a variety of functions, including exhibitions, meetings and a cafeteria. It is foreseen that such a range of activities will, in time, generate sufficient revenue to meet the costs of the upkeep of the restored Palace and the garden as a whole.

WHY ADAPTIVE REUSE IS RELEVANT

HCP's approach to the reuse of historic buildings has developed as a result of the Programme's involvement in preservation planning and conservation projects since its inception. There can be no doubt that this is one of the most pressing issues in decaying historic areas throughout the world, and certainly no less so in the context of Islamic cities.

A first question is why adaptive reuse is relevant in the effort to preserve historic areas. It is in this light that HCP's approach and practice can be best understood, particularly with regard to the choice of a functional programme and its philosophy of intervention, as well as the implementation modalities followed.

Inexorable Decay and Rapid Development

Two opposites – inexorable decay and rapid development – reinforce each other and bring about a vicious cycle that is very hard to break in historic areas. Because the old fabric is so fragile – sometimes on the verge of collapse – urgent intervention appears justified. But when intervening, the only alternatives considered in most cases are radical modernization or total substitution. There are numerous reasons for this.

Global changes caused by rapid urbanization and development have brought about social displacement as well as the loss or transformation of historic places and natural sites around the world. New building models and materials that are associated with progress are used extensively in new and old areas alike, in spite of the fact that they are often expensive and ill-suited to local conditions. The gradual disappearance of traditional builders and artisans, and the emergence of contractors who are often unable to cope with old structures is, of course, another difficulty. They find it easier and more lucrative to demolish and rebuild.

Inside the Queen's Palace in Kabul there is an exhibition and performance space. The skills of a sizeable team of Afghan craftsmen in a range of building techniques were developed in this reconstructive and adaptive process.

A dancing lesson under way at the
Darb Shouglan Community Centre in Cairo,
which serves the residents of the
Darb al-Ahmar neighbourhood. The Cultural
Programme provides an excellent example
of young people expressing themselves and
developing a sense of pride.

An Alternative to Radical Destruction and Change

In the face of this unfortunate state of affairs, the rehabilitation and adaptation of old buildings for new uses can be a powerful means of demonstrating that there is an alternative to radical and destructive change and that old buildings, particularly those that still hold a symbolic significance for the communities concerned, need not be associated with poverty and neglect.

Such buildings are, in fact, still capable of playing a useful role in contemporary life. Their reuse can help stimulate the revitalization of traditional crafts and create new employment, and they can offer a strong attraction for residents and visitors alike.

In sum, adapting old buildings to new uses can be a source of pride, as well as economic and social benefits for the surrounding communities. For this reason, the exemplary, demonstrative value of successful rehabilitation and reuse projects can inspire the community and serve as a tangible demonstration that old is far from bad.

Definition of the Functional Programme

In adapting an old building, the first question is what to do with an old structure, often underused and sometimes derelict or abandoned. HCP's approach has always been to identify a functional programme that will be useful and relevant, self-sustainable, and not disruptive.

HCP's approach has been that of researching and promoting discussion within communities to identify uses that are relevant and that benefit residents. Libraries, health centres, adult education facilities, recreational and children's day-care places are but a few among the functions that can find a place in structures awaiting rehabilitation, particularly in declining historic areas where services are rare. The more these structures can be made part of the life of a neighbourhood, the more they will be appreciated and cared for, and the more they will serve as a demonstration that old buildings can continue to have a useful purpose.

Income-Generating Components

Once rehabilitated, if buildings are not maintained, within the span of just a few years they will be back where they started. Ensuring financial support for their continued maintenance is thus essential. However socially relevant they may be, such new uses per se cannot guarantee a building's long-term sustainability. In fact, socially relevant uses may bring in little revenue. A mix of activities is thus essential, some not or less profitable, others definitely to generate revenue. HCP therefore seeks to identify income-generating components for its adaptive reuse schemes, dedicating between one third and one half of the usable space to this purpose. Depending on the specific situations and the results of preliminary market studies, the inclusion of spaces that can be rented out for commercial or office use or as studio accommodation has proven an effective means of ensuring that revenue for the operation of the buildings is available. A further strategy that has proven effective in ensuring sustainability is adaptive reuse schemes that are not overly specialized. Spaces that are versatile and adaptable over time are more likely to remain occupied. If a given use fails or is no longer profitable, it can be replaced with another. Uses that are not overly specialized are also less likely to disrupt a historic structure.

In Keeping with the Past

The third prerequisite in defining a successful and acceptable functional programme is that a new use must be compatible with the historic character of the building. This is best achieved by avoiding total transformations. The ideal solution is one where the same use and spatial organization can be reinstated. But this is rarely possible. Even reusing an old house for the same purpose requires modifications and upgrading to accommodate changes in family structure, as well as the need to insert modern utilities. No matter how different the proposed new use may be from the original, the new use of the space should be compatible with the nature of the spaces and the architectural character of the old building. Preservation of the structure's circulation, hierarchy of spaces, decorative features, proportions and scale must inform the brief for its adaptive reuse, and not vice versa. This does not mean that change is excluded, but that it must be compatible in order to allow the building in question to remain true to its essence – both within, so as not to disrupt the interior articulation and significance of spaces, and without, so as not to alter the surrounding context.

Philosophy and Approach

The philosophy of intervention adopted by HCP in its rehabilitation and adaptive reuse initiatives has been to apply internationally agreed conservation criteria and standards, and to identify the best ways in which these can be adapted to the particular conditions of the site in question.

Respecting the existing fabric, including alterations to the building over the course of its evolution, is a major element of the approach. In general, the existing situation is, as much as possible, retained as found, particularly where there is no evidence of the previous

The timber carving on the facade of the Old Dispensary in Zanzibar is unlike any other in the Stone Town in its sheer abundance and vivacity.

A ceremony taking place in front of the new Caravanserai at Bagh-e Babur in the Old City of Kabul. Funds generated through activities at the Caravanserai are one means of making the garden self-sustaining.

configuration. In cases where evidence of a different, earlier condition is found, the relative advantages and disadvantages of the observable transformations are carefully assessed, and, if justified, the original configuration is re-established. HCP has sought to conserve rather than replace any salvageable component of the building. In cases where replacement is unavoidable, techniques and materials used are compatible with the original ones. In particular, the use of cement is avoided as it is never compatible with traditional mortars. In cases where new components are inserted, such as with sanitary facilities, electrical works and other technical installations, these changes are rendered reversible and do not alter in any substantial way the building's existing configuration. Through new interventions, HCP seeks to improve the quality of the fabric and its long-term conservation whenever intrinsic structural faults are detected.

Back to the Future

HCP seeks to fit the proposed new uses around the original building so as to avoid any disruption, loss or disfigurement of the traditional fabric, as well as avoid any alteration of the building's established patterns of use. This approach usually determines the fundamental choices to be made in preparing the adaptive reuse scheme, as well as important decisions to be made before and during intervention. Usually the nature of the interventions can be grouped into actions aimed at stabilizing and preserving the existing original building materials and features; eliminating accretions and inappropriate changes that are no longer justified; or re-establishing finishes and well-documented components that have been demolished or removed from the building. This occurs primarily in cases where the appreciation and presentation of the historic structure was seriously compromised by past demolitions. Interventions also aim to introduce services and modern conveniences or technical installations needed to enable the contemporary use of the building, without unnecessary emphasis and avoiding excessive juxtapositions. Ultimately, HCP's ambition is to reintroduce meaningful life to old buildings, and leave as few marks as possible.

Implementation and the Role of Training

Experience with local contractors in the contexts where HCP has been operating often reveals that conservation skills and experience are limited and that there is a need to disseminate effective conservation and repair techniques. This makes the development of training and apprenticeship programmes an essential aspect of the implementation of any building works. The complexity of integrating the training component with the building works process, as well as the need to identify and adapt new conservation techniques as the work proceeds, calls for the definition of implementation modalities especially tailored to the requirements and organization of each project.

Flexibility and Control

Often, HCP's project team retains control over the entire development of the construction work and, in different degrees, takes over the combined responsibilities of supervision architect and main contractor. Accordingly, the project team is responsible for planning the nature and schedule of works, coordinating labour and procurement of materials, and supervising the implementation of site activities and training, as well as monitoring the quality of the results achieved. Depending on the particular conditions, the work may be split into a series of separate components and implemented as work carried out by the apprentices, during or immediately following training, under the supervision of the trainers and project staff; through direct recruitment of experienced local craftsmen who are selected on the basis of their abilities and past experience; or by subcontracting discrete packages to specialized contractors selected on the basis of their competence and proven track record.

The combination of these different modalities of implementation makes it possible to maintain flexibility and control at all stages, thus enabling the project team to ensure good quality in the work performed, monitor and reduce costs, and facilitate close integration of the training component into the overall building conservation process.

Above, lime plaster to prevent water seepage is being applied to the dome of the Tomb of Isa Khan in the gardens of Humayun's Tomb in Delhi.

Below, workmen at the junction of the roof and wall on the south facade of the Great Mosque of Mopti, Mali, preparing to position new water spouts.

SYRIA
242–279

EGYPT
280–323

MALI
212–241

TANZANIA
190–211

CASE STUDIES

TAJIKISTAN
324–333

AFGHANISTAN
70–109

PAKISTAN
110–165

INDIA
166–189

KABUL

AFGHANISTAN

1 Bagh-e Babur   2 Timur Shah Mausoleum and Park   3 Asheqan wa Arefan   ■ Intervention areas

N
▲ ├──────── 500 m

FEATURED CASE STUDIES

BAGH-E BABUR

TIMUR SHAH MAUSOLEUM AND PARK

ASHEQAN WA AREFAN

Kabul Area Programme

Programme Scope / Objectives

The scope of programme activities includes documentation, the conservation of historic public and private buildings and the rehabilitation of historic landscape and reclamation of green open spaces. Also involved are the upgrading of basic infrastructure, the development of craft skills, and the promotion of activities intended to improve household incomes. Support for neighbourhood planning initiatives, technical assistance to institutions responsible for planning and urban management, and support for professional development are also part of the intervention.

Preceding pages:

A view of Kabul looking towards the north shows the historic quarters located in District 1 in the middle ground, Timur Shah Mausoleum along the river, and the presidential quarters in the distance.

The city of Kabul is thought to have grown around a Buddhist settlement mentioned by Ptolemy in AD 150. The fortified Citadel of Bala Hissar bears witness to its turbulent history, as do the defences along the ridge of the Sher Darwaza Mountain to the south, dating in part to the period of Hindu rule prior to the advent of Islam in AD 871. Kabul seems to have remained little more than a military outpost during the fourteenth and fifteenth centuries, when the cities of Ghazni and Herat witnessed significant prosperity and architectural innovation. It was not until the early sixteenth century, when the founder of the Mughal Empire Babur visited and laid out several gardens in and around the city (including the newly rehabilitated park now known as Bagh-e Babur), that Kabul seems to have grown in importance. While based in India, Babur's successors continued to show an interest in Kabul, with Shah Jahan's governor, Ali Mardaan Khan, building the covered Char Chatta bazaar in the centre of the commercial quarters in the mid seventeenth century. By the time that Timur Shah moved his capital from Qandahar to Kabul in the late eighteenth century, Kabul was home to approximately 60,000 people.

Accounts from nineteenth-century travellers to Kabul describe a dense settlement of traditional dwellings, accessed by means of narrow alleyways and divided into distinct quarters, some of which were walled. The only neighbourhoods in which this dense urban fabric has survived are Asheqan wa Arefan and Chindawol. Apart from the imposing brick Mausoleum of Timur Shah, built in the late eighteenth century, and the royal residences and walled gardens within the citadel, the bazaars and serais seem to have been the principal landmarks in the city. The Char Chatta bazaar was the target of a punitive raid on Kabul in 1842 by British troops, who returned in 1880 to destroy Bala Hissar Citadel, which until then had been the seat of power.

Shortly after this event, Amir Abdur Rahman Khan laid out a new palace north of the Kabul River, outside the confines of the historic city, whose population had by then risen to about 500,000. Merchant families who had previously lived close to the bazaars in the city centre began at this time to move to more spacious new homes built on market gardens to the north and west. Zarnegar Park, now in the centre of modern Kabul, formed part of a walled orchard in which a number of residences and pavilions used by the royal family and members of the court stood. The earliest suburbs of Kabul began to develop after the

Left, AKTC is working to preserve traditional housing stock in the war-affected historic quarters of the Old City. A typical street view within the project cluster in Asheqan wa Arefan shows restored external facades and access improvements.

Right , the process of planning involves consultations between government, professionals and community representatives.

1920s, when foreign architectural forms and styles began to prevail, most notably in the development by Amanullah Khan of a new government enclave at Darulaman, well to the south.

As part of subsequent efforts to modernize Kabul, the boulevard of Jade Maiwand was driven through the historic fabric in the 1940s, followed by further roads cut through Shor bazaar and Chindawol, in response to anti-government unrest in the late 1970s. The utopian Kabul Master Plan, originally drawn up in 1967, indicates multi-storey blocks in place of the historic fabric, with wide freeways replacing the network of narrow alleyways. The reality on the ground, however, remained one that differed little from nineteenth-century accounts, and it was in the traditional fabric of the Old City that much of the inter-factional street fighting took place in 1993–94, which forced the population to flee their homes. It was not until 1995 that families were able to return and reconstruct their war-damaged homes, after the area had been cleared of landmines.

It is in the war-affected historic quarters of Asheqan wa Arefan, Chindawol, Pakhtafu-rushi, Shanasazi and Kuche Kharabat, which together are home to some 18,000 people, that the Aga Khan Trust for Culture (AKTC) has undertaken a range of planning, conser-vation, upgrading, training and socio-economic initiatives since 2002. Within an area that is now the most densely populated in Kabul, a dozen historic public buildings – including mosques, shrines, a mausoleum, a *madrasa*, traditional *hammams*, and educational facilities – have been restored over the past seven years. During the same period, some fifteen important historic homes have been rehabilitated in these quarters, where more than seventy families have been able to undertake essential repairs to their traditional homes through a system of small-scale grants. This conservation work has provided opportunities for on-the-job training for more than a hundred carpenters, plasterers and masons, many of whom live in the historic quarters.

Much of the fragile stock of traditional housing in the Old City is subdivided and residents, half of whom are tenants, have access to only the most rudimentary services, due to decades of under-investment and neglect, as well as more recent conflict-related damage. In order to address the abject conditions facing the majority of residents in this area, AKTC has invested in repairs or construction of drains, paving of alleyways and streets, and safer water supplies, benefiting nearly 20,000 inhabitants since 2002. These interventions have generated significant employment within the resident communities, who have also benefited from a range of measures aimed at promoting small-scale

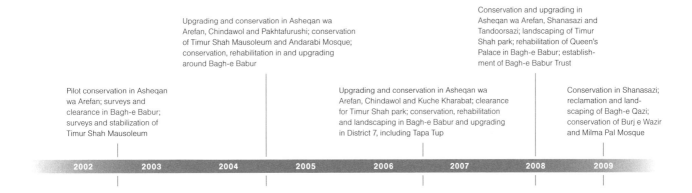

Pilot conservation in Asheqan wa Arefan; surveys and clearance in Bagh-e Babur; surveys and stabilization of Timur Shah Mausoleum

Upgrading and conservation in Asheqan wa Arefan, Chindawol and Pakhtafurushi; conservation of Timur Shah Mausoleum and Andarabi Mosque; conservation, rehabilitation in and upgrading around Bagh-e Babur

Upgrading and conservation in Asheqan wa Arefan, Chindawol and Kuche Kharabat; clearance for Timur Shah park; conservation, rehabilitation and landscaping in Bagh-e Babur and upgrading in District 7, including Tapa Tup

Conservation and upgrading in Asheqan wa Arefan, Shanasazi and Tandoorsazi; landscaping of Timur Shah park; rehabilitation of Queen's Palace in Bagh-e Babur; establishment of Bagh-e Babur Trust

Conservation in Shanasazi; reclamation and landscaping of Bagh-e Qazi; conservation of Burj e Wazir and Milma Pal Mosque

2002 2003 2004 2005 2006 2007 2008 2009

economic activity, especially among women. Together with the jobs created through conservation projects, these investments have contributed to the process of recovery across these quarters, where self-built repairs and infill construction are on the increase. In the context of a process of urban recovery that since 2002 has been largely ad hoc and uncontrolled, AKTC works with Afghan institutions and residents to prepare neighbourhood plans to guide reconstruction and development within specific quarters, while ensuring that such initiatives are consistent with wider planning processes for the metropolitan area of Kabul. An important contribution to the planning process was made through the formulation in 2005 of a joint planning framework for the residential neighbourhood of Chindawol, which remains under intense pressure from commercial development in adjoining areas. Initial mapping of land use, infrastructure and services was followed by a series of intensive participatory planning exercises with municipal staff and representatives from Chindawol, leading to identification of development priorities over a five-year period, along with assignment of institutional responsibilities.

It was in order to address the issue of responsibilities for planning and urban management that an Old City Development Commission was formed in 2004, with a view to ensuring more effective collaboration between concerned institutions. With participation from ministerial and municipal staff, academics, professionals and community representatives, the Commission serves as a clearing house for information and provides a valuable platform for consultations between professionals and residents on critical development and technical issues. Its efforts to contribute to the process of planning, however, have been less successful, due both to a lack of professional capacity and persistent institutional rivalries.

As pressure on urban land and housing mounts, and uncontrolled 'development' encroaches on the surviving historic fabric, the future of the Old City requires action at a variety of levels: formulation of effective national policy on urban heritage; promotion of consultative processes of planning; more effective urban management; enhancement of professional and craft skills; technical support for families to repair or upgrade traditional homes; and promotion of economic activity to enable them to afford these. In all of these aspects, it is important to maintain a balance between conservation and development, by basing interventions on a sound understanding of the past, while allowing for new needs and opportunities to emerge, in response to the aspirations and resources of Afghans themselves.

In the process of upgrading Kabul's infrastructure, attention has been paid to unsanitary and dangerous street drainage in the historic quarter. Above, drainage works are being undertaken in Chindawol in the Old City; below, residents benefit from AKTC's intervention.

Background

BRIEF HISTORY OF PROGRAMME AREA

Settled since the 1st century AD, Kabul did not develop as a major conurbation until the 16th century. By the late 18th century the city comprised a series of defensive enclaves that were home to some 60,000 people. By the late 19th century the urban population had grown to 500,000 with settlement expanding beyond the historic quarters, to the north of the Kabul River. There was significant development in District 7 during the 1960s, but few investments in infrastructure in District 1, where living conditions deteriorated until 1993, when factional fighting caused widespread damage in both areas. It was not until 1995 that families were able to resettle and, since 2001, ad hoc reconstruction of property has continued, although investment in repair or extension of infrastructure has been negligible.

Challenges

PROGRAMME RISKS

While significant physical gains have been made in conservation of historic property and upgrading of community infrastructure, and self-built residential (re) construction is widespread, the process is largely ad hoc and rarely conforms to the outdated Master Plans that continue to serve as an official reference for urban development.

SITE CONDITIONS

Districts 1 and 7 have some of the highest densities in the city, and access is primarily by means of narrow alleyways between fragile traditional homes or on steep hillsides. This poses a challenge for both conservation and upgrading works, as did the clearance of unexploded ordnance that was necessary during the early stages of the programme.

DEMOGRAPHICS

The historic quarters in District 1 have some of the highest recorded residential densities in Kabul, at more than 300 persons per hectare. AKTC baseline surveys indicate a 15% increase in residential population in District 1 between 2003 and 2005, with a slightly smaller increase in District 7 for the same period.

HOUSEHOLD ECONOMY

Nearly half of households occupy rented property, with two thirds of families dependent on a single income (usually derived from casual labour) and often in debt.

STATUS OF HEALTH AND EDUCATION

Within the programme area there are several major government health facilities to which residents have access if they can afford care and medicines. Recorded school attendance is nearly 80%, although significant numbers of children work in workshops, depots and bazaars in the commercial area of District 1.

AVAILABILITY OF DRINKING WATER AND PROPER SANITATION FACILITIES

The coverage of the piped water network in Districts 1 and 7 is limited, and more than a third of families rely on public sources, where contamination is common. There is no mains sewage, and nine out of ten families rely on basic sanitation facilities.

ENVIRONMENTAL CONCERNS

With extensive war damage and limited access to basic infrastructure and services for those living in informal areas, environmental conditions are generally poor.

INFRASTRUCTURE

A legacy of under-investment in drainage, water supply and electrical networks, coupled with extensive war damage, requires significant investments to achieve even the most basic levels of service coverage for the fast-growing population of Districts 1 and 7.

ACCESS TO OPEN SPACE

Deterioration of and encroachment on key open spaces is widespread. Public parks or open spaces have generally not been effectively maintained, and are often used for parking or the disposal of domestic waste. With many areas of the Old City laid waste as a result of factional fighting, property disputes are common and encroachment on public open spaces is widespread.

BUILDING CONDITIONS

The combination of lack of maintenance and war-related damage means that the bulk of the housing stock, which is largely traditional, is in a poor state of repair. Added to this, high levels of occupancy in subdivided homes in District 1 pose a challenge to efforts to improve living conditions for the occupants.

Significant Issues and Impact

MASTER PLANNING PROCESS

The historic fabric within District 1 is designated for comprehensive 'redevelopment' in the various Master Plans drawn up for Kabul since the 1960s, but is now widely acknowledged to merit 'special heritage zone' status – even though there is no urban heritage policy to frame this. Along with adjoining areas, a new plan for District 7 has been under formulation since 2006.

PLANNING ISSUES

While several proposals for the rehabilitation of the historic quarters of Kabul have been drawn up since 2003, none has been formally adopted, nor have 'neighbourhood plans' been officially endorsed. Instead, the process of urban planning in Kabul continues to be ad hoc, and precise responsibilities for formulation and implementation remain unclear.

BASELINE STANDARDS

Since 2005, baseline surveys have been conducted in residential areas of Districts 1 and 7, covering more than 30,000 people. In addition to the monitoring of physical transformations in the area, several surveys of informal commercial activity have been undertaken in District 1 since 2004.

SOCIO-ECONOMIC INITIATIVES

In addition to some 200 craftsmen trained through apprenticeships during the course of conservation works in Districts 1 and 7, more than 100 women continue to take part in vocational training aimed at improving household livelihoods in the programme area. The generation of employment through conservation and upgrading activities, as well as development of skills within communities in Districts 1 and 7, continues to be a priority within AKTC's programme.

CONSERVATION ASPECTS

Significant progress has been made since 2003 in the conservation of a cluster of historic buildings situated between the Timur Shah Mausoleum, on the banks of the Kabul River, and the neighbourhood of Asheqan wa Arefan in District 1, aimed at halting the transformation of the traditional fabric and deterioration of often-fragile buildings. Other important monuments were also conserved during the rehabilitation programme in Bagh-e Babur between 2002 and 2008.

QUALITY OF LIFE

It has been addressed through investments in urban squares (Asheqan wa Arefan, Kuche Kharabat), the reclamation of historic gardens (Bagh-e Babur, Timur Shah Mausoleum and Bagh-e Qazi), as well as landscaping measures in degraded municipal open spaces such as Zarnegar Park. Since 2003, investments in upgrading of infrastructure and support for small-scale housing repairs have benefitted some 25,000 people in the programme area. Some investments have been made in improving public water sources and grants for improvements in household sanitation have been made available.

POST-IMPLEMENTATION PLANS

Building on the experience gained in the formation of an independent Trust that now operates the restored Bagh-e Babur, the establishment of a dedicated Kabul Old City Trust (to succeed the existing Old City Commission), might ensure effective oversight of development in the historic fabric. The Trust might also have a role in coordination of the upkeep of key historic public facilities and facilitation of community-managed maintenance of infrastructure.

Partners

PUBLIC PARTNERS

Kabul Municipality, Ministries of Urban Development, Information and Culture, and Religious Affairs.

PRIVATE PARTNERS

Property owners, businessmen, traders, NGOs.

COMMUNITY PARTNERS

Community representatives.

Authoritative Framework

'Memoranda of Understanding' between Kabul Municipality, the Ministry of Information and Culture and AKDN signed in 2002, relating firstly to urban conservation programme covering the area around Timur Shah Mausoleum and historic neighbourhoods to the south and east and secondly to the restoration of the historic landscape of Bagh-e Babur and rehabilitation of surrounding area in District 7.

Opposite page:

A craftsman at work in the Milma Pal Mosque in Bagh-e Bala, Kabul, which is being restored as a joint training exercise with the Ministry of Information and Culture.

Bagh-e Babur

KABUL, AFGHANISTAN

Laid out in the early sixteenth century by the Mughal emperor Babur, the site now known as Bagh-e Babur was rehabilitated between 2002 and 2008. The natural landscape was central to the life of Babur's court, and he was buried in the garden in around 1540. Among his successors, both Jahangir and Shah Jahan commissioned works on this site, in honour of Babur.

Accounts of nineteenth-century travellers suggest that the garden subsequently fell into disrepair, and its perimeter walls were reportedly damaged in an earthquake in 1842. Repairs were carried out at the turn of the century, during the reign of Amir Abdur Rahman Khan, who constructed a complex for use by his family within the garden. Further transformations took place during the twentieth century, when European-style elements were introduced into the landscape and a swimming pool and greenhouse were built on an upper terrace. By the time fighting broke out in Kabul in 1993–94, the character of Bagh-e Babur was much altered and the site was in a poor state of repair. Situated on the front lines between factions, the garden and surrounding area was laid waste, and it was not until 1995 that the clearance of mines could begin, and residents return to their war-damaged homes.

In 2002 an agreement for the rehabilitation of the eleven-hectare garden was signed between the Aga Khan Development Network (AKDN) and the Transitional Afghan Administration. In parallel with clearance of remaining unexploded ordnance, work began in 2003 on conservation of Babur's grave enclosure, which had been significantly altered over time. Apart from the carved headstone erected by Jahangir in 1607, few original elements survived and the marble enclosure recorded by nineteenth-century travellers had disappeared. Following archaeological excavations, levels around the grave were lowered and a wall rebuilt around the original grave platform, after removal of a modern concrete structure. Based on marble fragments found in the grave area, it was then possible to erect a replica of the marble enclosure around Babur's grave, inside the walled area.

The war-damaged marble mosque dedicated by Shah Jahan in 1675 was re-roofed with lime mortar and cracked marble elements were replaced, while the *mihrab* wall was refaced with marble in 2004. Among other historic buildings subsequently restored were the nineteenth-century Garden Pavilion and

The landscaping aims to restore the character of the original garden through the introduction of flowing water. Above, a water channel is seen flowing from the Garden Pavilion in the distance.

Opposite page:
The same area is seen during the early stages of the rehabilitation.

Following pages:
The Kuh-e Sher Darwaza hill settlements provide a dramatic view of Bagh-e Babur.

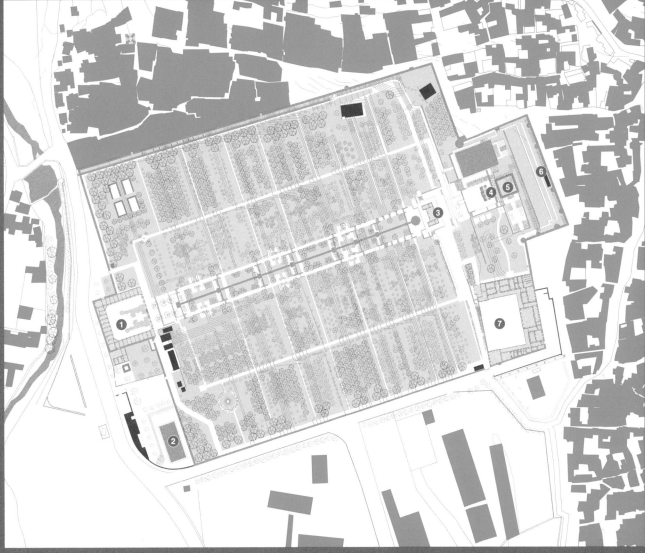

1 Caravanserai Complex   3 Garden Pavilion   5 Babur's Grave Enclosure   7 Queen's Palace
2 Swimming Pool   4 Shah Jahan Mosque   6 Perimeter Wall

N   100 m

Project Scope / Objectives

Documentation, archaeological excavation, grading, replanting and the installation of irrigation systems have been undertaken here. The reconstruction of perimeter walls and the central axis, as well as the conservation of the Shah Jahan Mosque, was also involved. The reconstruction of Babur's grave enclosure, the rehabilitation of the Queen's Palace and Pavilion, construction of the Caravanserai and new swimming pool, and development of an operational plan and procedures for the site were also carried out.

Phasing 2002 → 2008

| Surveys and project design; site clearance and grading; reconstruction of perimeter walls | Archaeological excavations; restoration of Shah Jahan Mosque; landscaping and installation of irrigation system; construction of a Caravanserai | Reconstruction of Babur's grave enclosure and central axis; rehabilitation of Garden Pavilion and Queen's Palace; landscaping and installation of irrigation | Upon completion of rehabilitation, a 'Memorandum of Understanding' for the formation of the Bagh-e Babur Trust was signed; imple-mentation of operational plan and procedures |

| 2002 | 2003 | 2004 | 2005 | 2006 | 2007 | 2008 |

Along the central axis, water descends through a series of channels, water chutes and ponds, before being filtered and pumped back to the main holding tank at the base of the Garden Pavilion.

the Queen's Palace, both now in use for public functions. Excavations in the western end of the garden in 2003 revealed stone foundations of a seventeenth-century gateway, around which was constructed a Caravanserai complex, using traditional forms and techniques, which now houses an interpretation centre and other facilities.

It is thought that Babur had massive walls built around the perimeter of his entire garden and nearly 1.5 kilometres of traditional compacted earth wall were rebuilt or repaired during 2003–04, generating significant employment among residents of the surrounding neighbourhood.

Archaeological excavations in 2004–05 revealed sections of a marble-lined water channel and a series of water tanks along the central axis, which provided the basis for the design and reconstruction of a system that again allows water to flow the length of the centre of the garden, as it did in Babur's time.

The landscaping aims to restore the character of the original garden, through the reintroduction of flowing water and the grading of adjoining terraces that have been replanted as distinct orchards. Stone pathways and stairs have been laid on either side of the central axis, which is flanked by an avenue of plane trees, interspersed with pomegranates, apricots, apples, cherries and peaches. Outside this zone, the terraces have been planted with mulberry, apricot, fig and almond trees, with copses of walnut along the reconstructed perimeter walls.

Opposite page:

Top, 1.5 kilometres of walls were rebuilt or repaired around the garden where people stroll and relax. Stone pathways and stairs have been laid on either side of the central axis.

Right, work undertaken since 2002 on Babur's marble grave enclosure, which comprises a central arched opening flanked by pairs of marble lattice, or *jali*, screens, aimed to re-establish the original character of the grave area, seen also in section, below.

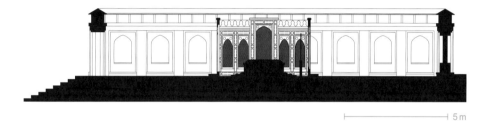

| | 5 m

Right, the war-damaged marble Mosque dedicated by Shah Jahan in 1675 was re-roofed with lime mortar and cracked *marble* elements were replaced, while the *mihrab* wall was refaced with marble in 2004. A plan and elevation of the Mosque are also shown, below.

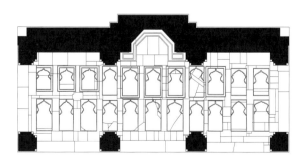

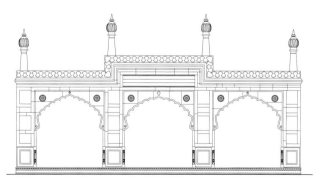

| | 5 m

Above, people take advantage of the weather to relax in the garden of Bagh-e Babur, where the enhancement of craft skills, including weaving (above right), is encouraged.

Below, a view from the upper terrace of Bagh-e Babur reveals the restored Garden Pavilion and Shah Jahan Mosque, while, on the right, the swimming pool, relocated during the restoration process, is a popular attraction in the warmer months.

In parallel with the garden rehabilitation, support has been provided for improvements in living conditions for the 10,000 residents of the surrounding neighbourhoods, through community-managed upgrading of storm-water drainage, water supplies and access. In 2007 a series of vocational training courses for women and men were initiated, in order to contribute to improving household livelihoods in the district.

Upon completion of the rehabilitation work, the signature in early 2008 of a 'Memorandum of Understanding' between Kabul Municipality, the Ministry of Information and Culture and AKDN paved the way for the formation of the independent Bagh-e Babur Trust, which now operates the garden. Revenue derived from the growing numbers of visitors to the garden and the hire of restored facilities is used to meet the costs of the operation.

Many visitors to Bagh-e Babur remark on how it represents for them a symbol of cultural recovery in Afghanistan: the challenge is to retain the unique character of the landscape and monuments while ensuring continued access to the public.

Background

BRIEF HISTORY OF PROJECT SITE

The garden was laid out in the early 16th century by the founder of the Mughal empire, Babur, who was buried on the site in 1540. His successors continued to enhance and invest in the site which, by the mid 19th century, seems to have fallen into disrepair. Some 50 years later, several new buildings were constructed and, through to the 1940s, parts of the historic landscape were transformed in imitation of European gardens. Already in a poor state of repair, both monuments and landscape were badly damaged during fighting in 1993–94. Following minor repairs in the late 1990s, a comprehensive rehabilitation programme was initiated in 2002.

Challenges

SITE CONDITIONS

The presence of unexploded ordnance in Bagh-e Babur and the surrounding area posed an initial challenge, as did encroachments against the perimeter walls of the garden and the need to keep the site open to the public during the course of the rehabilitation work.

DEMOGRAPHICS

Having been largely depopulated, the residential neighbourhoods in the environs of Bagh-e Babur are now home to some 28,000 people. With an urban growth rate in Kabul of 5%, there is growing pressure on land and housing across the city, with indications that residential densities (recorded in 2007 to be 290 persons/hectare) in District 7 continue to rise.

HOUSEHOLD ECONOMY

More than a third of households rely on wages from daily casual labour for their primary income, and less than a third of households report having a secondary income. Fewer than 5% of families report having any savings.

STATUS OF HEALTH AND EDUCATION

While there are few public health facilities in District 7, access to education is not a major specific challenge, with a number of large schools operational. Despite this, nearly a quarter of children resident in the District do not attend school. Nearly half of household heads in the settlement around Bagh-e Babur are illiterate.

AVAILABILITY OF DRINKING WATER AND PROPER SANITATION FACILITIES

Only 15% of residents have access to a piped water source (often a public standpipe), while others rely on shallow wells, many of which are contaminated. Nearly all families rely on traditional pit latrines, with more than a quarter of residents sharing these and washing facilities with others.

ENVIRONMENTAL CONCERNS

As elsewhere in Kabul, the depletion of groundwater resources remains a concern, and efforts are being made to recycle waste water for irrigation in Bagh-e Babur. In the context of limited collection of domestic waste by the Municipality, most of this is now disposed of in the Kabul River.

INFRASTRUCTURE

While investments have been made in storm-water drains on the slopes above Bagh-e Babur, the growth of illegal settlement in this area poses a continuing risk. Repairs have been made to a local water network supplied from wells in the garden, and key sections of drains upgraded, but more investments are required if access to basic infrastructure for residents of war-damaged neighbourhoods in District 7 is to improve significantly.

ACCESS TO OPEN SPACE

The destruction of Bagh-e Babur denied residents of Kabul access to what had been one of the city's largest public open spaces.

BUILDING CONDITIONS

Families continue to invest in the self-built reconstruction and repair of war-damaged housing, which is largely traditional, but overcrowding is common and living conditions are generally poor.

Significant Issues and Impact

DATA COLLECTION/SURVEYS

Baseline surveys have been conducted in District 7 since 2005, while the profile of visitors to Bagh-e Babur is recorded through regular interviews. Over the past four years, during and since the completion of the rehabilitation, the garden has been visited by some 800,000 visitors.

MASTER PLANNING PROCESS

The Kabul Metropolitan Area Plan foresees District 7 remaining a largely residential area, with a light industrial zone designated to the south of Bagh-e Babur. Despite the provisions of this and previous Master Plans, however, growth continues in an ad hoc manner and changes in land use remain unchecked.

PLANNING ISSUES

Drawing on the results of physical and social surveys, a number of joint neighbourhood planning exercises have been initiated in District 7, involving community representatives and municipal staff.

HISTORIC BUILDINGS/MONUMENTS CONSERVED

Among the monuments conserved during the course of the project are Babur's grave enclosure; Shah Jahan Mosque; Queen's Palace; Garden Pavilion and the noon-day gun platform; and Burj e Wazir in Guzargah Village. All of the major buildings within Bagh-e Babur have been restored or reconstructed, and are in regular use.

NEW BUILDING FACILITIES

New construction includes the Caravanserai (housing the Bagh-e Babur visitor centre and other functions) and a public swimming pool and related facilities situated outside the precinct of the garden.

COMMUNITY INVOLVEMENT/PROGRAMME

Building on experience gained during community-managed upgrading between 2003 and 2006, a number of small-scale enterprises were established in 2007, with the objective of contributing to household incomes in the neighbourhood.

VOCATIONAL TRAINING/CAPACITY BUILDING

In order to address the initial lack of conservation experience, the Bagh-e Babur rehabilitation project served as a platform for the development of skills among Afghan craftsmen and professionals. This has been followed since 2007 by community training initiatives in District 7, where carpentry and tailoring workshops have been established with AKTC support. Survey and neighbourhood planning exercises with municipal staff and others have contributed to the development of capacity within counterpart institutions.

CONTRACTING METHODS

With the exception of two subcontracts for specific tasks within Bagh-e Babur, all works have been carried out with direct labour recruited (usually from the resident community) and supervised by AKTC professional staff. Upgrading work undertaken by AKTC in District 7 between 2002 and 2008 generated some 400,000 workdays of labour, in addition to that generated from the rehabilitation of the garden.

RELEVANT CODES/STANDARDS ADOPTED

All conservation work has been undertaken in accordance with the relevant international charters and Afghan domestic law. The formulation of operational procedures drew on documented examples of similar types of site management elsewhere in the region.

EXTERNAL ASSESSMENT

A dossier for the possible inclusion of Bagh-e Babur on the World Heritage List is being prepared by UNESCO consultants.

Partners

PUBLIC PARTNERS

Kabul Municipality, Ministry of Information and Culture.

PRIVATE PARTNERS

Property owners, NGOs.

COMMUNITY PARTNERS

Community representatives.

Donors

Federal Republic of Germany, Royal Norwegian Embassy, United States Embassy, Save the Children.

Authoritative Framework

'Memorandum of Understanding' between Kabul Municipality, the Ministry of Information and Culture and AKDN signed in 2002, covering the rehabilitation of Bagh-e Babur and upgrading measures in District 7. A tripartite 'Memorandum of Understanding' was signed in 2008 between the same parties. The purpose of this agreement was to establish terms for a joint programme aimed at the effective management and upkeep of Bagh-e Babur.

Timur Shah Mausoleum and Park

KABUL, AFGHANISTAN

One of the largest surviving Islamic monuments in central Kabul, the Mausoleum of Timur Shah marks the grave of the son of Ahmad Shah Durrani, who effectively united Afghanistan in the late eighteenth century. Born in 1746, Timur Shah served as governor of Herat before facing down a military challenge to the throne from his elder brother, and then moved his capital from Qandahar northeast to Kabul. His son Zaman Shah laid him to rest in 1793 in a garden on the banks of the Kabul River, but it was not until 1817 that the actual construction of the Mausoleum began.

Timur Shah's Mausoleum comprises an octagonal structure with two intersecting cross-axes organized on six levels. Above a crypt in which the grave stands is a square central space surrounded by an octagonal structure, with four double-height *iwans* on the main elevations. There are sixteen brick-vaulted spaces of varying size on the first floor, encircling the central space, with a flat roof above, surrounding the sixteen-sided drum under the domes. Following the central Asian tradition, the Mausoleum has an outer dome constructed on a high drum above a ribbed inner dome.

Surveys of the structure in 2002 revealed that part of the upper dome had partially collapsed and that rainwater had penetrated parts of the supporting drum. This area was therefore the focus of the initial conservation work, once the damaged roof sheeting and timber structure had been removed. Examination of the upper dome revealed that it had been built in stages, using 'skins' of brick masonry laid in relatively weak lime mortar. After the erection of a bamboo platform over the lower dome, and installation of two tension belts around the drum, a reinforced-concrete beam was poured around the inside, anchored into the brickwork with forty-eight stainless-steel anchors. Unstable sections of brickwork in the upper dome were removed, and repairs undertaken to match the original structure, using special bricks laid in lime mortar. The original geometry, comprising six layers of brickwork at the springing, reducing to two at the apex, was reproduced in the repairs.

As the upper roof was not part of the original scheme, a new geometry was devised for its profile, based on a harmonic curve that matched the proportions of the main structure. A total of thirty-two laminated timber rafters, measuring up

The open space surrounding the Mausoleum has been reclaimed and landscaped to provide much-needed green space in Kabul.

Opposite page:
Below, sections of the damaged dome were removed during conservation work; above, the restored Mausoleum can be seen with its new terrace at ground level.

Project Scope / Objectives

Documentation and conservation of the Mausoleum, together with upgrading of community infrastructure, formed the basis for this intervention. Grading, replanting and installation of irrigation system in the adjoining park were also in the scope of the project. Construction of perimeter walls and the hosting of cultural events in the restored Mausoleum were carried out in parallel with negotiation for an operational plan for the site.

Phasing 2002 → 2009

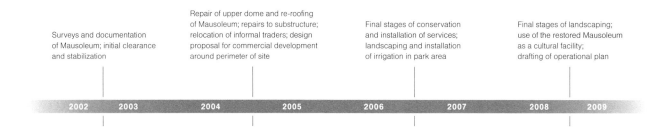

Surveys and documentation of Mausoleum; initial clearance and stabilization

Repair of upper dome and re-roofing of Mausoleum; repairs to substructure; relocation of informal traders; design proposal for commercial development around perimeter of site

Final stages of conservation and installation of services; landscaping and installation of irrigation in park area

Final stages of landscaping; use of the restored Mausoleum as a cultural facility; drafting of operational plan

2002   2003   2004   2005   2006   2007   2008   2009

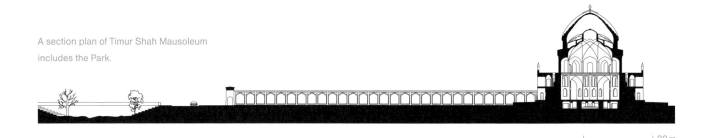

A section plan of Timur Shah Mausoleum includes the Park.

20 m

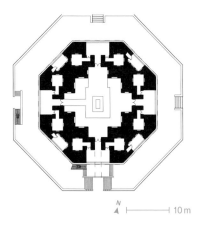

N   10 m

The ground-floor plan shows the Mausoleum's octagonal structure with two intersecting cross-axes.

to thirteen metres in length, were produced to support a new 'shell' roof, which now spans the repaired dome. Timber boards were then screwed in a circumferential pattern over these rafters, prior to the fixing of galvanized sheeting.

While work proceeded on the main dome, repairs were carried out on the flat roofs and supporting vaults. Areas of facing brick on the elevations were also repaired, as were the soffits of the main vaults, where there was a high quality of brick masonry. In order to protect the lower sections of masonry and facilitate public access, a seven-metre-wide brick platform was built around the Mausoleum.

During the course of conservation work, negotiations took place for the relocation of the two hundred or more informal traders who had encroached on what had been the garden around the Mausoleum. A range of options was explored aimed at incorporating the traders into a new development on or adjoining the garden of the Mausoleum, but these were not approved by the Municipality, and the traders were removed in 2005. Since then, a perimeter wall has been constructed to protect the site, which has been planted with an orchard of mulberry trees – matching those seen in historic photographs – and laid out with paths for pedestrian access through the garden.

Since its restoration, the central space of the Mausoleum has been the setting for lectures, seminars and exhibitions, and discussions are under way with the relevant authorities for the space and reclaimed garden to be used for cultural events on a regular basis. Despite the challenging physical and institutional context in which the project was realized, it stands as an example of how an important historic monument can help to encourage a wider process of regeneration in a fast-changing urban setting.

Timber planking was fixed to the radial rafters over the upper dome, supporting a protective outer layer of galvanized iron sheeting.

The informal commercial market, with over 200 traders, which occupied the original municipal park surrounding the Mausoleum, was relocated. Pedestrian paths and orchards have been placed in this new green space.

Challenges

SITE CONDITIONS
The limits on access to the Mausoleum posed a significant challenge, as did encroachments around the monument and across the adjoining park area.

DEMOGRAPHICS
The Mausoleum now stands in one of the busiest commercial areas in central Kabul – a fact that affected the negotiations leading up to the reclamation of the Park that had been encroached upon by informal traders.

ENVIRONMENTAL CONCERNS
The reclamation of the Park has contributed to improving the environmental situation in an important commercial neighbourhood. The state of the Kabul River remains a concern.

INFRASTRUCTURE
The poor state of infrastructure in the area around the Mausoleum and Park represented a challenge.

ACCESS TO OPEN SPACE
Encroachment by informal traders on a park (now reclaimed) that had originally surrounded the Mausoleum meant that the public was denied access to an important public green space.

BUILDING CONDITIONS
The poor condition of the Mausoleum, and the structural instability of its upper dome, represented a major challenge.

Significant Issues and Impact

DATA COLLECTION/SURVEYS
A range of surveys were conducted within the commercial areas that surround the Mausoleum and Park.

MASTER PLANNING PROCESS
Under the Kabul Master Plan, this area of District 1 has been designated a commercial area, although there are questions as to the future of the pockets of residential property to the west, and the Kabul River to the north.

PLANNING ISSUES
The reclamation of the Park has restored the designated land use, although the lack of proper controls on properties around the site could affect its use as a public green space.

HISTORIC BUILDINGS/MONUMENTS CONSERVED
The conservation of the largest surviving Islamic monument in central Kabul has contributed to the rehabilitation of this area.

VOCATIONAL TRAINING/CAPACITY BUILDING
The conservation work on the Mausoleum provided opportunities for the development of skills among Afghan craftsmen and professionals. The continuing use of the building for student lectures contributes to developing their awareness of cultural issues.

CONTRACTING METHODS
Given their specialist nature, conservation work was undertaken with direct labour, supervised by AKTC professional staff.

RELEVANT CODES/STANDARDS ADOPTED
All conservation work has been undertaken in accordance with the relevant international charters and Afghan domestic law. The formulation of operational procedures draws on experience gained during the course of establishing the Bagh-e Babur Trust.

Partners

PUBLIC PARTNERS
Kabul Municipality, Ministry of Information and Culture.

PRIVATE PARTNERS
Informal traders, shopkeepers.

COMMUNITY PARTNERS
Community representatives.

Authoritative Framework

'Memorandum of Understanding' between Kabul Municipality, the Ministry of Information and Culture and AKDN signed in 2002, covering a range of urban conservation measures in District 1, Kabul.

Asheqan wa Arefan

KABUL, AFGHANISTAN

The neighbourhood of Asheqan wa Arefan takes its name from two historic graves at which Afghans come to worship and pay their respects to this day. As with the conservation of ten other buildings of religious significance in the area, the project was vital in building confidence within the community during the initial stage of the programme of the Aga Khan Trust for Culture (AKTC) in the Old City of Kabul in 2002. Found to be in a poor state of repair, the distinctive colonnaded entrance and passage that leads to the grave of Asheq required extensive structural repairs, while the lower grave of Aref, which retains its traditional wooden enclosure, was re-roofed, as were those of the adjoining summer and winter mosques. The courtyard of the shrine, which provides an important focus for residents in the area and visitors alike, was landscaped and improvements made to the public water supply and ablution facilities located at its perimeter.

The mosque of Sedukan, which in its present form dates from the mid nineteenth century, lies to the north-east and was identified by residents as a priority in 2005. Here, it was necessary to entirely reconstruct flood-damaged sections of the lower brick masonry structure, including the traditional hypocaust that provided underfloor heating to the ground-floor prayer space that is mainly used in winter. This was followed by the restoration of a finely carved wooden colonnade that divides the upper prayer space and the timberwork on the main east elevation. Drawing on the experience gained in Sedukan, a further ten community mosques, along with a large brick-domed *madrasa*, were restored in the Old City between 2002 and 2010.

Work began in early 2004 on the early twentieth-century house of Muhammad Amin, one of eleven historic homes to have been restored in the area. Still inhabited by the son of its original builder, who was a carpenter, the dwelling is arranged on three levels around a courtyard, whose elevations retain the characteristic vertical-sliding timber shutters. Subsidence under sections of the structural timber-frame of the house was addressed, and then repairs were carried out to load-bearing external brick masonry. Following this, mud-brick infill between the lightweight timber framing – a widely used technique to strengthen structures in this earthquake-prone zone – was repaired on the upper levels. A more complex process of restoration was followed in the Wasay House, which is

The entrance portico to Asheqan wa Arefan Shrine, with its series of decorated plaster niches, was uncovered during the course of repairs and restored.

Opposite page:
A view inside the Ulya Madrasa shows the extent of damage to the structure as a result of conflict. Work is proceeding fast on restoring the building, which will be returned to community use.

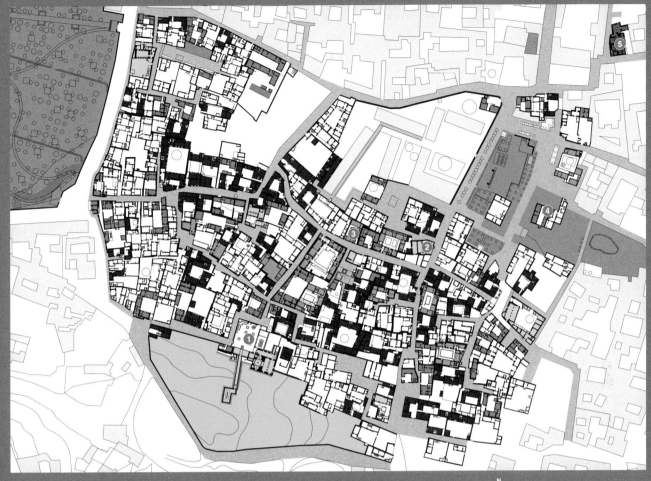

1 Asheqan wa Arefan Shrine
2 Sedukan Mosque
3 Muhammad Amin House
4 Wasay House
5 Shuturkhana Hammam

■ Conservation of religious buildings
■ Conservation of other public buildings
■ Full-scale residential conservation
■ Small-scale residential repairs
■ Public access and infrastructure improvements
■ Other properties documented
■ Public green space

N ⊢———————————⊣ 100 m

Project Scope / Objectives

The scope of the intervention includes documentation and conservation of historic buildings, together with the reclaiming and landscaping of public green space. Basic infrastructure has been upgraded, while the development of craft skills, measures to enhance household livelihoods and support for neighbourhood planning initiatives also lie within programme.

Phasing 2002 → ongoing

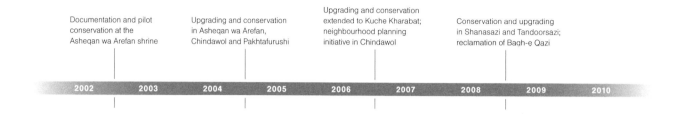

Documentation and pilot
conservation at the
Asheqan wa Arefan shrine

Upgrading and conservation
in Asheqan wa Arefan,
Chindawol and Pakhtafurushi

Upgrading and conservation
extended to Kuche Kharabat;
neighbourhood planning
initiative in Chindawol

Conservation and upgrading
in Shanasazi and Tandoorsazi;
reclamation of Bagh-e Qazi

| 2002 | 2003 | 2004 | 2005 | 2006 | 2007 | 2008 | 2009 | 2010 |

A drawing of the highly decorated door
of Asheqan wa Arefan Shrine.

thought to date from the mid nineteenth century and required stabilization of the entire structure. Historic photographs of the dwelling enabled the project team to ascertain the original decorative scheme, on which basis war-damaged parts of the internal moulded plaster decoration – including a series of recessed niches or *chinikhana* used for the display of porcelain – and timber screens within the main space on the first floor were restored. Here, as in other conservation projects, the documentation of the building has enabled a better understanding of the diversity of construction and decorative techniques used in the Old City over the past 120 years.

Even with some of its finest historic buildings restored, living conditions for many residents of the Old City remain poor, with widespread overcrowding and limited access to services within homes. The rehabilitation of traditional bathhouses or *hammams*, many of which were no longer operational, offered a means of improving family health and hygiene. For instance, the war-damaged domed structure of the *hammam* in the Shuturkhana neighbourhood was entirely rebuilt, and the traditional hypocaust system of heating its semi-subterranean spaces was rehabilitated. Reopened in late 2006 and managed by private operators, the *hammam* is used by more than 150 residents a day on average, and generates revenue that is used for upgrading public infrastructure in the surrounding area.

As part of efforts to improve living conditions for the residents of the Old City, nearly six kilometres of underground and surface drains have been repaired or rebuilt over the past eight years, while an area of more than 22,000 square metres of pedestrian alleyways and streets have been paved within the historic fabric.

The opportunities provided for residents to develop their skills and to find employment have been as important as the physical outcome of the conservation and rehabilitation work in Asheqan wa Arefan and adjoining residential neighbourhoods in the Old City. To date, nearly 320,000 workdays of skilled and unskilled labour have been generated among communities in the Old City, while more than 150 young men have undertaken apprenticeships as carpenters, masons and plasterers, working alongside highly skilled Afghan craftsmen. As part of an initiative aimed at improving family livelihoods, more than two hundred women from the neighbourhood have attended courses in tailoring, embroidery and kilim-weaving, along with literacy classes.

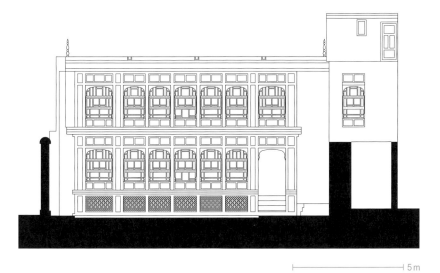

Top left, repairs being undertaken
at Asheqan wa Arefan Shrine.

Top right, drainage works are a priority for
the inhabitants of Asheqan wa Arefan.

Bottom right, a carpenter repairs a timber
lattice-work screen.

Left, a sectional plan of Wasay House,
located in Asheqan wa Arefan.

⊢————————————————⊣ 5 m

Opposite page:
The fine timber work of Muhammad Amin House in the Asheqan wa Arefan district of the Old City has been restored.

Right, a view taken inside the restored Wasay House features the Goldaste Kharabat orchestra, formed as part of the music initiative in Kabul.

Challenges

PROJECT RISKS
Growing pressure on city-centre property presents a continuing threat, as does the absence of a coherent framework for urban development for Kabul as a whole.

SITE CONDITIONS
With some of the highest densities in the city, and access primarily by means of narrow alleyways between fragile traditional homes, conservation and upgrading faced significant logistical and technical challenges.

DEMOGRAPHICS
At more than 300 persons per hectare, the historic quarters have some of the highest recorded residential densities in Kabul. Surveys indicate a 15% increase in residential population in District 1 between 2003 and 2005 alone.

HOUSEHOLD ECONOMY
With nearly half of households occupying rented property and two thirds of families dependent on a single income (usually derived from casual labour), the Old City is one of the poorest areas in Kabul.

AVAILABILITY OF DRINKING WATER AND PROPER SANITATION FACILITIES
The piped water network in District 1 suffered extensive war-related damage, and more than a third of families rely on public sources, where contamination is common. There is no mains sewage.

INFRASTRUCTURE
Decades of under-investment in drainage, water supply and electrical networks, coupled with extensive war damage, means that significant investments are required to achieve even the most basic levels of service coverage for a fast-growing population in District 1.

BUILDING CONDITIONS
Lack of maintenance, together with war-related damage, results in the bulk of the traditional housing stock being in a poor state of repair. Added to this, high levels of occupancy in subdivided homes pose a challenge to efforts to improve living conditions.

Significant Issues and Impact

DATA COLLECTION/SURVEYS
Since 2004, regular baseline surveys have been conducted in District 1, covering more than 30,000 people.

MASTER PLANNING PROCESS
The historic fabric within District 1 is designated for comprehensive 'redevelopment' in the various Master Plans drawn up for Kabul since the 1960s, but is now widely acknowledged to merit 'special heritage zone' status – even though there is no urban heritage policy to frame this.

PLANNING ISSUES
While several proposals for the rehabilitation of the historic quarters of Kabul have been drawn up since 2003, none has been formally adopted, nor have 'neighbourhood plans' been officially endorsed.

HISTORIC BUILDINGS/MONUMENTS CONSERVED
Since 2002, more than a dozen public buildings and 15 historic homes have been conserved within a cluster of historic fabric in the Old City.

COMMUNITY INVOLVEMENT/PROGRAMME
All conservation and upgrading activities have been undertaken in close collaboration with community representatives, who have also assisted in managing and securing contributions to certain projects.

VOCATIONAL TRAINING/CAPACITY BUILDING
More than 100 craftsmen have been trained through apprenticeships during the course of the conservation work, and some 60 women continue to take part in vocational training.

CONTRACTING METHODS
With the exception of minor subcontracts for Bagh-e Qazi, all works have been carried out with direct labour recruited (usually from the resident community) and supervised by AKTC professional staff.

QUALITY OF LIFE
The deterioration of open spaces has been addressed through investments in urban squares, the reclamation of historic gardens, and landscaping measures in degraded municipal parks.

Partners

PUBLIC PARTNERS
Kabul Municipality, Ministries of Urban Development, Information and Culture, and Religious Affairs, Kabul Old City Commission.

PRIVATE PARTNERS
Property owners, businessmen, traders.

COMMUNITY PARTNERS
Community representatives.

Donors

Federal Republic of Germany, Royal Norwegian Embassy, United States Embassy, USAID Afghanistan, British Embassy, Aga Khan Foundation.

Authoritative Framework

'Memorandum of Understanding' between Kabul Municipality, the Ministry of Information and Culture and AKDN signed in 2002 for urban conservation programme in District 1.

BAR DURRANI

OUTBE CHAQ

MASJID JAME

MOMANDHA

ABDULLAH MESRI

1 Ansari Shrine Complex   ■ Intervention areas

N   ⊢————⊣ 250 m

FEATURED CASE STUDY

**ANSARI SHRINE COMPLEX,
LOCATED NORTH-EAST OF THE OLD CITY**

Herat Area Programme

Programme Scope/Objectives

The scope of programme activities includes the documentation and conservation of historic public and private buildings. Also involved are the upgrading of basic infrastructure, the development of craft skills, support for neighbourhood planning initiatives and technical assistance to institutions responsible for planning and urban management. Support for professional development has also been extended.

Preceding pages:

The restored Chahar Suq Cistern provides the backdrop for a street scene in the Old City of Herat.

From its origins as an outpost of the Achaemenid Empire, the repeated strengthening of the Citadel of Qala Ikhtyaruddin, and the setting out of a walled settlement by the Ghaznavids, the city of Herat has had a turbulent history. Situated at the crossroads of regional trade, in the midst of rich irrigated agriculture, the area has been a prize for successive invaders. The city became a centre for Islamic culture and learning during the reign of Timur, whose successors commissioned several monumental buildings, but it then fell into decline under the Mughals. Considered part of Persia during the Safavid era in the eighteenth century, it was not until 1863 that Herat was incorporated into the emerging Afghan state.

The distinctive rectilinear layout of the city of Herat was delineated by massive earth walls that protected the bazaars and residential quarters that lay within. This was the extent of the city until the middle of the twentieth century, when administrative buildings were constructed outside of the walls to the northeast. In time, wealthier families moved away from the densely-inhabited historic fabric into suburbs that spread across what had been gardens to the north. The historic quarters remained home to some 60,000 people by the time that unrest broke out in 1979, resulting in the depopulation of the western quarters, where traditional buildings soon fell into disrepair or collapsed and infrastructure was looted or damaged. It was not until 1992 that clearance of mines and unexploded ordnance began, enabling families to resettle in the war-affected historic quarters and begin the process of rebuilding.

With a rapid increase in the urban population since 2002, pressure on central residential neighbourhoods has intensified, even though the state of infrastructure and the few public facilities result in poor living conditions for most inhabitants. In many cases, returnee families who had become accustomed to modern dwellings while in exile have demolished their traditional homes and, in the absence of building controls, built incongruous concrete structures, dozens of which now rise above the skyline of the Old City. Residential areas that adjoin main roads are rapidly being commercialized, with the construction of multi-storey 'markets' which have both an environmental and visual impact on the historic fabric.

In order to address these transformations, the programme of the Aga Khan Trust for Culture (AKTC) in Herat has since 2005 involved processes of documentation, building conservation and upgrading, in parallel with measures to

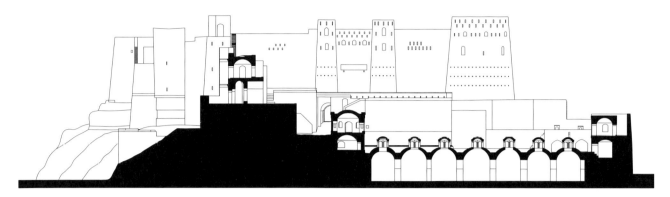

10 m

Above, the largest restoration project undertaken by AKTC has been the Citadel of Qala Ikhtyaruddin, seen here in section.

Bottom, a view of the Citadel of Qala Ikhtyaruddin shows work being done on a wall under scaffolding, with a tower in the background.

strengthen the capacity of and coordination between key institutions. Given the pace of change, one of the first priorities was to map the historic fabric and establish systems for monitoring demolitions and new construction. A survey of more than 25,000 residential and commercial properties in the Old City, undertaken in 2005–06, yielded important information on the current urban environment, and this has now been mapped and linked to a database, which has proved to be a useful resource for identifying priorities for intervention and could also be invaluable for physical planning.

The prime focus of AKTC's conservation work has been on two clusters of historic fabric, extending across the Bar Durrani and Abdullah Mesri quarters, where investments have been made in the conservation of key public buildings – mosques, cisterns and bazaars – as well as historic houses. A system of small-scale grants and building advice was also established, aimed at enabling some fifty owners of traditional homes to undertake basic repairs, which has resulted in improved living conditions while protecting the integrity of the historic fabric. As well as safeguarding historic property, these projects have provided a platform for the training of craftsmen, while demonstrating the potential of conservation and adaptive reuse in a context where there is a growing tendency to demolish historic property and 'redevelop'.

At the centre of one such cluster lies the domed Chahar Suq Cistern, constructed in 1634, which, along with smaller cisterns, remained the primary source of water for inhabitants of the Old City until the 1970s. The massive structure supports a brick dome that spans nearly twenty metres over a square reservoir which, at the time of initial surveys, was filled with domestic waste. Extensive repairs were carried out on the war-damaged dome and the masonry substructure that had been weakened by encroachments from adjoining shops. An urban square has been created in front of the north entrance, after the relocation of shops that had encroached on this area. Since its conservation, the Chahar Suq Cistern has been in regular use for cultural events, including exhibitions and music recitals.

Of the other cisterns that have been conserved in the Old City, one is being used as an art gallery, another is being converted into a public library, while another serves as a study space for students of a *madrasa*. Among other initiatives aimed at promoting the adaptive reuse of historic buildings is the Karbasi House, now a school for traditional music and crafts, and the Yu Aw Synagogue that is now used as a kindergarten. Among the thirty other public buildings that have been conserved in the Old City are the historic

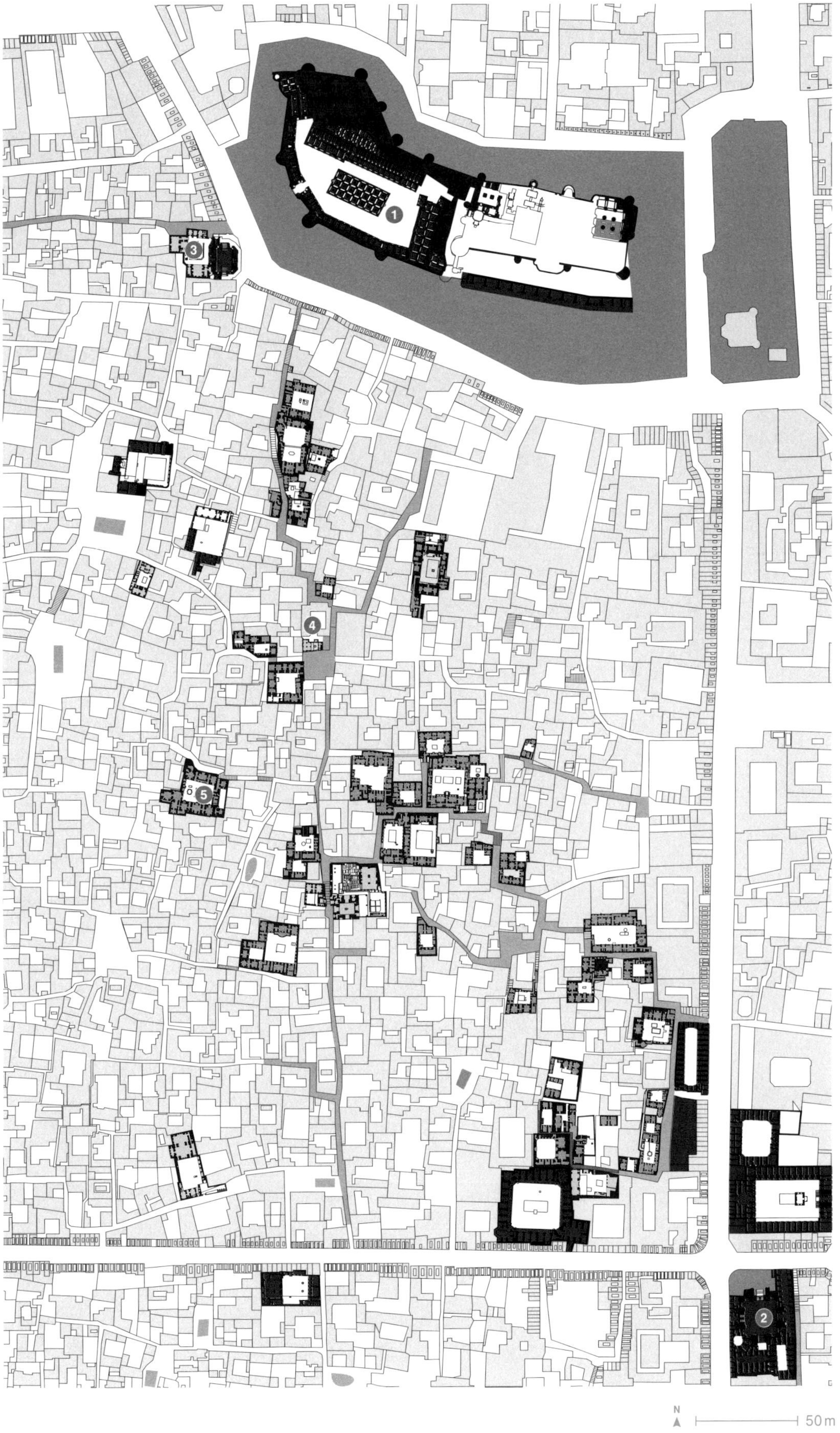

Conservation of
religious buildings

Conservation of
public buildings

Full-scale residential
conservation

Small-scale residential
repairs

Public access and
infrastructure improvements

Public space upgrading

1 Qala Ikhtyaruddin
2 Char Suq Cistern
3 Malik Cistern and Mosque
4 Urban Upgrading
5 Karbasi House (Aga Khan
Music Initiative School)

N
↑

├─────────┤ 50 m

Before work could begin on Chahar Suq Cistern, seen from the north-west
during restoration in 2005 (left) and after completion (right), encroachments
on the site had to be cleared and traders relocated.

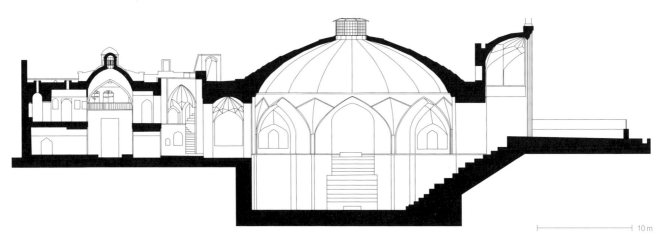

Chahar Suq Cistern, seen here in section,
is now much used for cultural events.

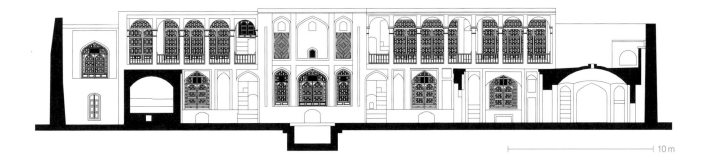

mosques of Hazrat Ali and Khaja Rokhband as well as several shrines, synagogues and a *hammam* or bathhouse. The largest single project to be undertaken in Herat by AKTC is the conservation of parts of the historic Citadel of Qala Ikhtyaruddin, where work began in late 2008 and is due for completion at the end of 2010.

Together with conservation of historic homes, these initiatives have provided opportunities for training in traditional construction and decorative techniques. Among the most significant of these dwellings is the Attarbashi House, which dates from the early twentieth century and retains distinctive northern and southern ranges of rooms (for use in summer and winter respectively), arranged around a courtyard. Traces of decorated plasterwork and intricate lattice *orosi* screens were found in a partially collapsed section of the house, which has been reconstructed, along with a small *hammam* for use by the family. To the south, in the Abdullah Mesri quarter, a very unusual painted mural was discovered in 2008 in the Ghulam Haider Posteen Doz House. Once the home of a wealthy family, the complex was found to be in a poor state of repair, and conservation work is under way on the structure, following documentation and stabilization of the mural.

As much as building conservation, however, the upgrading of infrastructure is critical to the future of the Old City of Herat. In order to contribute to the improvement of living conditions, nearly five kilometres of underground and surface drains have been repaired or rebuilt, and more than 6000 square metres of pedestrian alleyways and streets paved to facilitate access through the historic fabric. Together with the building conservation work, this has generated more than 240,000 workdays of skilled and unskilled labour, largely drawn from residents of the Old City, since 2005. These investments have directly benefited at least half of the population of the Old City, prompting community-implemented improvements in some quarters that were not covered under AKTC's urban conservation programme.

Aside from the physical challenges facing the historic fabric and the need for additional investment to render the Old City more habitable, the issue of management of the urban environment is now more critical than ever. Despite assurances that new development will be rigorously controlled, and appropriate plans drawn up to ensure safeguarding of the unique fabric of the Old City, city officials seem unable or unwilling to act to halt demolitions or inappropriate 'redevelopment'. Given that many such officials lack the professional training or experience to effectively manage urban growth in this sensitive context, AKTC staff provide technical assistance to a Commission for the Safeguarding and Development of the Old City of Herat, comprising representatives from key institutions and professional bodies. While it has made limited progress on the reform of systems of building permits and the monitoring of new construction or demolitions, the Commission

Top, a section of Attarbashi House.

Middle, a mural that was painstakingly restored in Posteen Doz House.

Bottom, a carpenter works on the restoration of Attarbashi House.

Left, masons work on the facade of the south wing of the central section of Attarbashi House during its rehabilitation.

Right, street-paving work in the Old City. About 6000 square metres of pedestrian alleyways and streets have been paved to facilitate access through the historic fabric.

provides a platform for discussion between key stakeholders, and a clearing house for information. While some progress has been made in involving communities themselves in the safeguarding of historic property, the absence of effective leadership on the part of civil servants has often handicapped these initiatives.

Most of the key historic monuments in the Old City have now been formally registered as part of an ongoing collaboration between AKTC and the department of Historic Monuments of the Ministry of Information and Culture. In order to build local professional skills, students from Herat University have been engaged in on-the-job 'further education' through the AKTC programme, which also supports site visits and lectures about conservation, planning and urban management issues. It is hoped that this cadre of young Afghan professionals will be in the vanguard of continued efforts to safeguard and develop their city, and possibly other historic centres in Afghanistan.

The challenge for the AKTC programme has been to find a balance between meeting often urgent conservation needs while addressing poor living conditions and simultaneously strengthening institutional capacity. This requires work at a variety of levels: with central government in Kabul to promote administrative reform and accountability; with local government to promote the rule of law, effective coordination and basic professional standards; among the wider Afghan professional community to raise awareness and build partnerships; among community representatives to assist in the implementation of rehabilitation work; and among donors and international organizations to draw attention to the threats posed to the fragile historic fabric of the Old City of Herat.

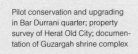

Pilot conservation and upgrading in Bar Durrani quarter; property survey of Herat Old City; documentation of Guzargah shrine complex

Upgrading and conservation in Abdullah Mesri and Momandha quarters in Herat Old City; conservation of Abdullah Ansari Shrine, Namakdan Pavilion in Guzargah

Completion of Chahar Suq Cistern and Guzargah complex; initiation of conservation on Qala Ikhtyaruddin

2005   **2006**   **2007**   **2008**   **2009**   **2010**

Challenges

PROGRAMME RISKS
While significant progress has been made in conservation of historic property and upgrading of community infrastructure, the lack of control over private 'development' continues to affect the integrity of the surviving historic fabric of the Old City.

SITE CONDITIONS
Residential areas in the Old City are densely populated, with homes often overcrowded, and access is primarily by means of narrow alleyways. This posed a challenge during the course of both conservation and upgrading works, as did the presence of unexploded ordnance.

DEMOGRAPHICS
With an average of 285 persons per hectare, the residential quarters in the Old City have some of the highest densities in Herat, and there are indications that this is increasing as the value of property rises, and families are forced to move into overcrowded homes in what remains the most affordable part of the city.

HOUSEHOLD ECONOMY
A significant proportion of residents in the Old City inhabit rented property, and rely on casual labour for their livelihoods.

STATUS OF HEALTH AND EDUCATION
There are very few educational or health facilities within the Old City, and residents have to travel elsewhere to have access to these services.

AVAILABILITY OF DRINKING WATER
AND PROPER SANITATION FACILITIES
More than a third of families in the Old City do not have access to a supply of safe piped water. While there is a system of underground drains, which has been upgraded in some quarters, most liquid waste flows into the 80 open cesspools that lie within the historic fabric.

ENVIRONMENTAL CONCERNS
With extensive war damage and limited access to basic infrastructure and services for residents of the Old City, environmental conditions are generally poor.

INFRASTRUCTURE
A legacy of under-investment in drainage, water supply and electrical networks, coupled with extensive war damage, requires significant investments to achieve

even the most basic levels of service coverage for the resident population. Added to this, there are significant technical challenges in laying drains through the dense historic fabric of the Old City.

ACCESS TO OPEN SPACE
Deterioration of and encroachment on open spaces in the Old City is widespread.

BUILDING CONDITIONS
The combination of lack of maintenance and war-related damage means that the bulk of the traditional housing stock is in a poor state of repair.

Significant Issues and Impact

MASTER PLANNING PROCESS
The historic fabric of the Old City has been ignored in the various Master Plans drawn up for Herat since the 1970s and, although there is widespread support for it to be given some form of 'special heritage zone' status, there exists no legal framework in which this might occur.

PLANNING ISSUES
A range of planning proposals for key clusters within the Old City has been drawn up, but none has been formally endorsed. Instead, development takes place in a largely ad hoc manner.

BASELINE STANDARDS
In 2005–06 a property survey was conducted in the Old City, covering more than 25,000 premises. Subsequent monitoring within the historic fabric has enabled physical transformations that continue to be tracked.

SOCIO-ECONOMIC INTIATIVES
Some 150 craftsmen have been trained through apprenticeships during the course of conservation works in Herat. The generation of employment through AKTC's conservation and upgrading activities over nearly five years has, therefore, made an important contribution to the urban economy.

CONSERVATION ASPECTS
With many historic buildings in Herat and the environs requiring conservation, efforts have been focused since 2005 on clusters of historic property within the Old City, as well as the shrine complex in Guzargah, which dates from the Timurid era. All works have been undertaken in partnership with Afghan counterpart

staff, in order to ensure that both crafts and professional skills are developed during the course of the works.

QUALITY OF LIFE
Efforts are being made to transform the area around Qala Ikhtyaruddin into a public green space.

POST-IMPLEMENTATION PLANS
An Old City Commission has been established during the course of the conservation programme and is officially mandated to monitor development in the Old City and to oversee future planning initiatives.

Partners

PUBLIC PARTNERS
Herat Municipality, Office of the Governor, Departments of Urban Development, Information and Culture, and Religious Affairs.

PRIVATE PARTNERS
Herat Old City Commission, property owners, businessmen, traders, NGOs, Herat Professional Shura.

COMMUNITY PARTNERS
Community representatives.

Donors

Federal Republic of Germany, United States Embassy, Royal Norwegian Embassy, Prince Claus Fund.

Authoritative Framework

'Memorandum of Understanding' between the department of Historic Monuments of the Ministry of Information and Culture and AKTC signed in 2005, covering the urban conservation works in the Old City. Separate agreement covering the conservation work on Qala Ikhtyaruddin signed with the Ministry of Information and Culture in late 2008.

Ansari Shrine Complex

HERAT, AFGHANISTAN

The shrine complex of Khwaja Abdullah Ansari in Guzargah, north-east of Herat, is both an important example of Timurid architecture and a popular place of pilgrimage. Having spent a life of contemplation and writing in and around the village, Ansari was buried here in 1089. Records suggest that a *madrasa* was established in Guzargah in the late twelfth century, and this was probably the complex reconstructed by Shah Rukh in 1424 and which now makes up the shrine complex.

The large courtyard of the *hazira* of Abdullah Ansari, with its arched *iwans* on the main axes and rows of study rooms between, takes a form that is more commonly associated with a *madrasa*. Both the main entrance arch and the high *iwan* that rises above Ansari's grave retain sections of fine glazed tile epigraphy and areas of geometric decoration. Some of the finest extant Timurid decoration in the region has been documented here as part of the limited intervention of the Aga Khan Trust for Culture (AKTC) in the complex.

Beginning in 2005, repairs were carried out to all roofs of the Shrine, which had been poorly maintained risking damage to the fragile internal plaster decoration in parts of the complex. During the course of this work, evidence emerged of alterations that had been made over time to the eastern *iwan*, which rises more than eighteen metres above the surrounding village. The removal of concrete that dated from the 1970s permitted a detailed structural analysis, on which basis a series of brick buttresses was constructed on the eastern side. At the same time, three vaulted rooms in the north-east corner of the complex, which were found to be unstable, were reconstructed on the same footprint as the original, using traditional materials. One of these rooms houses an intricately decorated basalt grave known as the Haft Qalam. It is foreseen that these spaces will in time be used to display important objects from the Shrine.

In order to facilitate the visits of pilgrims, original sections of marble paving were relaid at the main entrance. Incongruous aluminium doors were replaced with traditional wood, along with other doors leading on to the courtyard. To establish improved records, the historic gravestones that now fill this courtyard were methodically documented, prior to repairs and consolidation of the most vulnerable graves. Brick paving was also laid in key areas, to enable access and

Abdullah Ansari's tomb is under restoration in the complex courtyard and the historic gravestones have been documented.

Opposite page:
Above, the entrance *iwan* to the Shrine retains sections of fine glazed-tile epigraphy and areas of geometric decoration.

Below, an axonometric of the Shrine complex.

Project Scope / Objectives

The restoration of the Shrine complex at Guzargah involved structural analysis, detailed surveys, roof repairs and landscaping, together with reconstruction and restoration to better enable pilgrim visiting and document the surviving Timurid decoration.

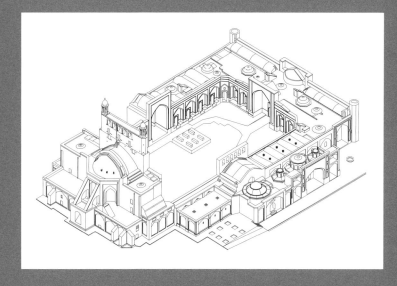

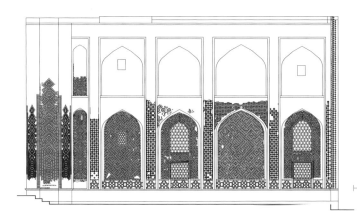

Left, work is being done on reconstructing the Haft Qalam room. The *haft-qalam* (seven pens) is a black marble gravestone marking the grave of one of Sultan Hussain Baiqara's sons. It refers to the seven styles employed in the decoration and design of the gravestone.

Above right, the fine detail of tile-work on the facade of the Shrine can be seen.

Right, a drawing of the tile-work.

Opposite page:
The restored Namakdan Pavilion once again represents the structure its Timurid builders had intended and work is now being undertaken on landscaping a formal garden around it.

2,5 m

guard against the removal of historic stones when new graves are dug within the courtyard. Discreet external lighting that is regularly used at night for religious ceremonies has also been installed around the courtyard

Following a detailed survey of the existing structure, restoration work on the Namakdan Pavilion, which dates from the fifteenth century, was initiated in late 2005. The two-storey, twelve-sided brick structure, built around an octagonal central space, had been much altered and was found to be in a poor state of repair. Following repairs to the ribbed dome, a modern intermediate floor was removed, restoring the original double-height central space, where traces were found of a water pool and channel, which were subsequently reconstructed. In order to ensure the stability of the brick superstructure, a system of horizontal steel reinforcement was introduced at several levels of the Pavilion, in some places using the apertures that had originally housed timber ties. During the course of removal of modern plaster, traces of glazed-tile decoration were found on two external elevations, and have been restored. After more than four years of painstaking conservation, the Namakdan Pavilion again resembles the structure that its Timurid builders intended, while work continues on landscaping the surrounding area.

Among other works carried out in the Guzargah complex were repairs to the structure and roof of the Zarnegar *khanqah*, which lies to the south-west of the Shrine. The central domed space of this building retains fine painted decoration, entirely in deep blue and gold, with bands of complex calligraphy.

Challenges

PROJECT RISKS
The principal risk in conserving the Shrine complex was in securing acceptance from the resident community and the many pilgrims who visit the site.

ENVIRONMENTAL CONCERNS
The principal environmental challenge lay in the protection of the historic garden and graveyard, which risked being encroached upon.

BUILDING CONDITIONS
Poor maintenance of the Shrine complex resulted in the various buildings being in a highly vulnerable condition at the start of the works.

Significant Issues and Impact

HISTORIC BUILDINGS/MONUMENTS CONSERVED
All significant historic buildings within the Shrine complex have been conserved, although there remains significant work to be done on the tile and plaster decoration.

COMMUNITY INVOLVEMENT/PROGRAMME
All conservation work was undertaken in close collaboration with the *mir* of Guzargah and other community representatives, who played a critical role in facilitating the works.

VOCATIONAL TRAINING/CAPACITY BUILDING
Dozens of craftsmen were trained during the course of the conservation works.

CONTRACTING METHODS
With the exception of landscaping, all works were carried out with direct labour supervised by AKTC professional staff.

RELEVANT CODES/STANDARDS ADOPTED
All conservation work in Guzargah has been undertaken strictly in accordance with the relevant international charters and Afghan domestic law.

Partners

PUBLIC PARTNERS
Ministry of Information and Culture.

PRIVATE PARTNERS
NGOs.

COMMUNITY PARTNERS
Mir of Guzargah, community elders.

Donors

Federal Republic of Germany.

Authoritative Framework

'Memorandum of Understanding' between the department of Historic Monuments of the Ministry of Information and Culture and AKTC signed in 2005, covering amongst other things the conservation of the Shrine complex of Abdullah Ansari in Guzargah.

GILGIT-BALTISTAN

PAKISTAN

1 Baltit Fort 2 Altit Fort 3 Shigar Fort 4 Khaplu Palace 5 Hunza Villages Rehabilitation   Intervention areas   N   ⊢———————⊣ 50 km

FEATURED CASE STUDIES

BALTIT FORT

ALTIT FORT

SHIGAR FORT

KHAPLU PALACE

HUNZA VILLAGES REHABILITATION

Gilgit-Baltistan
Area Programme

Programme Scope / Objectives

The goal of the programme is sustainable development through culture and strategic investments. These are social, economic and institutional processes that aim to protect, manage and promote cultural heritage as an integral part of sustainable development. The hope is to enable effective and participatory community stewardship of heritage and environmental resources, and to create income and enterprise opportunities for communities based on proactive cultural heritage management. This has entailed the restoration of monuments and the improvement of living conditions through housing, sanitation, local capacity building, revival of arts and crafts, and the creation of new employment and income opportunities.

Preceding pages:

A view through a pair of carved wooden windows in Khaplu Palace to the valley and the Karakoram Mountains beyond.

Gilgit-Baltistan, spread over 69,930 square kilometres, brings together a land of majestic mountain ranges and deep gorges with raging rivers and a heterogeneous population of a million whose origins are lost in the myths of antiquity. Defining the region are the Karakoram Mountains and the Indus River with its several tributaries, with the Himalayas extending in the south and the Hindu Kush range in the east while the Pamirs cordon the north.

It is home to the high mountain valleys of Hunza and Baltistan, located in the upper catchment area of the Indus River and deep within the Karakoram, where nature with its peaks, glaciers, rivers and streams is omnipresent. Terraced fields draw water from a great distance through extremely well-engineered irrigation channels, attesting to efforts to make the best use of nature under harsh living conditions.

The location of the region is sensitive and strategic because of its boundaries with Afghanistan (Wakhan territory), with China and with Indian-held Kashmir. The construction of the Karakoram Highway (KKH), connecting Islamabad with Kashgar over the Khunjerab Pass (over 4700 metres), added to its importance, while the construction of further roads connecting Skardu with the KKH has given this region even more significance. The hydroelectric power potential of the Indus river system in Gilgit-Baltistan is another reason for the region's significance.

The area may be perceived as impenetrable, but it has historically provided conduits for trade between Central Asia and South Asia, with some of the strands of the Silk Road passing through it. This vast mountainous region is populated by heterogeneous communities and tribes of fairly distinct ethnic and linguistic groups, deriving their origin from Aryan, Scythian, Mongolian, Tibetan, Turanian and Caucasian stock.

The earliest forms of religion reaching this region seem to be Hinduism, in time supplanted by Buddhism, before the spread of Islam between the ninth and the fourteenth centuries. The languages spoken in the region are Shina around Gilgit, and Balti, a form of Tibetan in Baltistan. People of Hunza and Nagar speak Buruskaski. Other languages or dialects spoken in Gilgit-Baltistan are Wakhi, Khowar, Turki, Kashmiri and Gujri. Urdu is understood and spoken in almost all areas, while English is gaining ground, particularly with the young.

Altit Fort is typical of building construction in the Gilgit-Baltistan area, with reinforcing cribbage structures at the corners and horizontal cators stabilizing the walls.

Opposite page:
Baltit Fort in 1996, after restoration, looks out over the Hunza Valley.

Over time these peoples developed life styles that meshed fully with local environmental conditions. Frugality, self-dependence, optimal use of resources, and community endeavour emerged as their bedrock. The mountainous terrain is such that barely 1.5 per cent of the land is available for habitation. Water, though running in mighty rivers, was too far down to be readily harnessed. Streams were tapped and brought to parcels of land such as alluvial fans for seasonal crops through ingenious water channels. Only 'useful' trees were planted and looked after, with the apricot being a favourite, while quick-growing poplar was preferred for use in construction. The insufficiency of precipitation and the consequent lack of natural forests, particularly in Hunza, coupled with the burden of creating stone from huge rocks and the scarcity of available land resulted in the construction of multi-purpose single-room dwellings. These, typically, have a storeroom attached, and are made of mud and stone with no chimney or window, only a square hole in the centre of the roof over a fireplace where the cooking was done. Walls are tied in at various levels by wooden beams. A typical Hunza house presents a unique architectural design combining space, security and comfort, with a second storey for summer use. These houses clustered together to form settlements built on barren land that was of no use for the cultivation of crops. Their small size helped conserve energy required for heating as well as other resources. The cluster was also intended to provide security, as protective walls and watchtowers witness.

The first habitations in Hunza are reported to be those of Ganish, Altit and Baltit (since 1960 Karimabad), where *khuns* (fortified settlements) were formed, and water from the Ultar was taken to irrigate land. Over time watchtowers were added and the forts at Altit and Baltit took their present form. Skilled artisans from Baltistan reportedly carried out the work.

With easier access to and from Kashmir and having historical links with Tibet, Baltistan developed at a faster pace than Hunza. It generally also has bigger open spaces compared to Hunza, and has better resources in terms of land, or tree cover. Of the five valleys of Baltistan, Shigar is perhaps the most attractive. The valley is fertile with abundant water. Situated at an elevation of over 2440 metres, Shigar and the Shigar River drains the waters of the glaciers, feeding into the Indus. The Baltoro glacier, one of the largest in the Karakoram, begins at the north-west end of the valley. This is the main route for mountaineers headed to K2 and the Gasherbrums.

The other important valley in the area is Khaplu, which has borders with Ladakh (Indian-held territory). The average elevation of this valley is 2740 metres. Mountaineers on their way to the Masherbrums and the Saltoro range have to pass through Khaplu. Traditional housing here shows a great range in the use of timber, and has larger spaces as well as two-storey structures that use innovative wooden pillars. The palaces and forts are better developed and places of religion also testify to the rich architectural heritage that is regionally standard. A number of these forts or palaces, though relocated to lower sites during the Dogra regime, offered opportunities for restoration and adaptive reuse.

Our inventory of important cultural buildings in Gilgit-Baltistan includes eight major forts and palaces and nearly twenty minor ones; forty-five *khanqahs* (Sufi retreats), 150 mosques, over fifty archaeological sites, thirty important tombs and fifty traditional polo grounds. Gilgit-Baltistan contains a very rich and pluralistic heritage – representative of Muslim cultures, but also of Buddhist and Hindu influences.

As mentioned, strands of the Silk Road passed through the Hunza and Indus valleys. Commerce, art, skills, ideas, religious faiths, languages and technology passed between East and West through these mountains. The cross-fertilization that occurred facilitated

Phasing 1991 → ongoing

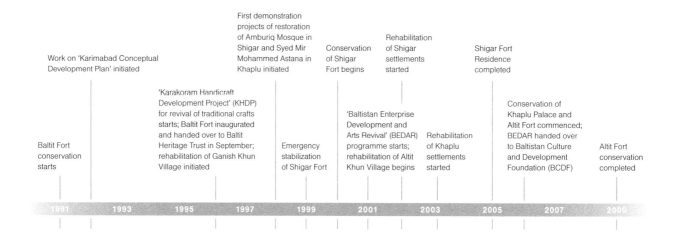

an unprecedented exchange of ideas and the development of a unique culture, which deserves to be preserved and shared.

The cultural enclaves of central Hunza, Shigar and Khaplu were focused upon for Area Development, as these offered a sufficient level of heritage that could collectively permit a discernible improvement in the quality of life. Landmark monuments provided the centrality while the traditional settlements and the heritage and traditions surrounding these forts or palaces allowed for community-based conservation and rehabilitation efforts. The fact that these cultural enclaves were rapidly being transformed from a rural to an urban setting underscored the need to ensure that cultural heritage and values informed the inevitable transition to modernity.

Conservation work started with the most identifiable landmark buildings, such as the Baltit and Altit forts in central Hunza, and Shigar Fort and Khaplu Palace in Baltistan. These forts or palaces, through their gifting by the *mirs* and rajas, transformed private hereditary assets into public resources that benefit local communities.

The experience of conservation of Baltit Fort, and rehabilitation of the traditional settlement just below it, indicated that meaningful restoration work needs to be associated with rehabilitation of traditional settlements as well as promotion of building techniques that can thus have an area development effect.

Conservation of the Fort/Palace and the improvement of living conditions in the adjoining settlements was started simultaneously in Shigar and Khaplu, while in Altit, community-based built-environment upgrading and rehabilitation – a process for conserving historic villages and settlements by providing basic sanitation, water supply, electrification and street paving – was undertaken. Community spaces were restored prior to the conservation of the Fort itself. Economic empowerment of the community involving the revival of skills, particularly those of masons and carpenters, and the creation of modern skills, such as engaging young men and women in documentation functions, were part of the process.

It became clear that a broad range of activities was needed to complement these efforts, including the revival of arts and crafts through an enterprise process. Meaningful

cultural development necessitating the involvement of local partner organizations, such as the Town Management Societies, the Karakoram Area Development Organization and the Baltit Heritage Trust, proved essential to building ownership and sustainability in the future for these projects.

Between 1992 and the present, not only have the three forts of Baltit, Altit and Shigar been conserved and put to use for the benefit of the communities, but work on Khaplu Palace is continuing, with completion expected in 2012. Sixteen historic settlements have been rehabilitated, a number of monuments and houses have been stabilized, and seven public buildings built, demonstrating traditional construction techniques and the use of local building materials. Two major enterprises were established: one in Hunza for embroidery and rugs, and one in Baltistan for apricot kernel oil and production of wood products (carving, construction and furniture). These efforts were backed up with the establishment of a number of new institutions.

The revival of traditional crafts, such as weaving and embroidery, has been an important part of the socio-economic programmes. Trades such as carpentry have been fostered, and the handing down of household traditions has been encouraged.

Background

BRIEF HISTORY OF PROGRAMME AREA

Hunza, nestling in the shadows of the Karakorams, first gained notoriety and fame from its location, the possession of which was coveted by the two expanding rival empires during the 19th century in Asia: Russia under the czar in Central Turkistan advancing towards the Indian borders, and the British Indian empire expanding to the north. In 1842 Sikhs who held Kashmir as part of their domain entered Gilgit, opening the way for the Dogra rulers to get a foothold in the region. The latter had acquired Kashmir after the British had broken the Sikhs' power in the Punjab and the treaty of Amritsar was signed, in accordance with which Kashmir (which included the territories of Baltistan and Astore) was transferred in 1846 to Maharaja Gulab Singh, the Dogra chief from Jammu. Realizing its strategic importance, in 1876 this area was taken away from the maharaja under a treaty by the British. The region was directly administered by the British, while Baltistan continued to be administered by Kashmir State as part of Ladakh, which was conquered by Sikh and Dogra troops before 1842. In December 1891 a successful campaign was conducted against Hunza/Nagar. The main battle was fought at a place called Nilt in Nagir. In 1935 the Government of India arranged with the maharaja of Jammu and Kashmir a lease for 60 years whereby all the territory except Baltistan and Astore areas would be administered by the British Raj. In 1947 (independence of India and Pakistan) the whole area was returned under the control of the maharaja of Jammu and Kashmir who appointed a Governor in Gilgit with military garrisons in Gilgit and Baltistan. On 31 October 1947 the control of the Jammu and Kashmir administration was wrested from the maharaja's representative in Gilgit and his troops were routed by a successful 'War of Liberation' in favour of Pakistan. On the request and invitation from the people of Gilgit-Baltistan, the Government of Pakistan took over the administration in mid November 1947, which in 1948 was extended to Baltistan following its liberation.

Challenges

DEMOGRAPHICS

In 1974 the overall population for Gilgit-Baltistan was estimated to be half a million, now estimated to be one million. The rate of population growth is estimated to be 2.5%. Gilgit and Skardu are the main towns with populations estimated at a 100,000 each.

ENVIRONMENTAL CONCERNS

The construction of the Karkoram Highway (KKH) which connected Islamabad to Kashgar, and the construction of other roads linking all the major towns with Gilgit, also opened the area up to outside influences. The ease of having construction materials at hand, such as cement and corrugated iron sheets, had a major negative impact, as, rather than relying on local materials such as stone, poplar wood and mud bricks that were suitable for the extreme climatic conditions, these so-called modern constructions started to encroach into the area. Arresting this trend and steering design and construction to respect local materials and traditional construction techniques is an area of focus for AKTC work in Hunza and Baltistan.

_____

Significant Issues and Impact

MASTER PLANNING PROCESS

In Hunza, the process was based on participatory inputs. Meetings and detailed follow-ups by experts with the community and with government planning departments were held and options explored, resulting, in the case of Karimabad, in the 'Karimabad Conceptual Development Plan'. In Shigar, with the community and government representatives on board and in collaboration with other agencies such as World Conservation Union (IUCN), land-use plans were generated.

BASELINE STANDARDS

These relied on 'Aga Khan Rural Support Programme' (AKRSP) surveys in most cases for data on the socio-economic conditions. For physical surveys, teams were trained locally and employed. Some of these teams, especially women-based ones, were further supported and have since 2005 been carrying out excellent survey work.

SOCIO-ECONOMIC INITIATIVES

The first initiative was the Swiss-funded 'Karakoram Handicraft Development Programme' (KHDP), with a focus on reviving the traditional art of embroidery work, which has since been subsumed by the Karakoram Area Development Organization (KADO) in Hunza. KHDP was initiated in 1996 as an action-research programme, when the community in Hunza, the Swiss Development Cooperation Agency (SDC) and AKCS-P decided to revive crafts and promote enterprise and economic development with a special focus on women. The success of the action-research phase in 1996 and the formation of a regional body – KADO as a local institutional body representing Hunza Valley – offered AKCS-P the opportunity to transfer the operational responsibility for KHDP to KADO in a staggered manner. Capacity building for KADO during the early phase of the project, especially in administrative and financial skills, facilitated this handover. KHDP allowed 3000 women, working out of their homes, to enhance their incomes through production of embroidery work – a craft which Hunza women had prided themselves on for over generations but which was dying out. In Baltistan, a similar organization, the 'Baltistan Enterprise Development and Art Revival' (BEDAR) was set up by the Baltistan Culture Foundation (BCF) and AKCS-P with funding from the SDC. BEDAR is the Urdu word for "awakening" and was chosen for its symbolic connotations with regard to the resurrection of traditional values. Initiated in July 2003, BEDAR selected a number of product lines. Of these, woodwork has achieved the best results, while responding to a local and regional demand using the comparative advantage strategy to effect. In woodworks, woodcarving and production of *jalis* (perforated screens) – a traditional skill that was recently on the verge of extinction – have been revived by apprenticing young trainees with *ustads* (masters) and the products are being sold in the markets. The small workshop was expanded and now furniture and construction carpentry are the main products. This allows for substitution of imported goods, since furniture items were trucked in all the way from Islamabad, a road journey of two days. Producing local poplar-wood furniture of a reasonable standard in Baltistan helps the local economy. The large numbers of poplars planted with the help of AKRSP are becoming an economic resource, and plenty of wood-related employment opportunities are emerging.

QUALITY OF LIFE

In order to meet the ever increasing needs for proper sanitation systems, an initial project was conceived and launched in Karimabad to cater for the needs of people living in the historic settlements. Based on positive results, these efforts were extended and through a community-led initiative the historic villages of Karimabad, Ganish and Altit now have these facilities. In Baltistan, the Shigar community preferred to use traditional community toilets; these have been improved through better design and better locations. In Altit, Shigar and Khaplu clean drinking-water projects were launched that provide water for the restored landmark monument while also supplying water to the adjoining settlements.

_____

Partners

COMMUNITY PARTNERS

Karimabad Town Management Society, Altit Town Management Society, Ganish Khun Heritage and Social Welfare Society, Shigar Town Management and Development Society, Khaplu Town Management and Development Society, Karakoram Area Development Organization, Baltistan Culture and Development Foundation.

_____

Authoritative Framework

Frameworks – known as 'Terms of Partnership' (TOP) – were negotiated for each of the project interventions with the beneficiary community. These TOPs laid down the roles with AKCS-P invariably having technical responsibility while the community would be responsible for the social aspects and for subsequent use of the project.

Opposite page:

The carved wood balcony of Khaplu Fort,

which is being transformed into a guest house,

is undergoing restoration.

Baltit Fort

GILGIT-BALTISTAN, PAKISTAN

Baltit Fort not only towers over Karimabad, but is also the sentinel of the Hunza Valley. Under the protective presence of the Fort, the houses of the traditional settlements of the old Baltit (now Karimabad) Village are gathered along the slopes beneath it. The Fort forms the backdrop and the focus to these settlements. Restoration and reuse of the 700-year-old Baltit Fort as a cultural and historical museum, and the conservation of its context, the historic settlement of Karimabad, are best seen within the perspective of changes that started in the second half of the twentieth century with the independence of Pakistan and accelerated from the 1970s onwards.

Many of the traditional social conventions that held the community together in the past had been weakened first with the abolishment of the mir in 1974 and then when Hunza, which had remained largely insulated from external forces, was opened up in 1979 with the construction of the Karakoram Highway (KKH) that links Islamabad to Kashgar.

It was recognized that, if not managed properly, forces of change resulting from development could spoil the impressive natural setting and the cultural heritage that was Karimabad's major resource. Preservation of the outstanding physical and environmental qualities was deemed essential to the well-being of central Hunza. The peaks of the Ultar, Rakaposhi and others, the terraced fields, the irrigation channels, the clustered settlements, the wealth of historic buildings and the rich cultural heritage needed to be protected and made to act as drivers for development.

The rapid change from a secluded rural area into a semi-urban one, with the attendant issues of infrastructure, traffic, commercial activities, tourism and new construction modes, all affected the physical environment and charm of Karimabad. These facts needed to be taken into account as part of the programme that had started with the restoration of Baltit Fort.

Baltit Fort had been abandoned in the early 1950s and a new palace constructed where the mir had moved with his family. In the 1980s the Fort was fragile and if it had been permitted to collapse Hunza would clearly have lost its major landmark and an important part of its cultural identity. However, before conservation work could be started, it needed to be transferred from private to

The restored Baltit Fort seen from the south-west.

Opposite page:
A view of Baltit Fort's southern facade from below highlights its early 20th-century wooden additions.

1 Baltit Fort   **2** Karimabad   **3** Visitor Parking

N |—————————————————————| 100 m

Project Scope / Objectives

The physical conservation of Baltit Fort was conceived to meet several interrelated objectives. The first of these was to restore and reuse the Fort as a museum and cultural centre and to protect and manage the built environment of Karimabad. A second objective was to train local people in conservation and related disciplines, establishing a pool of professionals capable of undertaking future restoration projects. Third, the project is meant to serve as a demonstration of excellence in conservation and to stimulate awareness and understanding of the significance of restoration and reuse of similar monuments.

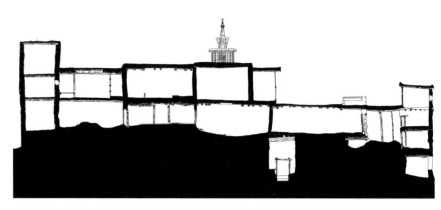

⊢————————⊣ 10 m

Right, a latitudinal section of Baltit Fort
and, below, floor plans of the roof (top),
the upper level and the bottom level.

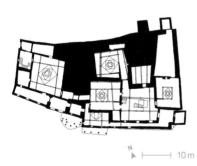

N
⊢————⊣ 10 m

Opposite page:
Pathways lead up to the entry of Baltit Fort
after restoration. The village of Karimabad
appears at the base of the structure.

public ownership. The mir on behalf of his family graciously decided to gift the Fort and the land surrounding it to the newly formed Baltit Heritage Trust (BHT) enabling a physical programme of works to be initiated.

From the beginning it was intended that the conservation should retain the historic character and appearance of the Fort. The restoration of missing features would be based on sound archaeological evidence. It was also realized that if the restored Fort were to enhance and promote cultural values of a living culture it needed to contribute to economic opportunities for the residents and to generate sufficient income to sustain operation and maintenance costs. Accordingly, the main uses selected for the restored Fort were those of a museum and active cultural centre.

While work started on Baltit Fort, a strategic framework for the orderly physical growth and development of Karimabad, and for the maintenance of its environmental and cultural assets, home to a population of around 5000, was developed, resulting from the analysis of its situation in 1992, and leading to the development of the 'Karimabad Conceptual Development Plan' (KCDP).

Although the plan for Karimabad, as conceived in the KCDP, is still not enforceable by law, it increased the awareness of the community about the issues at stake, leading to a participatory development process and the need for a community-based institution. In order to anchor this process in the local community, the Karimabad Town Management Society (KTMS), a democratically elected body, was formed and registered under the Social Welfare Societies' Law. The KTMS promotes community involvement in planning efforts in Karimabad and also exercises influence on development projects that advance the KCDP land use, infrastructure and road planning components. The KTMS has also attracted donor funding for a sanitation project that has enabled full coverage to Karimabad and the lower village of Ganish. This was in line with the earlier pilot project of rehabilitation and sanitation project for a portion of Khurukshal Village that had succeeded in bringing people back to old settlements that were being abandoned.

With increased interest from the community and awareness about the need to plan for development and channel change, Karimabad is in far better shape now than it would have been without the KTMS. There is a new attitude towards the local environment that helps to preserve the farming terraces and encourages the introduction of improved standards of health and hygiene, while reviving sound traditional construction techniques.

Phasing 1991 → 1996

Creation of the Baltit Heritage Trust (BHT); transfer of Fort to BHT; beginning of survey work	Conservation plan completed; commencement of physical restoration work	Artefacts collected for display in the Fort museum	Establishment of Karakoram Handicrafts Development Centre	Restoration completed; inauguration of Baltit Fort; handover of the Fort to Fort to BHT	UNESCO conservation award
1991	1992	1994	1995	1996	2004

Left, a carpet-weaver works under the auspices of the 'Karakoram Handicraft Development Project'.

Right, the *mir*'s bedroom on the second floor, seen after restoration, is part of the visitor tour.

The 'Karakoram Handicraft Development Project', which was set up to complement the Baltit Fort project, and since 1999 managed by the Karakoram Area Development Organization (KADO), produces small embroidered gift items, *sharma* (local woollen rugs) and hand-knotted carpets, allowing for increased incomes for thousands of women. KADO also operates a solid-waste disposal programme in central Hunza.

By mobilizing community resources, providing incentives, and demonstrating evidence of short and long-term benefits, the restored Baltit Fort has transformed Karimabad into a focus of interest in northern Pakistan, while giving local culture a renewed legitimacy in the face of powerful factors of recent change. The project has helped to renew the residents' pride in their heritage. The restoration of Baltit Fort within its setting of the historic village of Karimabad demonstrates the ability to integrate conservation issues in the larger context of community and regional development.

Background

BRIEF HISTORY OF PROJECT SITE

Baltit Village is one of the three oldest known settlements in Hunza, the others being Ganish and Altit. Under the protective presence of the Fort, the houses of the traditional settlements of old Baltit (now Karimabad) Village are gathered up the slopes beneath it. Baltit Fort is dramatically located at the top of a natural amphitheatre formed by terraced slopes, and the site was carefully chosen to control the irrigation channels that emanate out of Ultar. It is a remarkably complex building resulting from more than 700 years of 'organic growth', starting possibly from a watchtower and an adjoining building. Traditional stories mention that it was never captured by outside powers until the advent of the British in 1991 after having defeated the joint Hunza-Nagir forces at Nilt, when Baltit Fort was opened up and the British took control.

Challenges

PROJECT RISKS

This was the first major project of its kind ever in Gilgit-Baltistan, where restoration expertise and skills were not available. Consequently, international expertise was called in for the conservation.

DEMOGRAPHICS

The historic settlements immediately below the Fort were being abandoned as households realized that rather than living in cramped and unsanitary conditions it was preferable to move to lands available in the orchards and terraces, where new housing could be constructed to meet needs of the increasing family size.

AVAILABILITY OF DRINKING WATER AND PROPER SANITATION FACILITIES

Traditionally the sources of water are the irrigation channels that tap the Ultar. The water in these channels was very carefully monitored to ensure judicious distribution, particularly during early spring when new crops were in need. Also it was ensured that these channels would not be polluted and no direct washing of clothes, bathing or throwing of rubbish would occur, as well as runoffs from fields into these channels. However, with changes leading to the establishment of the first piped water lines and the abolishment of the Mirdom, this restraint disappeared, resulting in the water channels no longer being clean. Also the traditional system of sanitation was being abandoned for modern systems by setting up crude cesspits.

ENVIRONMENTAL CONCERNS

A road was planned to go through the historic settlement that would have affected most of the households and would certainly have led to the total abandonment of the settlement.

BUILDING CONDITIONS

Baltit Fort was in a state of advanced decay, with the roof resembling a patchwork of holes. Rainwater was able to flow freely into all parts of the building and even down into the lowest storeys. Most of the timberwork had rotted, while renders were reduced to piles of soil collected on the floors. Many walls were tilting and others had settled because they did not have foundations or sat on the loose morraine soil.

Significant Issues and Impact

DATA COLLECTION/SURVEYS

A number of surveys were completed for the 'Karimabad Conceptual Development Plan' in the mid 1990s, in the physical and housing realms, as well as building typologies, demographics and economic conditions. For sanitation needs, surveys to determine routes and meet future needs were carried out. After restoration and its opening, Baltit Fort attracted large numbers of visitors (around 20,000), which, though, have declined sharply after "9.11" (11.09.2001). However, even in 2009 around 3500 foreign visitors and 8000 domestic visitors paid for access to Baltit Fort.

MASTER PLANNING PROCESS

The 'Karimabad Conceptual Development Plan' was commissioned in 1992, when it was realized that the traditional settlements were being abandoned, with the consequent implication of building new houses in the terraced land, resulting in the charm of the bowl of Karimabad being dotted with unappealing new constructions in concrete and at the cost of the farming terraces and orchards. New haphazard road constructions were being planned that would destroy old settlements and also lay Karimabad open to all sorts of commercial exploitation, taking away its charm and balance. The multi-faceted planning process had a number of objectives, including establishment of a representative local institutional body – the Karimabad Town Management Society – allowing for conservation of both the traditional settlements and the scenic environment and establishing an adequate road and service infrastructure to provide for appropriate land-use patterns while responding to a growth in population and changing economic trends.

PLANNING ISSUES

Abolition of Hunza State in 1974 led to an institutional vacuum, as no proper authority took over the responsibilities of the Mirdom that had existed since then. Further, the anomalous status of Gilgit-Baltistan within Pakistan has not allowed for a system of governance that responds to local needs. This was all compounded by the fact that Karimabad was not treated as a town or municipality, further affecting planning for its development. Thus, patchwork development projects implemented through annual development plans have been the norm. It is only in late 2009 that a deputy commissioner has been placed in Karimabad, and a more formal planning process is expected to start.

HISTORIC BUILDINGS/MONUMENTS CONSERVED

In addition to Baltit Fort, five historic houses in its vicinity, two mosques – including the Hanging Mosque on the pathway to the Fort – and the historic watermill that used to be the ground storey of the watchtower, as well as another watchtower, have been restored. For the Fort, remedies were found by putting a temporary protective cover on the roof, while structural problems of the foundations and load-bearing walls were tackled first, allowing for conservation of the architectural fabric and finishes later. Timber elements were procured and inserted at the identified critical intervention points, while modern interventions were also inserted for extra structural strengthening, such as synthetic polyurethane reinforcement meshes and polymer anchor cables. Additional importance was given to preserving the timber lacing and cribbage work, as a means of demonstrating the value of this unique engineering and construction system in resisting earthquakes and of reviving traditional local skills and crafts.

CONTRACTING METHODS

The Aga Khan Planning and Building Services (AKP& BS), then known as the Aga Khan Housing Board, was contracted to carry out work on Baltit Fort under the supervision of AKTC. Work on Baltit Fort and the rehabilitation of the historic settlements around it engaged over 200 unskilled persons.

QUALITY OF LIFE

With support from the community a modern sanitation system has been laid to cater for all the residents of Karimabad as well as Ganish, covering 1000 households. Piped water schemes have also been implemented, while the local community is encouraged to move animals to their fields.

LESSONS LEARNED

This being the first conservation and rehabilitation project brought a wealth of learning to other projects that were taken up subsequently. One major development was the bringing together of the conservation and rehabilitation processes so that planning and implementation were further improved.

Partners

PUBLIC PARTNERS

Government of Pakistan represented on the Baltit Heritage Trust.

COMMUNITY PARTNERS

The community of Karimabad.

Donors

PUBLIC PARTNERS

Government of Norway, Aga Khan Foundation, European Union, Getty Foundation, Sumitomo Foundation, Silver Jubilee.

Authoritative Framework

Agreement signed in 1991 with the Baltit Heritage Trust for the restoration of the Fort and its return to the Baltic Heritage Trust for its future safekeeping and use.

Altit Fort

GILGIT-BALTISTAN, PAKISTAN

Altit Fort is another of the great landmark monuments of Gilgit-Baltistan. Indeed, the *shikari* (watchtower) is some three hundred years older than the first phase of Baltit Fort, making it the oldest surviving standing structure in the western Himalayas. Arguably, it is also the most spectacularly sited fort, built on the very edge of the main Hunza gorge. It sits above 200-metre-high sheer cliffs and precipitous slopes that cascade down towards the river. Its importance stems from the control it exercised on the upstream communication routes.

The conservation strategy for Altit Fort was to preserve it in its 'found', state. Most conservation works therefore related to mending structural defects, stabilizing existing walls, reattaching render to the wall substrate, replacing some roofs, treating wood decay and providing a nominal amount of lighting. However, for the walls that were too unstable, the infill was removed to allow them to be jacked back to more vertical positions and the stone and/or adobe soil blocks replaced in their original positions – making use of detailed survey drawings and photographs. This rather purist concept, an exciting objective in its own right, is significantly different from solutions applied to Baltit Fort, Ganish Village and Shigar Fort.

The conservation strategy for Altit Fort also extended to the associated historic garden, to the north of the Fort. Today, the garden is being kept as it is. When one enters the garden it is like stepping back in time.

But before starting conservation of Altit Fort, it was decided to first rehabilitate Altit settlement, in order to allow for heritage-related values to take root more firmly, while reducing negative commercial pressures. The formation of the Altit Town Management Society (TMS), with a general body including forty per cent of women members and long deliberations about the impact of development, led to a clearer realization by the Altit community of the need to be proactive and involved in the cultural development process. As a result, the interventions in the environmental context, that is, in relation to the historic settlement, the ancient Fort and the built-up or agricultural land, took place under a citizen-managed land-use programme, prior to the monument conservation project.

Built on rocky, unproductive terrain, the settlement reflects traditional values of land use and conservation in a region scarce in agricultural land. Its historic

Altit Fort is located among the snow-capped mountains of Central Hunza .

Opposite page:
A view of the valley and Altit Village with the Fort in the background.

1 Altit Fort   **2** Altit Village   **3** Water Tank   **4** Garden

N

50m

Project Scope / Objectives

The scope of activities in the case of Altit Fort included documentation of the highest standards and development of a conservation plan that followed a strategy aimed at pursuing a 'purist' approach. Another goal was to fully tie the surrounding Altit Village to the Fort through social and economic bonds.

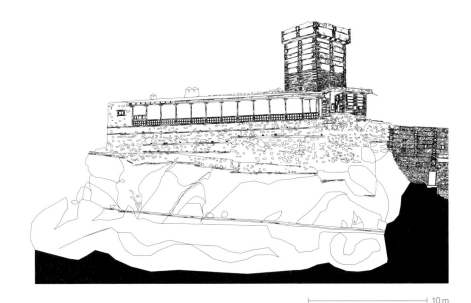

Right, a drawing of the north facade of Altit Fort, which is built on the very edge of the main Hunza gorge.

⊢——————————⊣ 10 m

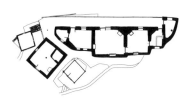

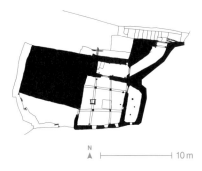

N
▲ ⊢——————————⊣ 10 m

Above, the Fort has three main levels: from the top, floor plans of level 1, level 2 and level 2B.

dwellings exemplify indigenous architectural forms, building techniques and materials well adapted to an environment whose hazards include earthquakes and bitterly cold winters. In addition, the historic settlement, with its compact design and common spaces, supports a culture of cooperation, respect and mutual interdependence that is one of Hunza's most unique and valuable assets.

By the late 1990s, the core settlement of Altit was being abandoned by its residents, largely because of unsanitary living conditions and the inadequacy of houses to support modern life. A consequence of this process was the building of new houses in the surrounding farmland, where families with the financial means could create dwellings with modern facilities and greater living space. The newer houses, with their cement-block construction and rudimentary sanitation systems, contributed to an increase in pollution and a decrease in social cohesion. Moreover, the new construction came at the detriment of the verdant farming terraces and centuries-old fruit orchards that cover the surrounding hillsides. The physical condition of the *khun* became increasingly dilapidated and its common spaces and historic houses were neglected.

Keeping in view the historic, cultural and architectural value of the village, an intervention was conceived that would enhance the value of the old settlement and demonstrate that people can sustain life at contemporary standards in harmony with the traditional built environment. The rehabilitation process included the piping of clean drinking water into each dwelling, the introduction of a modern sanitation system in difficult mountain terrain and the underground electrification of the settlement. In addition, the project undertook the revitalization of common public spaces, improvements to the exterior of the historic houses and the paving of lanes and cul-de-sacs with stone. The project was accomplished with a high level of community participation, and succeeded in changing the attitudes of the people towards the settlement, bringing many families back into their historic residences. It also created a new attitude towards the natural environment, and has thereby nearly stopped the demolition of historic buildings and the random construction of new houses in the scenic farming terraces. In addition to establishing new standards of health and hygiene, it has revived traditional crafts and building techniques developed over centuries.

Phasing 1999 → 2009

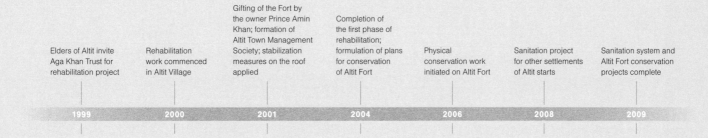

| | | Gifting of the Fort by the owner Prince Amin Khan; formation of Altit Town Management Society; stabilization measures on the roof applied | Completion of the first phase of rehabilitation; formulation of plans for conservation of Altit Fort | | | |

Elders of Altit invite Aga Khan Trust for rehabilitation project / Rehabilitation work commenced in Altit Village / Physical conservation work initiated on Altit Fort / Sanitation project for other settlements of Altit starts / Sanitation system and Altit Fort conservation projects complete

1999   2000   2001   2004   2006   2008   2009

Background

BRIEF HISTORY OF PROJECT SITE
Located in close proximity to the historic areas of Ganish and Karimabad, Altit is said to be one the earliest settlements of this region: most scholars agree that it was established in the 15th century AD. Altit's historic value lies in its having been the first capital of the ruling *mirs* of Hunza. The elders remember that the village once had a fortification and eleven *shikaris* (watchtowers), presently buried under the rubble of memory. The original fortified settlement (*khun*) of Altit is located at the base of the Fort, protecting its approaches.

Challenges

SITE CONDITIONS
The site of the Fort, with one side overhanging the cliff, limited the number of people who could be employed gainfully at any one time. Also, access to the east wall was not possible without putting up scaffolding. The installation of scaffolding on the cliff side was technically extremely challenging.

ENVIRONMENTAL CONCERNS
At the start of the project the dilapidated condition of the houses, their small size and the unsanitary atmosphere (due to a lack of modern facilities and to the practice of keeping livestock inside the house) had prompted many settlement residents to relocate outside the settlement. This, in turn, led to further neglect of the physical structures. Since the completion of the project, however, structural improvements to the exterior of many houses, together with the provision of piped drinking water, safer underground electrification and proper sewage facilities, have led many families to move back into their ancestral homes.

BUILDING CONDITIONS
The Fort was in an advanced state of decay. On the western side, it overlooked Altit Village. The danger of wall collapse onto the village was a real possibility, averted through emergency measures of tying and buffering the bulging walls of the Fort.

Significant Issues and Impact

PLANNING ISSUES
At the urging of AKCS-P, residents have relocated their animals to pens outside the settlement, making the houses more spacious and more sanitary. AKCS-P has also provided technical support to families wishing to renovate the insides of their homes using traditional materials and often incorporating elements of traditional craftwork.

COMMUNITY INVOLVEMENT/PROGRAMME
In the process of rehabilitating and upgrading the settlement, local traditions of community participation and collective labour were drawn upon, reinforcing the community's awareness of and pride in its heritage and the potential for self-sustainability. Skilled craftsmen from the community were recruited to train the volunteer unskilled labour in traditional crafts and techniques. Traditional social and political practices have been strengthened as former settlement residents have moved back into their ancestral homes, bringing the settlement back to the critical mass required for healthy sociability and democratic decision making. The Altit Town Management Society (TMS) draws on culturally sanctioned values and modes of collective discussion and decision making in its activities, creating continuity with the political traditions of the area. The Altit TMS also oversees the collection of revenue from the project beneficiaries – the settlement residents – for the maintenance of improvements and services. The revenue is collected monthly, generating a total of PKR 17,000 per month from 150 households. The maintenance has proved entirely financially self-sustaining, even generating revenue for future improvements. Monthly expenditures for maintenance come to PKR 6000, providing PKR 11,000 in monthly savings. In addition, the Altit TMS is already charging visitor entry fees to the rehabilitated Altit Village, thus generating additional funds.

VOCATIONAL TRAINING/CAPACITY BUILDING
The settlement and improvements are the common property of the resident community. For the physical upkeep of the structures and services, the Altit TMS is able to draw on the expertise of those villagers who were given training during the course of the project.

QUALITY OF LIFE
Provision of clean drinking water using the technical expertise of the 'Water and Sanitation Extension Programme' (WASEP) for all the residents of Altit Village, besides providing water to the educational institutions, has created a clean and hygienic village, where it is reported that sickness and disease have reduced considerably. All settlement homes now include a separate washroom.

LESSONS LEARNED
Providing tangible benefits to the local communities prior to carrying out work on a landmark project is most helpful in allaying their concerns and also reducing commercial tendencies.

Partners

COMMUNITY PARTNERS
The community of Altit.

Donors

Government of Norway, Government of Japan.

Authoritative Framework

In 2001 the owner Prince Amin Khan graciously gifted Altit Fort to AKDN while a sizeable portion of the orchard garden was purchased. The Tourism Promotion Services is to manage the Khabasi Café opened up in the summer house, while the Women Social Enterprise in collaboration with Altit TMS and with AKCS-P oversight are responsible for Altit Fort itself and the garden.

A detail of a column in a communal kitchen in Altit Village displays exquisite carving.

Shigar Fort

GILGIT-BALTISTAN, PAKISTAN

The four-hundred-year-old Shigar Fort was selected for adaptive reuse and restoration as a major strategic investment that would re-establish community identity and confidence by conserving and putting into use one of the major heritage assets of Baltistan, in the rugged high desert mountains of the Karakoram in northern Pakistan. The current function of the Fort/Palace complex as a heritage guest house and museum is having ripple effects in terms of economic benefits for the community, generating employment and training, both in artisanal skills and in tourism. The project provides an income stream for future maintenance of the Fort and to sustain local institutions. The value of cultural heritage has become evident in the region. Community-based planning and rehabilitation of the three traditional settlements of Khlingrong, Chinpa and Halapa surrounding Shigar Fort accompanied the restoration, with three additional villages – Giangpa, Chamaqpa and Agaipa – benefiting from similar rehabilitation efforts subsequently. The upgrading of the Shigar public bazaar and the construction of a community school building using traditional techniques and local materials at Sainkhore were also undertaken.

Built on a massive boulder, Shigar Fort is locally known as Fong Khar – literally the Fort on the Rock. Located on the right bank of a mountain stream, slightly elevated above the nearest hamlets of Shigar, it is at the foot of a steep rock formation, a hundred or so metres high, on top of which lie ruins of the original fort.

Raja Hassan Khan, the twentieth ruler of the Amacha dynasty, ascended the throne in 1634, but lost his kingdom to invaders. He managed to regain his throne with the help of forces of the Mughal emperor Shah Jahan. The raja brought various artisans including shawl weavers, carpenters, goldsmiths and stone carvers from Kashmir to Shigar and proceeded to build the Fort/Palace. Fong Khar was gradually abandoned in the 1950s in favour of more recent annexes, built in its immediate vicinity.

Shigar Fort in its 'received' state was an abandoned and neglected building that had undergone many changes. But it was also a wonderfully preserved statement of history. The idea of promoting a new type of environmentally conscious cultural tourism was decisive for the reuse design of Shigar Fort, both in

The reconstructed outer wall of the reception hall of the Shigar Fort/Palace complex is at terrace level.

Opposite Page:
A view of the Old House and Raja Mosque.

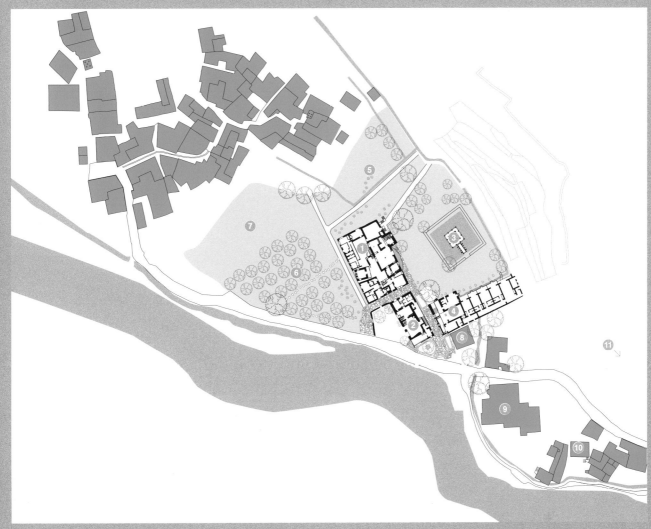

1 Shigar Fort   4 Garden House   7 Burpi Tzar   10 Khlingrong Mosque
2 Old House   5 Vegetable Garden   8 Raja Mosque   11 Water Filtration Plant
3 Baradar   6 Cherry Garden   9 Raja House

N   50 m

Project Scope / Objectives

The objectives for the Shigar Fort project were the restoration and reuse of the most outstanding land-mark monument in Shigar, leading to a revival of pride, identity and skills for the community. Also at stake was heightening the awareness of the importance and relevance of cultural and architectural heritage in the present; the initiation of conditions for socially responsible tourism and economic development of the area; and finally, the creation of revenues for the maintenance of the Fort, as well as for the community.

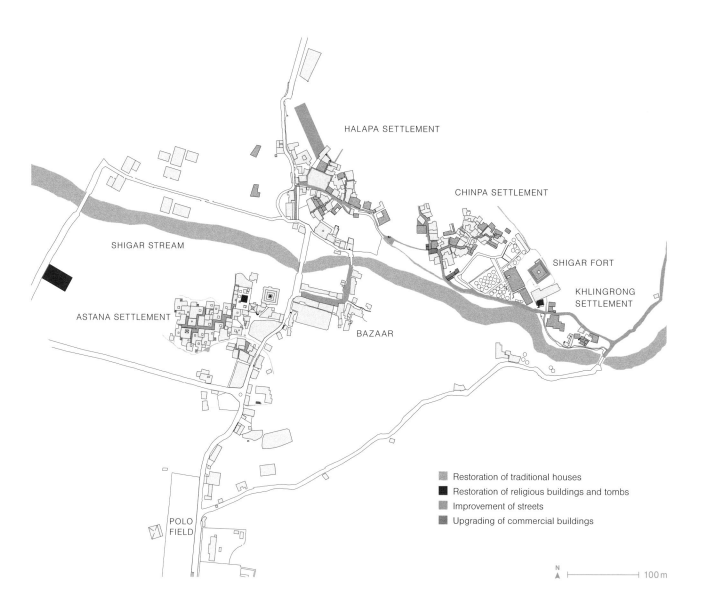

HALAPA SETTLEMENT

CHINPA SETTLEMENT

SHIGAR STREAM

SHIGAR FORT

KHLINGRONG
SETTLEMENT

ASTANA SETTLEMENT

BAZAAR

Restoration of traditional houses
Restoration of religious buildings and tombs
Improvement of streets
Upgrading of commercial buildings

POLO
FIELD

N
A ├─────────────┤ 100 m

Settlement plan for the area around
the Shigar Fort/Palace complex.

terms of providing new opportunities to residents and of ensuring financial self-sustainability for the restored building.

The adaptive reuse plan for the Fort was predicated on transforming it into an exclusive thirteen-room guest house with the grand audience hall and anterooms serving as a museum of Balti woodcarving and local living traditions. The guestrooms – some rather small, others having a comfortable suite character – retain the authentic character of the Fort/Palace as much as possible. Modern furniture and equipment in the rooms is minimal. Many guestrooms feature original or restored woodwork complemented by traditional craft objects and artefacts from the region. Accommodation is geared to an international clientele of connoisseurs, who look for a special experience.

The "Old House", located at the entry of the compound, has been redesigned and converted to cater for all service functions, including a reception area and museum ticketing. Inside, the building accommodates a kitchen and ground-floor restaurant with outdoor sitting space and an upper-floor lounge with balcony overlooking the stream, a meeting room and administration facilities. The Garden House, with no historic features,

Left, views of the Old House and Fort; right, individual
guest rooms in Shigar Fort Residence.

was refurbished and extended to offer seven additional guestrooms that are more 'conventional' and modern in character, that is, larger and more practical than the average guestroom in the Fort. However, most of the rooms overlook the garden and therefore have a charm of their own. Offering two alternate accommodations enables the complex to cater for different tastes and types of clients.

Beyond its architectural and environmental merits, this project is the first attempt to achieve a wider cultural development initiative in Gilgit-Baltistan based on the promotion of a new type of culturally and ecologically sensitive tourism. The location of Shigar on the access route towards some of the highest mountains in the world and the metalled road between Skardu and Shigar facilitates marketing of the guest-house complex. Guests have the opportunity to engage in short treks in the vicinity, or to indulge in trout fishing. They can climb Shigar rock, visit the hot springs at Chutron (two hours from Shigar), visit monuments in Shigar and Skardu, or take day-tours to Khaplu, Kiris and Kharmang, or Deosai.

The development of local institutional capabilities has been vigorously pursued by the Aga Khan Cultural Services-Pakistan (AKCS-P), resulting in the formation of the Shigar Town Management and Development Society (TMDS), an active partner for all projects and activities in Shigar. The TMDS as an institution that consolidates and brings together the thinking of the Shigar community on matters related to culture and tourism has been an essential mechanism, acting as a bridge and allowing for the articulation and discussion of views, while also allowing for information and news to reach the community in a considered and comprehensive manner.

The project provided an opportunity to act as a catalyst for a comprehensive improvement of the local economy, generating direct and indirect employment opportunities. Situated in the immediate proximity of a poor and unskilled village population, it was thought the Shigar Fort Residence project could raise the quality of life in the villages surrounding it, and boost economic enterprises in the bazaar area. This process was accompanied by a proactive village upgrading and rehabilitation programme that has reached almost twenty-five per cent of the households of Shigar's two union councils.

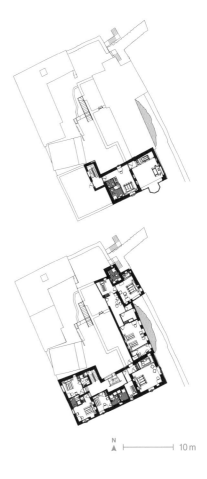

N
↑ ├─────────┤ 10 m

First- and second-floor plans after
conversion into Shigar Fort Residence.

133

The restored Khilingrong Mosque stands
near the Shigar Fort/Palace complex.

Gifting of the Fort by the owner Raja Azam Khan

Rehabilitation work on the settlements of Khlingrong, Chinpa and Halapa

Rehabilitation work in settlements completed

Work on Shigar community school started and rehabilitation of three more settlements; Shigar Fort Residence under TPS management

Work on school completed

Start of physical conservation work

Work on Shigar Bazaar

Completion of Shigar Fort restoration and opening to visitors

Rehabilitation work completed

1999   2000   2001   2002   2003   2005   2007   2008   2009

Background

BRIEF HISTORY OF PROJECT SITE
Fong Khar is the last remaining structure associated with the ruling Amacha family, which claims to have ruled Shigar for 32 generations. Sources describe the Amachas as having their origins in the "Hamacha" tribe of Ganish, Hunza. The present raja, Mohammad Ali Shah Saba, believes that the Amacha originally belonged to China. Buddhist ruins in the vicinity of Shigar Fort testify to the lengthy human occupation of the site.

Challenges

PROJECT RISKS
Since this was the first major project of its type in Baltistan, in order to create credibility and trust with the local community and demonstrate the procedures and benefits of culturally relevant rehabilitation, the restoration of Amburiq Mosque in Shigar, selected in consultation with the community, was carried out in 1998. The result of this conservation impressed the community significantly, paving the way for the restoration of Shigar Fort.

DEMOGRAPHICS
The two union councils of the town of Shigar, Marapi and Murkunja, collectively make up a total population size of around 10,000 and 1240 households spread over 21 villages. Rehabilitation projects have had a direct impact on almost 400 households with a population of around 3300 in eight villages.

HOUSEHOLD ECONOMY
In general household economy depends on agriculture, with some seasonal tourism-related activities when locals provide portering services. Shigar Fort Residence employs 25 local staff out of a total of 28.

STATUS OF HEALTH AND EDUCATION
Education has been recognized by the Shigar community as the most important element for improving their lives. After a visit to Hunza by the Shigar TMDS, the top priority it identified was education.

AVAILABILITY OF DRINKING WATER AND PROPER SANITATION FACILITIES
Like other valleys, provision of clean drinking water remains a major area of concern. Although there are a number of piped water systems, these carry untreated water.

BUILDING CONDITIONS
During the past two to three centuries Shigar Fort had already undergone many transformations and adaptions. As found in 1998, it was in a partially ruined condition, with some of the former rooms serving as cowsheds and a new ramp access leading directly into the former reception room.

Significant Issues and Impact

PLANNING ISSUES
A combined museum/guest-house option was selected for Shigar Palace that allowed AKCS-P to develop a different restoration philosophy, complementing the approach applied to Baltit Fort. The reuse aims helped to carry out a more proactive policy of consolidation, restitution and reconstruction based on the evidence uncovered during the consolidation process. All efforts have been made to preserve the patina of older elements, and newer elements and finishes have been executed to be in sympathy with this age value.

HISTORIC BUILDINGS/MONUMENTS CONSERVED
The positive impact of the conservation of Shigar Fort translated into practical action by the Shigar community. In one case the shrine of one of the saints in Shigar was restored by the community itself, winning a UNESCO award of merit. The larger community has started work on a Jamia Masjid using traditional design, materials and construction techniques.

NEW BUILDING FACILITIES
The Abruzzi Higher Secondary School Building has been built, designed to be compatible with local conditions and optimizing local materials. The most important aspect is that this is designed to be a school for both boys and girls, quite a transformation for a society considered conservative.

COMMUNITY INVOLVEMENT/PROGRAMME
The Shigar TMDS is the main forum for the community, which is spread over 20 villages/settlements and has a population of around 12,000 people in 1500 households. The establishment of the Shigar TMDS, with both a community development and planning function, brought the village upgrading operations into a far stronger relationship with the monument conservation project. It was from the villages of Khlingrong, Chinpa and Halapa, where village upgrading had first occurred, that most of the workers in the Fort project were drawn and continue to be drawn as the working staff of Shigar

Fort Residence. Furthermore, in 2009 PKR 3 million ($40,000) worth of purchases was made locally of groceries, fruit and vegetables, meat and poultry, thus helping to provide an economic boost to the local economy. Transport needs for Residence guests was met locally, with a sum of PKR 560,000 going to local transporters. 10% of this revenue was provided to Shigar TMDS.

VOCATIONAL TRAINING/CAPACITY BUILDING
Ten carpenters were trained in the art of carving and jali (perforated screen) work, besides reviving the skills of cribbage construction. Also five young women were trained in the field of documentation, including survey work.

LESSONS LEARNED
In order for local community institutions to have sustainability, the recourse to viable restoration and reuse projects, such as Shigar Fort Residence, are critical. Also utilizing the strengths of AKDN agencies provides synergies. The role of Tourist Promotion Services (TPS) in managing the Residence exceedingly well is a case in point.

Partners

COMMUNITY PARTNERS
The community of Shigar.

Donors

Government of Norway, Aga Khan Foundation, International Union for Conservation of Nature, Governments of Germany, Japan, Greece, Spain and Pakistan, American Express.

Authoritative Framework

Raja Azam Khan and his father Raja Mohammad Ali Shah Saba gifted the main Fort building and the land it sits on to AKDN in 1999, while the Old House and lands around it were purchased. The Garden House was taken on a six-year lease with access to the Amacha garden in exchange for building a house built for the Raja. The Tourism Promotion Services has been managing Shigar Fort Residence as a guest house since 2008.

Khaplu Palace

GILGIT-BALTISTAN, PAKISTAN

Khaplu is the easternmost part of Baltistan, with the Shyok River, a tributary of the Indus River dividing the valley. The steeply sloped valley has less land available than other valleys in Baltistan. However, in terms of architectural heritage and cultural expression it arguably has more treasures than Shigar, possibly as a result of its proximity to both Leh in Ladakh and Srinagar in Kashmir.

In Baltistan, a region rich in cultural heritage, Khaplu Palace is the finest surviving royal residence. Built by the Yabgo Raja Daulat Ali Khan in 1840, it replaced an earlier fort constructed 600 metres above the present location, of which little now remains. As a former seat of royal government, the Palace is exemplary in terms of its building typology and aesthetic and structural qualities.

Following the inauguration of the restored Baltit Fort in 1996, His Highness the Aga Khan visited Baltistan where he emphasized the role of culture in development and environmental management in an address to a large gathering, This led to an invitation to the Aga Khan Cultural Services-Pakistan (AKCS-P) to extend its activities to Baltistan. An exploratory expert mission was sent to Baltistan in 1997 to visit over eighty sites. This was followed up by systematic inventories in 1998 and following years establishing that the cultural heritage of Baltistan was worthy of international recognition.

Among the pilot projects that were implemented by AKCS-P in Baltistan, in Khaplu the upgrading of a typical traditional house, the construction of a community building and the restoration of the *astana* (or tomb and shrine of a venerated saint) of Syed Mir Mohammed were initiated in 1998. The surveys had established Khaplu Palace and Shigar Fort as the two landmark buildings with outstanding historic and architectural merit. While work following a successful dialogue with the raja of Shigar and the community was started on Shigar Fort, in the case of Khaplu the understanding for its restoration was reached when the benefits of restoration and reuse of Shigar Fort became visible in 2005.

Rehabilitation of the historic settlements of Hunduli and Banpi was initiated in 2002, using simple, low-cost interventions such as improved composting, the creation of community latrines and of places for washing clothes, as well as bathrooms for men and women. Piped water delivery was improved and stone paving of the pathways and streets was put in place. Meanwhile the establishment

The north facade of Khaplu Palace features projections in wood.

Opposite page:
The interior of the projecting room on the upper floor.

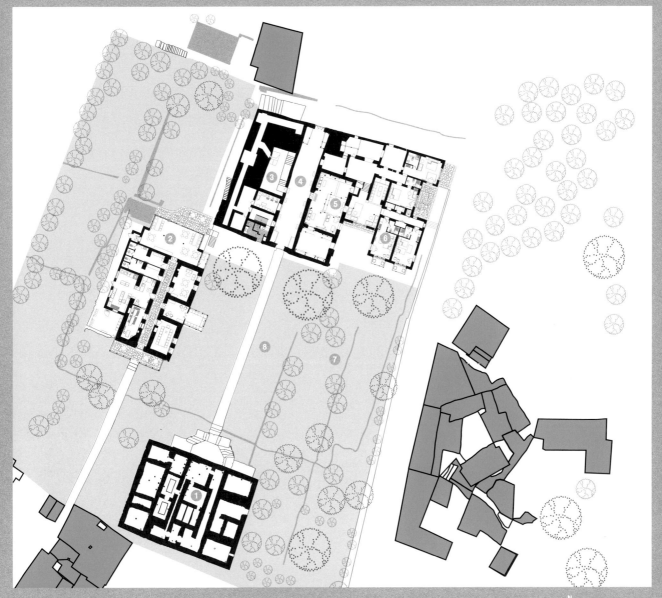

| 1 Palace | 3 Chaman House | 5 Stables | 7 Ra Tzar Garden |
| 2 Darbar House | 4 Wankoo | 6 Ra Tzar House | 8 Chaoni Tzar Garden |

N ⊢———————⊣ 10 m

Project Scope / Objectives

The Palace complex is being conserved or developed as part of a reuse project that will turn the property into an up-scale hotel – a 21-bed residential retreat. The aim of the project is to develop a tourism circuit based on cultural heritage and to generate economic and employment opportunities for locals.

Left, carpentry workshops prepared
workers for erecting house frames.

Right, a stone floor is being laid in one
of the complex's buildings.

of the Khaplu Town Management and Development Society (TMDS) as the local community institution, along the same lines as the TMS bodies nurtured in Hunza, allowed for
local ownership of the development.

In 2005 Khaplu Palace itself was gifted by the rajas Zakria Ali Khan and Nasir Ali
Khan to the Aga Khan Development Network (AKDN) and its agencies, the Aga Khan
Foundation (AKF) and AKCS-P, to facilitate the conservation of Khaplu Palace as a heritage site. In addition to direct benefit through a share in the profits (30%), the local
economy also benefits through employment, purchase of local goods wherever possible
and the stimulation of tourism services in the town. As was the case in Shigar, increased
visitor numbers resulted from this work.

The reuse plan drawn up for Khaplu Palace has at its core the intent to operate the
site as a guest house and restaurant similar in nature to Shigar Fort. The use of the complex
for a number of complimentary purposes is central to the reuse plan and future financial
sustainability of Khaplu Palace and Residence (KPR).

Khaplu Palace complex can be grouped into four main areas. The Palace (Yabgo
Khar) is four storeys high including the basement, and has been used as a seat of
governance, grain store and royal residence. From the outside, the building appears to
be one structural unit but detailed examination of the internal structure suggests that it
was built during a number of different construction phases. Its form and internal organization are strongly influenced by the Kashmiri manor-house typology, with rooms
arranged in a rectangular grid around a central courtyard.

Given its significance, the Palace is being treated as a Grade 1 listed building. Six
rooms at the rear of the first and second floors are being adapted with minimum compromise of conservation standards, to provide guest suites with modern comforts. The
more historically significant rooms at the front of the building that were used by the raja
as living and reception spaces are being incorporated into an interpretative museum
open to the public.

There are also ceremonial gardens (Chaoni Tzar, Ra Tzar) – two formally organized
garden spaces adjacent to the Palace – and historic landscape. The Chaoni Tzar, which
forms a key part of the ceremonial entrance sequence, was (according to an account by the
raja) formerly laid out as a *chahar-bagh* Persian garden, with geometrical areas separated
by watercourses. In more recent times it was used as a ceremonial gathering space beneath
the Palace where the raja could preside over celebrations and hold court.

———————————————| 10 m

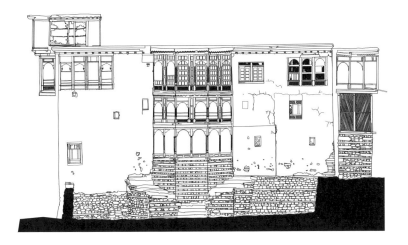

Top, distinctive features of Khaplu Palace
are the rooms projecting out from the north
facade (left) and the wooden balconies
on the south facade (right).

Left and above, an extended elevation
of the complex and a north elevation of
Khaplu Palace.

———————————————| 10 m

The complex of Khaplu Palace
can be seen in its dramatic natural
environment.

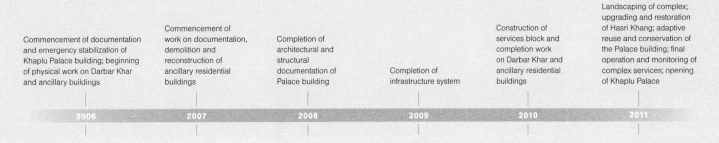

2006	2007	2008	2009	2010	2011
Commencement of documentation and emergency stabilization of Khaplu Palace building; beginning of physical work on Darbar Khar and ancillary buildings	Commencement of work on documentation, demolition and reconstruction of ancillary residential buildings	Completion of architectural and structural documentation of Palace building	Completion of infrastructure system	Construction of services block and completion work on Darbar Khar and ancillary residential buildings	Landscaping of complex; upgrading and restoration of Hasri Khang; adaptive reuse and conservation of the Palace building; final operation and monitoring of complex services; opening of Khaplu Palace

Background

BRIEF HISTORY OF PROJECT SITE

Until the creation of Pakistan in 1947, the territory of Baltistan was under the suzerainty of the Dogra maharaja of Kashmir. Khaplu was ruled by the Yabgo family of local rajas for a thousand years or more. Khaplu Palace was the family's residence as well as its seat of power and was built in the first half of the 19th century when the region had just fallen under the control of the Dogra rulers of Kashmir. In 1840, when the Dogras annexed the territory under Zorawar Singh, all the rajas in the Baltistan region were ordered to dismantle their ancient fortresses, many of which were located on strategic defensive heights. As a consequence, new palaces came to rise lower down in the valleys, including the one at Khaplu. Abandoned by the family in the late 1970s, the building had been decaying for several years.

LANDSCAPE

The town of Khaplu is in reality a group of rural settlements scattered about on an ancient alluvial fan along the course of the Shyok River some 90 kilometres upstream from its confluence with the Indus River. Watered by the Ghanche stream, this natural terrain has been turned over the centuries into an oasis of fertile terraced fields and apricot orchards.

Challenges

SITE CONDITIONS

The site is a series of agricultural terraces that long pre-date the construction of the Palace and its satellite buildings. The historicity of these terraces was a value that had to be protected and enhanced through appropriate treatment of the vegetation contained by them.

HOUSEHOLD ECONOMY

In general household economy depends on agriculture, with some seasonal tourism-related activities when locals provide portering services.

AVAILABILITY OF DRINKING WATER AND PROPER SANITATION FACILITIES

The downstream village of Doksa will be provided with clean drinking water and it is expected, as demonstrated in Shigar, that water-borne and gastrointestinal diseases will be reduced to statistical insignificance in this village.

INFRASTRUCTURE

Infrastructure services have aimed at providing clean drinking water from the filtration unit established for the project to the Doksa community down the slope. Infrastructure development has raised issues of conflict, related also to future employment opportunities, which were resolved by realignment, relocation of certain services, and changing their specifications.

BUILDING CONDITIONS

Most buildings that tend to the 'monument' status are built in stone or mud-block infill in a framework of heavy timber cribbage and seismic ties. Structurally the main Palace building posed serious challenges in being founded on cultural fill with the bearing strata in full access of a basement space. Decay of timber elements and rainwater and irrigation water ingress had resulted in serious decay of the building fabric and its timber elements. More modest buildings are built generally in massed rubble masonry or mud-block construction reinforced with horizontal timber ties and vertical poplar *ka'as* (columns embedded in masonry) or *khewphang* (vertical columns traversing more than one floor). Internally walls are provided with a thick plaster render of mud and straw which provides buildings with adequate insulation during the bitter winter months. Typically these techniques are not used any longer at the popular level, having been replaced by concrete blocks, reinforced concrete and corrugated sheet steel – all without any insulation – leading to numerous health and social issues.

Significant Issues and Impact

PLANNING ISSUES

As elsewhere, a voluntary civil society organization, the Khaplu Town Management and Development Society (TMDS), was helped into existence. Community-related issues, including land-use control, are partially regulated with the help of the Khaplu TMDS. However, since Khaplu is the headquarters of the Ghanche District, the Town Committee mandated by the Local Government Act also exists, and works in the same deficient manner as many such institutions in the public sector do. The Khaplu TMDS acts as a civil society balancing institution making up for many such deficiencies.

HISTORIC BUILDINGS/MONUMENTS CONSERVED

Among the main accomplishments is the conservation and recycling for reuse of the main Palace building, Yabgo Khar; the Darbar Khar, a building added on one of the terraces in 1929; and Hjta Khang, the old stables. Reconstruction of Chamanstar Khang, one of the older ancillary buildings, and demolition of the latest residential outhouse from about the 1960s and their replacement by a new designed structure, Ra'astar Khang, providing the majority of guestrooms. The Palace itself is being treated with great respect for its authenticity and its original fabric, composed as it is with source material from two or three older buildings. The reuse of the building has been kept as much as possible similar to its original residential use. Mechanical services are being installed with sensitive consideration for the building form and built fabric. Of the 21 guestrooms being created, only six are located in the Palace building, the remaining being housed in the ancillary blocks.

NEW BUILDING FACILITIES

The new buildings on the complex comprise Ra'astar Khang and the services blocks. Ra'astar Khang will offer nine of the 15 guestrooms outside Yabgo Khar, and has been designed as a new functional building but in the traditional material of natural stone and earthen mortars, laced with timbers for seismic stability. The two service blocks are located on land well removed from the main complex, and comprise the laundry building, which also includes a small cafeteria for staff, and the standby power building, which will house the standby generators, the transformer substation as well as living accommodation for six staff.

COMMUNITY INVOLVEMENT/PROGRAMME

Through the Khaplu TMDS, the community is benefitting from employment of labour at the construction site of the project. The Tourist Promotion Services has already started the process of selecting a cadre of employees who will work as trained hotel staff in the complete project.

VOCATIONAL TRAINING/CAPACITY BUILDING

About 30 staff drawn from the community is being trained in the hospitality trade as cooks, waiters, housekeeping staff, watch and ward staff, in mechanical equipment operation and maintenance, and other miscellaneous roles. During construction, hundreds from the local community have been employed as skilled and unskilled workers, many being trained as masons, carpenters, plumbers and electricians.

Partners

COMMUNITY PARTNERS

The community of Khaplu.

Donors

Government of Norway, Government of Japan.

Authoritative Framework

The main Palace building and the Darbar was bequeathed to AKDN. The ancillary buildings and the open land area were purchased by AKDN. One of the contiguous terraces has been leased for 25 years to retain control over further development. Additional land was purchased in the vicinity to establish service facilities. The property will be managed and operated as a residence guest house by the Tourist Promotion Services.

Hunza Villages Rehabilitation

GILGIT-BALTISTAN, PAKISTAN

While conservation of Baltit Fort, the first project of the Aga Khan Trust for Culture (AKTC) in the area, was undertaken it was determined that in order for the socio-economic benefits to be fully realized, thus allowing for community ownership of the process, the living conditions and overall welfare of the inhabitants of Karimabad would also have to be improved. Thus the Karimabad project undertaken as of 1992 was the first AKTC initiative using multiple inputs for community-based rehabilitation, village planning and area development.

Subsequent to the loss of the traditional institutional structures in 1974, with the abolishment of the Mirdom and the opening up of the KKH road that linked Pakistan with China in 1979, the physical environment in Hunza experienced a negative phase. Traditional wisdom called for the use of scarce land for agriculture, fruit growing and cash crops while 'dead' land was employed for housing, but these lessons were cast aside. This negative development had started to affect Karimabad as the traditional settlements in the neighbourhood of the Fort were being abandoned, mostly because of prevailing unsanitary living conditions and the inadequacy of the houses to support the desired standard of modern life.

New housing built on the open farm terraces with only rudimentary sanitary waste disposal was not only marring the physical scenic beauty but also reducing productive farm land. To steer this development away from these negative aspects, following discussions with the inhabitants of Karimabad, a framework for physical growth and for the maintenance of its environmental and cultural assets was formulated. This called for: the establishment of a representative local institutional base, the Karimabad Town Management Society (TMS), which could resolve upcoming social and community issues; the rehabilitation of the traditional settlements and their architectural heritage; a more balanced land-use development catering for future growth either by enlarging the existing settlements or by developing new sites suitable from an environmental and cultural sensibility; and the planning and setting up of service infrastructure to support the proposed land use.

An aerial view of a settlement
in the Hunza Valley.

Opposite page:
Elders dancing in the rehabilitated *jataq*, or
community space, in Altit Village.

1 Ali Gohar House
2 Tower
3 Kuyukutz Mosque
4 Rupikutz Mosque
5 Mamurukutz Mosque
6 Yarikutz Mosque
7 Kuyukutz Mosque
8 Shalkutz Mosque
9 Tower
10 Tower
11 Water System Improvements

N
▲

⊢————————⊣ 10 m

Project Scope Objectives

The aims of this project include improving living conditions in central Hunza, while protecting and retaining the natural and physical setting that is the attraction of the area. The conservation of its architecturaland cultural heritage is a clear goal, together with the rehabilitation of its traditional settlements through insertion of modern services (such as sanitation, water supply, paved pathways). These actions demonstrate the applicability of traditional housing, fostering responsible community-based institutions, and reviving traditional skills in crafts, while developing capacities in non-traditional areas for women.

Left, the restored *jataq*, or community space, in Altit.

Right, the traditional, flat-roofed houses adjacent to the Fort on which one can see plates of apricots drying in the sun.

The rehabilitation programme was extended to the historic village of Ganish initially and then spread to the villages of Chumerkhun, Sheraz and Altit. To sustain improvement in the quality of life brought about by these projects, Town Management Societies (TMS) were instituted following the Karimabad model in Ganish and Altit, with the charge of taking full responsibility for the rehabilitation projects in the settlements. In addition to the restoration and rehabilitation efforts, focus on reviving traditional skills, generating new employment opportunities through revival of arts and crafts, and training in non-traditional skills for women was also implemented.

Revival of the marketing of traditional crafts, such as weaving, embroidery and rug making, was also made possible through partnering with local organizations, such as the Karakoram Area Development Organization (KADO). Other KADO activities include the Hunza Environmental Committee which looks after the collection and disposal of waste in central Hunza. Another initiative is the Hunza Arts and Culture Forum, established to revive and promote music through apprenticeship of young students with masters in the old traditions, and production of indigenous musical instruments.

At the request of the Ganish community, the rehabilitation programme was extended to Ganish, one of the oldest villages in Hunza, an example of a traditional fortified settlement. Initiatives started with the conservation of an architectural ensemble of the four family mosques of Yarikutz, Rupikutz, Kuyukutz and Mamurukutz, organized around a historic open community space, the *jataq* – formerly the site of ritual and ceremonial activities. The programme was then extended to cover the whole historic village with its three other mosques, two *shikaris* (watchtowers), the historic village water reservoir and a number of historic houses. Sanitation and water supply schemes were also instituted. A concealed electric supply system was installed and the village lanes were stone-paved to complete the environmental upgrading.

Residential development outside the historic areas has allowed for the revival of sound building techniques based on tradition, drawing upon the experiences and research into appropriate forms of traditional cluster housing. This helps to provide a viable social setting, where inter-generational interaction is possible and encouraged, and where security of the individual and the family is ensured.

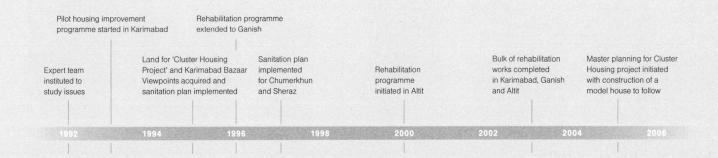

Pilot housing improvement
programme started in Karimabad

Rehabilitation programme
extended to Ganish

Expert team
instituted to
study issues

Land for 'Cluster Housing
Project' and Karimabad Bazaar
Viewpoints acquired and
sanitation plan implemented

Sanitation plan
implemented
for Chumerkhun
and Sheraz

Rehabilitation
programme
initiated in Altit

Bulk of rehabilitation
works completed
in Karimabad, Ganish
and Altit

Master planning for Cluster
Housing project initiated
with construction of a
model house to follow

1992   1994   1996   1998   2000   2002   2004   2006

Background

BRIEF HISTORY OF PROJECT SITE

The historic settlements of Ganish, Altit and Baltit are in central Hunza. A strand of the old Silk Route runs through Ganish where within walking distance are found the Sacred Rocks at Haldeikish, testimony to the many cultures, traders and travellers that traversed this route. The human effort to carve out a living in this incredibly beautiful yet harsh terrain, in harmony with the natural environment, led to the development of a mountain culture among the Hunzokutz which is visible in the many forts and fortified villages, the terraced farming lands, the irrigation channels that were constructed, the intricate water supply system that was implemented, the traditions and festivals that were adopted, the folklore and the language – Burushaski – the diet, dance and music, and the arts and crafts. The combination of the cultural heritage and the physical environment provide an enclave that is worthy of recognition as a world heritage site.

Challenges

DEMOGRAPHICS

The three villages of Karimabad, Ganish and Altit with their many settlements have a population of 11,000 with 1400 households.

ENVIRONMENTAL CONCERNS

The centuries-old harmony of human habitation and natural environment is being eroded by the construction of scattered housing in the productive terraced farmlands. A large number of these new houses use concrete blocks and large glass windows, alien to the traditional wisdom of using local materials, such as stone, poplar wood, mud adobe bricks and small-sized living spaces, and of being south facing, as well as importantly being built on so-called dead land that could not be made productive.

ACCESS TO OPEN SPACE

The Karimabad bowl-shaped land configuration enables wonderful scenic vistas. These vistas, because of commercial pressures on the scarce land, have been blocked as multi-storey buildings have come up in the main Karimabad Bazaar. The buildings on the lower side obscure these views. In an effort to provide visual corridors and prevent the feeling of traversing any other bazaar in Pakistan, a number of 'viewpoint' areas were acquired that have been retained to provide openings for people to absorb and get a wide-open feeling.

Significant Issues and Impact

DATA COLLECTION/SURVEYS

Surveys and data collection were centred on Karimabad. As the programme spread, village surveys and topographic surveys have also been done, through locally trained women and men.

MASTER PLANNING PROCESS

The 'Karimabad Conceptual Development Plan' was formulated through a very interactive process with the community, village organizations and government departments. Expertise and research work was also done through field work carried out by the Aga Khan Program for Islamic Architecture, where students from MIT and Harvard participated in the early 1990s.

HISTORIC BUILDINGS/MONUMENTS CONSERVED

The major forts of Baltit and Altit have been conserved. The fortified settlement of Ganish Khun has been fully rehabilitated, including recently the Ali Gohar House; so too the historic settlements of Karimabad and Altit. The various conservation and rehabilitation projects have so far won four UNESCO Asia-Pacific Awards for Cultural Heritage in central Hunza.

NEW BUILDING FACILITIES

In an attempt to demonstrate the modern usage of traditional construction techniques and materials, a number of new buildings have been constructed. These are the Amin Khan House, the Altit TMS building, the Altit gallery building, the Darbar in Aliabad, the office building in Karimabad, which houses the Karimabad TMS, and the model house in the 'Cluster Housing Project'. The latter and some other buildings that have used traditional building materials and construction techniques, relying on local materials thus also supporting the local economy, have been much appreciated by the communities. Already one sees greater use of locally available poplar wood, thus cutting down on deforestation, as well as use of local building materials in some of the new housing and buildings now being constructed.

VOCATIONAL TRAINING/CAPACITY BUILDING

The decision to restore the historic Baltit Fort as a museum and cultural centre in the early 1990s was the first major step that triggered the process of revival of traditional construction style and skills. The few master masons and carpenters then available were recruited, together with young apprentices under the supervision of international consultants and professional staff. This strategy of developing technical and skilled capacities in conservation and rehabilitation has been followed

since the beginning of the Baltit Fort restoration with 14 master carpenters and 23 master masons now practicing, some with 15 years of experience in conservation and rehabilitation. The Women Social Enterprise (WSE) has enabled 12 young women with school education, previously trained in technical documentation of heritage assets, now to work with master carpenters, masons, electricians and plumbers. These young women trainees are receiving both on-the-job practical training from master artisans as well as basic theoretical understanding from professional staff, such as engineers, architects and consultants.

QUALITY OF LIFE

Health indicators are much improved with the provision of proper modern sanitation systems through the coverage of the 1400 households of Karimabad, Ganish and Altit. Interestingly the treated effluents are being used for growing crops in the areas of the Hunza River bank with excellent harvests reported.

Partners

COMMUNITY PARTNERS

Karakoram Area Development Organization, Karimabad Town Management Society, Ganish Khun Heritage and Social Welfare Society, Altit Town Management Society.

Donors

Governments of Norway, Japan and Spain, Swiss Agency for Development Cooperation, Aga Khan Foundation, European Union.

Authoritative Framework

The underlying agreement for all community-based rehabilitation and enterprise projects is that communities would drive the project implementation, while AKCS-P would provide technical assistance and financial oversight. On completion the communities would take responsibility for the management of the concerned individual projects.

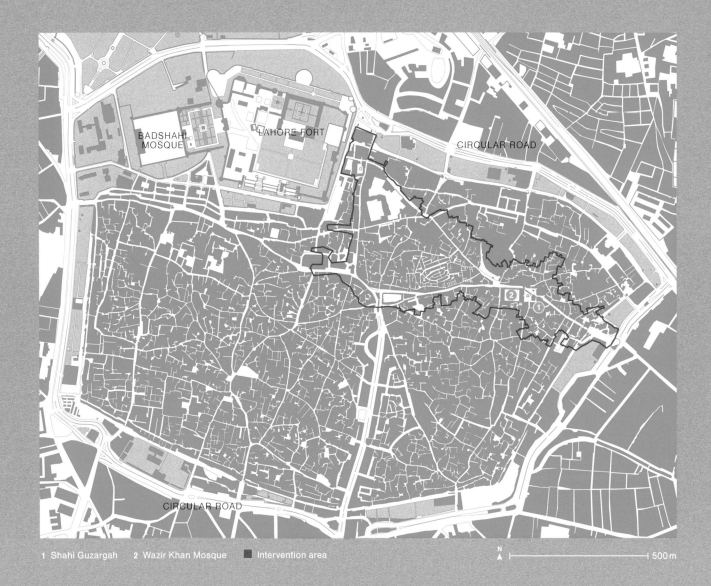

BADSHAHI MOSQUE

LAHORE FORT

CIRCULAR ROAD

CIRCULAR ROAD

1 Shahi Guzargah   **2** Wazir Khan Mosque   ■ Intervention area

N

500 m

FEATURED CASE STUDIES

SHAHI GUZARGAH

WAZIR KHAN MOSQUE

Lahore Area Programme

Programme Scope/Objectives

The Lahore Walled City project focused on the rehabilitation of the historic urban fabric and included the conservation of architectural heritage. Landmark monuments as well as public and private buildings were concerned, as was the improvement of infrastructure services in neighbourhoods and the living conditions of the residents. It also aimed at rehabilitating public (open) spaces within and around the area.

Preceding pages:

A view of Kotwali Bazaar looks west along the north facade of Wazir Khan Mosque.

This once fortified city is located in the north-west area of metropolitan Lahore, the capital of the province of the Punjab, and measures about 2.5 square kilometres. This historic core of Lahore has a concentration of monuments and buildings that reflect cultural diversity in architecture. Despite a dynamic and tumultuous past spanning several centuries, this area has retained much of its historic urban form.

The Walled City of Lahore project was initiated in 2006 by the Government of the Punjab and the World Bank. The following year the Aga Khan Trust for Culture (AKTC) entered a 'Public-Private Partnership Agreement' (PPP) with the provincial government to provide technical and financial assistance for the project and to undertake to build capacities in urban heritage conservation. In early 2008 AKTC signed a 'Memorandum of Association' with the World Bank. The Historic Cities Programme (HCP) has provided strategic planning services for the entire historic city while extending professional assistance for a pilot urban rehabilitation project that is integrated in a city-wide strategic framework for conservation and redevelopment.

The World Heritage Site of Lahore Fort (the Shahi Qila) and other equally spectacular monuments from the Mughal period, such as Badshahi Mosque (1683), Wazir Khan Mosque (1634) and the Wazir Khan Hammam, lend their splendour to the city. Additionally, several structures from the Sikh period and British colonial sites add to the city's charm, highlighting the importance the city held for a sequence of empires that ruled over South Asia. At present, the city possesses nearly two thousand buildings of significant architectural merit. Despite the lack of appropriate regulatory mechanisms pertaining to building demolition and construction, the Walled City is physically distinct, marked off from the surrounding colonial period city by the Circular Garden and the Circular Road.

In 1959 an excavation at Lahore Fort revealed the city's pre-Muslim occupation, dating back almost 1500 years. In the early eleventh century AD, Lahore became the seat of Sufi learning under Ali ibn Usman Hajweri, known as Data Ganj Bakhsh by his devotees. Lahore was subsequently conquered by the Ghaznavids under Sultan Mahmud in 1026, commencing the Muslim phase of its political history. Under the Mughal dynasty (1526–1789), Lahore flourished as an important provincial city periodically substituting for the Mughal capitals at Agra and Delhi. From 1789 onwards, Lahore was ruled by the Sikhs until the

Phasing 2007 → 2010

'Memorandum of Understanding' signed with the World Bank; several types of surveys begin, including assembly of a base map, building inventory, environmental quality assessment

Neighbourhood demonstration project through pilot home improvements initiated; GIS database assembly

Wazir Khan Mosque project preparation study; neighbourhood demonstration infrastructure project commences; Shahi Guzargah project implementation continues

2008   2009   2010

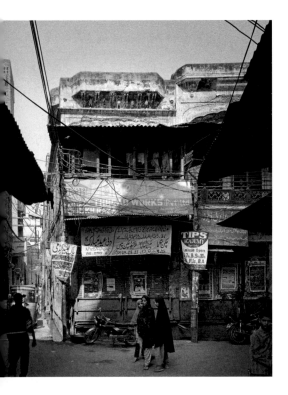

Sutar Mandi Chowk.

Opposite page:
The west facade of Naunihal Singh Haveli.

British annexation of the Punjab in 1849. In 1947 a substantial part of the Old City was destroyed as a result of communal strife and arson associated with the Partition of the South Asian subcontinent. This area is now home to intense commercial pressures resulting in the piecemeal demolition of the historic residential fabric.

The 'Strategic Plan' developed by HCP for the Walled City aims to redefine the city's role as a heritage site within Metropolitan Lahore. Promoting heritage-sensitive urban design, infrastructure improvement and residential land use, the Area Development framework integrates both landmark monuments and historic neighbourhoods. The framework provides for increasing residents' capacities to engage in the revitalization of the city and for generating opportunities for income. These broad priorities are being pursued at three levels.

The Walled City is surrounded by regional transportation functions that support local commercial markets. The 'Strategic Plan' proposes the gradual relocation of such metropolitan functions to more suitable sites elsewhere in Lahore in conjunction with associated land use such as wholesale and warehousing. This is being considered by the Punjab Government.

The Plan promotes the re-establishment of residential and other functions compatible with the city's historic character and makes provisions for reclaiming green areas in and around the Walled City. Special attention is being given to the restoration of the monumental complexes (and open spaces associated with them) and other architectural heritage as well as upgrading and expanding public utilities in neighbourhoods.

A legislative initiative is now underway to develop new planning and regulative processes. The framework also outlines building regulations in order to check the uncontrolled demolitions of historic building stock and their conversion into commercial entities.

The Plan outlines strategies for consolidating residential use and rehabilitating building stock. The overriding focus of attention concentrates on revalorizing *mohallas* in their historic and topographic context. Pilot initiatives integrate facade improvement, infrastructure upgrading and (historic) home improvement. Community-driven initiatives are also encouraged through training of local youth in spatial mapping and building trade skills as well as incentives for home improvement to owners through technical support.

Accompanying these efforts routine advice has been given to the Government of the Punjab on planning, legislative and administrative issues. Baseline surveys comprise a topographical map at the scale of the Walled City, an inventory of all 22,800 properties and a socio-economic survey of 1757 households across the city. An operational Geographic Information System (GIS) is in place.

The north-eastern minaret
of Wazir Khan Mosque seen
from Chitta Gate.

Background

BRIEF HISTORY OF PROGRAMME AREA

Lahore Walled City is the historic core of Lahore and began on the banks of the River Ravi at least 1500 years ago. In the early 11th century AD, Lahore became a seat of Muslim Sufi learning under Ali b. Usman Hajweri. Not soon after, in 1026, Lahore was conquered by the Ghaznavids under Sultan Mahmud. The centuries under the Delhi Sultanates (1187–1526) were turbulent, and physical evidence of the city's eminence from this period is scarce. Under the Mughals (1526–1789), Lahore was an important provincial city and several important monuments were built, including the World Heritage Site of Lahore Fort, the Mosque of Wazir Khan (1634) and the Badshahi Mosque (1683). From 1789 Lahore was under the control of the Sikhs until the British annexation of the Punjab in 1849. The colonial period saw the destruction of the city's fortifications and its gates, and the establishment of important institutions and the architecture associated with them outside the historic core. In 1947 significant areas of the Walled City were destroyed by arson and looting, leaving an indelible mark in the form of commercial developments that replaced what was lost. The new markets continue to expand agressively at the cost of the historic fabric. However, some 2000 non-monumental buildings of architectural merit still survive.

Challenges

PROGRAMME RISKS

The project seeks to address many existing conditions – physical, socio-economic, cultural and administrative. The single most imporant challenge it faces is the continued lack of an enabling administrative and governance apparatus, being mitigated by certain legislative and administrative steps being taken by the Government of the Punjab. Other challenges are related to this, such as the unimpeded demolition of the historic building stock and its replacement by commercial structures.

SITE CONDITIONS

The historic city is an artificial mound, 2.6 km^2 in area, with a rise of some 15 metres. The city is densely packed with nearly 23,000 parcels of land, and gross residential density is in the range of 550 persons per hectare. The city is surrounded by major inter-regional rail and road transporation functions in a symbiotic relationship with the regional markets inside the historic precincts.

DEMOGRAPHICS

According to the last census conducted in 1998, the Walled City's population stood at 160,000. However, a declining trend is in place due to increasing commercialization and loss of the residential fabric. In spite of this, the Walled City remains one of the most densely populated localities in the metropolis.

HOUSEHOLD ECONOMY

The Walled City is home to some of the poorest people in metropolitan Lahore and the lack of suitable job opportunities is a major concern amongst households – especially those who continue to educate their children. Common sources of income include employment as salesmen, vendors, daily wage earners and/or owners of small shops.

STATUS OF HEALTH AND EDUCATION

Common illnesses comprise diabetes and blood pressure, asthma, hepatitis B and typhoid. AKCS-P has introduced monthly health awareness sessions to address frequent concerns among women. Most public-sector schools are overcrowded, and lack playing areas and adequate sanitation facilities.

AVAILABILITY OF DRINKING WATER AND PROPER SANITATION FACILITIES

Drinking water is of poor quality with high traces of faecal contamination. Lack of appropriate measures to treat the water supply at source further exacerbates the problem. During the summer, significant parts of the Walled City suffer from water scarcity.

ENVIRONMENTAL CONCERNS

Prevailing environmental conditions negatively impact the quality of life of residents. Improvement in the services infrastructure and the enforcement of land-use controls are expected to improve the currently unacceptable health and environmental conditions.

INFRASTRUCTURE

The 150-year-old reservoir built at the city's highest point and some of the water mains of the old water supply network are still relied upon, and are part of a pressurised grid augmented by some 16 tube wells, dotted around the city. Failure of pressure in the system results in contamination and insufficient supply, leading to consumers installing small centrifugal pumps on the supply lines. The drainage system is mainly covered-over open drains, many large open drains on one or both sides of the main thoroughfares, and main sewers in some bazaars. It is a mixed sewage and storm-water system. The electrical and the telecommunication distribution systems need much reorganization and updating to acceptable standards. A city-wide programme of infrastructure development and guidelines for implementation have been prepared. These aim to improve the water supply system, introduce a new drainage system separating storm water from sewage, and rationalize the electrical and telecommunication distribution system, all at standards well above the prevailing ones.

ACCESS TO OPEN SPACE

The Circular Garden, established in 1912, has been heavily overrun by public and private sector unauthorized buildings, and by strip-commerce along Circular Road. Urban squares have also been overrun by unauthorized commerce.

BUILDING CONDITIONS

Most buildings are founded on cultural debris and structural failure is endemic. To stem this, it is proposed to provide a new drainage system that stops the percolation of water into the foundation-bearing soil.

OPEN SPACES

The Circular Garden along the Walled City serves as the main open space. However, it has been subjected to routine encroachments by commercial enterprises as well as public institutions.

Significant Issues and Impact

DATA COLLECTION/SURVEYS

Topographical surveys using EDM/CAD technology could only be carried out at night, owing to traffic conditions. Inventory of 22,800 individual buildings, recording some 172 attributes, is now part of a GIS database.

MASTER PLANNING PROCESS

Strategic Plan completed in February 2008, now due for a review and update.

PLANNING ISSUES

Ownership titles for properties are non-existent owing to land subdivision not having been recorded during colonial times; absence of land-use regulation; collapse of municipal governance; no clear demarcation of the municipal limits of the historic area; metropolitan and regional planning inadequacies negatively impact on Lahore Walled City.

HISTORIC BUILDINGS/MONUMENTS CONSERVED

AKTC and AKCS-P are carrying out the conservation of Wazir Khan Mosque. A home in one of the lanes of the Old City has been conserved as a demonstration project.

NEW BUILDING FACILITIES

A new urban infill building has been designed and site access is being negotiated.

COMMUNITY INVOLVEMENT/PROGRAMME

Community-based organizations have been formed based on discreet components of the urban morphology. One of the communities is currently directly involved in the conservation and upgrading of its neighbourhood.

VOCATIONAL TRAINING/CAPACITY BUILDING

Skills enhancement training programmes related to building trades and spatial documentation have been initiated in the project area. The programme provides on-the-job training for local youth – both male and female.

CONTRACTING METHODS

For large projects, national competitive bidding procedure; material and labour contracts for intermediate and small projects; labour only contracts with material purchased by AKTC; employed labour and hired unskilled labour with material purchased by AKTC.

NEW TECHNOLOGIES INTRODUCED

GIS; EDM/CAD real-time surveying and documenting techniques, with photo-orthorectifying software; SSPS analysis.

RELEVANT CODES/STANDARDS ADOPTED

International codes being recommended by consultants engaged by AKTC. Recommendations and guidelines prepared by AKTC being introduced.

LESSONS LEARNED

This is the first HCP project based on a 'Public-Private Partnership' framework approach. While the Government of the Punjab facilitates many aspects of the project that would otherwise be extremely difficult, the project has been characterized by changing levels of mutual understanding of its nature, purpose and philosophy, owing mainly to varying political and administration personalities that AKTC has had to work with.

Partners

PUBLIC PARTNERS

Government of the Punjab.

COMMUNITY PARTNERS

Several community-based organizations at the scale of micro neighbourhoods.

Authoritative Framework

'Public-Private Partnership Framework Agreement' was signed between AKTC and the Government of the Punjab on 2 July 2007. 'Memorandum of Understanding' between the World Bank and AKTC was signed on 6 March 2008.

Shahi Guzargah

LAHORE, PAKISTAN

The 'Pilot Urban Rehabilitation and Infrastructure Improvement Project' is being jointly implemented with the Government of the Punjab in one section of the Walled City of Lahore and constitutes eleven per cent of the Old City's footprint. The project, as initially conceived by the World Bank and the Punjab Government, aimed to rehabilitate a historic thoroughfare (starting at the Delhi Gate – one of the city's thirteen entrances and leading up to the Royal Fort) by putting services underground. Presently, this route comprises some of the major commercial centres serving the metropolis and the region. With the collaboration of the Historic Cities Programme (HCP), the project now has a broader set of goals. It comprises comprehensive regeneration of the area as heritage urbanism with special emphasis on the conservation of the historic residential areas associated with the bazaars, and includes the conservation of the main monuments and urban open spaces associated with them. This entails urban design, infrastructure upgrading, monument conservation and historic urban fabric rehabilitation with participation by the communities that constitute the residential areas.

Part of the site also represents a significant expansion of the area of the fortified city brought about by the addition of a new wall in the sixteenth century by the Mughal emperor Akbar (1542–1605). The site of Wazir Khan Mosque (see p. 160) used to be outside the old walls, and when the Mosque was constructed in 1634 it was one of the first to be inside Emperor Akbar's new walls. The urban open spaces associated with this monument are to be rehabilitated as part of the project.

The urban design aspect focuses on improving the visual and sensory features of the urban environment in conjunction with the rationalization and improvement of the visible elements of services infrastructure. The Aga Khan Trust for Culture (AKTC) is facilitating the improvement of bazaar facades (1.5 kilometres in length) and street surface improvement, the design and development of open spaces that have been heavily encroached upon by commercial entities, the provision of civic amenities and tourist facilities, urban landscaping, street furniture and related facilities including signage.

Regarding services infrastructure, AKTC has prepared an integrated infrastructure conceptual design for the Walled City as a whole. This conceptual design provides guidelines and parameters for the detailed design of infrastructure and

Infrastructural problems plague
Sutar Mandi Chowk.

Opposite page:
Delhi Gate, one of the thirteen entrances
to the Walled City.

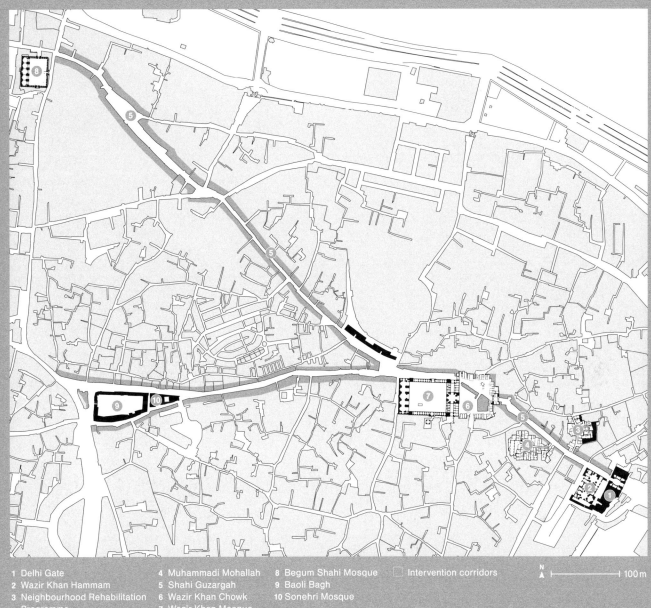

1 Delhi Gate
2 Wazir Khan Hammam
3 Neighbourhood Rehabilitation
   Programme
4 Muhammadi Mohallah
5 Shahi Guzargah
6 Wazir Khan Chowk
7 Wazir Khan Mosque
8 Begum Shahi Mosque
9 Baoli Bagh
10 Sonehri Mosque

Intervention corridors

N

100 m

Project Scope / Objectives

This project aims to rehabilitate the main bazaar thoroughfares as well as residential urban fabric in an integrated manner. This entails urban design work, infrastructure upgrading and historic building stock rehabilitation. Urban open spaces are to be rehabilitated and key landmark monuments located in the main thoroughfares are also to be restored as individual projects. The neighbourhood demonstration project involves testing of proposed designs on which basis the larger pilot project will be implemented.

A courtyard detail of an old *haveli*
in a state of decay.

allows for a higher degree of design and implementation control at the level of the project area. Upgrading and improvement of infrastructure for water supply, sewage disposal, storm-water disposal, electricity, telecommunications and natural gas in the pilot project pose a different range of problems at various levels of delivery. Standards and details of the infrastructure include carefully thought out solutions responding to the myriad problems posed by the special physical and geographical context of the Walled City.

The 'Neighbourhood Rehabilitation Programme' constitutes a key component of the 'Pilot Urban Rehabilitation and Infrastructure Improvement Project'. It proposes a holistic approach to urban rehabilitation with sustainable yet quality standards for the services infrastructure, and the structural consolidation and revalorization of the historic building stock. A strategy sensitive to the historic urban fabric has been developed and is being implemented in a residential lane off Delhi Gate Bazaar – Gali Surjan Singh and its cul-de-sac offshoot, Koocha Charakh Garan. Together, these two streets comprise twenty-five residential buildings housing approximately 150 people. The locality was chosen primarily because it represents the average conditions of infrastructure, building obsolescence, and the admixture of historic and contemporary houses among the historic neighbourhoods in the area.

The survey and documentation done by the Aga Khan Cultural Services-Pakistan (AKCS-P) in the project area revealed that, by and large, homeowners are willing to undertake home repair and maintenance works in small interventions in accordance with their income levels. However, the lack of adequate technical knowledge and necessary skills poses serious limitations on the scope of the work. A home restoration project carried out in 2008 demonstrated the full range of problems associated with building decay and mobilized the street community to take part in the project.

The rehabilitation strategy involves intensive social and technical extension work, and aims at setting a precedence for urban environmental rehabilitation. It addresses the socio-economic dynamics of the context with on-the-job training in various traditional building trade skills targeting local youth in the project area, who work alongside master craftsmen in masonry, carpentry, plumbing and electrical works.

The programme has three well-defined but interlinked components. First, facade improvement: since infrastructure elements such as electricity and telecom lines can only be attached to rehabilitated facades that can effectively bear the stresses of physical support, facade rehabilitation is considered an investment in the public realm. Intervening in house facades entails a modicum of structural consolidation and necessarily means engaging with the inner workings of a house too. A close relationship is thus developed between the owner-occupant of a house and the implementing agency, in this case AKCS-P, one that also encourages homeowners to make their own investments in undertaking home repairs. Second, infrastructure upgrading: this provides for improved waste and storm-water disposal where possible, systems for improved solid waste disposal, subsurface layout of gas pipes and new (re)organized electrical, telephone and television cable distribution networks. It is expected that better drainage facilities will reduce the extent of leakage or seepage into the bearing strata of the soil, therefore complementing efforts at structural consolidation of the surrounding buildings. Third, home improvement: this component addresses building problems in the internal spaces of a house and includes, to varying degrees, structural repairs and consolidation, replacement of dilapidated and/or dysfunctional installations, non-structural architectural intervention and finishes.

Left, drainage upgrading is being undertaken in Shahi Guzargah.

Right, restoration work is being done on original brickwork.

Above, a bird's-eye view of Sunehri Masjid (Golden Mosque),
Rang Mahal, in the Walled City (left) and a detail of a ruined facade
in Chehal Bibiyan Mohalla (right).

Below, elevations of Guzargah neighbourhood rehabilitation projects,
before and after intervention.

⊢————————————⊣ 10 m

Background

BRIEF HISTORY OF PROJECT SITE
The project site comprises those neighbourhoods of the historic city through which the route taken by Mughal royalty, from the entrance to the city to the gates of the royal palace, passes. This route now consists of some of the major commercial centres of the metropolis.

Challenges

SITE CONDITIONS
Neglect and inadequacy of the existing services infrastructure and the task of transforming it to meet acceptable standards is one of the biggest challenges of the project, particularly when seen in relation to the complex morphology of the Walled City. The state of the historic building stock is another key challenge, as a vast majority of the buildings reflect structural failure, traceable to foundation failure and bad plumbing which results in water seepage into the building fabric.

DEMOGRAPHICS
Approximately 8000 people live in the Shahi Guzargah project area. The neighbourhood demonstration project serves close to 150 people residing in the residential lanes, Gali Surjan Singh and Koocha Charakh Garan. The majority of residents are homeowners.

HOUSEHOLD ECONOMY
Lahore Walled City is home to some of the poorest people in metropolitan Lahore and a lack of job opportunities is a major concern. Common sources of income include employment as salesmen, vendors, daily wage earners, piece-rate workers (especially in the case of women), and/or small shops owned by residents. Socio-economic profiles of residents in Gali Surjan Singh and Koocha Charakh Garan are not much different from the rest of the Walled City.

STATUS OF HEALTH AND EDUCATION
Common illnesses comprise diabetes and blood pressure, asthma, hepatitis B and typhoid. In collaboration with the Aga Khan Health Service, AKCS-P has introduced monthly health awareness sessions and medical camps for residents in the project area and surrounding localities. Most public-sector schools are overcrowded, and lack playing areas and adequate sanitation facilities.

AVAILABILITY OF DRINKING WATER AND PROPER SANITATION FACILITIES
Drinking water is of poor quality with high traces of faecal contamination. Lack of appropriate measures to treat the water supply at source further exacerbates the problem. During the summer, significant parts of the Walled City suffer from water scarcity.

ENVIRONMENTAL CONCERNS
Improvement in the services infrastructure and the enforcement of land-use controls are expected to improve the currently unacceptable living conditions.

ACCESS TO OPEN SPACE
No open spaces suitable for women and children exist in the immediate vicinity of the Shahi Guzargah project area or the neighbourhood project site.

BUILDING CONDITIONS
Most buildings are founded on cultural debris and structural failure is endemic. A majority of the buildings are taken over by commercial enterprises resulting in significant deterioration. Homeowners continue to alter houses according to their needs but changes are generally inappropriate in the light of the age and condition of the buildings.

Significant Issues and Impact

DATA COLLECTION/SURVEYS
A full inventory of buildings has been completed and made a part of the GIS system. A topographical map of the area has been completed. Buildings displaying architectural merit are in the process of being documented. A 12% sample of households has been surveyed for establishing income and poverty levels and prevailing quality of life conditions. For the purposes of the demonstration project, detailed home documentation for all the houses in the two streets has been carried out along with the survey of existing services infrastructure. Baseline data pertaining to the socio-economic profile of all the households in the two streets have been compiled.

MASTER PLANNING PROCESS
The demonstration project is one of several 'Local Development Frameworks' that have been planned for the Walled City. It represents the full range of policies and interventions envisaged at this scale in the 'Strategic Plan' prepared by HCP.

PLANNING ISSUES
Governance, land use and zoning control are lacking. Necessary legislative frameworks to regulate building constuction are not in place. Traffic reorganization is in need of planning. Heritage conservation, urban design and rehabilitation of neighbourhoods and open spaces require an integrated approach.

HISTORIC BUILDINGS/MONUMENTS CONSERVED
A number of monuments are part of the project area. Monuments being targeted for conservation include Wazir Khan Mosque, the Sonehri (Golden) Mosque and the Maryam Zamani (Begum Shahi) Mosque. A single historic house (just over 100 years old) in Koocha Charakh Garan – the neighbourhood demonstration project area – was conserved in 2008. Rehabilitation of five additional historic houses are underway in the same locality.

NEW BUILDING FACILITIES
An 'urban infill' building has been designed and is part of the project. This will give back the scale and physical volume of a missing portion of the streetscape; create opportunities for appropriate level of commerce of a type aimed at visitors; and house certain infrastructure elements such as transformers and one tube well. Other new buildings are planned to manage the urban space outside the city's perimeters.

COMMUNITY INVOLVEMENT/PROGRAMME
Community-based organizations (CBOs) have been created in small units related to the topo-morphological characteristics of the neighbourhoods. These help in resolving local issues of conflict, in speaking to individual stakeholders, and in propagating the desirable values in development participation.

VOCATIONAL TRAINING/CAPACITY BUILDING
Youth residing in the project area are participating in the 'Skills Enhancement Programme' pertaining to building trades and spatial documentation. The programme provides on-the-job training to both males and females.

CONTRACTING METHODS
National competitive bidding under the guidelines of the World Bank. In the case of the neighbourhood demonstration project, material purchased and labour hired directly by AKTC; supervised by AKTC staff.

NEW TECHNOLOGIES INTRODUCED
EDM/CAD real-time surveying and documenting techniques, with photo-orthorectifying software; data analysis with GIS and SPSS. New standards for the infrastructure distribution networks have been introduced.

RELEVANT CODES/STANDARDS ADOPTED
Recommendations and guidelines prepared by AKTC being introduced.

QUALITY OF LIFE
In collaboration with the Aga Khan Health Service, AKCS-P has introduced monthly health awareness sessions and medical camps for residents in the project area and surrounding localities.

Partners

PUBLIC PARTNERS
Government of the Punjab.

Donors

The World Bank, German Foreign Ministry.

Authoritative Framework

'Public-Private Partnership Framework Agreement' was signed between AKTC and the Government of the Punjab on 2 July 2007.

Wazir Khan Mosque

LAHORE, PAKISTAN

Wazir Khan Mosque is the centrepiece of a historic urban ensemble in the Walled City of Lahore. The Mosque was built in 1634 by Hakim Alimuddin who was granted the title of Wazir Khan on Shah Jahan's accession to the Mughal throne in 1628. It is founded on the site of an old Sufi convent – associated with the saint Syed Ishaq Gazruni (d. AD 1284/AH 786) – between the limits of the Old City and the new city walls built a century earlier by Shah Jahan's grand-father, Emperor Akbar. In this still developing space, the Mosque complex was an ambitious and unprecedented piece of urban design. The grave of Syed Ishaq Gazruni was included in the fabric of the Mosque. At the time of its construction it was considered the largest mosque within the fortifications of Lahore and superseded the Begum Shahi Mosque (constructed by Emperor Jahangir in 1614) as the congregational mosque of the city.

Wazir Khan Mosque is located at a distance of about 260 metres from the Delhi Gate on the route to Lahore Fort and is surrounded by the thick urban fabric of the Walled City. The physical context comprises the Chowk (a square urban open space), Chitta Gate and the buildings fronting the square and the bazaar. The houses on the south side define the southern limits of the Mosque and street defines the border between the Mosque and the urban fabric on the west side. On the northern side the bazaar opens up at a fork to form the Kotwali Chowk, which was the space in front of the Mughal-period city police station, the *kotwali*, no longer existing. Historically, as part of the thoroughfare connecting Delhi Gate and Lahore Fort, Wazir Khan Mosque, together with its square, formed a singularly important element punctuating the urban fabric of the Walled City.

Of the fourteenth-century Sufi establishment nothing but three grave sites remain. Of these the grave of Syed Ishaq Gazruni was made part of the fabric of the Mosque, and is accessed by a staircase in the main courtyard, marked by an elaborate pavilion. The original level of his grave is about 2.5 metres below the level of the Mosque's courtyard.

The Mosque's layout comprises a large quadrangular plan, with the heavily built prayer chamber housing five in-line domed cells located at the *qibla* end of the courtyard. The main building of the Mosque and its inner courtyard is sup-plemented by a bazaar with two rows of shops – intended for calligraphers and

The eastern facade of the main prayer chamber of Wazir Khan Mosque, seen from the courtyard.

Opposite page:
Scaffolding has been erected to enable a thorough documentation of the building.

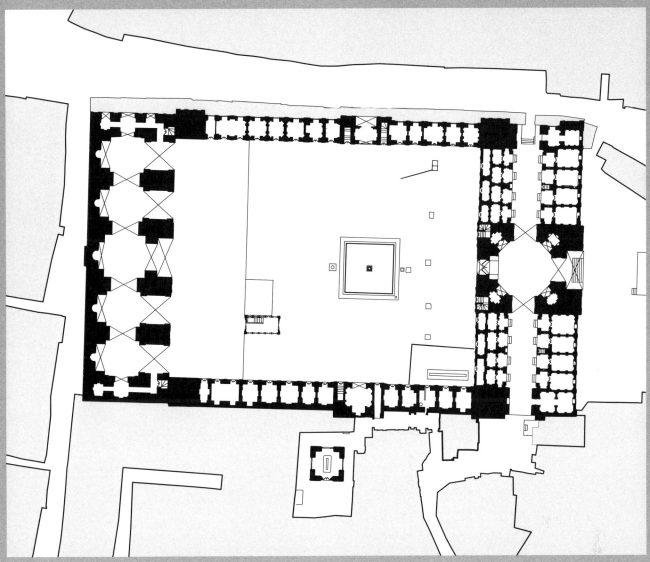

Project Scope / Objectives

AKTC is working on the conservation of Wazir Khan Mosque and providing planning assistance towards the reorganization of the space in front of the Mosque with the objective of improving the quality of the urban environment. Goals are the relocation of infrastructure underground and the return of the Mosque to its original urban setting.

book binders – at right angles to the axial direction upon entering the courtyard. The Chowk, a square open forecourt outside the Mosque, was part of a conscious attempt at formal urban design and an immediate precursor to other great urban compositions of Shah Jahan's time.

The chief architectural and artistic characteristic of the Mosque resides in its profuse surface decoration both on the exterior and in the interior. On the exterior, the decoration comprises a combination of fine exposed brickwork and a framework of plaster render with a thin layer of *faux* brickwork. This forms the overriding frame for dramatically coloured glazed-tile mosaics in floral and arboreal motifs as well as depicting calligraphic quotations from the Qur'an, the Hadith and other verses. Interior surfaces, entirely covered by fresco-work, have been touched up or painted over down the centuries by successive attempts at 'restoration', so much so that no original work appears to exist any longer. Of the delicate Mughal surface ornaments and decorative techniques, the most vividly displayed are the glazed-tile mural decoration and calligraphy which, despite its chromatic exuberance, recalls Safavid monuments in Isfahan (Iran), built only a few years before, and earlier Timurid architectural antecedents.

The Mosque has undergone serious damage. Heavy ingress of rain and waste water has damaged the floor of the rooms and the courtyard. Inappropriate commercial activity in the shops on the main facade poses a hazard to the building's fabric.

The four minarets, thirty-six metres in height from the street, have leaned out to varying but not alarming degrees. The movement of the two minarets adjacent to the main prayer chamber has caused cracks in the arches and roof structure of the end bays. Structural investigations suggest successive earthquakes as the cause of this behaviour. That the cracks existed prior to 1971 is confirmed from the record of repair work begun at that time.

Since March 2009 major architectural and damage documentation of the Mosque complex has been under way. Detailed electronic documentation of the building provides the basis for examining the nature and extent of damage and for assessing the extent of conservation measures. Geotechnical investigations have been completed and measures to carry out structural consolidation of the monument are being designed. Assessment of the building and the condition of its foundations indicate that major structural cracks are not related to ongoing structural behaviour. A programme for the conservation of the Mosque, to be implemented in several stages, is being developed.

Above, Wazir Khan Mosque is located in
a heavily built-up environment.

Below, the east-west section of the Mosque.

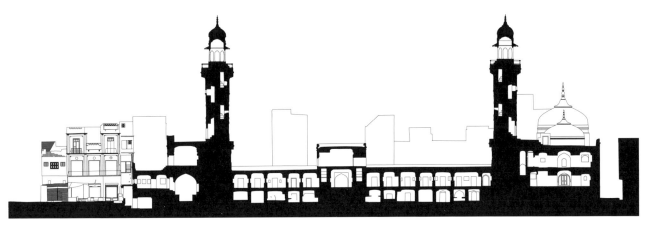

⊢————⊣ 10 m

163

Background

BRIEF HISTORY OF PROJECT SITE
Wazir Khan Mosque was built in 1634 by Hakim Alimuddin Ansari, the famous governor of the region under Emperor Shah Jahan. When still Prince Khurram, Shah Jahan had employed Hakim Alimuddin as his court physician. Upon ascending the throne, Shah Jahan appointed him governor of Lahore with the title Wazir Khan. A 14th-century Sufi convent associated with Syed Ishaq Gazruni existed on the site of the Mosque. The monument is noteworthy for its rich glazed-tile decorations.

Challenges

PROJECT RISKS
The minarets of the Mosque have leaned outwards. The base of the two western minarets, attached to the main prayer chamber, have induced structural cracks in the chamber. Structural investigations suggest that in all likelihood the cracks developed as a result of successive earthquakes. The conservation and restoration of the surface decorations in the Mosque, including its tile revetments, are costly and time-intensive operations and will require sustainable development of the appropriate skills. Pilot projects for key decorative crafts are proposed to be initiated. These are fresco murals, ceramic tiles and lime plasters. For post-conservation monitoring and maintenance, appropriate capacity in the maintenance agency is proposed to be developed.

SITE CONDITIONS
The diagonal connection from Chitta Gate to the gate leading out of the square on the north-eastern corner of the Mosque has now been transformed into a bazaar as a result of encroaching shops. A detailed survey has revealed that most of the shops, fronting the square on its eastern and northern sides, have encroached into the square. Some fragments of the original 17th-century shops on the perimeter of the square are nested deep within the new structures. The historical openness of the square has been seriously sacrificed to low-value structures. Increasing presence of commercial activities during the last four decades has resulted in ill-maintained shops and structures that have ultimately distorted the form of the open space and the monument.

INFRASTRUCTURE
The project aims to improve the existing infrastructure in the Mosque complex. Water supply, rain and waste water disposal, gas supply and electrification have all created serious problems since their introduction during past restoration efforts. An example of the negative impact is the settlement in the courtyard floor in various locations due to the heavy ingress of water resulting from inadequate drainage.

BUILDING CONDITIONS
As the street level has risen over the centuries most of the original shops on the northern side, rented out to an assortment of businesses, have lost accessibility from the steet and currently exist as storage space for shops built onto the face of the Mosque and encroach into the street space. Commercial activity, such as steel fabrication in the shops (on the main facade on the eastern side), is a huge threat to the structure of the Mosque. The Mosque has undergone serious damage due to inadequate maintenance and care.

Opposite page:
The interior of the main prayer chamber, looking north, and, on the left, a detail of a courtyard facade.

Significant Issues and Impact

DATA COLLECTION/SURVEYS
Since March 2009 major architectural and damage documentation of the Mosque complex is underway. Geotechnical investigations have been completed and measures to carry out structural consolidation of the monument are being designed.

MASTER PLANNING PROCESS
At the end of the documentation and analysis stage a master conservation plan is being prepared.

PLANNING ISSUES
The problems of building control and the regulation of the urban fabric, widespread in the Walled City, are equally applicable to the Wazir Khan Mosque complex. Equally important is how the present capacities for the protection and administration of the architectural heritage and levels of conservation skills presently available can be made more effective and sustainable.

HISTORIC BUILDINGS/MONUMENTS CONSERVED
A conservation programme for the Mosque is being developed and will be implemented over several stages. In the first stage structural and architectural investigations have been carried out.

COMMUNITY INVOLVEMENT/PROGRAMME
An initiative to involve the local community in the process of documentation and enhancing building skills has already been started and will be extended during the restoration of the Mosque.

CONTRACTING METHODS
The work will be carried out by employing skilled and unskilled workers, and the project management will be carried out by AKTC staff. Building contractors in the field of conservation do not exist in Pakistan.

NEW TECHNOLOGIES INTRODUCED
Real-time EDM/CAD documentation and photo-rectification software has been used for the first time in a protected monument in Pakistan.

RELEVANT CODES/STANDARDS ADOPTED
The 'International Charter for the Conservation and Restoration of Monuments and Sites' (the Venice Charter), 1964, is the principal document for the documentation and restoration of the monumental complex.

LESSONS LEARNED
The conservation of Wazir Khan Mosque and the rehabilitation of its Chowk are part of a larger Area Development Project in the Walled City of Lahore. It is part of a local development framework comprising the rehabilitation of the surrounding urban fabric and open space. The thrust of the project is aimed at urban regeneration and the economic uplift of the residential communities living in the neighbourhood of the project and offers lessons in conservation planning and methodology and capacity building.

Partners

PUBLIC PARTNERS
Government of the Punjab, Planning and Development Department, Sustainable Development of the Walled City of Lahore Project, Awqaf Department.

Donors

Kaplan Foundation Fund.

Authoritative Framework

'Public-Private Partnership Framework Agreement' was signed between AKTC and the Government of the Punjab in 2007. In 2009 formal permission to proceed was obtained from the Awqaf Department – the custodian of the property.

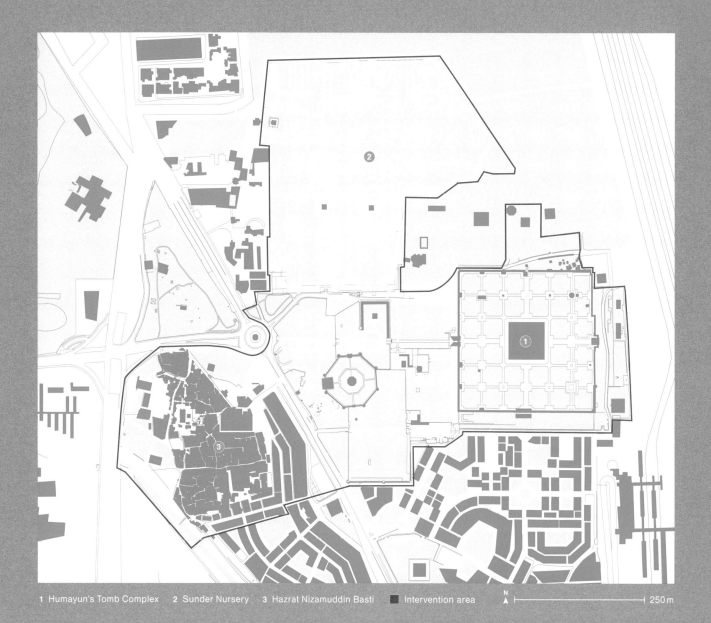

1 Humayun's Tomb Complex   2 Sunder Nursery   3 Hazrat Nizamuddin Basti   ■ Intervention area

N ▲   ├─────────────────────┤ 250 m

FEATURED CASE STUDIES

HUMAYUN'S TOMB COMPLEX

SUNDER NURSERY

HAZRAT NIZAMUDDIN BASTI

Delhi Area Programme

Programme Scope/Objectives

This is a conservation, socio-economic and environmental programme with key project components including the conservation of over 30 Mughal-era monuments and the creation of a city park with Delhi's first arboretum. Performance spaces, documentation and training in music traditions, assistance in the revival of craft skills, the strengthening of the municipal education and health infrastructure were also undertaken. The programme involved setting up vocational training programmes, building public toilets, assorted urban improvements, and conservation training for professionals and craftsmen.

Preceding pages:

A panoramic view from the north-east overlooks Humayun's Tomb complex. Sunder Nursery is on the right.

Located in the heart of New Delhi, in the setting of Humayun's Tomb World Heritage Site and dotted with over a hundred monuments, the project area may be the densest ensemble of medieval Islamic buildings in India. More importantly, the densely populated Hazrat Nizamuddin Basti is the repository of seven hundred years 'living culture' recognized for its pluralistic traditions.

On the occasion of the fiftieth anniversary of India's independence, as a gift of His Highness the Aga Khan, the Aga Khan Trust for Culture (AKTC) implemented the Humayun's Tomb Garden restoration. The successfully completed project led to a significant increase in visitor numbers and eventually culminated in a new public-private partnership project for a comprehensive urban renewal initiative in the area. With distinct conservation, socio-economic and environmental development objectives, this project aims to unify the three presently segregated areas of Humayun's Tomb, Nizamuddin Basti and Sunder Nursery into an urban conservation zone of considerable breadth and cultural significance while improving the quality of life for resident populations.

Heritage Conservation: Humayun's Tomb Complex

Conservation works aimed at enhancing the historic character and ensuring long-term preservation are now being undertaken on the mausoleum and associated gateways, pavilions and enclosure walls. Similarly the project, through landscaping and conservation, will focus on enhancing the setting of the World Heritage Site and possibly lead to the expansion of the site's boundaries.

Exhaustive archival research, site surveys, documentation using three-dimensional, state-of-the-art laser scanning technology, condition assessment and structural analysis preceded the preparation of detailed conservation proposals in keeping with established Indian and international conservation standards and guidelines. Conservation works then commenced in April 2008, following discussion and peer review. Significant completed works include the careful removal of over one million kilos of twentieth-century concrete from the roof and repairs to the dome, with its marble cladding repointed and cleaned and gold-plated finial repaired. The original Delhi quartzite paving of the lower plinth has now been restored, requiring the removal of concrete and manually lifting and resetting 12,000 square metres of stone blocks, most weighing over a thousand kilos.

Phasing 1997 → 2012

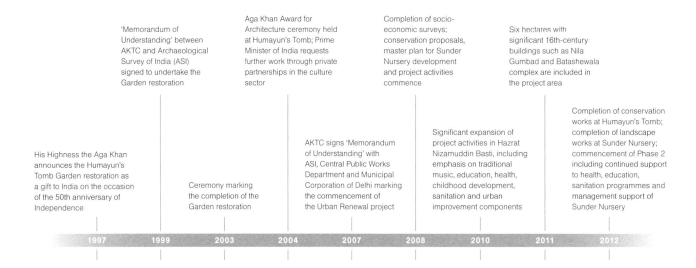

'Memorandum of Understanding' between AKTC and Archaeological Survey of India (ASI) signed to undertake the Garden restoration

Aga Khan Award for Architecture ceremony held at Humayun's Tomb; Prime Minister of India requests further work through private partnerships in the culture sector

Completion of socio-economic surveys; conservation proposals, master plan for Sunder Nursery development and project activities commence

Six hectares with significant 16th-century buildings such as Nila Gumbad and Batashewala complex are included in the project area

Completion of conservation works at Humayun's Tomb; completion of landscape works at Sunder Nursery; commencement of Phase 2 including continued support to health, education, sanitation programmes and management support of Sunder Nursery

His Highness the Aga Khan announces the Humayun's Tomb Garden restoration as a gift to India on the occasion of the 50th anniversary of Independence

Ceremony marking the completion of the Garden restoration

AKTC signs 'Memorandum of Understanding' with ASI, Central Public Works Department and Municipal Corporation of Delhi marking the commencement of the Urban Renewal project

Significant expansion of project activities in Hazrat Nizamuddin Basti, including emphasis on traditional music, education, health, childhood development, sanitation and urban improvement components

1997   1999   2003   2004   2007   2008   2010   2011   2012

During 2008 and early 2009 over a million kilos of concrete were removed from the roof terrace of Humayun's Tomb.

The project has also served as a platform for training programmes for conservation professionals and craftsmen. Over a hundred officers from across India have attended training modules focused on the preparation and use of lime mortar and high-definition survey techniques.

Sunder Nursery Monuments

Located immediately north of Humayun's Tomb, the twenty-seven-hectare Sunder Nursery stands on the historic Grand Trunk Road linking Lahore to Kolkata and hosting significant sixteenth-century monuments that exist there thanks to nearby Hazrat Nizamuddin Auliya's *dargah*.

Conservation works are ongoing on the unique sixteenth-century Sunderwala Mahal and have been completed on the eighteenth-century Mughal-era garden pavilion, which was on the verge of collapse and threatened with demolition for a roadway project. Its conservation required painstaking work by master craftsmen using traditional materials, skills and techniques.

Over the next few years conservation works will be carried out on Lakkarwala Burj and Sunderwala Burj – buildings considered to be of national importance. It is also planned to integrate the large Azimganj Serai, to the north of Sunder Nursery.

Hazrat Nizamuddin Basti

The densely populated Basti is named after one of India's most venerated fourteenth-century Sufi saints, Sheikh Nizamuddin Auliya. The conservation and rehabilitation of monuments and civic open spaces aim to restore its intrinsic cultural, historical and spiritual significance and enhance visitor experience for pilgrims and tourists.

Conservation works in the Basti commenced following the partial collapse, in July 2008, of the fourteenth-century Baoli (step-well), considered holy and visited annually by millions of pilgrims. This is the only step-well in Delhi still fed by underwater springs, albeit heavily polluted by sewerage and waste. Its collapse in July 2008 endangered the lives of both residents and pilgrims and necessitated urgent remedial measures. Prior to commencing conservation works on the Baoli, studies were carried out using state-of-the-art technology including a ground penetrating radar survey, high-definition 3D laser scans, and geotechnical assessments.

In keeping with the requests of the Pirzada's, or keepers of the shrine, the Baoli was also de-silted to its original levels and centuries of accumulations were manually removed requiring over 8000 man-days of work. The collapsed portions were rebuilt as per the original construction techniques and the entire wall surface was chiselled to remove a thick layer of epoxy. Prior to conservation works, a dwelling unit over the collapsed portion needed to be dismantled and an alternate residence built for the family.

Standing at the eastern edge of the Basti, the unique Mughal tomb known as Chaunsath Khamba, together with the tomb enclosure of Mirza Ghalib – South Asia's most renowned poet – forms the largest open spaces within the Basti. Both enclosures have been land-scaped so as to enhance its historic character and restore dignity while creating perfor-mance spaces for musical traditions associated with the area for over seven centuries.

Socio-economic initiatives

Aimed at improving the quality of life for the densely populated Hazrat Nizamuddin Basti, the project takes a synergistic, community-centric and collaborative approach to develop and strengthen essential urban services through interventions in core areas of education, health, sanitation and upgrading open space.

Education

The existing education infrastructure has already been significantly enhanced and im-proved. Interventions in key segments of education, such as the training of teachers and support for students, were extended to include a major refurbishment of a municipal pri-mary school building. This was in a dilapidated state and lacked functional toilets or drinking water. Aimed at creating a student friendly, secure school environment beneficial to the growth and development of pupils, 'Building as a Learning Aid' elements were incorporated and provisions made for drinking water, separate toilets for boys and girls, wider stair-cases and safety features, like additional exits, unbreakable window panes and new electrical systems. The renovated school and education initiatives have resulted in a 150-per cent increase in the enrolment of students in just over a year.

Health

Interventions at the municipal polyclinic have significantly improved the quality of avail-able clinical and preventive health care. A newly established pathology lab is capable of conducting thirty-four types of tests and more than 3500 people have used the facility to carry out over 11,000 tests in just over a year. The initiative has included placing add-itional doctors for consultations in Gynaecology, ENT and Eye Care.

Vocational Training

In response to community needs, vocational training, career development and employ-ability programmes have been developed and are being implemented. These are aimed at building skills that translate into employment for youth, and livelihood opportunities and financial independence for women.

Urban improvements

A year after socio-economic development programmes commenced in the Basti and interaction with residents had increased, a physical mapping was undertaken in 2009 with the intention to plan sensitive urban improvements including landscaping of open spaces and street improvement; plans for both are now being implemented.

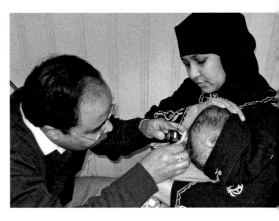

Top, classes are held in new classrooms at the Municipal Corporation of Delhi School.

Middle, people listen to a young Basti resident trained as a heritage volunteer at Chaunsath Khamba.

Bottom, a child is being examined at the Municipal Corporation of Delhi Polyclinic.

At Humayun's Tomb, young women practice the once near-extinct art and craft of *sanji*, or paper cutting, which was introduced to create income-generation opportunities in the district.

The parks along the western edge of the Basti will be landscaped to suit the needs expressed by the resident community in consultative meetings and as such there will be earmarked parks for women, children, cricket and other sports, community functions and weddings.

A key intervention for urban renewal in the Basti, the community toilet complex built in 2009 has improved access to hygienic sanitation for residents and pilgrims, who rely on public utilities. Also, over a hundred household toilets have been connected to the sewerage system and portions of the sewerage system relaid as part of the conservation works on the Baoli.

Cultural revival initiative

Exceptional by virtue of not just its vintage, the 700-year-old 'living culture' of the heritage area is a unique blend of secular and interfaith elements that encompass performing arts, classical music, poetry and traditional crafts in the setting of significant monuments. The project aims to revive and revitalize these components by documenting and recording their rich legacy and by making them viable in a contemporary milieu and to showcase this intangible heritage through music festivals held at the performance spaces created within the Basti. With the Qawwali music of fourteenth-century poet-composer Amir Khusrau Dehlvi originating here, it is the focus of documentation, training and outreach components of the project.

The initiative also aims to build awareness and generate interest in the built heritage on the Basti through activities like theatre, painting, craft workshops and guided walking tours – led by trained youths of the area. Basti women tutored in the traditional craft of paper cutting now augment family incomes with sales of their products.

Sunder Nursery: Developing a city park

The twenty-seven-hectare Sunder Nursery, established in 1912, is being developed as an urban park with distinct heritage, ecological and nursery zones. Works to enhance and showcase its ecological and historical heritage under a multidimensional landscape and conservation programme are now ongoing.

The landscape master plan includes a micro-habitat zone/arboretum to showcase Delhi's fast disappearing biodiversity. In a first for Delhi, the arboretum will house three hundred tree species representative of Delhi's native flora, trees and plants favoured by the Mughals and secure an important bird habitat. In addition, the park will emphasize its horticultural past with provisions for mist chambers, a tissue culture lab, glass houses, 3.6 hectares of nursery beds, a training centre, and dedicated spaces for flower shows and exhibitions.

With a two-kilometre-long peripheral road now complete, the park will be pedestrian. The central axis of the park, aligned to Humayun's Tomb entrance plaza, will draw in visitors and lead them through the many magnificent Mughal-period monuments set in lush environs, specialized gardens and ecological zones of the park. Additionally, Sunder Nursery will house educational facilities such as an Interpretation Centre on Ecology and Heritage, an amphitheatre for cultural events and a lakeside restaurant.

The three project zones of Humayun's Tomb, Nizamuddin Basti and Sunder Nursery will be interconnected by nature trails and heritage walks that link not just the three sites but also their history and culture. The resulting landscape will thus offer a unique experience for visitors while enhancing the cultural significance of the greater Niza-muddin area.

Background

BRIEF HISTORY OF PROGRAMME AREA

The Nizamuddin heritage precinct, comprising the three presently segregated areas of Hazrat Nizamuddin Basti, Sunder Nursery and the World Heritage Site of Humayun's Tomb, has had continuous building activity since the 12th century. The revered Hazrat Nizamuddin Auliya lived here in the early 14th century and following his burial the area witnessed centuries of tomb building, since it is considered auspicious to be buried near a saint's grave. The Mughal-era Grand Trunk Road linking Calcutta to Lahore passed through the site, which boasts one of the densest ensembles of medieval Islamic buildings in India, several of which stand within the densely populated Hazrat Nizamuddin Basti. Sunder Nursery, also dotted with Mughal-era monuments, was established as a plant nursery north of Humayun's Tomb in the 1920s to provide and experiment with plants for the British city of New Delhi.

Challenges

PROGRAMME RISKS

The programme has distinct conservation, environmental and socio-economic development goals. Significant progress has been made to realize diverse project objectives, but existing partnerships with public partners and the local community need to be strengthened and new partnerships with public and private agencies established.

SITE CONDITIONS

Located in the heart of New Delhi, the Hazrat Nizamuddin Basti is one of the city's densest settlements where three- to four-storey modern buildings stand alongside medieval monuments. The Basti is separated from the large open space of Humayun's Tomb and Sunder Nursery by a major road. Sunder Nursery has been a largely under-utilized green space with significant heritage and ecological assets.

INFRASTRUCTURE

The programme aims to build the required infrastructure at Sunder Nursery so it can function as a city park. Visitor facilities including an interpretation centre are required at Humayun's Tomb. In order to allow residents of Nizamuddin Basti better access to health, education, sanitation, open spaces and economic opportunities the existing infrastructure needs to be considerably strengthened.

ACCESS TO OPEN SPACE

Humayun's Tomb stands on the southern edge of a 40-hectare green zone that stretches to Humayun's Citadel named Dinpanah (now called the 'Old Fort'). The 10-hectare enclosed Garden immediately surrounding Humayun's Tomb was earlier restored by AKTC in partnership with the Archaeological Survey of India and the remaining portions of the 27-hectare complex will now be landscaped. North of Humayun's Tomb stands the 28-hectare Sunder Nursery and the five-hectare Batashewala complex, both of which will be landscaped and made accessible to the public as a result of the ongoing project there. Despite living on the edge of a garden city, few Nizamuddin Basti residents have access to the two hectares of neighbourhood parks on the western edge of the Basti. These parks, presently misused, are being landscaped in consultation with community groups, especially women and youth.

Significant Issues and Impact

MASTER PLANNING PROCESS

The Master Plan for Delhi (MPD) 2000 recognized the greater Nizamuddin Area (including Humayun's Tomb and Sunder Nursery) as one of five designated 'Conservation Areas' in Delhi. However, the status of the Hazrat Nizamuddin Basti, which should be that of an 'Urbanized Village', is unclear in the MPD 2021. Sunder Nursery has now been designated in the MPD as a 'District Park'. The entire project stands in Zone D of the MPD, alongside the British-era constructed area today known as the Lutyens Bungalow Zone. A preparation of a 'Local Area Plan' for the Nizamuddin Basti is now underway.

PLANNING ISSUES

A prime objective of the programme is to integrate the three presently segregated zones: Nizamuddin Basti, Humayun's Tomb and Sunder Nursery. Physical surveys of the entire project area and zones abutting the project have been completed. At the Tomb and Nursery this will be achieved by forming a single pedestrian entrance zone, emphasized by an interpretation centre. Heritage trails will link the Basti where, following detailed physical mapping and studies, the project will focus on urban improvements. The three project zones of Humayun's Tomb, Nizamuddin Basti and Sunder Nursery will be interconnected by nature trails and heritage walks that link not just the three sites but also their history and culture. The resulting landscape will thus offer a unique experience for visitors while enhancing the cultural significance of the greater Nizamuddin area.

BASELINE STANDARDS

A Quality of Life survey, aimed at establishing benchmarks for key interventions in the Hazrat Nizamuddin Basti was completed. A baseline for establishing benchmarks for early childhood care and development indicators was also carried out. In addition, monitoring and evaluation systems to track programme beneficiaries and changes due to implementation of interventions have been established.

SOCIO-ECONOMIC INTIATIVES

Significant efforts in the field of education, health, sanitation, vocational training and urban improvements coupled with cultural revival initiatives are being made to improve the quality of life for local residents and the pilgrimage experience. Major works have now been completed towards upgrading a primary school, establishing a pathology laboratory at the local polyclinic, building new community toilets, establishing vocational training programmes aimed at improving employability and setting up community self-help groups.

CONSERVATION ASPECTS

Over a hundred listed heritage buildings stand within the project area. In the last decades many others have been lost as a result of expanding urbanization, vandalism and neglect. Twenty-nine of the remaining are considered of national importance and protected by the Archaeological Survey of India. Other buildings of high historical and architectural significance were presented to the Municipal Corporation of Delhi as buildings of local importance, many suffering decades of neglect and inappropriate repairs. Though they provide a poor living environment, several are tombs and occupied as residences. Conservation work on at least 40 heritage buildings is being undertaken as part of the ongoing project. Boundaries of the MPD Conservation Area and the World Heritage Site are also to be defined.

POST-IMPLEMENTATION PLANS

Discussions are ongoing to ensure that revenue generated at Sunder Nursery is returned back into operations and maintenance of the park through the formation of a trust or 'Special Purpose Vehicle' and, furthermore, as support to the education, health and sanitation programmes established under the programme.

Partners

PUBLIC PARTNERS

Archaeological Survey of India, Ministry of Culture, Government of India, Municipal Corporation of Delhi, Central Public Works Department, Ministry of Urban Development, Delhi Development Authority.

Authoritative Framework

'Public-Private Partnership Memorandum of Understanding' signed by the Archaeological Survey of India, Municipal Corporation of Delhi and Central Public Works Department together with AKTC and the Aga Khan Foundation on 11 July 2007.

Conservation efforts on Humayun's Tomb complex involved the work of many skilled craftsmen, including stonemasons.

Humayun's Tomb Complex

DELHI, INDIA

The tomb of the second Mughal emperor, Humayun, one of the twenty-seven UNESCO World Heritage Sites in India, was the first of the monumental mausoleums to be built in the country. The *chahar-bagh,* or four-part paradise garden, is the earliest existing example of the Mughal garden tomb. The Tomb and Garden are considered one of the precursors of the Taj Mahal.

The restoration of the Garden was the first privately funded restoration of a World Heritage Site in India and was completed in March 2003 through the joint efforts of the Aga Khan Trust for Culture (AKTC) and the Archaeological Survey of India under the aegis of the National Culture Fund. The objective of the project was to revitalize the gardens, pathways, fountains and water channels of the *chahar-bagh* surrounding Humayun's Tomb according to the original plans of the builders.

The Garden is laid out in a classical *chahar-bagh* pattern. It is divided into quarters by raised causeways. The quadrants are divided, in turn, into eight plots, each with walkways. At the intersection of these walkways are octagonal or rectangular pools. Site works encompassed a variety of disciplines, including archaeological excavation, the application of conservation science and hydraulic engineering. Following the restoration of the Garden, visitor numbers increased tenfold. Building on the success of this project, in 2007 AKTC signed a 'Public-Private Partnership Agreement' to undertake the restoration of Humayun's Tomb complex.

Emperor Humayun was the son of Babur, the founder of the Mughal Empire. His tomb was built over nearly a decade beginning in about 1565. Influenced by Persian architecture, the Tomb stands on a 120-square-metre platform and reaches a height of forty-seven metres. Built of rubble masonry, the structure is the earliest example of the use of red sandstone and white marble in such great quantities.

Humayun's Tomb complex and its surrounding areas cover almost twenty-four hectares of land and include several significant monuments, such as Isa Khan's Tomb enclosure, Afsarwala Tomb and Mosque, the Arab Serai, Bu Halima's Tomb and several monumental gateways.

Exhaustive archival research, documentation using state-of-the-art laser scanning technology, condition assessment and structural analysis preceded

The central water channel and pool in the gardens of Humayun's Tomb complex in Delhi were restored by AKTC in 2003.

Opposite page:
Above, the restored plinth appears in a general view of Humayun's Tomb.

Below, work being done on Barber's Tomb in the gardens of Humayun's Tomb complex, a World Heritage Site.

Project Scope / Objectives

Humayun's Tomb complex is a UNESCO World Heritage Site. The mausoleum and its peripheral buildings were found to be in urgent need of conservation in order to retard deterioration and enhance the cultural significance of the building. The conservation process emphasizes original crafts and skills and aims to revive dying techniques and traditional art forms. The project includes the integrated development of the surrounding open spaces, provision for visitor facilities and an interpretation centre.

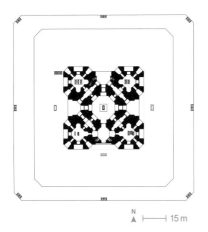

N △ ├——┤ 15 m

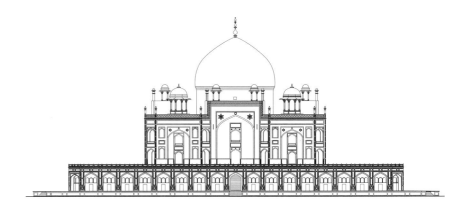

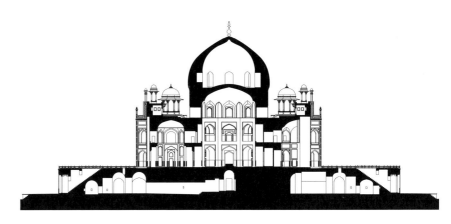

├————————┤ 15 m

Above, the floor plan of Humayun's Tomb which stands on a 120-square-metre platform and reaches a height of 47 metres.

Right, its elevation and section.

Opposite page:
The first part of the project involved the revitalization of the Tomb Garden which is laid out in a classic *chahar-bagh* pattern. Here, people relax on benches.

the preparation of conservation proposals. Conservation works commenced in April 2008 and included restoration of the mausoleum, the monumental gateways, pavilions and tomb structures. The project also includes the integrated development of the surrounding open spaces and provision of visitor facilities and an interpretation centre.

The project vision is to link up the Tomb complex with the site where the Nila Gumbad, a seventeenth-century tomb, also restored by AKTC, is located, just outside the eastern enclosure wall, and Sunder Nursery, which the Trust is converting into a park. Together, this ensemble will create a vast area of monuments, green space, facilities and services.

Once completed, the restoration of Humayun's Tomb complex will return a significant amount of enhanced green space to the city and the surrounding community, with its constituent parts returned to their historically authentic format. The project is expected to increase interest in and visits to the Tomb, the Garden and the associated visitor facilities, which together form a large complex next to a major urban highway in Delhi. It will serve the local residents of Nizamuddin district as a community green area on one level, and the population of Greater Delhi as well as tourists on another level. Humayun's Tomb and Garden has rekindled interest in the rich history of Mughal rule and presents Delhi's heritage in a dignified and cohesive setting worthy of this capital city.

Phasing 1997 → 2012

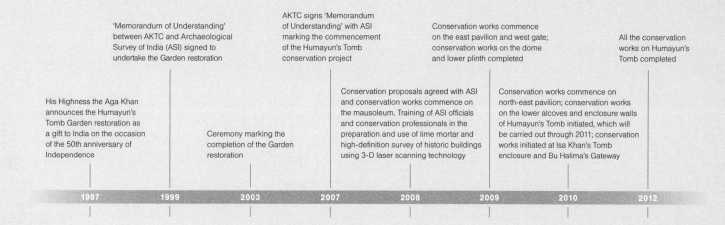

'Memorandum of Understanding' between AKTC and Archaeological Survey of India (ASI) signed to undertake the Garden restoration

AKTC signs 'Memorandum of Understanding' with ASI marking the commencement of the Humayun's Tomb conservation project

Conservation works commence on the east pavilion and west gate; conservation works on the dome and lower plinth completed

All the conservation works on Humayun's Tomb completed

His Highness the Aga Khan announces the Humayun's Tomb Garden restoration as a gift to India on the occasion of the 50th anniversary of Independence

Ceremony marking the completion of the Garden restoration

Conservation proposals agreed with ASI and conservation works commence on the mausoleum. Training of ASI officials and conservation professionals in the preparation and use of lime mortar and high-definition survey of historic buildings using 3-D laser scanning technology

Conservation works commence on north-east pavilion; conservation works on the lower alcoves and enclosure walls of Humayun's Tomb initiated, which will be carried out through 2011; conservation works initiated at Isa Khan's Tomb enclosure and Bu Halima's Gateway

1997   1999   2003   2007   2008   2009   2010   2012

Background

BRIEF HISTORY OF PROJECT SITE

Since it is considered auspicious to be buried near a saint's grave, following the burial of Hazrat Nizamuddin Auliya this area saw seven centuries of tomb building. The greatest is Humayun's Tomb. The complex now includes several other prominent buildings such as Isa Khan's Tomb enclosure, Bu Halima's Tomb, Nila Gumbad and tombs in the Batashewala complex, all dating from the 16th–early 17th century. The Arab Serai, originally part of the complex, today functions as an Industrial Training Institute. The Yamuna River, on the banks of which Humayun's Tomb was built, shifted eastwards in the 19th century leaving the site landlocked. Humayun's Tomb became a World Heritage Site in 1993.

Challenges

PROJECT RISKS

All conservation works at the World Heritage Site are undertaken as part of an established process that ensures cultural significance is retained and visitor experience is enhanced. Almost a million tourists and school children visit Humayun's Tomb annually and as such all works are carried out in a manner that causes minimum disturbance to visitors.

SITE CONDITIONS

Because of the large number of visitors, vehicular and machine movement is not possible within the complex. Manual movement of material is the only other option; it often requires a group of 20 craftsmen a whole day to lift a single piece of stone to the roof. On a larger scale, the inappropriate earlier application of concrete removed from the roof of Humayun's Tomb and the earth expected to be removed from the Isa Khan–Bu Halima complex pose significant logistical challenges.

BUILDING CONDITIONS

Most monuments within the complex are in urgent need of conservation works ranging from removal of 20th-century cement and concrete to stitching of cracks and restoring missing plaster, stones and ceramic tiles.

Significant Issues and Impact

DATA COLLECTION/SURVEYS

Conservation works at Humayun's Tomb commenced following the peer review and approval of the 'Conservation Plan' in May 2008. The 'Conservation Plan' included detailed measured drawings of all structures utilizing high-definition 3D Laser scanning equipment, research of archival photographs, drafting of a statement of significance and detailed conservation proposals on the basis of national and international conservation charters.

HISTORIC BUILDINGS/MONUMENTS CONSERVED

Conservation works are ongoing on Humayun's Tomb and its attached gateways, pavilions and enclosure walls. Work has now commenced on Isa Khan's Tomb enclosure.

NEW BUILDING FACILITIES

An interpretation centre is proposed at the entrance zone of Humayun's Tomb complex.

COMMUNITY INVOLVEMENT/PROGRAMME

Youth from Hazrat Nizamuddin Basti are being trained to become tour guides for visitors to Humayun's Tomb and adjoining sites. Also women, from Nizamuddin Basti, are being trained to learn craft techniques such as paper cutting that will enable them to make products inspired from motifs on the monuments for sale to tourists.

VOCATIONAL TRAINING/CAPACITY BUILDING

The project is being used as a platform for training of conservation professionals and craftsmen. Regular training workshops on the use of lime mortar have been attended by over 150 officers of the Archaeological Survey of India from countrywide locations. To mitigate risks a craftsmen training programme has been included in the programme and monthly reviews of work are held by a panel of experts with annual independent peer reviews.

CONTRACTING METHODS

All conservation works are implemented directly by master craftsmen employed by the project.

NEW TECHNOLOGIES INTRODUCED

Use of 3D high-definition laser scanning technology to document all monuments prior to conservation works, and a training workshop to introduce this technology was also held in India.

Partners

PUBLIC PARTNERS

Archaeological Survey of India.

Donors

Sir Dorabji Tata Trust, World Monuments Fund.

Authoritative Framework

'Memorandum of Understanding' signed on 11 July 2007.

Opposite page:

Pointing work is being done on the dome of Humayun's Tomb during the final stages of its repair and restoration.

Sunder Nursery

DELHI, INDIA

Sunder Nursery was established by the British to experiment with the trees proposed to be grown in the new capital in Delhi. It is a large, enclosed nursery on the north side of Humayun's Tomb, owned and operated by the Central Public Works Department. Located in south central Delhi and spread over twenty-eight hectares, the development of Sunder Nursery into a sustainable park is part of a larger socio-economic development programme that includes the urban regeneration of Nizamuddin Basti and restoration of Humayun's Tomb complex (a World Heritage Site).

The Sunder Nursery abuts Humayun's Tomb complex, with which its shares a common entrance zone, and stands on the historic Grand Trunk Road. Within the Nursery stand nine Mughal-period tombs, of which three are protected by the Archaeological Survey of India. The work of the Aga Khan Trust for Culture (AKTC) will aim to enhance nursery functions; create a significant arboretum; restore the monuments; create new attractions; and provide visitor facilities. At the same time, plans are in place to link up the Nursery site with Humayun's Tomb complex, creating a vast green space, a 'cultural heritage park', in the heart of the capital city.

A flat, extensive and underused green space lies in Nizamuddin, a designated heritage zone comprising Lutyen's Garden City, its extensions and a number of significant heritage areas, such as India Gate, Humayun's Tomb complex, Lodhi Gardens and the Old Fort. The Nursery is bordered by Humayun's Tomb to the south, the National Zoological Park to the north, the Bharat Scouts and Guides Centre to the east and the prominent Delhi Public School to the west. The area's position between Humayun's Tomb complex and Nizamuddin Basti provides the opportunity to create a larger Area Development Project connecting Humayun's Tomb and its outer precinct.

The design of the new Park is organized along a central axial spine around which gardens and landscapes are arranged. From formal garden to informal settings for families to enjoy picnics, the Park will offer a variety of recreational and cultural venues. Water features, ponds and lakes are part of the master plan, which includes nursery beds, a flower showcase, arboretum, rose garden and orchards.

More than just a green space in the heart of the city, Sunder Nursery literally stands in the midst of history. The monuments located here are being carefully conserved using traditional materials and building crafts. Lakkarwala Burj with its landscaped garden is shown above.

Opposite page:
Conservation work on the ceiling of Sunder Burj.

1 Nursery Beds   4 Graves Platform   7 Sunder Burj   10 Interpretation/
2 Lakkarwala Burj   5 Garden Pavilion   8 Sunderwala Mahal   Training Centre
3 Glasshouse   6 Arched Gateway   9 Flower Show Area

N ⊢————————————————⊣ 100 m

Project Scope / Objectives

The conversion of Sunder Nursery into a public park containing visitor facilities and restored Mughal-era monuments is part of a development programme that seeks to create a larger Area Development Project connecting with Humayun's Tomb and Hazrat Nizamuddin Basti.

Phasing 2007 → 2013

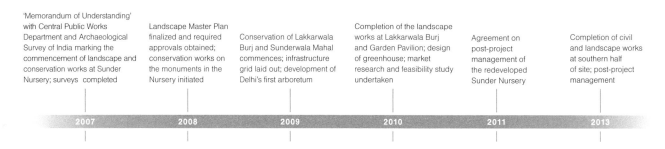

'Memorandum of Understanding' with Central Public Works Department and Archaeological Survey of India marking the commencement of landscape and conservation works at Sunder Nursery; surveys completed

Landscape Master Plan finalized and required approvals obtained; conservation works on the monuments in the Nursery initiated

Conservation of Lakkarwala Burj and Sunderwala Mahal commences; infrastructure grid laid out; development of Delhi's first arboretum

Completion of the landscape works at Lakkarwala Burj and Garden Pavilion; design of greenhouse; market research and feasibility study undertaken

Agreement on post-project management of the redeveloped Sunder Nursery

Completion of civil and landscape works at southern half of site; post-project management

2007   2008   2009   2010   2011   2013

The 18th-century Garden Pavilion was in a ruinous condition and threatened with demolition to make way for a 'tunnel roads' project. Today this unique building is being considered for protection, thanks to the conservation work carried out by master craftsmen.

Opposite page:
Aligned on an axis with Sunder Burj and culminating at the foot of Azim Ganj Serai, the Central Vista will provide a seamless pedestrian connection between Humayun's Tomb and Sunder Nursery, at the same time creating an extraordinary visual delight.

As part of the Nursery development project all of the historic structures located in the Nursery will undergo conservation to enhance their significance and restore their architectural integrity. Landscaping the setting of the monuments is an important element of the conservation works and the master plan for the Nursery. Over 140 tree species presently exist at Sunder Nursery, some of which are unique to the Delhi region. It is proposed to add a similar number of species mostly comprising vegetation that has been lost to the Delhi region. A 3.6-hectare nursery has been established along the northern edge of Sunder Nursery; glasshouses, mist chambers, tissue culture labs, and a training centre are also proposed to be built. As part of the project a micro-habitat zone – an arboretum – is being created, simulating a microcosm of Delhi's landscape, including Kohl (hilly), Khadar (riverine), Bangar (alluvial) and Dabar (marshy) zones.

The proposed Interpretation Centre on ecology and heritage in Sunder Nursery will host education programmes. A newly created amphitheatre will host musical and cultural performances and a café and restaurant will provide refreshments and food for visitors. The buildings will be eco-friendly and sustainable, having minimum impact on the site's environmental character, and vehicular traffic will be limited to the periphery to allow visitors to enjoy the natural and built heritage of the new Park.

Transforming the Nursery into a Park will create employment opportunities for the residents of Nizamuddin Basti. In keeping with AKTC's wider objectives of improving built environments in largely Muslim communities, it is expected that the surplus income generated from the Park would be used to restore and develop the Basti's urban infrastructure, such as schools, training centres, home improvements and public spaces.

Additionally, the future Park will provide a platform to educate children through the conservation and development of tangible and intangible heritage and awareness of cultural identity with the creation of interpretive programmes complementary to the visits. On an environmental level, the revitalization and efficient utilization of more than twenty-eight hectares of land in the middle of Delhi will help reduce pollution and increase air quality.

Background

BRIEF HISTORY OF PROJECT SITE
Sunder Nursery is located inside an important archaeological zone between the 16th-century fort built by Mughal ruler Humayun and his tomb. The Mughal-era Grand Trunk Road passed through the area. The Nursery was established by the British to cultivate trees for the new capital in Delhi.

Challenges

SITE CONDITIONS
Sunder Nursery is nearly flat and shares an entrance with Humayun's Tomb complex. Within the Nursery remain nine Mughal-period tombs, and the archaeological remnants of several other structures. The Nursery is bordered by the National Zoological Park to the north, the Batashewala complex to the east and the Delhi Public School to the west.

Significant Issues and Impact

DATA COLLECTION/SURVEYS
A detailed survey and database of all existing trees was prepared prior to commencement of the master-planning process. Over 140 tree species exist at Sunder Nursery, some of which are unique to the Delhi region. A plan for conservation works on several monuments was similarly prepared at the onset of the project.

MASTER PLANNING PROCESS
The landscape Master Plan emphasizes developing the ecology, heritage and nursery functions of Sunder Nursery and received approval of the Delhi Urban Art Commission.

PLANNING ISSUES
The new park design is organized along a central axial spine around which gardens and landscapes are arranged. From formal gardens to informal settings, the park will offer a variety of recreational and cultural venues. Water features, ponds, lakes, nursery beds, a flower showcase, arboretum, rose garden and orchards are all incorporated in the design. Landscaping settings for the monuments is an important element of the work too. A number of original species of vegetation currently lost are being considered for replanting. A traffic study is underway to minimize the impact of the six-metre-wide road that divides Humayun's Tomb from Sunder Nursery.

HISTORIC BUILDINGS/MONUMENTS CONSERVED
Conservation works are ongoing on the Lakkarwala Burj, Sunderwala Burj and Sunderwala Mahal, all 16th-century buildings. Work was completed on the 18th-century Mughal-era Garden Pavilion, which was on the verge of collapse and threatened with demolition for a roadway project. The project also aims to incorporate the five-hectare Batashewala complex with three buildings of national importance within the future Sunder Nursery.

NEW BUILDING FACILITIES
Amongst the first project activities was a two-kilometre peripheral road to ensure that vehicular access to the public areas is limited. An Interpretation Centre on ecology and heritage will host educational programmes and a greenhouse will be constructed to showcase plant species from different climates. A newly built amphitheatre is to host musical and cultural performances. A food-court and restaurant will provide refreshments and food for visitors. The buildings will be eco-friendly and sustainable, having minimum impact on the site's environmental character, and vehicular traffic will be limited to the periphery. The project also envisages improvements in irrigation, electrical supply, and drainage and visitor facilities.

COMMUNITY INVOLVEMENT/PROGRAMME
The development of the Nursery into a park will create direct and indirect employment opportunities for the residents of Nizamuddin Basti. In keeping with AKTC's wider objectives of improving built environments and raising living standards, it is hoped that the surplus income generated from the park can be used to support the Basti's urban infrastructure, such as the municipal school, polyclinic, community toilets and public spaces.

NEW TECHNOLOGIES INTRODUCED
Large portions of Sunder Nursery and Humayun's Tomb complex have been surveyed using ground-penetrating radar to discovery archaeological remnants prior to earth works. Several monuments were surveyed and documented using laser scanning.

Partners

PUBLIC PARTNERS
Central Public Works Department, Archaeological Survey of India.

Donors

Khaplan Foundation Fund, US Ambassadors Fund for Cultural Preservation.

Authoritative Framework

'Memorandum of Understanding' signed on 11 July 2007.

Hazrat Nizamuddin Basti

DELHI, INDIA

Located in the heart of New Delhi, adjacent to Humayun's Tomb complex and Sunder Nursery, Hazrat Nizamuddin Basti is named after the revered saint Hazrat Nizamuddin Auliya, who lived here in the early fourteenth century. A settlement developed at this location during the saint's lifetime and it has been continuously inhabited.

Following the successful restoration of Humayun's Tomb Garden in 2004, the urban renewal project commenced with the signature of a public-private partnership 'Memorandum of Understanding' on 11 July 2007. The non-profit partnership includes the Archaeological Survey of India, the Central Public Works Department, the Municipal Corporation of Delhi (MCD), the Aga Khan Foundation (AKF) and the Aga Khan Trust for Culture (AKTC).

Nizamuddin Basti comprises a resident population of approximately 20,000. A synergistic, community centred and collaborative approach has been adopted to improve the quality of life for residents through a series of multi-input projects that aims to improve the urban environment, conserve monuments, develop public parks, strengthen basic services through interventions in the three core areas of health, education and environmental sanitation and engage community participation through a regular series of cultural activities and performances. In so doing, the project seeks to integrate conservation, socio-economic development and urban and environmental development objectives in consultation with local communities and relevant stakeholders. All programmes commenced following a quality of life assessment study.

In 2009 a physical mapping/survey of the Basti was undertaken to document the area with the intention of planning sensitive urban improvements. The survey has led to the preparation of street improvement plans which will be implemented by the Municipal Corporation of Delhi. Small public parks are being planned along the western edge of the Basti in areas that are deteriorating and are no longer safe and clean. These spaces will be landscaped to fulfil the needs expressed by the resident community. These parks will bring much needed community space and nodes of civic life back to the area and improve pedestrian circulation through the Basti, and there will be parks earmarked for women, children, cricket, community functions and weddings.

Craftsmen are fitting sandstone *jali* screens at the Baoli.

Opposite page:
Children are being taught at the refurbished Municipal Corporation of Delhi Primary School.

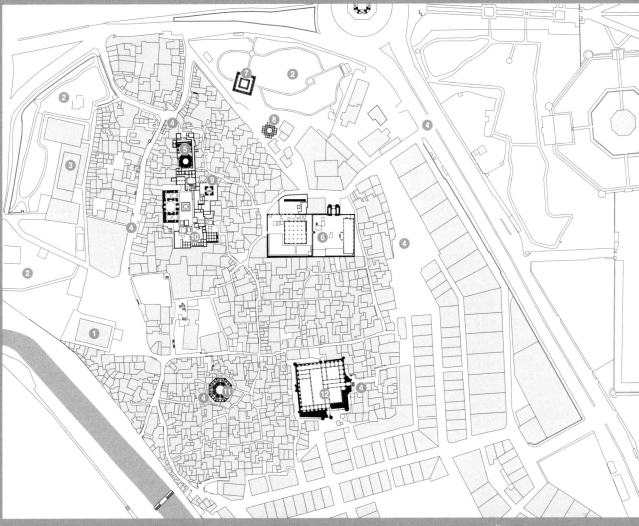

1 School
2 Open Space Restoration
3 Construction of Community Toilets
4 Street Redevelopment
5 Conservation of
  Hazrat Nizamuddin Baoli
6 Conservation of
  Chaunsath Khamba
7 Barah Khamba
8 Lal Mahal
9 Atgah Khan's
  Tomb
10 Dargah of Hazrat
   Nizamuddin Auliya
11 Tilangani's Tomb
12 Kali Mosque

N
100 m

Project Scope / Objectives

The project combines conservation with a major socio-economic development effort that is being implemented through a community-centred, collaborative approach. The objective is to improve environmental conditions and strengthen essential urban services with interventions in the core areas of education, health and sanitation.

Above, noted poet Mirza Ghalib's tomb setting was enhanced by landscaping the court and creating an enclosure with stone *jali* screens to be used for *mushairas* (poetry readings) and other performances.

Below left, conservation works on the Baoli were initiated following the collapse of portions of this 13th-century stepped well; right, a view of the Baoli after the work.

The conservation of monuments and the rehabilitation of open spaces in the Basti aim to restore their intrinsic cultural, historical and spiritual significance. Using state-of-the-art technology, including ground-penetrating radar survey, high-definition 3D laser scanning and geotechnical assessments, conservation started on the fourteenth-century Baoli (step-well).

At the eastern edge of the Basti stand two important tombs: the Chaunsath Khamba, a Mughal tomb, and the tomb of Mirza Ghalib, South Asia's most renowned poet. Together, they form one of the largest open spaces in the Basti. Landscape works at both tombs have enhanced the historic character, restored dignity to these monuments and provided much needed community gathering spaces in this dense setting.

Social programmes in conjunction with the AKF have focused on education, training, health and the environment. In the first place the major effort towards primary education improvement has included a refurbishment of the MCD primary school, interventions to improve quality of education through professional development of faculty, improved classroom processes/child centred to teaching-learning process, better school management and strengthened school community approaches interface. Secondly, vocational training programmes for young people include a career development centre (NIIT Institute of Technology), the teaching of the English language (British Council) and training of heritage guides to give tours of the Basti and its history, while learning support

to students in the age group of fourteen to sixteen years is given in Maths and English ('English Access Micro-Scholarship Programme' co-funded by the US Embassy).

In parallel with these procedures health interventions in the Basti include upgrading the MCD Polyclinic to ensure better diagnosis and treatment, reduce referrals and build the capacity of a community health outreach team for preventive health care, as well as the creation of a pathology laboratory. Finally, newly built public toilets – a key intervention for urban renewal in the Basti – have improved access to hygienic sanitation for residents.

As part of the urban renewal project there is a focus on cultural initiatives. A rich cultural vein, particularly in music and poetry, has existed in the Basti for centuries and drives the lifeblood of the community. This is where Amir Khusrau, musician, poet, scholar, Sufi mystic and spiritual disciple of Hazrat Nizamuddin Auliya, started Qawwali music traditions in the thirteenth century. This tradition continues to this day. The 'living culture' of the area is a unique and vibrant blend of secular and interfaith elements that encompass the performing arts, classical music, poetry and traditional crafts. Improvement in the life of the residents must also include initiatives that embrace the creativity and talent nurtured in this environment and that are core to its identity. Steps are being taken to revive and revitalize these components highlighted at festivals, performances, discussions and through recordings.

A series of initiatives are spurring a cultural revival in the Basti. Here, Chaunsath Khamba (right) is lit up at night during a concert of Qawwali music at the Jashn-e Khusrau festival.

The Basti's narrow streets are host to many shops and markets.

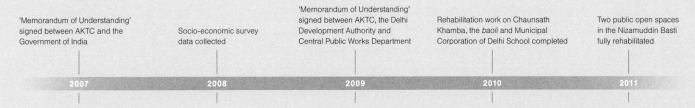

'Memorandum of Understanding' signed between AKTC and the Government of India

Socio-economic survey data collected

'Memorandum of Understanding' signed between AKTC, the Delhi Development Authority and Central Public Works Department

Rehabilitation work on Chaunsath Khamba, the *baoli* and Municipal Corporation of Delhi School completed

Two public open spaces in the Nizamuddin Basti fully rehabilitated

2007   2008   2009   2010   2011

Background

BRIEF HISTORY OF PROJECT SITE

Ghiyas-ud-din Balban, Sultan of Delhi in the 13th century, built the palace of Lal Mahal in what is now Hazrat Nizamuddin Basti. In the early 14th century, the revered saint, Hazrat Nizamuddin Auliya, lived and was also buried there, initiating seven centuries of tomb building in the area. During the building of New Delhi the agricultural lands attached to the Basti were acquired and the area declared an urban village. The area was declared a conservation area in the 2021 Master Plan of Delhi.

Challenges

PROJECT RISKS

Low levels of literacy, high number of immigrants, rampant drug usage and peddling have led to high crime. Though there is a presence of several NGOs working in Hazrat Nizamuddin Basti, there are no active resident associations/youth groups or community groups.

DEMOGRAPHICS

Hazrat Nizamuddin Basti is one of the most densely populated areas in Delhi, especially when the floating pilgrimage population who reside there for short periods is taken into account. Approximately 64% of the populace is in the productive employment age group but only 41% participate.

HOUSEHOLD ECONOMY

Over 50% of families in Hazrat Nizamuddin Basti have a single wage earner – largely employed in petty trades or as casual workers. A similar number of men in the 15 to 25 age group are working and only 6% of women hold jobs. During community discussions, life skills, career counselling and vocational training opportunities emerged as key needs.

STATUS OF HEALTH AND EDUCATION

Lack of access to quality clinical facilities has resulted in extremely poor health conditions. During baseline research, reported illness in the previous two weeks was 54% among females and 29% among males. The project continues to implement interventions to improve health care including both clinic-based and outreach activities, and plans to address health issues of the elderly and the disabled. While literacy rates remain high, raising the quality of education, and increasing enrolment and completion rates of existing programming are a project focus.

AVAILABILITY OF DRINKING WATER AND PROPER SANITATION FACILITIES

Household water connections are unreliable and 33% of households access water from public taps, which are in a poor condition. Public toilets are used by 11% of households and 14% share toilets. In addition, the large floating population of pilgrims puts further strain on the system.

ENVIRONMENTAL CONCERNS

Rapid physical densification and population growth put enormous strain on the infrastructure at Hazrat Nizamuddin Basti, especially in terms of environmental sanitation and waste management. Frequent flooding and blockages in sewage lines are common and provide public health concerns.

INFRASTRUCTURE

Water supply and sewage disposal systems are present but well below required capacity.

ACCESS TO OPEN SPACE

Encroachment and misuse of open spaces and parks are widespread.

BUILDING CONDITIONS

In Hazrat Nizamuddin Basti limited living space per family, poor ventilation from densification, inadequate sewerage and water connections compounded by large numbers of pilgrims have increased the dependence on public utilities and building facilities.

Significant Issues and Impact

DATA COLLECTION/SURVEYS

The project activities commenced following detailed physical mapping of the project area, documentation of the monuments and socio-economic surveys, which needed to be managed sensitively by senior programme staff to explain objectives. The physical surveys in the community were met with repeated resistance from the community. They could only be completed in 2009 after establishing confidence building programming in health, education, sanitation and vocational training.

PLANNING ISSUES

With the renovation of open spaces and landscaping of parks coupled with community mobilization, ownership and their involvement in management of these spaces, it is hoped that children, women and residents in Nizamuddin Basti will be able to safely access these spaces. The project has incorporated interventions such as connecting households to sewer lines and there are plans to improve housing stock in need of repairs, especially those surrounding significant monuments and public spaces such as the Baoli and the *nallah* respectively.

HISTORIC BUILDINGS/MONUMENTS CONSERVED

Several monuments dating from the 12th-century onwards are located within Nizamuddin Basti. Conservation works to date in the Basti have focused on a 13th-century step-well or *baoli* that partially collapsed in July 2008 and on the conservation and landscaping of the tomb of the famous poet Mirza Ghalib. In 2011, conservation works will continue on the *baoli* and also expand to the 16th-century structures known as Chaunsath Khamba and Atgah Khan's Tomb.

NEW BUILDING FACILITIES

One block of community toilets has now been built and is in operation. Work on an additional, much larger toilet block is planned to commence in 2011.

COMMUNITY INVOLVEMENT/PROGRAMME

The project has begun to strengthen civil society, based on consultative planning and implementation, as well as the formation of interest and user groups. Self-help groups have been established and community management of public facilities such as toilets has commenced. The project continues to implement interventions to improve health care, including both clinic-based and outreach activities, and plans to address health issues of the elderly and the disabled.

VOCATIONAL TRAINING/CAPACITY BUILDING

With only 21% of youth having completed senior secondary education, the vocational training programmes being implemented are designed for improving employability. Market linkages with tourists arriving at Humayun's Tomb are being established for craft and embroidery products by local women. Whilst literacy rates are reasonably high, increasing enrolment and completion rates and the quality of education are a project focus.

CONTRACTING METHODS

All conservation works and renovations are implemented directly by master craftsmen employed by the project.

Partners

PUBLIC PARTNERS

Archaeological Survey of India, Municipal Corporation of Delhi, Delhi Development Authority.

Donors

Ford Foundation, German Embassy, United States Embassy, Canadian International Development Agency.

Authoritative Framework

'Memorandum of Understanding' signed on 11 July 2007. In 2009 additional 'Memorandums of Understanding' were signed with Delhi Development Authority and Delhi Government's Public Works Department to allow landscaping of parks and *nallah* respectively.

ZANZIBAR

TANZANIA

1 Old Dispensary   2 Forodhani Park   ■ Intervention area

N   ⊢——————————⊣ 250 m

FEATURED CASE STUDIES

OLD DISPENSARY

FORODHANI PARK AND SEAFRONT

Stone Town
Area Programme

Programme Scope/Objectives

Documentation, land and building surveys, historical research, social and economic surveys, and inventories of historic buildings and cultural resources were all undertaken here. On this basis, the development of general planning proposals and regulations, as well as detailed projects for buildings and major public areas, were elaborated. The 'Conservation Plan' provides the planning and legislative framework needed to encourage appropriate development in line with the Stone Town's historic character and today's requirements.

Preceding pages:

The balcony of the House of Wonders offers dramatic views of the restored Forodhani Park and the sea off Zanzibar.

The Stone Town of Zanzibar, the historic core of the capital city of the island of Zanzibar, located thirty-eight kilometres off the coast of East Africa, has been a regional cosmopolitan crossroads for centuries, reflected in its unique fusion of Swahili, Islamic, Hindu and European culture arising through trade and travel. Its principal waterfront cornice displays the front line of a dense array of arresting coral stone/lime structures which are both individualistic in character and yet highly integrated into a larger urban morphology of historic importance.

Although certain institutions of the Aga Khan Development Network (AKDN) trace their history in Zanzibar to the turn of the twentieth century, the first involvement of the Aga Khan Trust for Culture (AKTC) in Zanzibar dates to 1988, when the Aga Khan Award for Architecture organized an international seminar on the island. This event raised the Trust's interest in the rehabilitation of the old Stone Town, which led to an agreement of protocol of collaboration in the Stone Town between AKTC and the Government of Zanzibar.

AKTC's sustained involvement in Zanzibar over several years made it possible to develop a coherent, long-range strategy and set of initiatives aimed at the revitalization of the town's historic core, from the definition of general policies to the implementation of specific building projects and area plans.

The Old Dispensary

The listed Old Dispensary building in the Stone Town was the second major historical building to be restored by the Historic Cities Programme (HCP) after its establishment in October 1992. As such, it provided a model for similar initiatives carried out both in the Stone Town and elsewhere during subsequent years. The design aimed to respect the existing historic fabric, while taking into account the different building phases, thus avoiding arbitrary interventions and unnecessary alterations. Great attention was paid to ensure that all materials used in the works corresponded to or were compatible with the original ones. Any changes deemed necessary for technical reasons were carefully recorded and identified. In terms of new uses, changes were considered for their compatibility and opportunity vis-à-vis the existing fabric. The final adaptive reuse choice was to transform the Old Dispensary into a combined service, retail and cultural centre. These new uses sought to enhance the building's original qualities in the context of a culturally meaningful public function, while at the same time generating the income necessary to ensure the Centre's future maintenance.

Phasing 1990 2010

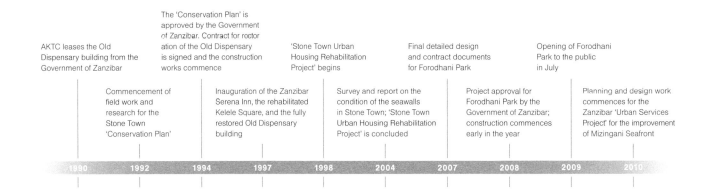

AKTC leases the Old
Dispensary building from the
Government of Zanzibar

The 'Conservation Plan' is
approved by the Government
of Zanzibar. Contract for rector
ation of the Old Dispensary
is signed and the construction
works commence

'Stone Town Urban
Housing Rehabilitation
Project' begins

Final detailed design
and contract documents
for Forodhani Park

Opening of Forodhani
Park to the public
in July

Commencement of
field work and
research for the
Stone Town
'Conservation Plan'

Inauguration of the Zanzibar
Serena Inn, the rehabilitated
Kelele Square, and the fully
restored Old Dispensary
building

Survey and report on the
condition of the seawalls
in Stone Town; 'Stone Town
Urban Housing Rehabilitation
Project' is concluded

Project approval for
Forodhani Park by the
Government of Zanzibar;
construction commences
early in the year

Planning and design work
commences for the
Zanzibar 'Urban Services
Project' for the improvement
of Mizingani Seafront

1990   1992   1994   1997   1998   2004   2007   2008   2009   2010

The 'Stone Town Urban Housing
Rehabilitation Programme' included the
rehabilitation of Mnazi Mmoja, the former
Royal Hotel.

Conservation Planning

A number of wider urban planning and conservation efforts complemented the Old Dispensary initiative to guide future development in the historic area of Zanzibar. In particular, following earlier efforts sponsored by UNCHS/Habitat, AKTC developed, in close cooperation with the Zanzibar Stone Town Conservation and Development Authority (STCDA), the national authority responsible for the historic area, a number of urban surveys, research activities and planning proposals centred on Zanzibar's historic area.

This area, traditionally known as the Stone Town, measures approximately 125 hectares, including the eighty-seven hectares that constitute the town's built-up historic core. The Stone Town accounts for only about five per cent of greater Zanzibar's total urban area. Within its confines, however, are concentrated the vast majority of Zanzibar's monuments and registered buildings, as well as principal public and commercial facilities.

Staring in 1992, a joint initiative between the STCDA and AKTC led to the preparation of a 'Conservation Plan' for the Stone Town. The Plan was formally adopted by the Zanzibar Government in 1994. It includes controls on the use and development of land, measures to protect individual buildings, street elements and open areas. The Plan also contains a set of measures designed to improve infrastructure, parking and circulation in and around the Stone Town. These proposals are complemented by a set of new building regulations, which constitute an integral part of the Plan, as well as proposals to improve and develop the principal public spaces of the Stone Town.

Forodhani Park and the Seafront

Two such public spaces are the Zanzibar Seafront and Forodhani Park which were, and still are, the object of sustained AKTC work. Forodhani Park lies at the heart of the historic seafront district of the Stone Town. Approval to rehabilitate Forodhani Park was given in January 2008 and work on the Park proceeded from February 2008 to January 2009, together with the restoration of the historic seawall adjoining the Park, initiated in late 2008 and completed in May 2009. The Park was reopened in July 2009 and has since turned a fairly derelict public open area into a major and highly successful concourse for residents and visitors. It reconciles aspects of both rehabilitation and revitalization to create a contemporary urban space, whilst reviving a historic sense of place. Such is the success of the Park that the initiative led the government to request the World Bank to include financing for the rehabilitation of the adjacent stretch of seafront, the Mizingani area, into its 'Zanzibar Urban Services Project' (ZUSP) loan. In this case, AKTC will provide design and advisory services to the STCDA towards the implementation of the initiative.

The lesson which can be drawn from this experience is that sustained commitment and the ability to realize projects that generate local pride and international visibility are powerful catalysts for urban regeneration. Moreover, such projects are capable of raising complementary support from governments and international institutions in areas that are normally excluded from financing because they are not considered a priority, such as culture and conservation. On the contrary, the Forodhani initiative and its expected follow-up along Zanzibar's seafront show that reinforcing connections with the city's past and its cultural traditions, and combining them with the economic regeneration of significant urban areas, can bring business and jobs, as well as increased revenue from tourism. In this respect, the Zanzibar experience can be extended to other cities in the region and provide an alternative model of urban development, one that reinforces the distinct character and authenticity of places over the look-alike, heavy-handed developments that are currently applied in so many city centres internationally.

In the new Park design, large trees were retained along the foreshore of the Park to function as focal points.

Housing Rehabilitation

In parallel to the various activities outlined above, a 'Stone Town Urban Housing Rehabilitation Programme' was conducted over the period 1998–2004. Co-funded by the Swedish Development Cooperation Agency (SIDA), the urban rehabilitation programme has benefited approximately five hundred of the poorest residents of Stone Town, who lived in publicly owned houses or in houses administered by the government-controlled religious charity board (*Waqf*). By the time the community-based rehabilitation programme was completed, nine large publicly owned houses had been rehabilitated, serving more than a hundred families.

The Kiponda Caravanserai is one of these. It was home to nineteen households with a total population of seventy people. Before rehabilitation it only had two functioning toilets: one for a family of six and one for the remaining sixty-four inhabitants. Now there are six working toilets and there are separate washing facilities. Cooking was done in the corridors or inside the rooms. Now it is done in the central courtyard. More importantly, perhaps, is that the tenants, who did not have any security regarding the length of their stay, now have formal ten-year contracts with the housing authorities. The Urban Village

Kiponda Caravanserai (top) and
Nyumba Ya Moshi (bottom) before (left)
and after (right) rehabilitation. In the
experience of the Historic Cities Programme,
housing improvement has proved crucial in
the process of urban regeneration.

Tenants' Committees that were called into life by this programme have played an important role in community mobilization and empowerment. In concert with the programme, courses in building repair and lime stucco technology were run for tradesmen, their content later being collated and published as practical repair guidelines made available in both English and Swahili.

Although limited to the initial phase of activities carried out by AKTC in the Stone Town, the housing rehabilitation initiative underlines another important aspect of the Zanzibar experience: the importance of housing in the context of urban regeneration projects. There is in fact no doubt, as other AKTC work has shown in places such as Cairo, that the single, most important catalyser for disadvantaged communities is improved housing conditions. If results can be achieved in this sector, even if numerically limited but significant in quality, community support and mobilization for conservation will follow. Rehabilitation of housing remains a central aspect of urban conservation and it is vital for the sustainability of urban regeneration in this and other cities of the Islamic world.

Indian Ocean Maritime Museum

Future cooperation initiatives between AKTC and the Government of Zanzibar that build upon this foundation include the creation of a maritime museum through the adaptive reuse of the Orphanage building, an early twentieth-century structure located in close proximity to Forodhani Park. As a contribution to this museum, Zanzibar authorities entrusted the Sultan's Barge to AKTC for restoration and eventual display. That work has already been completed. Also in this case, the thematic exploration of the maritime traditions of the region can become a major attraction for visitors to the island and an important educational springboard for local residents. Although Zanzibar already has two important museums aimed at local history and the past, a maritime museum focusing on the Indian Ocean would bring an international perspective and context to the island and return to the town the sense of its historical role in the development of the important commercial links that for centuries has united it to the rest of the Indian Ocean and beyond.

The facade of the building chosen to house the Indian Ocean Maritime Museum: the site, which had been the local orphanage, now relocated to new premises, is located next to Forodhani Park.

Background

BRIEF HISTORY OF PROGRAMME AREA

The Stone Town of Zanzibar is the centre of the greater city of Zanzibar, located half-way down the western coast of Unguja, the largest island of the Zanzibar archipelago. The Stone Town is the economic, political and cultural centre of the island and contains most of the Zanzibar government and administrative buildings. As the largest and best-known historic settlement in East Africa, the town is the result of a complex stratification of spaces and uses dating back at least three centuries. It was only after 1830, however, that Zanzibar's Stone Town took on a wholly urban character and that stone buildings were built in consistent numbers. Today, the Stone Town measures approximately 125 hectares (size of gazetted area) and houses an estimated 16,000 inhabitants. The 1992 inventory identified a total of 1453 traditional structures, including Indian-, Omani- and European-influenced structures, as well as thousands of architectural and streetscape features.

Challenges

PROGRAMME RISKS

The poor condition and adverse developments affecting the Stone Town spurred growing concern about the future preservation of the town and led to the Zanzibar Government's request for AKTC's support in the preparation of a conservation plan. The measures contained in the Plan were aimed at reversing the decline and guiding future development in the historic area.

SITE CONDITIONS

In the historic Stone Town land values are highest and the pressure for change is greatest. The 1992 survey ascertained that scores of buildings were built between 1982 and 1992 and that over one third of the old structures had been altered substantially. Also the condition of the infrastructure was poor and in need of major repairs and improvement.

DEMOGRAPHICS

The average population density in the Stone Town at the time of the 1992 survey was 183 persons per hectare. The same survey ascertained that, while the population of greater Zanzibar was expected to double by the year 2020 (reaching 414,000), population growth in the Stone Town would increase at a more moderate rate, reaching 18,000 by 2020.

HOUSEHOLD ECONOMY

With a total of 2700 households, the average size of household in 1992 was 6.10 with an average of 1.1 persons per room. More than half of the men living in the Stone Town were self-employed. Of these, half were involved in commercial activities, one quarter were skilled tradesmen and the rest were occupied in tourism or transport. The remaining half were salaried men working in the governmental sector, private commercial enterprises or construction.

STATUS OF HEALTH AND EDUCATION

In 1992 the Stone Town contained six primary and five secondary schools, with a total enrolment of about 12,000 children. Because of the scarcity of educational facilities outside the central area, these 11 government schools serve a much wider area. Approximately 5500 students commute to the Stone Town daily, putting additional pressure on the ageing school buildings and aggravating traffic problems in the central area. The city's major health facility is located within the boundaries of the Stone Town in the Mnazi Moja hospital complex located in Vuga South.

AVAILABILITY OF DRINKING WATER AND PROPER SANITATION FACILITIES

The quality of the water supply system has deteriorated steadily since 1982. The irregular supply of water and low water pressure has caused increasing installation of water pumps and storage facilities. The combination of unhygienic water-storage practices and seepage of contaminated groundwater into the mains when water pressure is low have led to the pollution of drinking water. This is considered the most serious water-related public health problem in the Stone Town. In 1992, 64% of households had at least one flush toilet; 17% shared a toilet with other households; and a further 18% had no flush toilet.

ENVIRONMENTAL CONCERNS

The poor condition of basic infrastructure and services for Stone Town inhabitants remains an issue of concern. Some limited repairs and upgrading took place in the mid 1990s with support from the German Technical Cooperation Agency (GTZ). Since then, no new investment has taken place and services have substantially deteriorated, especially the supply of electricity which is erratic and subject to major black-outs.

INFRASTRUCTURE

Investigation of the town's infrastructure focused on the supply of electrical and water services as well as the condition of drainage and sewage disposal systems. The information was used to determine the capacity and adequacy of existing systems and to identify remedial measures to be put into effect within the framework of the 'Conservation Plan'.

ACCESS TO OPEN SPACE

The Stone Town has few open public spaces within the built fabric; however, there are several large green areas adjacent to the town along or near to Creek Road. Within the Stone Town, there are several small but highly significant open spaces directly on the waterfront, which includes Forodhani Park (approx. 1.5 ha) and Mizingani Road. The public gardens and open areas are critical spaces for the inhabitants of Stone Town for leisure activities, for sport and exercise and for social interaction, due to the generally dense living conditions. Public parks or open spaces at the time of the Plan's formulation were generally poorly maintained and often used inappropriately or encroached upon by private development.

BUILDING CONDITIONS

The building condition survey carried out in 1992 found that over 84% of buildings in the Stone Town were in deteriorating or poor condition. These data were based on an assessment of exterior and interior building components, such as walls, floors, roofs and exterior features.

Significant Issues and Impact

MASTER PLANNING PROCESS

The master planning process aimed at developing two distinct but complementary levels of proposals: the first was the establishment of broad conservation and development policies for the Stone Town. These included controls on the use and development of land, and measures to protect individual buildings, street elements and open areas. It also included a set of measures designed to improve parking, circulation and public infrastructure in and around the Stone Town. The second level of proposals aimed at identifying priority areas and developing preliminary planning proposals for four Action Areas (the Seafront and Forodhani Park; the Port area; the Central Market and a new mixed-use complex in Malindi). These areas correspond to the most critical parts of the Stone Town, which were in need of a comprehensive and integrated planning approach. Preparation of the Plan was accompanied by public hearings and participatory initiatives designed to increase awareness and concern for the significance of the historic area and the importance of ensuring its long-term preservation and appropriate development.

PLANNING ISSUES

The 'Conservation Plan' advocated a model of balanced growth for the Stone Town, in which the central area maintains its capital and cultural role and its traditional urban character. The policies of the Plan were designed to curb the uncontrolled proliferation of commercial land use, decentralize inappropriate activities, reinforce residential use, promote sympathetic reuse of historic buildings, reorganize and improve the principal public open spaces, repair and ameliorate the infrastructure and delivery of public services, and rethink circulation and parking. The approval of the Plan enabled the identification of open areas to be subjected to greater public control and improvements, and eventually led to public initiatives towards their rehabilitation, such as the case of Forodhani Park, whose comprehensive upgrading was completed in 2009 with the financial and technical support of AKTC.

BASELINE STANDARDS

A complete field survey of the Stone Town was carried out in 1992. Its purpose was to update previous surveys and gather new information needed to formulate the 'Conservation Plan'. All investigations were conducted on a plot-by-plot basis by teams of three or four surveyors. Several forms were completed concurrently to gain a complete understanding of the Stone Town's physical fabric. These included a block survey form, a building survey form and forms documenting building conditions, and streetscape and open space features. In addition, the survey comprised interviews with a representative 10% sample of households living in the historic area. The findings provided information about household sizes, employment, tenure, occupancy, in- and out-migration, schooling and access to public services.

SOCIO-ECONOMIC INITIATIVES

A number of young Zanzibari professionals were trained and participated in the development of the Plan from its inception. They represented the core team of planning professionals who subsequently assumed positions of responsibility within the STCDA.

CONSERVATION ASPECTS

The planning approach and policies were consistent with the relevant international charters for the conservation of historic areas, with special reference to the UNESCO 'Recommendation Concerning the Safeguarding and Contemporary Role of Historic Areas' (Nairobi, 1976). The Stone Town 'Conservation Plan' also pioneered the establishment of ad hoc legislation and planning policies for the safeguarding of Zanzibar's urban heritage. The Plan introduced categories of significant listed monuments and buildings (Grade I and Grade II). Grade I structures (24 in total) were noted for their outstanding architectural, historical and cultural value. Grade II was assigned to structures of architectural significance (191 in total), including the identification of individual architectural features to be protected. The Zanzibar Stone Town 'Conservation Plan' was the first comprehensive town plan for a historic urban area to be developed by AKTC and formally adopted by the national authorities. As such, it provided a model for similar planning initiatives carried out by the organization in the region and elsewhere.

QUALITY OF LIFE

Access to open-space for the Stone Town population has improved substantially with the rehabilitation of Forodhani Park (completed in 2009) and the planned expansion of the open-space improvement programme, with the creation of a public seafront promenade along Mizingani Road and the amelioration of smaller gardens and open areas located in the southern portion of Zanzibar's seafront.

Partners

PUBLIC PARTNERS

Ministry of Water, Construction, Energy, Land and Environment, Stone Town, Stone Town Conservation and Development Authority.

Authoritative Framework

Exchange of letters and protocols between AKTC, the Ministry of Water, Construction, Energy, Land and Environment and the Stone Town Conservation and Development Authority (1992–94). Public hearings and regular reviews were scheduled throughout 1993 and the early part of 1994 towards the formal approval and ratification of the Plan. Peer reviews and workshops were also scheduled during the Plan's development process.

Old Dispensary

ZANZIBAR, TANZANIA

The Old Dispensary in Zanzibar was the first project of the Aga Khan Trust for Culture (AKTC) in the Stone Town, part of a larger programme of rehabilitation for the historic buildings along the seafront, which also included the restoration of the Old Customs House. The name of the building comes from its former use as a charitable dispensary, built in the nineteenth century by a prominent local businessman, Sir Tharia Thopan. The foundation stone was laid in 1887 to mark the jubilee of Queen Victoria, and Thopan's intention was for it to be used as a hospital. He died before it was completed and the building was sold off after a family quarrel. Originally, the Old Dispensary housed a dispensary on the ground floor, with a pharmacy and a resident doctor. The two upper floors were subsequently subdivided into apartments. This mixed use of the building continued until the revolution in 1964, when the inhabitants fled the island and the dispensary fell into disuse. As with most other structures in Zanzibar, the Old Dispensary passed into government ownership and control.

Since its inauguration, more than one hundred years ago, the Old Dispensary has been hailed as a symbol of the multicultural architecture of Zanzibar. And in fact it is an astonishing hybrid of styles combining Indian and European influences. The ornately carved wooden balcony and other intricate details are characteristic of Indian buildings, but laid over a highly disciplined European Neoclassical scheme. The building's design, rich decoration and construction techniques are of exceptional quality. The plan is U-shaped with a three-storey-high courtyard in the centre. The interior is partitioned into a series of rather small, mostly independent rooms arranged along arcades facing the courtyard. The shape of the site was difficult to deal with, yet the architects turned it to advantage and created a stunning interior space characterized by the exaggerated sense of perspective produced by the side walls converging halfway along the length of the court. This is suddenly reversed by one wall breaking forwards to introduce a diverging line, complemented on the other side of the courtyard by the introduction of a one-storey block that narrows the space yet further. "The timber carving is unlike any other in the Stone Town in its sheer abundance and vivacity, and contrasts with the more restrained plaster work. Carved tendrils and stalks twist and curl through gables, flowers erupt from the brackets, and

The Old Dispensary has been adaptively reused as the Stone Town Cultural Centre.

Opposite page:
A view of the Dispensary before restoration and the removal of modern encroachments. The building was in an extremely dilapidated condition with the main verandas in danger of collapse.

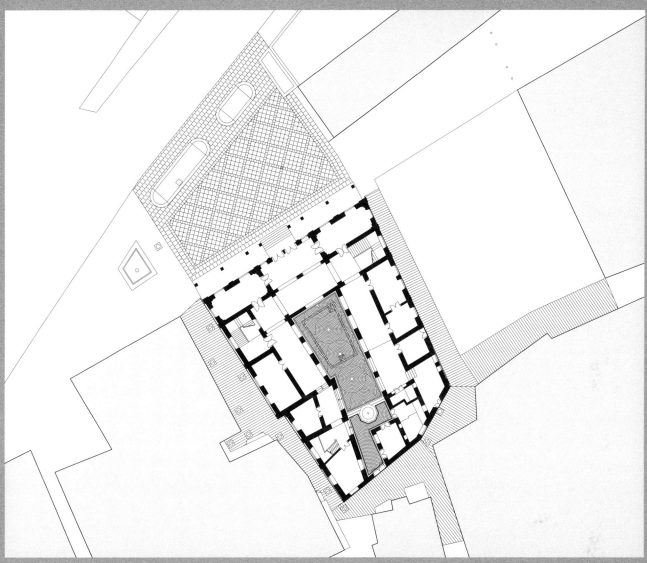

N
|————————————————————| 10 m

Project Scope / Objectives

The Old Dispensary is hailed as a symbol of multi-cultural Zanzibari architecture. The aim of conservation was to respect the historic fabric of the existing building and to try to understand and record the different building phases. With this information in hand, it was possible to make the building habitable, ensuring rental income for its upkeep and maintenance.

pineapples sprout from the ridges. Amidst the carved foliage, bright red, green, and blue panes of glass glitter like jewels. Eight massive columns, each one a single piece of timber forty centimetres square and over five metres long, support the principal beams running perpendicular and parallel to the facade." Inside, two suspended bridges span the courtyard and, together with the horizontal plaster mouldings, define and unify the interior space, articulated at ground, first and second floor levels by the strong piers surmounted by arched openings.

Prior to the AKTC intervention, the building had been badly neglected and hardly maintained for more than thirty years. Rising damp and moisture had taken a heavy toll on the timber and plasterwork. The first stage of the conservation process involved the identification of the original features of the building through patient research and recording. The internal anatomy of the building was systematically examined in order to establish which materials were originally used and the methods and techniques by which they had been applied. Eventually, the restoration aimed at reinstating the building's original fabric while respecting its different construction phases. All materials used in the restoration corresponded to, or were compatible with, the original ones. At the same time, the building envelope was made weather-tight to avoid the water penetration and leaks that had been the main causes of the building's deterioration. Where limited changes became necessary to improve the resistance and quality of the structure, these were carefully recorded and identified as newly added elements to distinguish them from the original ones.

Upon its completion in 1997 the restored Old Dispensary was converted into the Stone Town Conservation Centre. The new uses did not alter the historic features of the building, but rather sought to enhance its original qualities and make them accessible to a wider public in the context of a culturally meaningful public function. At the same time, these new uses had to generate the income necessary to ensure the building's future maintenance. Thus, the adaptive reuse of the structure transformed the Old Dispensary into a combined service, retail and cultural centre. The design took advantage of the special qualities of the ground-floor courtyard to convert it into a public open space

The restored inner courtyard, with its
bridge linking the upper floor, seen from
the balcony.

providing access to new retail outlets and offices. This public use was extended to the upper-floor balconies and reception rooms. The latter, in particular, were made accessible to visitors, with their superb views of the sea through the ornate framing of the balcony. Some of the rooms on the first floor became available as exhibition spaces for the new Stone Town Cultural Centre, a function that can be extended also to the ground-floor courtyard and first-floor balconies. Other rooms on the first floor have been adapted to become business offices compatible with the cultural functions prevailing in the rest of the building. On the further end of the upper-floor arcades, at some distance from the cultural centre, two small double-height studios have been provided for lease to resident staff or visitors. The existence of two parallel staircases, originally meant to create different circuits for men and women, gave the opportunity to separate the flow of visitors between the various functions of the building. The combination of shops, retail outlets, business areas and studio apartments is intended to create a lively interaction between a variety of functions and return the building to full use after many years of abandonment and neglect.

AKTC's efforts in Zanzibar did not end with the completion of the Old Dispensary. In response to the renewed interest in the historic area and improved prospects for tourism and private investment in Zanzibar, the need became apparent for an integrated plan for the conservation and development of the Stone Town. In 1992 the Trust assisted the Stone Town Conservation and Development Authority (STCDA) in launching an in-depth survey of the Stone Town and preparing a comprehensive conservation town plan, which not only identifies the heritage to be conserved, but also sets standards for appropriate new development, both at the level of individual plots and at the level of the overall townscape.

Phasing 1991 → 1997

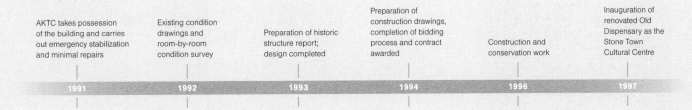

1991	1992	1993	1994	1996	1997
AKTC takes possession of the building and carries out emergency stabilization and minimal repairs	Existing condition drawings and room-by-room condition survey	Preparation of historic structure report; design completed	Preparation of construction drawings, completion of bidding process and contract awarded	Construction and conservation work	Inauguration of renovated Old Dispensary as the Stone Town Cultural Centre

Background

BRIEF HISTORY OF PROJECT SITE

The Old Dispensary was built by a prominent local businessman, Sir Tharia Thopan. The foundation stone was laid in 1887 to mark the jubilee of Queen Victoria. Thopan intended the building to be a hospital, but he died before it was finished. The building was completed in 1894 and purchased by a rich Zanzibari in 1900, who used it as a charitable institution housing a dispensary, a pharmacy and a resident doctor. The two upper floors were subdivided into apartments. This mixed use of the building continued until the revolution in 1964, when the residents fled and the dispensary fell into disrepair. As with most structures in Zanzibar, the Old Dispensary passed into government ownership and control. In October 1991 AKTC leased the Old Dispensary from the government in order to restore it and reuse it as a cultural centre.

Challenges

PROJECT RISKS

The poor condition of the building and the limited experience in the development of restoration and adaptive reuse projects in Zanzibar in the 1990s constituted a risk which had to be carefully evaluated prior to implementation. Eventually, the restoration and conversion of the building proved to be a seminal experience for the realization of similar projects in the Stone Town.

BUILDING CONDITIONS

A building condition survey was carried out following the decision to restore the structure in 1991. It revealed that water infiltration combined with rising damp, lack of maintenance and inappropriate repairs were the main causes of deterioration. Exterior problems included highly eroded plaster exposing the core of the walls, a severely tilted front balcony, leaking roofs and blocked drains. Inside, most of the windows were broken, with the openings shuttered. In addition, the initial inspections revealed inappropriate interior partitioning and evidence of poor use and vandalism throughout the building. The detailed assessment of exterior and interior building conditions formed the basis for the subsequent formulation and implementation of an appropriate and effective conservation process.

Significant Issues and Impact

DATA COLLECTION/SURVEYS

More than 300 drawings at various scales were produced to document and record the plans, elevations and details of the building. In addition, a condition survey of all major components of the building fabric was finalized, including an analysis of the original materials and methods of construction. Laboratory samples were obtained and analyses carried out on the materials, as well as historical research in the Zanzibar Government Archives. The latter provided important information about the original design and use of the building. The ensemble of these investigations made it possible to distinguish new from old, and track the stages of interventions and transformations which took place in the building through time.

DESIGN CRITERIA

The design aimed at respecting the existing historic fabric, as well as taking into account the different building phases in order to avoid arbitrary interventions and unnecessary alterations. Great attention was paid to ensure that all materials used in the works corresponded to or were compatible with the original ones. Any changes which were deemed necessary for technical reasons were carefully recorded and identified. In terms of new uses, changes were considered for their compatibility and opportunity vis-à-vis the existing fabric. The final adaptive reuse choice was to transform the Old Dispensary into a combined service, retail and cultural centre. These new uses sought to enhance the building's original qualities in the context of a culturally meaningful public function, while at the same time generating the income necessary to ensure the Centre's future maintenance. Each aspect of the work grew out of the interaction of professional advice and the experience of craftsmen on site, as well as extensive and repeated testing.

VOCATIONAL TRAINING/CAPACITY BUILDING

The Old Dispensary works generated numerous opportunities for local employment, training and capacity building. The restoration sought to revive as much as possible of the original construction and detailing process, even in cases where the local crafts base was considered insufficient and had to be complemented by external expertise. Master builders from India, knowledgeable about the traditional construction and detailing methods, were able to train a Zanzibar group in traditional skills and thus contribute to replenishing the local pool of craftsmen.

CONTRACTING METHODS

Technical and professional decisions were made by AKTC after extensive consultations with its team of consultants and guest advisors. The work was implemented by contractors and subcontractors selected on the basis of their capacities and proven track record of conservation work in the region or other geographical areas, such as India, where the original construction technologies had been developed and are still being practised.

NEW TECHNOLOGIES INTRODUCED

The state-of-the-art restoration of the Old Dispensary included research and adaptation of the original building technologies to ensure effective and long-lasting results. Through a series of trials, a repertory of solutions to most problems was developed: methods of repair, appropriate mixes and materials, and ways of joining, covering and finishes were agreed upon.

RELEVANT CODES/STANDARDS ADOPTED

The restoration standards and practices applied in the Old Dispensary works reflect the approach and methodologies contained in major international charters and recommendations. Peer reviews took place during the course of the project's implementation, as well as regular meetings with the STCDA and Ministry authorities.

LESSONS LEARNED

The restoration and adaptive reuse of the Old Dispensary was the first building project carried out by AKTC in Zanzibar. As such, it provided a model for similar initiatives carried out both in the Stone Town and in the region during subsequent years.

Partners

PUBLIC PARTNERS

Ministry of Water, Construction, Energy, Land and Environment, Stone Town Conservation and Development Authority.

Donors

Ford Foundation, UNESCO.

Authoritative Framework

Exchange of letters and protocols between AKTC, the Ministry of Water, Construction, Energy, Land and Environment and the Stone Town Conservation and Development Authority (1991–94).

Forodhani Park and Seafront

ZANZIBAR, TANZANIA

The 1994 'Conservation Plan' identified a number of schemes for Zanzibar's open spaces in order to ensure their protection, upgrading and rehabilitation. In particular, the work carried out by the Aga Khan Trust for Culture (AKTC) targeted three areas: Kelele Square, Forodhani Park and the Mizingani Seafront. Kelele Square was completed in 1997, following the adaptive reuse of the ex-Telecom Building into the Zanzibar Serena Inn, which defines part of the square. The much larger and ambitious rehabilitation of Forodhani Park, the most visible portion of Zanzibar's seafront, was completed in 2008–09, while the rest of the seafront, along Mizingani Road, is currently being planned and its rehabilitation is scheduled to begin in 2011. Together, these open areas represent almost seventy-five per cent of the public open spaces along Zanzibar's seafront and are the most visible and frequented public areas in the Stone Town.

Forodhani Park

Forodhani Park and the Mizingani Seafront form a continuous public open space along the Indian Ocean, stretching from the Orphanage House, at the southern end of the seafront, to the port at the opposite end. The area has the highest concentration of monuments and significant historic buildings in the Stone Town.

Prior to its rehabilitation, Forodhani Park was in very poor condition. It had, however, kept its original organization and layout from the time of its creation on the occasion of King George V's Silver Jubilee in 1935. The design for the rehabilitation of the gardens was aimed at reconciling current uses and needs with the historic significance and traditions of the garden. To that end, its original elements were preserved and restored and some new features added. The aim was to create a contemporary urban space, while enhancing the original features and historic character of the place. Accordingly, the Park's layout includes new paths lined with benches, linking together the original elements of the garden with a new organization and structure. Today, as in the past, Forodhani Park functions both as an active meeting place and passive promenade. At the same time, it maintains and defines separate areas intended for pedestrian movement, food vending, sports, contemplation and repose. The layout of the Park and proportions

The Park and Seafront, together with Kelele Square, represent almost 75% of the public open spaces along Zanzibar's seafront.

Opposite page:
The original informal food bazaar at the northernmost end of the Park was polluted and unhygienic.

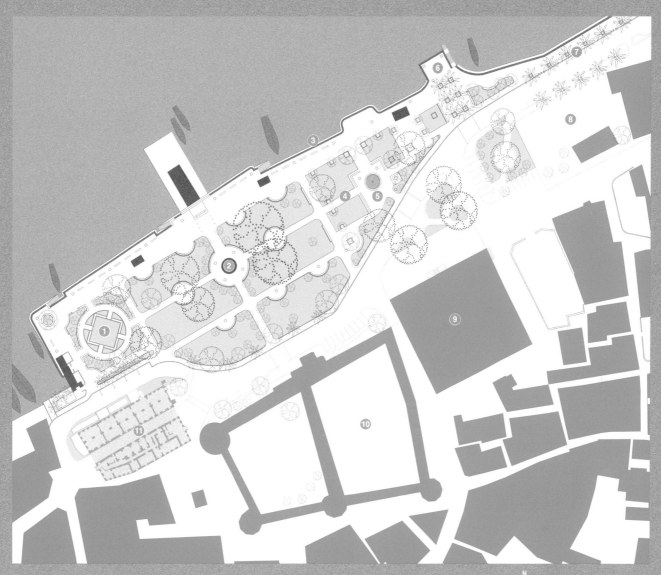

1 Children's Play Area   4 Food Vendors   7 Mizingani Seafront   10 Old Fort
2 Bandstand   5 Fountain   8 Palace Museum Garden   11 Orphanage House
3 Rebuilt Seawall   6 Sultan's Landing   9 House of Wonders   (future Maritime Museum)

N ⊢—————————⊣ 25 m

Project Scope / Objectives

The rehabilitation of Forodhani Park was part of a wider programme for comprehensive seafront rehabilitation in Stone Town. The rehabilitation of the Park was intended to be a logical extension of the work already completed along the seafront. The aim of the rehabilitation project was to upgrade social and recreational amenities in this historic park setting while providing for economic activity that will contribute to the sustainability of the Park. Considering its value for the local community, its attraction for visitors to the island, and the interaction of the Park with the landmark buildings facing the sea, the Park is expected to be a catalyst for broader social, cultural and economic development in the area.

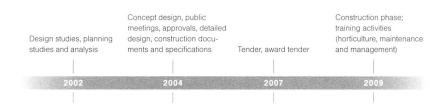

Design studies, planning studies and analysis	Concept design, public meetings, approvals, detailed design, construction documents and specifications	Tender, award tender	Construction phase; training activities (horticulture, maintenance and management)
2002	2004	2007	2009

Opposite page:
In the newly rehabilitated Forodhani Park, its original elements, such as the bandstand, the fountain and the pier, have been retained and new paths lined with benches have been added to link these elements together. *Baraza* seating, following traditional examples, was also installed.

of lawn, paving and planting were derived from the main cross-axes defined by the fountain, bandstand and pier, all pertaining to the original configuration of the garden. These simple geometries were reinforced by structured plantings of palms and umbrella shade trees. Detailing was designed in a robust but understated manner, with a formal vocabulary and materials typical of the Stone Town. The paving has an exposed coral aggregate finish, a reminder of weathered surfaces found elsewhere in the historic area, while the park lighting is derived from the original cast-iron lamps manufactured in Glasgow. The *baraza* seating, modelled after traditional examples, accommodates the need for social interaction and provides the opportunity to simply enjoy the gardens in comfort. The remaining ship cannons scattered about the site were carefully restored and repositioned as a six-gun shore battery.

A survey and restoration programme was carried out for the historically significant buildings, such as the Bandstand, the Fountain, the Arch, and one of the kiosks. The other buildings were demolished due to their dangerous structural conditions or as a result of the significant regrading of the site, and subsequently rebuilt in keeping with their original footprint and style. A new pedestrian bridge linking the Park to the Orphanage House was added to the scope of works to replace the original bridge that was structurally unstable.

Horticulture was a very significant aspect of the park design, and Forodhani Park has the good fortune of having maintained several very large original trees. The trees form an almost continuous green canopy across the Park and make a large shaded area in the central zone around the bandstand. When construction began, the old trees were in very poor health due to neglect and mistreatment. One of the first measures was to rescue the historic trees: they were monitored by a horticultural specialist, and actions taken to bring them back to good health. Old compacted soils and accumulated waste were removed from around the trunks and roots and replaced with new soil and nutrients, followed by a programme of irrigation and pruning. All the trees were saved, and a healthy green canopy has now developed. New planting was also used extensively throughout the Park, with over 130 new trees. The new specimens were selected to restore the green structure, colour and ambience of a classic public garden, as well as reflect the botanical character of the island.

In addition to the paths, lawns and trees, some modifications were made to optimize and redefine spaces for contemporary use, such as a secure playground and a multi-purpose park plaza available to food vendors. The southern area of the Park, opposite the Orphanage building, serves today as an intensive play area. It has been designed to withstand constant use, with lighting installed to extend its use after dark. The informal food bazaar, which is one of the most popular attractions in the Stone Town, occupies the

A comparison of the Park before and after intervention.

northernmost part of the Park. It has been repaved to withstand heavy pedestrian traffic and properly lit to extend the use of the area into the night, which is the busiest time for vendors. These various improvements are also flexible enough to accommodate additional uses in the future.

The Park infrastructure is entirely new and includes a much needed irrigation system, a new electrical network and new street and park lighting. Storm-water drainage is natural due to the slope of the site, with the water flowing over the paving directly into the ocean. The seawall is an integral part of the Park: its condition was very poor as a result of erosion, loss of material, subsistence and collapse of the park grounds. Today, it has been extensively restored, as well as rebuilt to stabilize and reinforce the Park's edge along the sea. The historic portion is made of sandstone material, while the rebuilt portion is made of hand-textured and custom-coloured cement blocks to replace the unstable coral rag wall. Initially, it was intended to use stone from the same source as the original construction. To this end, an environmental study was commissioned. Its results confirmed the compatibility of the coral stone with the original fabric of the wall, but indicated that exploitation of the quarry was inappropriate from an environmental standpoint. A mix of concrete or 'cast stone' was therefore formulated to resemble the original sandstone as closely as possible in both colour and texture. Each block was cut by hand to its final dimension, employing traditional masonry methodology and tools. This solution was specifically designed to match the appearance of the original seawall and reflect the status of the Stone Town as a UNESCO World Heritage Site.

The Forodhani project includes a programme to assist the local authorities in managing the Park and identifying opportunities for future financial sustainability. The management staff is supported by AKTC with training in specific areas of expertise. This support is considered essential to maintain the Park in the long term as a well-functioning public amenity for the residents and visitors of the Stone Town.

The Mizingani Seafront

The Mizingani Seafront project, which is due to start in 2011, will extend the public space of Forodhani Park, creating a linear promenade almost 360 metres in length. The project is part of the 'Zanzibar Urban Services Project' (ZUSP) financed by the World Bank and comprises the entire width of the Mizingani Road from the seafront to the foot of the buildings located along the road, including the seawall, pavement and carriageways. It includes the construction of a new seawall extended approximately five metres further out beyond its existing boundaries, with the necessary backfill and foundation work; and the refurbishment of the underground infrastructure including water, sewer, storm sewer and electrical and telecommunication lines. These will be located below the roadbed of Mizingani Road. In addition, the project foresees the resurfacing of the road and introduction of traffic calming measures. The road will be of sufficient width to accommodate two-way travel, parallel parking and a small pavement along the base of the buildings. Finally, a three-metre-wide pedestrian promenade is to be established, including planting, street lighting and street furniture along the seaside. Some densely planted areas will be included to create shaded areas for gathering along the promenade. The materials and details will be the same as those employed in Forodhani Park.

Background

BRIEF HISTORY OF PROJECT SITE
In the 1800s the park site was occupied by warehouses and bombarded by the British in 1896 in reaction to the political takeover by Seyyed Khalid. In 1935 the site was transformed into the Jubilee Gardens to commemorate the occasion of King George V's silver jubilee. The large trees now seen in the park date from this period; in 1936 the bandstand and the concrete shade structures were added. The site deteriorated throughout the 1980s and 1990s, in dire need of maintenance, controls and upgrading. It was recognized and identified in the 1994 'Conservation Plan' as a significant public open space to be improved. In 2004 AKTC committed both technical and financial assistance for the restoration of Forodhani Gardens with the support and collaboration of the Revolutionary Government of Zanzibar. In July 2009 His Highness Prince Karim Aga Khan and His Excellency President Karume of Zanzibar inaugurated Forodhani Park.

Challenges

PROJECT RISKS
Studies were carried out during the early 2000s in order to minimize risks to the Park in light of the planned upgrading and rehabilitation. The main risks were not properly addressing the needs of the public and intervening in ways that were insensitive incompatible with the historic context. The 1994 'Conservation Plan' formed the basis of the various subsequent design and social studies, and informed the meetings and consultations with local authorities and citizens.

SITE CONDITIONS
Prior to works commencing, the Park was in very poor condition from overuse, lack of controls and limited maintenance over many years. The historic trees were suffering due to the compaction of the soil around the roots, and lack of care, nutrients and irrigation. The seawall was much deteriorated, allowing water to erode the park creating dangerous sinkholes.

ENVIRONMENTAL CONCERNS
Environmental concerns for Forodhani Park include proper solid waste management, improving the health of the tree specimens, and increasing the coverage of areas with shade trees. Another important environmental concern in Forodhani Park is erosion from the sea. The existing seawall system is required to protect the city land from the sea and the effects of erosion. The poor condition of the old seawall, due to erosion and voids in the masonry, has allowed for sinkholes to be created in most areas along the Stone Town seafront.

INFRASTRUCTURE
The Park lacked functioning infrastructure prior to the rehabilitation.

BUILDING CONDITIONS
There are only four small buildings in the Park boundary: a washroom block and three kiosks. The kiosks, containing traces of the original reinforced-concrete gazebos from the 1930s, were in dangerous structural condition due to decades of exposure to water and salt. The washroom block was a concrete block structure in very poor condition. A fifth structure, the bandstand, was in good condition when the project began.

Significant Issues and Impact

DATA COLLECTION/SURVEYS
A topographic survey of the seafront zone from Africa House to the Old Dispensary was undertaken during 2004, which provided comprehensive physical data of site grades and contours for roads, open spaces and beaches; spot elevations inside building entrances; positions and alignments of roadbeds, sidewalks and curbs; location of public utilities and infrastructure; location and size of all trees; defined footprints of buildings, with details such as entrance locations, stairs and *barazas*. Subsequently, individual buildings within the Park were documented for restoration and rehabilitation proposals, and a detailed stone by stone survey of the cut limestone seawall in Forodhani was performed in 2003.

MASTER PLANNING PROCESS
Forodhani Park is located in one of the four Action Areas identified and defined in the 'Conservation Plan' of 1994. The design studies for Fordhani Park have adhered to and affirmed the planning guidelines legislated in the 'Conservation Plan'. Furthermore, the formal public review process has provided a forum for the exchange of ideas so that the final approved design was able to integrate any concerns that were raised, all the while maintaining conformity to the original approved master planning principles.

PLANNING ISSUES
The planning strategy for the Park layout sought to maintain and strengthen the site's historic character while incorporating the contemporary needs and uses of the community. The Park's historic elements and general organization provided the main nodes around which the new plan evolved. A three part 'zoning' strategy was developed in the project shown in the 'Conservation Plan' of 1994, which clearly delineated areas for specific uses within the Park bounds. However, the overall geometric structure and organization of the Park was enhanced through the organization of pathways, plantings and seating areas. The main zones are a secure play area to the south; a central passive leisure area with lawns and benches organized around the bandstand; and a multi-purpose paved plaza organized around the historic fountain. A densely planted garden along the street and pavement provides a buffer from traffic, while the broad promenade along the Seafront provides seating, open views and swimming access to the Indian Ocean.

HISTORIC BUILDINGS/MONUMENTS CONSERVED
Several significant historic elements and social traditions related to the Park were identified, affirmed and preserved during the rehabilitation process. The old seawall bounding the park edge was fully restored (south-west portion), rebuilt (north-west portion) and maintains its original alignment throughout. Original architectural elements such as the bandstand, the fountain, and the arch at the landing were all restored, while the historic trees were saved and brought back to health. Perhaps the most significant social tradition identified and preserved was the evening food market in Forodhani, where local vendors sell grilled fish, sugar-cane juice and roasted cassava among other things. The Forodhani food market has evolved over several decades to become one of the most identifiable aspects of Forodhani Park for both Zanzibaris and visitors.

COMMUNITY INVOLVEMENT/PROGRAMME
Preparation for the design of Forodhani Park involved public hearings intended to increase awareness and raise comments and insights about the significance of the seafront area.

VOCATIONAL TRAINING/CAPACITY BUILDING
AKTC has undertaken training and support activities for park maintenance, park operations and park management, and for horticulture and gardening. Furthermore, training in food preparation and hygiene for the vendors was also instituted. All of the activities were done in collaboration and conjunction with staff, workers and professions from the Municipality and the STCDA.

CONTRACTING METHODS
Public tender.

RELEVANT CODES/STANDARDS ADOPTED
The Stone Town 'Conservation Plan' provided the main legislative framework for the project's terms of reference. Furthermore, the UNESCO charter informed all technical and theoretical project parameters so as to guarantee compliance with international guidelines for restoration.

LESSONS LEARNED
In the context of HCP, the 'Forodhani Park Rehabilitation Project' continues the mandate of providing enhanced open public spaces for the use of the community, a programme of governance and maintenance through a comprehensive management plan and the continuity of support achieved though agreements for financial and institutional sustainability. Forodhani Park's success demonstrates that a programme of aesthetic and functional improvements can resonate deeply in a community when the social traditions associated with a particular place are fully integrated into the design.

Partners

PUBLIC PARTNERS
Ministry of Water, Construction, Energy, Land and Environment, Stone Town, Stone Town Conservation and Development Authority, Zanzibar Municipal Council, Ministry of Information, Culture, Tourism and Sport.

Donors

The World Bank.

Authoritative Framework

Seafront Trust Deed under development.

EARTHEN ARCHITECTURE
PROGRAMME
MALI

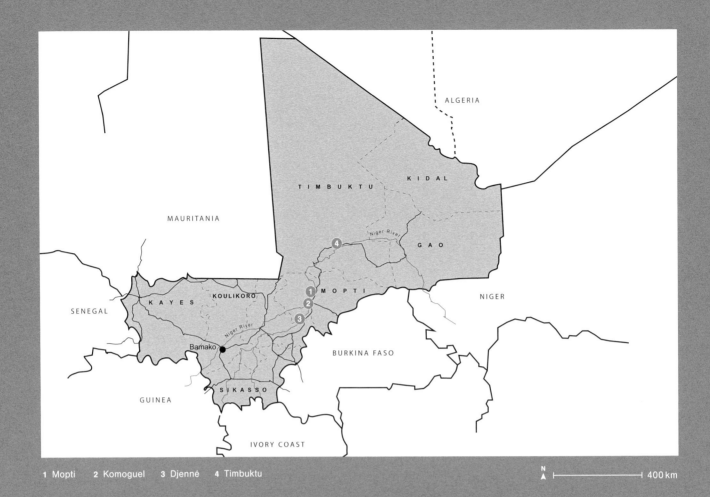

1 Mopti   **2** Komoguel   **3** Djenné   **4** Timbuktu

N
▲   ⊢————————⊣ 400 km

FEATURED CASE STUDIES

GREAT MOSQUE OF MOPTI

**KOMOGUEL WATER AND SANITATION
PROGRAMME, MOPTI**

GREAT MOSQUE OF DJENNÈ

DJINGAREYBER MOSQUE, TIMBUKTU

Earthen Architecture Programme

Preceding pages:

In 2009, heavy rains caused the collapse of a portion of the south-eastern facade of the Great Mosque of Djenné.

Much of what we know of Mali's past comes from oral histories passed down from one generation to the next by *griots*, or bards, whose profession is to memorize and recite events of the past. One of the first travellers to write an eyewitness account of Africa was Ibn Battuta travelling from Morocco to Mali in 1352. Since the late nineteenth century, archaeology provides us with clues of the past; we know that people lived in the region of present-day Mali as far back as a time when the Sahara Desert had abundant rainfall to support a lush forest, grasses and animals – long before it became a desert. In Djenné-Djeno, near present-day Djenné, there have been many archaeological finds despite a considerable amount of looting in the past. These finds indicate that Djenné-Djeno was inhabited as early as the third century BC. Urban life developed as early as the first century BC along the Inland Niger Delta (located between the Bani and Niger rivers in present-day south-western Mali) and for more than 2000 years it has been a crossroads of culture and trade and has seen the rise and fall of great empires.

Trade became an essential element in the rise and fall of the successive great West African empires of Ghana (Wagadu), Mali and Songhay. By about AD 300 camel caravan routes began to be established through West Africa and the Sahara Desert linking West African cities with Europe and the Middle East. Under the most famous of its emperors, Mansa Musa, Mali's influence expanded over the large city-states of Timbuktu, Gao and Djenné, which were all major trading cities along the trade routes, as well as cultural centres for the whole of West Africa. It was in these cities that vast libraries were built and *madrasas* (Islamic schools) were endowed.

Little remains from the medieval grandeur in Timbuktu or Djenné except their congregational mosques, situated on the sites of earlier mosques, and some of the urban fabric in their cities. Constructed in mud, like the vast majority of Mali's building stock, the mosques of Mopti, Djenné and Timbuktu are among the world's largest and finest examples of earthen architecture and form an essential part of Mali's cultural heritage.

With these important landmarks of Mopti, Djenné and Timbuktu the Aga Khan Trust for Culture (AKTC) commenced the activities of its 'Earthen Architecture Programme'. The Trust strategy hinges on close cooperation with local institutions and stakeholders, and the direct participation of experienced local masons and

Left, at Djingareyber Mosque *golettes*
(pieces of wood placed between beams)
are used for the roof of the Mosque.

Right, the *golettes* are being put into place.

specialists in restoration activities, ensuring a practical, hands-on approach and providing much needed training and job opportunities for local craftsmen.

The oldest mosque in the entire sub-Saharan region, the Djingareyber Mosque in Timbuktu, built in 1325, is still in use by the community. When the Trust commenced a survey and studies, the Mosque, made of tuff stone and mud subject to the depredations of a harsh arid climate, was in a process of advanced degradation due to deterioration of the mud plaster mix, associated with rainwater ingress into the stone and mud masonry and termite infestation of the timber beams; moreover, the accumulation of mud fill resulting from years of maintenance threatened to weaken the structure to the point of collapse.

The Great Mosque of Djenné, constructed in 1906, lies in the core of the historic city on an elevated platform overlooking the city's main market square. Its construction technique is most unusual since it was built entirely of small cylindrical mud bricks called *djenne-fey*, a tradition that local masons grouped in a corporation called *barey-ton* are responsible for maintaining. As well as their technical skills, the traditional masons in Djenné hold magical powers, giving them social importance in the community. In spite of the yearly festival of *crépissage* during which the community replasters the facades of the Mosque, work by AKTC brought to light the poor inner structure of the walls and roof and proposed a comprehensive conservation plan.

The Great Mosque of Mopti, commonly called the Mosque of Komoguel, built between 1936 and 1943, was also in poor condition; it had been damaged by the inappropriate use of cement in a previous restoration effort in 1978. In an attempt to address further decay of the building, the community had applied a cement crust to the upper part of the walls, preventing the building from breathing and threatening to weaken the structure to the point of collapse.

Following the completion of the Great Mosque of Mopti, the Trust has implemented an infrastructure and habitat improvement programme that aims to raise the quality of the urban environment and the standard of living for residents in Komoguel. This programme involved the installation of an infrastructure network of water and sewage, street paving using blocks manufactured with recycled plastic bags, vocational training in building

Heavy scaffolding covers the
Great Mosque of Mopti in the early
stages of its restoration in 2005.

Phasing 2004 → 2010

Start of Great
Mosque of Mopti
conservation

Completion of
Great Mosque
of Mopti
conservation

Start of Timbuktu
Djingareyber
Mosque
conservation

Start of Djenné
Great Mosque
conservation

Completion of
Timbuktu Djingareyber
and Djenné Mosques;
opening of the Centre
for Earthen Architecture
in Mopti

| 2004 | 2006 | 2007 | 2009 | 2010 |

crafts, the creation of a dyke to prevent annual flooding along the Pagué Danawal Lake and the creation of a community and visitor centre, public toilets and green open space for the public.

The 'Earthen Architecture Programme' has reversed the deterioration process and achieved the restoration of three important landmarks in Mopti, Djenné and Timbuktu, providing valuable experience in the technical, organizational and community-related aspects of preserving earthen structures in the country. Specifically it has succeeded in firstly identifying best practices of earth building grounded in local traditions and materials, introducing conservation methods and processes. In spite of the apparent vulnerability of earth architecture, the recourse to adequate mixes and organic additives, such as *karité* butter or baobab fruit powder, greatly improves the performance of traditional mud building. Secondly it has created a database of architectural, archaeological and technical documentation via first-hand knowledge of unique historic sites. Thirdly it has improved the local capacity to manage a precious architectural heritage, training locals in the skills of building with earth and reviving the traditions of handing down knowledge of restoration methods and materials to future generations. Finally it has generated economic benefits in terms of the development of local supplies, employment and tourism.

Great Mosque of Mopti

MOPTI, MALI

The Great Mosque of Mopti is an earthen structure built in the traditional Sudanese style between 1936 and 1943 on the site of an earlier mosque dating from 1908, and is commonly called the Mosque of Komoguel. At the time the Mosque was constructed, the Komoguel neighbourhood was in development as a result of the decision by the French settlers to use Mopti as Mali's central hub for trade along the Niger River.

When it became apparent, after preliminary studies and surveys, that the seventy-year-old Great Mosque of Mopti was in danger of collapsing, the Aga Khan Trust for Culture (AKTC) was asked to assist in its rehabilitation. Like other earthen buildings in Mali, the Great Mosque of Mopti had been maintained by the community with a traditional plaster of mud and rice chaff, but in recent years an incompatible layer of cement had been applied.

The first phase of the work on this important landmark focused on repairing the roof and stabilizing the upper part of the building, which had been damaged by the use of cement in 1978. Because cement adds additional loads to the structure and integrates poorly with the traditional materials, earthen buildings clad with cement often suffer water infiltration and structural damage over time – a process which, in this case, had weakened and seriously compromised the stability of the monument. Fissures in the cement cladding had been infiltrated by water, which had led to structural damage.

Preserving this unique landmark could only be guaranteed by the return to traditional earthen architecture techniques. Works included restoration of earth masonry, carpentry, roofing and technical installations; together with earthen plaster these aimed to re-establish its historical condition.

Starting in 2004, local masons worked to remove the cement layer and replace damaged areas with traditional mortar and bricks, which are made by mixing earth with rice. Roofing timbers and other structural and aesthetic elements made of wood were replaced. Then a fresh application of the traditional earthen plaster returned the building to its historic condition. To ensure that the Mosque remains structurally sound and that it is properly maintained well into the future, training courses were offered in traditional building crafts – skills that risked being forgotten in the region – and contemporary conservation methods

The Great Mosque serves the community of Komoguel in Mopti.

Opposite page:
Above, an aerial view of the Great Mosque after restoration.

Below, workmen intent on removing the detrimental cement render on the roof.

Project Scope / Objectives

Works on the Great Mosque included the restoration of earth masonry, carpentry, roofing and technical installations, together with earthen plaster. The aim was to help to re-establish Mopti Mosque's original condition and historic status.

├─────────────────────────┤ 5 m

The Mosque elevation showing the cement
render that had to be removed.

Opposite page:
The AKTC intervention has restored the
elegant lines of the Mosque after they had
been deformed by many years of refacing.

to more than sixty local masons and craftsmen. Literacy classes were provided to all
implementation crew and foremen were trained in basic computer skills.

The Trust strategy hinged on close cooperation with local institutions and stakeholders,
as well as on the direct participation of experienced local masons and specialists in restoration activities, thus ensuring a practical, hands-on approach and providing much needed
training and job opportunities for locals. Efforts in Mopti have expanded to include a
'Water and Sanitation Programme', in the Komoguel district surrounding the Mosque,
that aims to raise the standard of living for residents. In the process the Centre for
Earthen Architecture, a community centre and public toilets were constructed.

The rehabilitation of the Great Mosque of Mopti has in many ways become a model
for AKTC's other interventions in earthen architecture in Mali. Much of the knowledge
gained during AKTC's two years of work in Mopti found its way into the 'Memorandum of
Understanding' that was drawn up between AKTC and the Mali Ministry of Culture that
paved the way for expanded restoration and conservation activity at other sites in the
country. The work on the Mosque was conducted in conjunction with the Direction Nation-
ale du Patrimoine du Ministère de la Culture du Mali, regional authorities, the City of
Mopti and the Mosque's Committee. The local authorities also helped with the selection
of experienced masons and young apprentices who are being trained on the job. The
model was replicated at Djenné and Timbuktu. Training is an important aspect of AKTC's
international work and mission. In 2006, following the Mosque's restoration, the site was
included in the National Heritage List of Mali.

Background

BRIEF HISTORY OF PROJECT SITE
Mopti is one of Mali's larger cities, with a population of approximately 100,000. The Great Mosque of Mopti was built between 1936 and 1943 on the site of an earlier mosque dating to 1908. It is an earthen structure with similarities to the Great Mosque of Djenné. Komoguel neighbourhood, with its 10,000 residents, has developed around the Mosque since the beginning of the 20th century. In 2006, following Mopti Mosque's restoration, the site was included in the National Heritage List.

Challenges

SITE CONDITIONS
Preliminary studies performed in 2004 showed that the Mosque was subject to deterioration mainly due to the inappropriate application of cement plaster.

INFRASTRUCTURE
Mopti has no proper sanitation system and waste waters flow through its narrow streets before reaching the Bani River. Solid waste accumulates on the shores of the Bani River, forming a fill on top of which lives the poorest segment of the population. The district of Komoguel, surrounded by Lake Danawal, likewise lacks all basic infrastructure services, and consequently suffers from related health and environmental hazards. Prior to the project, sewage water flowed down the middle of streets leading to Lake Danawal, which acted as a filtration basin.

BUILDING CONDITIONS
The Mosque's wall-bearing system was weakened by the application of a cement coat. The roof leaked owing to defective slopes and accumulation of earth fill.

Significant Issues and Impact

DATA COLLECTION/SURVEYS
The AKTC project performed the first architectural surveys of the Mosque in 2004, followed by a topographic survey of its surroundings.

PLANNING ISSUES
It was determined that the Mosque's preservation could only be guaranteed by a return to traditional earthen architecture techniques.

HISTORIC BUILDINGS/MONUMENTS CONSERVED
Conservation of the historic Mosque was the main objective of the AKTC project in the period 2004–06.

VOCATIONAL TRAINING/CAPACITY BUILDING
A group of 150 community masons and labourers was trained in earthen conservation methods, plumbing, carpentry and street paving.

CONTRACTING METHODS
Due to a lack of qualified contractors for monument conservation in Mali, the work was entirely in-house managed. This also enabled direct quality control, flexibility in the resources and on-the-job training.

Partners

PUBLIC PARTNERS
Ministry of Culture, Municipality of Mopti, Republic of Mali.

COMMUNITY PARTNERS
Comité de gestion de Komoguel.

Authoritative Framework

'Memorandum of Understanding' signed in 2004 between AKTC and the Ministry of Culture, providing the framework for an Earthen Architecture Programme in Mali.

Komoguel Water and Sanitation Programme

MOPTI, MALI

Situated at the junction of the Bani and Niger rivers, the city of Mopti in Central Mali has developed over the past one hundred years from a modest settlement into an important urban and administrative centre that reaches out to both the north and east of the country. In addition to its access to river traffic, the city is also well connected to Mali's road network. A twelve-kilometre causeway across an area of seasonally flooded agricultural land, which was constructed during the French colonial period, links Mopti with the national road network. More recently an international airport was added, which receives a fair number of foreign tourists whose main destinations are principally the Pays Dogon and the nearby historic city of Djenné.

Mopti's strategic location at the confluence of two major rivers has also become its major constraint to further development. During the months of November to February, when the waters of the Niger and Bani are at their highest levels, the city becomes a virtual island with only the causeway as its connection to firm ground. Mopti's population, currently estimated at more than 125,000, is squeezed during this period into an area of not more than 2.5 square kilometres. Not surprisingly, a parallel city has developed over the years at Sévaré, at the other end of the causeway, where there are no restrictions to growth.

As a result of population pressure and overall low levels of development, living conditions in Mopti, particularly in the areas around the harbour and in the adjacent districts of Komoguel and Gangal, have steeply declined over the past decades. Water and sanitation are in a very poor state, a situation that is being aggravated by the absence of a proper system for waste collection and by unpaved streets with open sewers.

The major objective of the intervention of the Historic Cities Programme (HCP) in Komoguel is to improve existing living standards in a limited geographical area of Mopti by focusing on improved health and sanitation conditions. In order to achieve this, a series of limited interventions aimed at improving existing sanitation conditions in an area confined to the immediate surroundings of the Great Mosque of Mopti have been implemented since June 2006.

HCP has based its intervention strategy on close cooperation with the inhabitants of the neighbourhood, local religious authorities and government

The streets are being paved with bricks made from recycled local refuse, such as plastic bags.

Opposite page:
The Centre for Earthen Architecture was inaugurated in 2010. The interior space includes exhibits interpreting the earthen architecture projects undertaken by AKTC.

Project Scope / Objectives

This project's objective was to develop the built environment and improve local health standards through upgraded water supply, sanitation systems and street paving. This included the creation of toilet and shower facilities in a newly constructed community centre and the creation of the Centre for Earthen Architecture.

Phasing 2007 → 2010

Start of 'Water and Sanitation Programme', Phase 1	Start of embankment for flooding protection	Completion of 'Water and Sanitation Programme', Phase 1	Opening of Komoguel Park and the Centre for Earthen Architecture
2007	**2008**	**2009**	**2010**

Open sewers and poor drainage were serious health hazards in Komoguel.

Opposite page:
Successful efforts have been accomplished in Komoguel to improve the infrastructure. New paving has been made from recycled waste materials.

officials. Following the complete and successful rehabilitation of Mopti's Great Mosque by HCP in early 2006, substantial goodwill had been created with the local population and with the authorities to justify the launch of a major initiative for the area. The Mosque's Committee in particular welcomed plans for improvement of the environment in the immediate surroundings of the Great Mosque.

The activities are being carried out in phases. A first phase, which started in mid 2006 and continued until December 2009, focused on physical improvement of a relatively small area around the Great Mosque. In close collaboration with the local Mosque Committee, improvements have been realized to provide protection against periodically rising river water by constructing a flood barrier with 3200 square metres of landfill. In addition to this, several public water points were established to increase access to safe and clean drinking water; an underground sewerage system was established and connected with individual households; a treatment facility for raw sewerage was installed; 4000 square metres of streets were paved with locally manufactured bricks (made from recycled polythene bags and sand); and a system for collecting solid waste was introduced. These improvements made to the built environment during the three and a half years that it took to implement Phase 1 also generated training opportunities for 345 people in construction techniques, plumbing, masonry, brick manufacturing, carpentry and metalwork.

Following the completion of Phase 1, HCP commenced with the construction of public toilets, a community centre and a visitor centre on the landfill. The latter will house a permanent exhibition on earthen architecture and will also serve as a small museum, thereby generating income for the maintenance of the local water and sanitation system.

Based on information collected through an extensive baseline survey carried out during the first phase, a complementary second phase – involving also the Aga Khan Foundation (AKF) and the Aga Khan Agency for Microfinance (AKAM) – will follow, pending the availability of co-funding. The successful completion of the first phase for Komoguel has opened the possibility for further improvement of water and sanitation conditions in the quarter. During a second phase, a much larger area will be targeted for improvement. During Phase 2, two new sewage treatment facilities will be constructed, underground sewage will be put in place for 2000 beneficiaries and 8000 square metres of street will be paved with bricks. This second phase will include other socio-economic development issues related to public health, education, family income and possibly also open space development. During this phase cross-cutting issues such as gender, environment and the organizational and institutional development of civil society will also be addressed.

Background

BRIEF HISTORY OF PROJECT SITE

The district of Komoguel is located in north-east Mopti and borders the inner Lake Pagué Danawal. The project area encompasses Mopti's Great Mosque, built in the 1930s and now considered a prime example of quality earthen architecture in West Africa. The local built environment is semi-protected, with a limit placed on building height to protect the skyline.

Challenges

PROJECT RISKS

Water and sanitation development activities could continue through a number of phases to eventually encompass all watersheds in Mopti town, but local capacities to manage the complex of individual watersheds remain limited. With the island town's growing population and no further space for expansion, there is a risk of increased urban development along the town's outer edges, outside the established watersheds.

SITE CONDITIONS

Komoguel has one of the highest recorded residential densities in Mali (over 400 persons per hectare). Conservation and upgrading works faced significant logistical and technical challenges due to tight access via the narrow alleyways connecting fragile traditional homes.

INFRASTRUCTURE

The piped water network is insufficient. Untreated sewage, which currently is allowed to flow into inner Lake Pagué Danawal, poses a major health threat to the population. Acting as a large evaporation basin, the lake is in danger of disappearing altogether under layers of sediment made up of untreated sewage. Decades of under-investment in drainage, water supply and electrical networks, coupled with extensive war damage, means that significant investments are required to achieve the most basic levels of service coverage for a fast-growing population.

BUILDING CONDITIONS

Lack of maintenance, together with war-related damage, has left the bulk of Komoguel's traditional housing stock in a state of advanced disrepair. Additionally, high occupancy levels in subdivided homes pose a challenge to improving living conditions.

Significant Issues and Impact

DATA COLLECTION/SURVEYS

Since a first baseline survey in 2007, regular sample surveys have been conducted in the area and progress has been measured, covering more than 30,000 people. Nearly 40% of the population is 15 years old or less. Average household size is eight to nine people.

MASTER PLANNING PROCESS

A comprehensive master plan for Mopti is not available. There are remedial plans, however, for improving the port and some parts of the built environment.

PLANNING ISSUES

Mopti's relative isolation limits its future development. Ideally located for river traffic, it can only be reached by road via a single 11-km-long causeway passing through the floodplains to connect it with Sévaré. All future planning must take accessibility into account, balancing the needs of a relatively large population with a limited geographical space (around 2500 hectares).

COMMUNITY INVOLVEMENT/PROGRAMME

All sanitation improvement and construction activities were undertaken by or in close collaboration with community members. Community members are also assisting in managing and securing contributions to certain projects.

VOCATIONAL TRAINING/CAPACITY BUILDING

More than 300 craftsmen have been trained through apprenticeships during the course of the activities. Capacity building at organizational and institutional level involves the local counterpart CAK/Cogest (Comité d'Assainissement de Komoguel/Comité de Gestion).

CONTRACTING METHODS

All works were carried out with direct labour recruited (usually from the resident community) and supervised by AKTC professional staff. Subcontractors were used for moving earth (digging and transportation).

NEW TECHNOLOGIES INTRODUCED

Production of paving bricks manufactured from recycled plastic bags.

RELEVANT CODES/STANDARDS ADOPTED

All construction and installation work was undertaken in accordance with the relevant international charters and domestic laws.

Partners

PUBLIC PARTNERS

Ministry of Culture, Municipality of Mopti, Republic of Mali.

PRIVATE PARTNERS

Chambre des Métiers de Mopti.

COMMUNITY PARTNERS

Association pour l'assainissement de Komoguel.

Donors

Canadian International Development Agency, United States Department of Agriculture.

Authoritative Framework

'Memorandum of Understanding' with the Ministry of Culture (2006); various agreements with the Municipality of Mopti town.

Great Mosque of Djenné

DJENNÉ, MALI

Constructed by the community in 1906 on the remains of a pre-existing mosque, the Great Mosque of Djenné is the largest historical mud mosque in the sub-Saharan region and is considered by many to be the greatest achievement of the Sudano-Sahelian architectural style. It is located in the centre of Djenné alongside the marketplace, making it the city's focal social point. In 1988 the site was included in UNESCO's World Heritage List, together with the entire Old City.

Djenné is a small town of 13,000 inhabitants, located away from the main streams of development of Mali. The main income sources on which the local community is dependent are limited to the weekly marketplace and foreign tourism. While urban life is divided by neighbourhoods, the local community leaders play a major role in the city's decisions. The city has no proper sanitation system and waste waters flow in the middle of the tiny streets before reaching the Bani River, causing major environmental hazards. Solid waste is being accumulated on the shores of the river, forming a fill on top of which the poorest segment of the population has settled.

The Mosque has been preserved till now thanks to the yearly community effort of maintenance coordinated by the *barey-ton,* the local corporation of traditional masons, holding technical capacities in earthen architecture but also considered to have magical powers.

In spite of its yearly maintenance campaigns, the Mosque was in poor condition in terms of structural load-bearing walls and the roof. Based on a full documentation via topographic and architectural surveys, a damage assessment was drafted. The project scope was to guarantee the stability of the building by consolidating the carpentry and wall-bearing system. The Mosque interior was also subject to full conservation including rehabilitation of the Mosque's interior and exterior surfaces, eviction of the bats, and replacement of the defective sound, ventilation and lighting installations.

Due to a lack of qualified contractors for monument conservation in Djenné, the work was entirely in-house managed. This also enabled direct quality control, flexibility in resource allocation and on-the-job training in conservation methods to more than 120 community masons.

People are gathered for market day in Djenné with the Mosque in the background.

Opposite page:
A view of the facade with an area for making *banco* to reface the Mosque in front of it.

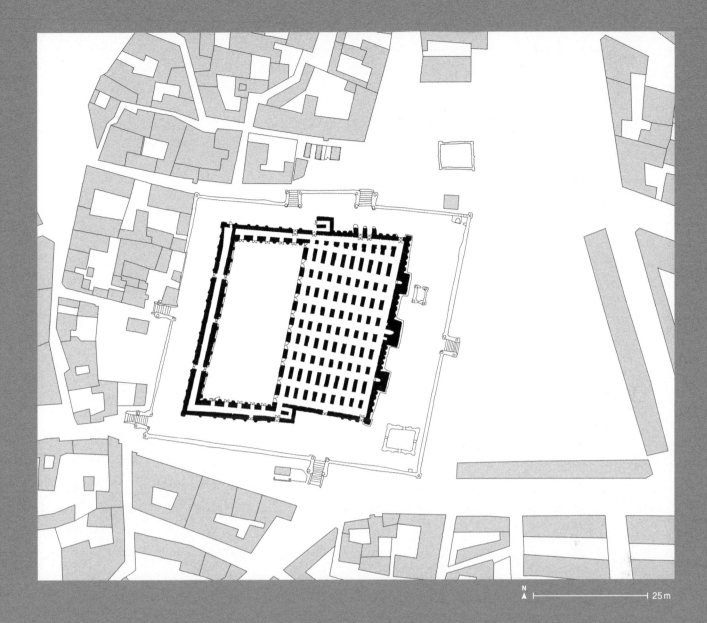

Project Scope / Objectives

This conservation project guaranteed Djenné Mosque's stability by consolidating carpentry and the wall-bearing system. The Mosque's interior and exterior surfaces were rehabilitated, and sound, ventilation and lighting systems installed.

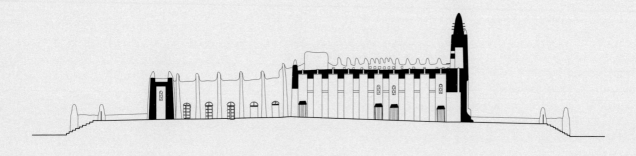

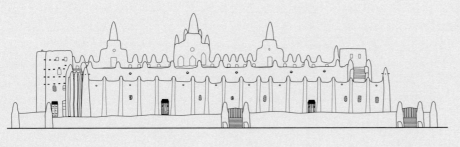

├──────────┤ 10 m

Above, the north-south section of the Great Mosque in Djenné showing the main prayer hall and the courtyard.

Below: the west elevation of the Mosque.

Opposite page:
Minarets feature on this part of the east facade of the Great Mosque in Djenné, before restoration.

Background

BRIEF HISTORY OF PROJECT SITE
Djenné is a small town (13,000 inhabitants), remote from the main stream of development in Mali but well-known for the number of its *madrasas*, where young pupils receive a basic education grounded in Qur'anic reading. The main income sources are limited to the weekly marketplace and foreign tourism. Built by the community in 1906 on the remains of a pre-existing mosque, the Djenné Mosque is the largest historical mud-brick mosque in the sub-Saharan region. Its symmetrical layout and arches reflect European influence. The Mosque has been preserved thanks to the yearly community maintenance effort coordinated by the *barey-ton*. This local corporation of traditional masons have technical abilities but are also believed to possess magical powers. In 1988, the site was included in UNESCO's World Heritage List, together with the entire Old City.

Challenges

PROJECT RISKS
Urban life is divided by neighbourhoods, with local community leaders playing a major role in the town's decisions. Located in the heart of the town, the Mosque is a focal point, making its conservation a highly sensitive issue to Djenné residents.

INFRASTRUCTURE
Djenné lacks a proper sanitation system. Waste waters flow through its narrow streets before reaching the Bani River.

BUILDING CONDITIONS
The Mosque suffered from the weakened structure of the wall-bearing system; water ingress in the roofing due to defective slopes and accumulation of earth fill; and accumulation of earth plaster on walls, hiding architecture and filling windows and doors.

Significant Issues and Impact

DATA COLLECTION/SURVEYS
The AKTC project performed the first topographic and architectural surveys of the Mosque in 2008. Documentation of the work in progress is compiled on a regular basis and a set of as-built drawings is being prepared.

HISTORIC BUILDINGS/MONUMENTS CONSERVED
Conservation of the historic Mosque was the main objective of the AKTC project. Its interior area of 1400 m², as well as 800 m² of courtyard spaces was fully restored.

COMMUNITY INVOLVEMENT/PROGRAMME
The community and its leaders played an important role in the decision-making process of the conservation through regular information and discussion sessions.

VOCATIONAL TRAINING/CAPACITY BUILDING
Some 120 community masons and labourers were trained in earthen conservation methods. Literacy classes were offered to members of the implementation crew and foremen were trained in basic computer skills.

CONTRACTING METHODS
Due to a lack of qualified contractors for monument conservation in Mali, the work was entirely in-house managed. This enabled on-the-job training, direct quality control and flexible use of local resources.

NEW TECHNOLOGIES INTRODUCED
New sound, electrical and ventilation systems were installed in the Mosque's interior.

RELEVANT CODES/STANDARDS ADOPTED
Although there are currently no building codes applicable to earthen architecture, the project is in line with conservation principles drawn up by ICOMOS and calls on the best practice of earth architecture specialists.

Partners

PUBLIC PARTNERS
Ministry of Culture, Republic of Mali.

COMMUNITY PARTNERS
Comité de gestion de Djenné.

Authoritative Framework

'Memorandum of Understanding' signed in 2004 between AKTC and the Ministry of Culture, providing the framework for an Earthen Architecture Programme in Mali.

Djingareyber Mosque

TIMBUKTU, MALI

The Djingareyber Mosque is known to have been constructed in 1325 by the Andalusian architect Abou Ishak, at the initiative of King Hadj Moussa, upon his return from pilgrimage to Mecca. Since then the Mosque has experienced a number of modifications, resulting from the organic nature of earthen architecture and its vulnerability to weathering. Archaeological test pits carried out in 2009 in the main prayer hall have shown that at least three successive buildings have occupied the site. The main earthen ornaments on the *qibla* wall and some pillars may date back to the sixteenth century. In 1988 the site was included in UNESCO's World Heritage List, together with the city's other two historic mosques, Sidi Yahya and Sankore.

The Mosque is located at the southern edge of Timbuktu's historic city, forming the core of modern Timbuktu, the home of 30,000 inhabitants and capital city of Mali's Northern Province.

Lying at the meeting point between the Niger River Delta and the Sahara Desert, Timbuktu and the Sahelian environment is affected by growing desertification. Trees that used to form raw materials for the Mosque's carpentry are no longer available. Wind erosion and accumulation of sand deposits in the city's open spaces are also of concern for the integrity of the urban fabric and public open spaces.

Built in mud and tuff stone, Djingareyber Mosque was in poor condition when it was first documented by the Aga Khan Trust for Culture (AKTC) in early 2007: a full topographic and architectural survey, first performed on the Mosque, was the basis for a damage assessment. It revealed that the building was in weak structural condition, particularly the roof and wall-bearing systems, due to water ingress in the roofing. This occurred because of defective slopes and accumulation of earth fill and the mediocre quality of local mud plasters due to the decline of familiarity with traditional crafts.

The project first focused on consolidating the mud masonry and carpentry, making the roofing watertight. Then the project aimed to conserve decorative earthen motifs and plastered surfaces in the interior spaces of the Mosque's covered prayer hall and replace the defective sound, ventilation and lighting installations.

The corner elevation of Djingareyber Mosque.

Opposite page:
Restoration work being done on the interior.

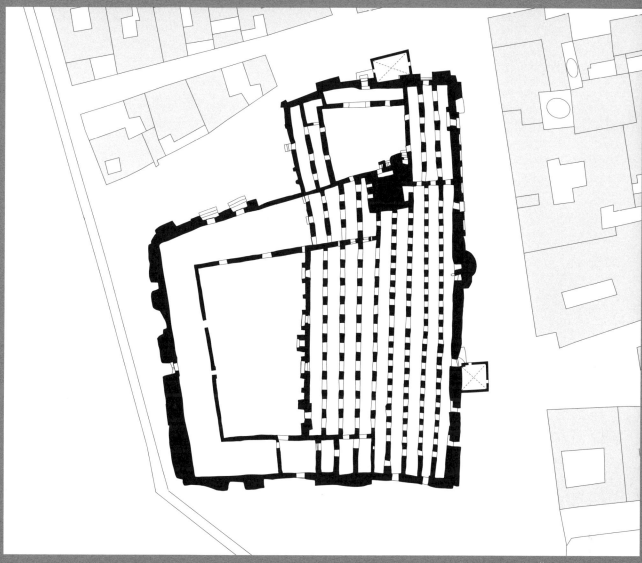

Project Scope/Objectives

Built in mud and tuff stone, Djingareyber Mosque was in poor condition before the intervention. The project focused on consolidating mud masonry and carpentry, making the roofing watertight, conserving decorative earthen motifs and plastered surfaces in the Mosque's interior, and also replacing the defective sound, ventilation and lighting systems.

N

⊢——————⊣ 10 m

A minaret of Djingareyber Mosque after restoration. The Mosque was built in mud and tuff stone, evident in the foreground of the shot.

Opposite page:
The east elevation and longitudinal section of the Mosque.

Timbuktu is a remote location posing challenging logistical conditions. Sourcing quality construction materials in the immediate environment is difficult due to the decline of appropriate mud construction techniques. Logistics and local transportation, combined with the lack of skilled mid-level labour and security threats, are also challenging.

As a result, the work on Djingareyber Mosque was entirely in-house managed, employing traditional masons active in the neighbourhood's corporation. This mode of operations also enabled direct quality control, flexibility in resource allocation and on-the-job training in traditional building crafts and contemporary conservation methods to more than 140 community masons and craftsmen. Literacy classes were offered to all implementation crew and foremen as well as training in basic computer skills.

|————————| 10 m

Background

BRIEF HISTORY OF PROJECT SITE
Timbuktu, a town with 30,000 inhabitants, is head of the Regional Council for the Northern Provinces of Mali. The population comprises a variety of ethnic groups, with a majority of Songhai, followed by Touaregs, Peuls, Bambaras and small proportions of other ethnic groups. Djingareyber Mosque was built in 1325 by King Hadj Moussa upon his return from a pilgrimage to Mecca, and has experienced a number of modifications over time. The main earthen ornaments on the *qibla* wall and some pillars may date to the 16th century. Archaeological test pits carried out in the main prayer hall revealed that at least three previous buildings occupied the site. In 1988 the Mosque was included in UNESCO's World Heritage List.

Challenges

PROJECT RISKS
Timbuktu is remote. Sourcing quality construction materials, transportation and finding skilled labour can be a challenge. In recent years security has become an increasing concern too.

SITE CONDITIONS
Timbuktu lies at the crossroads between the Niger River Delta and the Sahara Desert, an area affected by growing desertification. Trees that once served as the raw materials for the Mosque's carpentry are no longer available. The organic nature of the Mosque's earthen architecture makes the building vulnerable to weathering elements. Wind erosion and accumulations of sand deposits in the city's open spaces are of concern for the safeguard of the Mosque and overall city fabric.

INFRASTRUCTURE
The systems of water and sanitation in Timbuktu Old City are based on infiltration pits and built on sandy soil, posing hygiene hazards.

BUILDING CONDITIONS
Djingareyber Mosque's structure is threatened by a weakened wall-bearing system, water ingress in the roofing due to defective slopes and accumulation of earth fill, and the mediocre quality of local mud plasters associated with the decline in usage of traditional building techniques.

Significant Issues and Impact

DATA COLLECTION/SURVEYS
The AKTC project performed the first topographic and architectural surveys of the Mosque in 2007. Documentation of the work in progress is regularly compiled to form the basis of a set of as-built drawings.

HISTORIC BUILDINGS/MONUMENTS CONSERVED
Conservation of the historic Mosque was the main objective of the AKTC project. An interior space of 2000 m², together with 800 m² of courtyard spaces, was fully restored. The roofing system was improved using tie beams to evenly distribute the roof loads (lime-based mortar and layers of mud insulation).

COMMUNITY INVOLVEMENT/PROGRAMME
The community and its leaders play an important role in the decision-making process of the conservation through regular information and discussion sessions.

VOCATIONAL TRAINING/CAPACITY BUILDING
A group of 100 community masons and labour was trained in extensive earthen conservation methods. Literacy classes were offered to all implementation crew and foremen were trained in basic computer skills.

CONTRACTING METHODS
Due to a lack of qualified contractors for monument conservation in Mali, the work was in-house managed. This enabled direct quality control, on-the-job training and flexible use of resources.

RELEVANT CODES/STANDARDS ADOPTED
Although there are currently no building codes applicable to earthen architecture, the project is in line with conservation principles drawn up by ICOMOS and calls on the best practice of earth architecture specialists.

Partners

PUBLIC PARTNERS
Ministry of Culture, Republic of Mali.

COMMUNITY PARTNERS
Comité de gestion de Tombouctou.

Authoritative Framework

'Memorandum of Understanding' signed in 2004 between AKTC and the Ministry of Culture, providing the framework for an Earthen Architecture Programme in Mali.

National Park of Mali

BAMAKO, MALI

Bamako, the capital of the Republic of Mali, is located in the Niger River Valley. The city covers approximately forty square kilometres and it is estimated that its population has exceeded one million inhabitants. Since colonial times, Bamako has experienced significant population growth and this, in turn, has stimulated a constant growth of the urban area and demand for residential and public facilities.

The site defined and proposed for Bamako Urban Park lies within a larger protected forest reserve of 2100 hectares, a green belt of some magnitude and significance in this large but mainly arid country. The project site itself covers a total of 103 hectares comprising an inner active, cultural core zone of forty-nine hectares and an outer, more passive ecological buffer zone of fifty-four hectares. It is a large, semicircular canyon area that lies beneath the terraced outcrops of the Koulouba plateau between the National Museum and the Presidential Palace complex in a protected forest that remains in a relatively natural state. The central portion comprises the existing botanical garden, arboretum and zoo. The remainder is composed of the terraces and slopes beneath the 410-metre contour containing geological features such as caves, prehistoric habitats and an important range of flora and fauna.

The existing botanical garden, initiated in the 1930s, used to serve as a conservatory of local botanical species and a nursery for imported ones. A series of dams were constructed along the small riverbed to protect the area from devastating floods during the rainy season. The zoo, developed in a later stage, houses a number of African animals in cages. Small buildings were constructed throughout the period in the arboretum and zoo to accommodate maintenance staff and technical installations. What remains today of this earlier landscape are an arboretum affected by lack of irrigation with alignments of trees covered by alien vegetation, a dilapidated zoo and several small semi-neglected buildings.

Given its natural attractions, its large size and its location next to the museum complex, it was envisioned that the Park could become a large open space for leisure and educational activities, focused on the general public, school groups and tourists. The project brief called for the unification of the sites of the National Museum, the existing Botanical Garden and the Zoo into a single cultural/ecological park of significant value, with natural and cultural attractions.

People relax and stroll along a pathway of the Park.

Opposite page:
Children making the most of the playground equipment.

Preceding pages:
A fountain attracts children on a path leading from the entrance to the National Park of Mali.

1 National Museum of Mali   4 Park Boutiques   7 Children's Centre   10 Freedom Entrance
2 Parking   5 Park Pavillon   8 Tea-House   11 Sports Centre
3 Koulouba Entrance   6 Balasoko Restaurant 9 Medicinal Plants Garden 12 Environmental Centre

N
△ ⊢――――――――――⊣ 200 m

Project Scope / Objectives

The Bamako Park project encompassed the creation
of a high-quality, self-sustainable open space of 90
hectares allowing for cultural, sports, educational
and family recreation activities. The scope of activities included a major site survey, hydrology study,
detailed design of civil and electrical infrastructure,
road and path works, landscaping and facilities design
and construction. Reservoirs, a lake, pump stations,
an effluent treatment plant for recycled water, the
construction of perimeter fencing, and a range of new
buildings were all created. New botanical elements
include a medicinal garden, tree collections and
extensive planting of indigenous plant species.

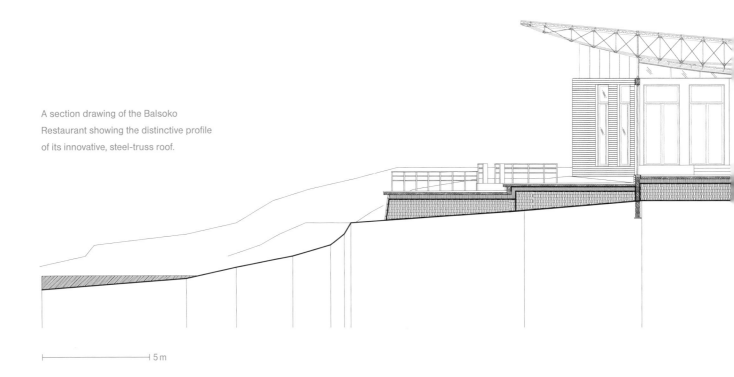

A section drawing of the Balsoko
Restaurant showing the distinctive profile
of its innovative, steel-truss roof.

⊢—————⊣ 5 m

Gardeners nurture seedlings
at the Park nursery.

In 2008 the Aga Khan Trust for Culture (AKTC) developed detailed planning and a sche-
matic design for Phase 1 of the project, while technical and economic feasibility studies
were advanced for the totality of the proposed project. Phase 1 is seventeen hectares in
area and contains a number of new building facilities, as well as rehabilitated open
spaces and gardens.

There is a comprehensive pedestrian circulation network and formal promenades
throughout the Park. The Park contains fitness, jogging, cycling and mountaineering
tracks of varying difficulty and diverse interpretive awareness trails for botany, birds and
nature. This pedestrian network provides easy access to the full extent of the 103 hectares
of parkland and connects existing successful nodes, such as the National Museum, with
other attractions, such as the amphitheatre dedicated to education or the performing arts.

An important part of Phase I planning includes the redevelopment and integration of
approximately eight existing buildings, to be used for internal park operations, food and
beverage points and storage. Built facilities, designed by Diébédo Francis Kéré, an Aga
Khan Award for Architecture recipient in 2001, will include entry structures (a primary and
secondary gate and entry building), a youth and sports centre cluster, a restaurant, public
toilets and kiosks.

The garden spaces offer varied types of indigenous flora in different settings, from
open lawn areas to flower gardens, wooded areas and a medicinal garden with
explanatory signage. The installation of a range of interpretive educational material, in
signage or display, and the potential for the development of trained guides could reveal
a new depth of educational experiences to all visitors. By combining an environmental
undertaking of a high standard with leisure and cultural facilities, all possibly under a
public-private partnership approach, an important development model can be put in
place in a favourable political context.

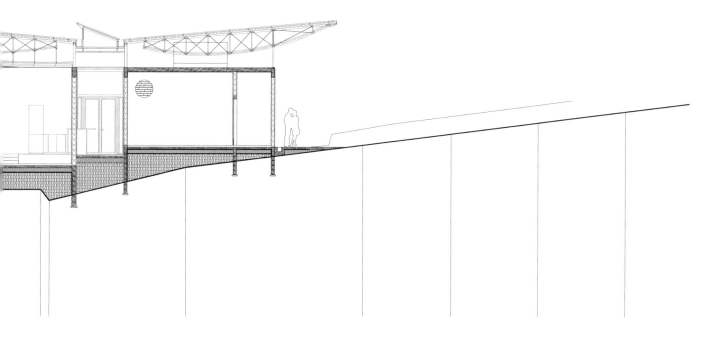

Park buildings, including the Balasoko Restaurant, in front of which there is a series of cascading water pools, were designed by the highly respected architect Diébédo Francis Kéré.

Opposite page:
The Maison du Thé in the Park is one of the existing
buildings that has been restored and reused.

Phasing 2007 → 2013

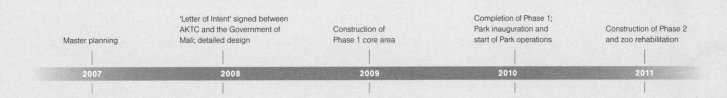

Master planning	'Letter of Intent' signed between AKTC and the Government of Mali; detailed design	Construction of Phase 1 core area	Completion of Phase 1; Park inauguration and start of Park operations	Construction of Phase 2 and zoo rehabilitation
2007	2008	2009	2010	2011

Background

BRIEF HISTORY OF PROJECT SITE

The Park site is situated in a valley that during Mali's colonial era was designated as part of a 'storm-water mitigation' system. The site eventually became a formal Park, and subsequently a scientific estate with a zoo, botanical garden and the National Museum. A small road bisected the area separating the Park and Museum components. The seasonal watercourses crossing the site were dammed at intervals and stone footpaths constructed to link various park features. Many indigenous trees were conserved, largely along the main stream, and formal, open lawns were set out between axial footpaths. Over time, poor maintenance and invasive trees and shrub species transformed the Park into overgrown thicket with insufficiently drained paths that became muddy in the rainy season. Since sports and family recreation are culturally important and the Bamako population lives in dense, often informal settlements, the Park nonetheless remained popular as a quiet shady refuge.

Challenges

PROJECT RISKS

Periods of extreme heat, interspersed with two intense rainy seasons, limit the window of opportunity for both construction and horticulture. The surrounding wooded slopes are subject to ad hoc burning to encourage grass for cattle, and such fires can spread uncontrolled. Informal collection of tree bark for medicine and wood for fuel threatened the mature trees on site.

SITE CONDITIONS

Virtually no formal facilities remained operational, including the original irrigation system. The planning process identified opportunities to reunite the Park and Museum through road closure and to restore, upgrade and enhance the natural facilities and activities offered by this dramatic valley site.

ENVIRONMENTAL CONCERNS

Water is a precious resource here and potential depletion of groundwater is an issue. Physical testing indicated that planned boreholes and water consumption were sustainable.

INFRASTRUCTURE

The municipal infrastructure did not have capacity for potable water, sewage treatment or irrigation requirements. Electricity supply was erratic.

BUILDING CONDITIONS

Access to building materials was limited due to the remoteness of the location.

Significant Issues and Impact

DATA COLLECTION/SURVEYS

The documentation prepared before the interventions included an evaluation of all site features: rock outcrops, specimen trees, boundary condition, various trail opportunities, offsite views, adjacent development proposals and catchment dynamics. Prototypes of construction materials and details were produced early in the planning process to inform design and define acceptable levels of workmanship. Engineering flood-line calculations were required to establish a no-build zone.

MASTER PLANNING PROCESS

A general programme was detailed, stating intervention priorities, integration of capital works and management objectives such as sustainability. This led to the preparation of area plans, descriptions of works, operational standards and budgets.

PLANNING ISSUES

Site works were programmed to take advantage of dry weather for building and infrastructure, and natural rains for plantings. Shift work enabled paving manufacture and construction to take best advantage of the seasons. Elements such as roofs and street furniture were prefabricated to expedite works and counter seasonal installation constraints. Natural stone was easily available and an on-site factory for cutting stone pavers and wall-facing blocks was established. These finishes served as a unifying theme. An autonomous water-related infrastructure was planned with bore holes, water treatment reservoirs, pumps and a package sewage treatment plant. Scour valves were installed in existing dams and new flood detention basins created. Standby electricity generators were also included in the infrastructure package. As long as the Park remained unfenced, informal public use continued. Completion of

the perimeter fencing was necessary to secure the site and ensure public safety. Grazing is excluded from the park area. Loss of mature trees was a consideration in the planning and the minimum number, largely alien species, were felled to assimilate the design. Many new plantings have been provided as an offset. The vast majority of required plant material was obtained from local sources or grown on site. Emphasis was placed on the proactive conservation of existing mature vegetation to preserve the Park's character. The Park's natural fabric – valley gorges, rock outcrops, woodland and riverine forests, and a rich birdlife habitat – was preserved and will now be protected and enhanced.

HISTORIC BUILDINGS/MONUMENTS CONSERVED

Administration and maintenance functions were dispersed at the Park edge. Several buildings were rehabilitated for new use as boutiques, a food kiosk, tea-house, crèche and environmental education centre. A range of buildings including formal entrance points, a gym and youth club, an environment centre, boutique, administration office, two cafés and ablution facilities were either erected or rehabilitated and the National Museum landscape was redesigned.

Partners

PUBLIC PARTNERS

Ministry of Culture, Ministry of Environment and Sanitation, Republic of Mali.

COMMUNITY PARTNERS

Associations of Park Users, Sports Club, Environmental Club.

Authoritative Framework

'Letter of Intent' signed in April 2008 between AKTC and the Government of Mali. A 'Public-Private Partnership Agreement' with the Government of Mali was signed in 2010.

Damascus Houses

DAMASCUS, SYRIA

Considered one of the oldest continuously inhabited cities, Damascus displays in its urban fabric the remains of the successive civilizations inhabiting its site, the latter being, before contemporary times, the Ottomans, who have profoundly marked the city during their four hundred years of presence. Among the most significant palaces constructed during the classical Ottoman period in Damascus are Bait Sibai and Bait Nizam. They are typical Syrian courtyard residences, the result of intensive reconstruction works after the earthquake of 1759 and refurbished several times according to the fashion of the time. Instead, Bait Quwatli, built in 1868, contemporary to the arrival of telegraph communication and rail transport, shows Western influence adapted to the local taste and construction methods.

The involvement of the Aga Khan Trust for Culture (AKTC) in Damascus commenced in the last quarter of 2008 following the signature of project framework agreements in August 2008. AKTC and the Tourism Promotion Services of the Aga Khan Fund for Economic Development (AKFED) embarked on the development of two hotels of distinct nature: one converting the Aleppo municipal Serai dating from the early twentieth century; the other in the Old City of Damascus reusing three historical palaces – Bait Sibai, Nizam and Quwatli – that were carefully restored prior to conversion into a boutique hotel.

The properties, owned in the past by prominent Damascene families, had become government owned in 1974 and since then, in spite of temporary use as film sets or for receptions and high-profile events, had deteriorated to the point of collapse. Although major restoration was carried out by the authorities on Bait Sibai and Bait Nizam in the 1980s and on Bait Quwatli in the early 2000s, lack of use and maintenance led to rapid damage. When AKTC initiated architectural surveys and condition assessments, the analysis revealed that much of the damage was related to lack of use and maintenance. The buildings had also been subject to a large number of recent alterations.

The conceptual approach to the conservation of the palaces and adaptive reuse as a boutique hotel associated a cultural dimension of heritage conservation aimed at conserving the authenticity of the fabric and at ensuring long-term conservation and a for-profit activity of hospitality, providing economic opportunities

A bird's-eye view of the interior courtyard of Bait Sibai.

Opposite page:
A detail of the wall decoration in the *qa'a* off the second courtyard of Bait Nizam, sometimes known as the "Grapes Room".

Preceding pages:
The main *qa'a* of Bait Quwatli, one of three historical palaces the Trust is converting in Damascus.

1 Bait Sibai   **2** Bait Quwatli   **3** Bait Nizam

N

20 m

Programme Scope/Objectives

AKTC's role is to survey and document three Ottoman houses in Damascus's Old City, and then preserve, restore and rehabilitate them for reuse as a boutique hotel. The project aims to illustrate the potential for beneficial change and to create architectural prototypes that strengthen typical Damascene structures against seismic activity. Overall, this is an attempt to create an asset for sustainable tourism in Damascus that can inspire urban regeneration in neighbouring areas.

Top left, a view of the main *qa'a* of Bait Nizam.

Bottom left, the *qa'a* off the second courtyard.

Right, the courtyard and water fountain.

Opposite page:
A view from above of the interior
of Bait Quwatli.

and social development in the area: employment, training, open-space upgrading and tourism. Conversion into a hotel facility, therefore, not only continues the previous use of the palaces as private residences but also guarantees to the authorities that the asset will be managed and maintained.

In functional terms, the large culturally-sensitive halls, located mainly on the ground floor around vast courtyards, are used for public functions, while the first-floor spaces were converted into high-standard guest rooms. To minimize the impact of modern hotel services in the existing buildings, a large portion of back-of-house, technical services and guest rooms were accommodated in two new buildings designed on adjacent plots in substitution of two obsolete concrete buildings: an elementary school and a fire brigade.

The Syrian authorities view this project as an opportunity to set high standards in the country for adaptive reuse initiatives in sensitive buildings, a booming trend in Syria that poses quality challenges. Thus, emphasis is given to project methodology and process, calling for a large variety of specialists, both Syrian and international, and an important component of training and capacity building of local professionals and craftsmen.

Background

BRIEF HISTORY OF PROJECT SITE
Damascus, with six million inhabitants, is considered one of the world's oldest continuously inhabited cities. This site is profoundly marked by 400 years of Ottoman presence. Bait Sibai and Bait Nizam are typical Middle-Eastern courtyard residences, the result of intensive reconstruction works after the earthquake of 1759. Bait Quwatli, contemporary to the 19th-century arrival of telegraph communication and rail transport, shows Western influence adapted to local taste and construction methods.

Challenges

PROJECT RISKS
New uses for historic buildings might result in rising prices in the neighbourhood, and consequently induce gentrification. Socio-economic programmes are intended to balance such reactions. Heavy vehicular access, intensive commerce and a recent increase in international tourism can undermine the historical value and monumental qualities of the site.

SITE CONDITIONS
The Old City of Damascus remains an important centre of urban activity.

INFRASTRUCTURE
Parts of the site's infrastructure date to the Roman era, but most of its electricity, water and sewage networks were built during the French Mandate period and require upgrades for future needs. Sewage and water leakage is seeping into and damaging the historic built fabric.

BUILDING CONDITIONS
Bait Sibai and Bait Nizam have undergone previous conservation works, using methods such as cement repair and synthetic varnish that damaged the historic fabric. Bait Quwatli was used as a school and a Palestinian refugee camp before being abandoned, and is today in very poor condition.

Significant Issues and Impact

DATA COLLECTION/SURVEYS
A comprehensive architectural survey of the three houses was conducted by a local team of young professionals, trained in total station and rectified photography.

HISTORIC BUILDINGS/MONUMENTS CONSERVED
In addition to Bait Sibai, Bait Quwatli and Bait Nizam, neighbouring remnants of an Ayyubid wall and a *sabil* (public fountain) were included in the conservation project.

NEW BUILDING FACILITIES
Two modern, but obsolete structures were replaced by new buildings to accommodate the site's infrastructure while displaying a form and scale more appropriate in design for the Old City.

VOCATIONAL TRAINING/CAPACITY BUILDING
The architectural survey and restoration project (including conservation works in stone, wood, plaster and paint) provided several recently graduated architects and other building professionals with an opportunity

to acquire skills required for monument preservation, a field with potential in a city that includes a World Heritage Site.

CONTRACTING METHODS
Conservation work on areas with significant decoration or morphological value was carried out by labour directly recruited by AKTC. Reconstruction works were left to contractors under AKTC supervision.

Partners

PUBLIC PARTNERS
Ministry of Tourism, Ministry of Culture, Directorate General of Antiquities and Museums, Governorate of Damascus, Directorate of Old City of Damascus.

Donors

Tourism Promotion Services.

Authoritative Framework

'Tourism Investment Contract' between the Aga Khan Fund for Economic Development and the Government of Syria for the sites of the Damascus Hotel and Yalbougha Hammam and Serai Hotel in Aleppo, signed in August 2009.

ALEPPO

SYRIA

1 Citadel of Aleppo   2 Citadel Perimeter   3 Bab Qinessrine   ■ Intervention areas

N

200 m

FEATURED CASE STUDIES

CITADEL OF ALEPPO

CITADEL PERIMETER

BAB QINESSRINE

Aleppo Area Programme

Programme Scope/Objectives

In Aleppo, AKTC aims to revitalize the Old City and to bring social and economic benefit to its residents by restoring the Citadel and adding a visitor centre. The conservation and adaptive reuse of a historic *hammam* and government building into a hotel are also involved, as are the upgrading and landscaping of public space around the Citadel perimeter. The creation of a sustainable public park with development initiatives taking place in adjacent neighbourhoods is also part of the programme. This initiative relies on a 'Public-Private Partnership Framework', which is new to Syria.

Preceding pages:

As part of the Aleppo Area Programme, the Perimeter of the Citadel of Aleppo has been upgraded.

The Aga Khan Development Network (AKDN) has made a long-term commitment to working with the people and Government of Syria to support and contribute to the improvement of prospects for economic, social and cultural development. These efforts are undertaken within a 'Framework for Development Cooperation Agreement' between AKDN and the Government of Syria, which was ratified by the Syrian Parliament in 2002.

AKDN programmes in Syria span six provinces (Aleppo, Damascus, Hama, Lattakia, Sweida and Tartous), and serve both rural and urban populations. Priority areas include rural economic development, employment and enterprise development, enhancing the quality of services, strengthening civil society organizations, protecting cultural heritage and developing sustainable tourism.

The Aga Khan expressed the interest for AKDN in Syria: "My interest in working in Syria is to take the various lead countries of the *umma* and say, let's start, let's move together, let's revive our cultures so that modernity is not only seen in the terminology of the West, but in the intelligent use of our past."

The Historic Cities Programme (HCP) has been active in Syria since 1999, when the Government of the Republic of Syria approached the Aga Khan Trust for Culture (AKTC) for assistance in the restoration of the three citadels of Aleppo, Masyaf and Salah al-Din. A partnership agreement was signed with the Syrian General Directorate of Antiquities and Museums in 1999. Consistent with the Area Development approach developed by AKTC in Egypt, Pakistan and elsewhere, under the agreement AKTC would also work to improve the area around the Citadels. During the early stage of the Citadel restoration projects, HCP expanded the initial scope of pure conservation work to include the contextual dimensions of the three sites. Building on its work on the Citadel of Aleppo, HCP expanded its mandate to include the planning and landscaping of the Citadel Perimeter, the creation of a new Park, and social development projects in the Old City.

One of the oldest cities in the Middle East, Aleppo developed as a crossroads between East and West, straddling important trade routes linking the desert to the sea. Until 1930 the city remained more or less confined within its medieval boundaries, limited by its walls and early suburbs, which were surrounded by pistachio, fig and olive groves.

Today, approximately 100,000 people, or five per cent of the population of the city as a whole, live in the historic Old City. A great many monuments are

Phasing 2000 → 2010

Opposite page:

The work done at the Citadel (here, the entrance to the bridge tower) is a key component in the expansion of tourism in Syria.

Start of Aleppo Citadel conservation	Completion of Aleppo Citadel conservation	Start of Aleppo Citadel Perimeter urban upgrading	Completion of Aleppo Citadel Perimeter urban upgrading	Detailed design of BabQinessrine Park
2000	2006	2007	2009	2010

Above, a mason carries out arch consolidation work on an Ayyubid room at the Citadel.

Below, protective work on wood at Tower 42 is being carried out.

found amidst the historic fabric of the city and it was recognized by UNESCO as a World Heritage Site in 1986.

Within this World Heritage Site lies the Citadel of Aleppo, located at the heart of the Old City. The area around the Citadel used to act as an oversized roundabout, with a constant stream of vehicles cutting off access from and into the historic town and creating a rupture in the urban fabric. In 2006, HCP initiated a planning project on the Perimeter of the Citadel, working in close collaboration with the Old City Directorate and the German Technical Cooperation Agency (GTZ). The scope of the planning project includes major infrastructure improvements, traffic management plans, landscape design and proposals for the reuse of key historic structures.

In 2007, a 'Memorandum of Understanding' was signed between the Governorate of Aleppo and AKTC to create a Park located at the edge of the Old City and to formulate a socio-economic project in the surrounding neighbourhoods. Bab Qinessrine Park will be an important gateway to the Old City. Capitalizing on the efforts already undertaken on and around the Citadel, the Park will attract locals and tourists, thereby providing opportunities for employment and services.

Although Aleppo is the second largest city in Syria and receives over four million tourists every year, proceeds from tourism have not led to a status of relative well-being for the population living around the Citadel. Aleppo's population to the east and south of the Citadel is considered amongst Syria's most marginalized, with income levels per capita that are often below the level of US $1 per day. The reasons for this are numerous, but foremost amongst them are a general lack of employment opportunities, low education levels due to high drop-out rates and inadequate upkeep of residences.

Three key areas of socio-economic intervention have been established in the two neighbourhoods immediately adjacent to the future Bab Qinnesrine Park, with local needs researched through a baseline survey. These initiatives include increasing literacy levels amongst those above fifteen years of age; ensuring education for potential school drop-outs; increasing access to health and promotion, as well as revival of cultural heritage; raising family incomes through vocational training and employment; providing linkages with micro-credit; the improvement of access to and upgrading of open spaces; and the physical improvement of dwellings.

The thrust of these efforts in Aleppo is to enhance the historic urban fabric and stitch together two attractive poles on the northern and southern ends, realizing the potential for these projects to become significant contributors to the economic development of the Old City.

Citadel of Aleppo

ALEPPO, SYRIA

The Citadel of Aleppo is one of the remarkable examples of military architecture in the Middle East. The recently discovered Temple of the Storm God dates human use of the hill from the beginning of the third millennium BC. The Citadel of Aleppo, which has been built on a natural limestone hill, is the result of numerous constructive phases, large changes and destruction. The record of these changes is still recognizable in a few structures. Most of what remains today is from the Ayyubid and Mamluk periods. The monument represents a unique cultural heritage for the quality of the architecture, the variety and quality of the materials, and for the complexity of the historical stratifications.

The Citadel rises above the Old City of Aleppo, which since 1986 has been a UNESCO World Heritage Site. In the same time, the Citadel is the landmark for the new Aleppo, a city with almost two million inhabitants that attributes a strong symbolic value to the Citadel. Indeed, the site is one of the most famous monuments of Islamic architecture and one of the most visited sites in Syria.

The Aga Khan Trust for Culture (AKTC) signed a 'Memorandum of Understanding' with the Directorate General of Antiquities and Museums in Syria (DGAM) on 1 December 1999 to propose support in the restoration of three citadels in Syria (Aleppo, Masyaf and Salah al-Din).

The Citadel of Aleppo is a very large complex containing a series of buildings and monuments with different historical features, which call for a diversified approach and different forms of conservation and maintenance targeted to the specific requirements of each structure or category of structures. These can be listed as the bridge and the main gateway; the ring walls and the towers; the mosques; the cisterns; the palace complex; the arsenal; the *hammam*; the barracks; the tunnels; and the new theatre.

Three major axes of implementation were developed by AKTC from 2000 to 2008, after the finalization of the Master Plan in 2000.

The main goal of the Trust was to develop several levels of intervention: upgrade the local staff in the preservation of the masonry; the development of a real tourist infrastructure; and intervention in place of the local Directorate of Antiquities when foreign expertise was needed.

The bridge leads to the entrance complex.

Opposite page:
Above, the plan highlights the phases of work accomplished on the restoration of the Citadel.

Below, an aerial view of the Citadel that illustrates its position on top of a natural outcrop.

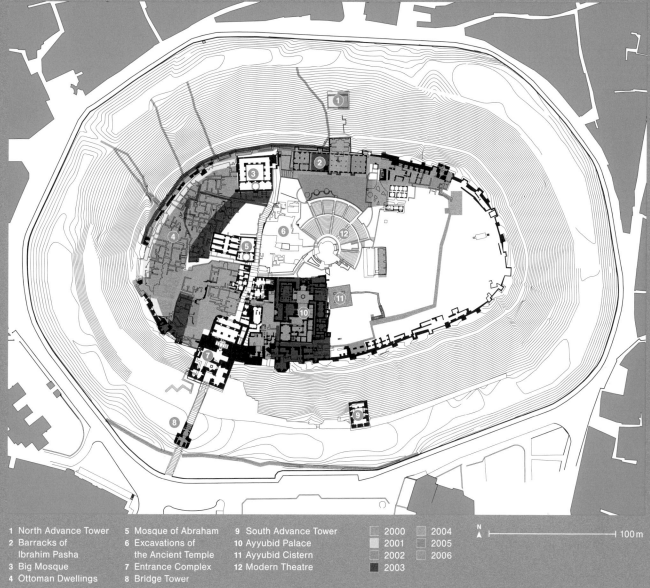

1 North Advance Tower	5 Mosque of Abraham	9 South Advance Tower	▢ 2000 ▢ 2004
2 Barracks of Ibrahim Pasha	6 Excavations of the Ancient Temple	10 Ayyubid Palace	▢ 2001 ▢ 2005
3 Big Mosque	7 Entrance Complex	11 Ayyubid Cistern	▢ 2002 ▢ 2006
4 Ottoman Dwellings	8 Bridge Tower	12 Modern Theatre	▢ 2003

N ⟶ 100m

Project Scope / Objectives

The goals of this restoration project are to train local Antiquities staff, engineers, contractors and craftsmen in up-to-date conservation techniques. The programme provides guidance on proper environmental protection and management of complete sites, the creation of visitor routes of tourist interest in neglected areas, and the creation of a visitor centre, equipped with documentation and guidebooks for visitors.

Top left and right, comparative views of
the Ottoman room and Arsenal entrance,
before and after restoration, exemplify
visitor path reclamation.

Bottom left and right, comparative views
of the main *qa'a* of the courtyard of the
Ayyubid palace, with a wall fountain in the
niche inside the northern *iwan*.

The Trust initiated a restoration project that included the preservation of remaining elements. This task concerns essentially the preservation of the medieval ruins, and consisted in a traditional but necessary exercise of masonry conservation. These interventions were completed over the years, through the training of the Antiquities staff, local engineers, contractors and craftsmen in up-to-date conservation techniques.

The Trust developed the visitor infrastructure, including the creation or upgrading of a ticket office, a visitor centre, paths, rest points and view points, signage, sanitation services, brochures and a guidebook. Through this initiative, the Citadel, along with those of Masyaf and Salah al-Din, was the first monument in Syria, to provide visitors with a comprehensive visit.

The Trust invested its expertise in the preservation of some highly sensitive buildings, such as the Ayyubid cistern and well. Plural-disciplinary teams were involved in the conservation of these two subterranean structures. High-technology techniques such as geo-radar analysis were used. The results of these analyses permitted the Trust to choose suitable techniques of conservation.

Since that time, in the Citadel of Aleppo, a considerable amount of work has been completed through cooperation with the Antiquities authorities. Only a number of historically or spatially coherent areas within the site were selected to become the focus of conservation efforts, with the intention that the DGAM would continue work elsewhere using methodologies and skills acquired during the implementation of the joint project.

The work has developed along the lines of international standards and methodology of restoration and rehabilitation. The choices made were the result of a careful analysis of the monument's history, of its present physical and figurative state, and of its conservation

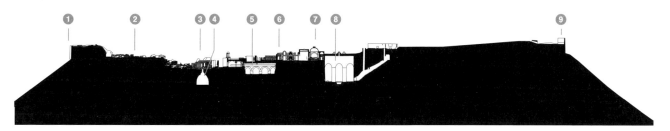

1 West Ring Wall Fortifications
2 Ottoman Dwellings and Streets
3 Hammam Nur al-Din

4 Souk Cistern
5 Persian-Byzantine Hall
6 Ayyubid Palace

7 Palace Hammam
8 Ayyubid Cistern
9 East Ring Wall Fortifications

⊢————————————————⊣ 100 m

A cross-section of the Citadel hill shows surface landmarks and underground spaces.

status. During these years in fact detailed surveys were carried out with the analysis of materials and systems of decay. The reconstruction or restoration of structures has sought to avoid the creation of facsimiles of how they might once have appeared as much as possible. The limited reconstruction of specific elements has been carried out only where it was absolutely necessary.

AKTC's work started in 2000 on one of the towers of the ring walls. From 2000 to 2008 the Trust initiated a large mission of surveys, to obtain documentation on the complete site. From 2001 to 2004 the Trust carried out sizeable works on large sections of the walls, including underpinning and important structural stabilization, as well as the consolidation of the northern advanced tower. During the years 2001 and 2002 the western area was the subject of a mission of archaeological excavation and conservation of the Ottoman remains discovered. In 2002 and 2003 pilot projects were developed on some major gullies located on the glacis. From 2002 to 2004 an important effort was made on the preservation of the Ayyubid Palace, a large complex including residential and reception functions. During these works the pavement of the central part of the main reception hall was restored. From 2002 to 2006 efforts were also concentrated on the development of the visitor infrastructure. In 2005 a reinforcement of the cladding stone of the glacis was implemented. From 2005 to 2007 the Trust worked on the conservation of the Ayyubid cistern and well, tasks that included structural reinforcement as well as architectural interventions. In 2007 the portal of the throne hall was completely cleaned. During 2008 a large mission of upgrading and cleaning the site was undertaken. The World Monuments Fund provided support for the work on the Ayyubid complex, some intervention on the ring walls, and participated in the archaeological excavations in the area of the temple, the Ayyubid cistern and the portal of the throne hall.

The Trust finalized its intervention by the definition of a cultural site management plan for the DGAM: a maintenance programme includes the routine upkeep of the structures and periodic checks to ensure that all mechanical systems are in working order, as well as repairs to materials and components that are subject to predictable wear and tear. But it was also important to include unplanned maintenance in this programme, in case

Recent excavations and subsequent conservation work have preserved a substantial Ottoman residential network in the western half of the site. This settlement featured a well-developed street and drainage network, and substantial improvements have been made to visitor pathways to enable access.

structural or mechanical components of a building are seriously impaired without prior warning. In these exceptional cases, prompt and effective interventions using appropriate equipment and personnel are crucial. The main maintenance-related problems in the Citadel could be subdivided into two major categories: management and technical.

Within the site, several archaeological excavations are still ongoing; the Citadel will be the subject of historical and archaeological research for several years. A first example is the Storm God Temple. Here the excavations are now almost concluded with the last two years' works funded by AKTC and the World Monuments Fund. The future use of the site once the work is completed should be considered beginning with the preliminary management phase. The most likely solution foresees the creation of an archaeological museum presenting the results of the excavations and the many important elements found during the excavations in the temple area, which will receive a 'roof' whose characteristics are still to be defined. Another example is the eastern part of the citadel: the reopening of this large archaeological area could eventually be undertaken by the DGAM at a later stage.

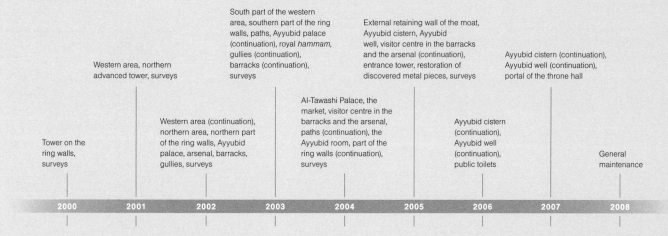

South part of the western
area, southern part of the ring
walls, paths, Ayyubid palace
(continuation), royal *hammam*,
gullies (continuation),
barracks (continuation),
surveys

External retaining wall of the moat,
Ayyubid cistern, Ayyubid
well, visitor centre in the barracks
and the arsenal (continuation),
entrance tower, restoration of
discovered metal pieces, surveys

Ayyubid cistern (continuation),
Ayyubid well (continuation),
portal of the throne hall

Western area, northern
advanced tower, surveys

Al-Tawashi Palace, the
market, visitor centre in the
barracks and the arsenal,
paths (continuation), the
Ayyubid room, part of the
ring walls (continuation),
surveys

Western area (continuation),
northern area, northern part
of the ring walls, Ayyubid
palace, arsenal, barracks,
gullies, surveys

Ayyubid cistern
(continuation),
Ayyubid well
(continuation),
public toilets

Tower on the
ring walls,
surveys

General
maintenance

2000   2001   2002   2003   2004   2005   2006   2007   2008

Background

BRIEF HISTORY OF PROJECT SITE

The Citadel of Aleppo stands at the centre of the Old City of Aleppo, which was recognized as a World Heritage Site by UNESCO in 1986. Situated on top of a natural limestone hill, the Citadel rises some 40 metres above its surroundings. Its high walls, imposing entry-bridge and great gateway remain largely intact, and continue to dominate the Aleppo skyline, a powerful symbol of the city's heroic past. The earliest archaeological evidence of occupation found in the Citadel date to the third millennium BC, although it is likely that the site was occupied even earlier. Most of what remains today are the ruins of military, ceremonial and residential structures built by the city's Ayyubid (12th to 13th centuries) and Mamluk (13th to 16th centuries) rulers.

Challenges

PROJECT RISKS

In addition to its status as a cultural and tourist attraction, the Citadel of Aleppo, was, is and will continue to be an archaeological site of great importance. These require different but compatible strategies concerning architectural preservation, structural safety, archaeological excavations, tourism, cultural events and maintenance.

SITE CONDITIONS

The ring wall foundations of the Citadel were in poor condition. Most of the area within the walls, including remnants of old buildings, was covered with earth, debris and overgrown vegetation.

INFRASTRUCTURE

The medieval drainage was full of debris and the long-neglected landscape prevented surface rainwater drainage, resulting in major leakage at the foot of the ring walls. Although several high-power electrical lines cross the site, no suitable electricity network existed within the Citadel.

BUILDING CONDITIONS

A succession of invasions, bombardments and earthquakes have taken their toll on the area within the ring walls, but amongst the ruins stand two fine mosques, a *hammam* and the remains of a palace and houses, dating to the Zengid, Ayyubid, Mamluk and Ottoman periods.

Significant Issues and Impact

DATA COLLECTION/SURVEYS

AKTC carried out architectural, structural and topographical surveys of the majority of the Citadel structures, moat and slopes. Areas of intervention were documented detailing conditions before, during and after restoration, conservation and rehabilitation works. Separate project documents were prepared in advance to any works.

MASTER PLANNING PROCESS

Prior to the work, a Master Plan was defined for future interventions. This plan was based on strategies related to emergency measures, drainage problems, archaeological areas, visitor infrastructure and the logical phasing of interventions.

PLANNING ISSUES

One of the project's aims was interpretation, to develop tourists' understanding of the site. Particular attention was paid to developing a tourist route (with signage) linking the major historical monuments in the Citadel. The trail is interspersed with shaded rest points and viewpoints with panoramas of the Citadel and city. A new visitor centre was equipped with information panels, brochures and guidebooks detailing the Citadel's historical evolution. Rubbish bins were installed and efforts made with the Directorate General of Antiquities and Museums (DGAM) of Syria to achieve better on-site waste collection but follow-up work is still required.

HISTORIC BUILDINGS/MONUMENTS CONSERVED

A large sector of the Citadel has now been preserved. The main structures are the Ayyubid complex, the western area, sections of the ring walls, the Ottoman barracks, the Ayyubid cistern, the well and the medieval paths. The monument's preservation entailed the revival of traditional building methods (such as lime-based mortar injection) that had disappeared during the last decades.

NEW BUILDING FACILITIES

Prior to AKTC interventions, there were no suitable structures for tourists. In cooperation with the DGAM of Syria, AKTC equipped the Citadel with a visitor centre and upgraded sanitation facilities in addition to rehabilitating the cafeteria located within the Citadel walls.

COMMUNITY INVOLVEMENT/PROGRAMME

At the project's outset, meetings were held with the DGAM of Syria to define and agree on interventions for the Citadel's major historical sites.

VOCATIONAL TRAINING/CAPACITY BUILDING

AKTC initiated training sessions and programmes to provide the DGAM of Syria, contractors and craftsmen with instruction in methodologies for documentation and conservation. Specialized and accredited international and local experts conducted the training.

CONTRACTING METHODS

The choice of contractors was based on tender procedures after selected invitations.

RELEVANT CODES/STANDARDS ADOPTED

Local codes and international standards.

Partners

PUBLIC PARTNERS

Directorate General of Antiquities and Museums, Governorate of Aleppo, Municipality of Aleppo, Directorate of Old City of Aleppo.

Donors

World Monuments Fund.

Authoritative Framework

On 1 December 1999, AKTC signed a 'Memorandum of Understanding' with the Directorate General of Antiquities and Museums of Syria for providing support and expertise to the 'Restoration of Three Citadels in Syria'. One of these sites was the Citadel of Aleppo.

Citadel Perimeter

ALEPPO, SYRIA

The Citadel of Aleppo is the centre of a historic city, which is registered as a World Cultural Heritage Site. The conservation project undertaken by the Directorate General of Antiquities and Museums (DGAM) and the Aga Khan Trust for Culture (AKTC) within the Citadel of Aleppo underlined the need for an intervention at its perimeter. Within the scope of the 'Project for the Rehabilitation of the Old City of Aleppo', an urban design study was implemented for the Perimeter of the Citadel of Aleppo, in cooperation with the Old City Directorate and GTZ (German Technical Cooperation Agency). The City of Aleppo and AKTC signed a protocol in 2003 detailing the objectives and conditions of this study.

One of the main objectives of the Citadel Perimeter project involved the planning and control of the spread of commercial functions in ways that might jeopardize the comfort, economy and environment of the adjacent residential areas. It was also important to open new cultural development opportunities through the reuse of existing historic buildings and to steer tourist and commercial functions into a direction that is beneficial to the particular areas involved and the Old City in general.

Condition of the Perimeter of the Citadel of Aleppo

The traffic situation of the Aleppo Citadel Perimeter was no longer suitable for the quality of such an exceptional site. An appropriate traffic management system supported the function of the central commercial zone created by the souks of the Old City. The optimization of traffic permitted the creation of the main public spaces as a representative cultural zone for the whole city.

The main objectives for the Old City comprise reorientation of the traffic in and around the Citadel area, including pedestrian issues, public transport networks and parking areas; the control of future planning and the protection of the physical and historical environment of the Citadel Perimeter; the control of the spread of commercial functions in ways that might jeopardize the comfort, economy and environment of residential areas; steering the commercial development in a direction that is most beneficial to the particular areas involved and the Old City in general as tourism activity; protecting the surrounding residential areas, especially from the pressure of commercial functions; adoption of a land-use

The area outside the Citadel has become a popular spot for people to gather and relax. The site was planted with palm trees and seating was added (opposite).

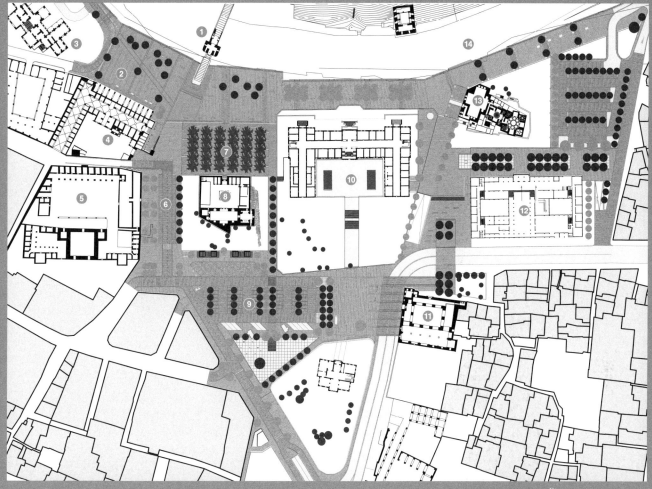

1 Bridge and Tower (entrance to Citadel)
2 Esplanade with outside cafés
3 Old National Hospital converted into a hotel
4 Khan ash-Shoune (handicraft market)
5 Mosque al-Khosrowiya (religious school)
6 Esplanade (parking and access to the Old City quarters)
7 Esplanade (pedestrian area planted with palm trees)

8 Madrasa al-Sultaniya (mosque)
9 Future underground parking and above ground bus station
10 New Serai (former governorate offices soon to be a hotel)
11 Djami' al-Otrush (mosque)
12 Justice Palace
13 Hammam Yalbougha al-Nasri
14 Moat

N ⊢———⊣ 50 m

Project Scope / Objectives

The scope of work included topographical, traffic, architectural, land-use and economical surveys as well as historical research of each component of the Citadel of Aleppo site. Project development included the creation of a vast pedestrian area at the foot of the entrance to the Citadel, and an appropriately scaled landscape suitable for the urban spaces located on its perimeter.

Before its development, the Perimeter was clogged with traffic, as pictured above, while now (opposite) it has become a people-friendly area and the New Serai, seen in the background, is currently being transformed into a hotel.

plan that enhances the tourist and cultural functions and complements rehabilitation efforts; proposition for future use of each of the major public or vacant buildings; and the improvement of public spaces, infrastructure elements, landscaping, pavements, lighting, details and so on.

Potentials of the Perimeter of the Citadel

The Citadel and its surroundings are one of the most famous cultural heritage sites in the Near East. They are at the heart of a lively historic town and the traditional administrative centre of the city. The Citadel is the landmark of a city of two million inhabitants and of high value for the image of the city. Together with its surroundings, the Citadel is a recreational area for residents and visitors, a cultural attraction of international and national standing, and an archaeological site of great importance for scientific research.

An Urban Study

The Citadel Perimeter envelope is a conglomeration of attractive historic buildings and plain new structures, creating a facade unified only through the use of limestone as its main building material. Its open spaces were poorly defined and badly employed. A privileged zone of the Aleppo Citadel Perimeter was the southern area of the project and in particular the area between the souk entrance and Yalbougha Hammam. This newly created pedestrian plaza now serves as a recreational and pleasure outlet for area residents, and for those of the city as a whole. It also acts as an attractive tourist activity zone. The proper conception of the overall design, details of the surface treatment, urban furniture and other essential elements in a pedestrian public space for creating an amiable urban area were essential to the success of the project. Reference to the traditional urban landscape was a priority, but as a voluntary spirit of continuity and not as an effort to create facsimiles or copies. The project completes the signature of each historical building from the different eras in a real sense of local modernity. Preferences were always given to local techniques and materials with durable qualities implemented by local labour.

Implementation

The implementation of the traffic concept under existing conditions proved to be a complex exercise in its own right. Accordingly the execution of the whole project was divided into five phases. Zone 3, the plaza across from the Citadel entrance, was funded by AKTC and is now completed. Zones 1 and 2 were funded by the Directorate of the Old City and completed in 2010. Zones 4 and 5, the car parks and the completion of the pedestrian zones, will be the subject of a tender procedure after final approval of the local authorities.

Background

BRIEF HISTORY OF PROJECT SITE

The Citadel of Aleppo is one of the most remarkable examples of Islamic military architecture in the Middle East and one of the foremost visited sites in Syria. It is also a landmark of strong symbolic value for Aleppo's two million inhabitants. Its periphery features buildings from a range of periods (13th to 20th centuries).

Challenges

PROJECT RISKS

The spread of commercial activities in the Citadel Perimeter may jeopardize the comfort, economy and environment of the adjacent residential areas, and therefore requires planning and controls.

SITE CONDITIONS

The area defined by Aleppo Citadel and its periphery was a large open space subject to heavy vehicular and pedestrian traffic. Many of the buildings on the Citadel Perimeter were used for administrative functions unrelated to the Old City and with no positive impact on the area.

INFRASTRUCTURE

Drainage, water supply, electricity and telephone systems were inadequate in varying degrees and in need of upgrades. The quality of the water network was very poor, often interrupted, and leakage had damaged buildings, especially at basement levels. Replacing the visually disruptive power cables crossing the site with an underground network presented a major challenge.

Significant Issues and Impact

DATA COLLECTION/SURVEYS

In addition to a detailed topographical survey, basic field data was collected for the demography and environment; existing traffic conditions; existing and future land use; definition of interesting buildings and houses; future functions of specific buildings and legal status of the lots.

MASTER PLANNING PROCESS

A study for a new concept of traffic in the Old City and in particular for the Citadel Perimeter was performed in cooperation with GTZ (German Technical Cooperation Agency) and the Directorate of the Old City. Based on the analysis of these data, the Master Plan was developed. The principal objective was to divert through traffic away from the Old City by proposing an efficient public transport system, providing appropriate parking facilities, offering an environmentally attractive design for the newly gained pedestrian areas between the Citadel and the New Serai, and beneficially redirecting the spread of commercial activities around the Citadel Perimeter. The esplanade in front of the entrance to the Citadel would provide the only public open space in the Old City. The integrative urban concept was prepared, with special attention paid to landscaping quality, and presented to the local authorities.

PLANNING ISSUES

Convincing the local authorities to suppress a major traffic axis and replace it with a mainly pedestrian area was difficult, but successful. Cultural development opportunities were generated by reusing existing historic buildings on the perimeter and steering tourist and commercial functions in a direction beneficial to the Old City. The project has resulted in an increased value of the lots within the Citadel Perimeter and revived commercial investment in the area.

HISTORIC BUILDINGS/MONUMENTS CONSERVED

The historical, architectural and cultural value of each building on the Citadel Perimeter was evaluated. Public administrative functions were relocated to the modern city centre and the buildings rehabilitated to serve tourist or cultural functions. The quality of both the stone available in the area and the stonework produced by local masons was outstanding and lent coherency to the project.

NEW BUILDING FACILITIES

A tourist centre, exchange points and public toilets were integrated in the project as were electricity substations to solve the lack of electricity supply in the area.

COMMUNITY INVOLVEMENT/PROGRAMME

Decisions regarding the reorientation of traffic in and around the Citadel area, developing pedestrian areas and creating controlled service roads were the result of meetings with the inhabitants, businesses and local authorities. Workshops with inhabitants and local authorities were organized throughout the development of the final design and during execution.

CONTRACTING METHODS

The choice of contractors was based on tender procedures after selected invitations. The sense of architectural micro-detail was a constant issue of discussion with the contractors and their teams, in the expectation that this approach might impact future projects developed by the city.

RELEVANT CODES/STANDARDS ADOPTED

Local codes upgraded by international standards.

Partners

PUBLIC PARTNERS

Directorate of Old City of Aleppo, Directorate General of Antiquities and Museums, Ministry of Tourism, Directorate of Electricity, Directorate of Water.

Donors

GTZ (Deutsche Gesellschaft für Technische Zusammenarbeit).

Authoritative Framework

Protocol signed between AKTC and the City Council in 2003.

Bab Qinessrine Park

ALEPPO, SYRIA

The Bab Qinessrine Park project is the result of a previous engagement by the Aga Khan Trust for Culture (AKTC) in the conservation of three historic citadels in Syria over 1999–2005, including the Citadel of Aleppo and the planning and redesign of the latter's urban Perimeter space. This first phase of engagement by the Trust in Syria was marked by the inauguration of the Citadel of Aleppo by His Highness the Aga Khan in 2008. The seventeen-hectare site of the future Park lies in a strategic location, just outside the city's historic walls, and takes its name from the south-western gate itself. The site is just a hundred metres from the Grand Mosque and traditional souk and only another forty metres from the Citadel of Aleppo.

The proposal for the redevelopment of the mostly barren site into a municipal Park was one advanced by the Government of Syria following a visit of high-level officials to Azhar Park in Cairo (see p. 310). Similarities between the former condition of the site in Cairo and that of Bab Qinessrine are striking: in their pre-existing states, these two sites represented mostly marginalized inner urban land, just outside the historic city walls, adjacent to economically challenged but vibrant communities, with considerable topography and poor soils. The Syrian authorities were keen to apply similar methods used in Cairo to this disadvantaged but central site.

Beyond the above-mentioned physical constraints, impediments to the project existed in the site's western edge where mid-rise multi-family housing blocks had experienced differential settlement, a large percentage of which had already been condemned, residents relocated and the buildings demolished. A remaining series of buildings await similar evacuation. Park design proposals also need to take into account the mosque and small cemetery located on the site's north-western corner and two known caves which run roughly north-south in the chalk strata below the site.

As is often the case, certain site constraints can be advantages, such as the high elevation of the central part of the site which affords views northwards towards the city gate and the Citadel. With careful master grading, the site will allow for a three-dimensional landscape with terracing of planted and walking areas and facilities that will provide interesting views over the city and city walls.

A bird's-eye view from the main retail spine shows the upper plateau, the lake and Bab Qinessrine Gate in the distance.

Opposite page:
The area where the Park will be developed is currently in a state of neglect.

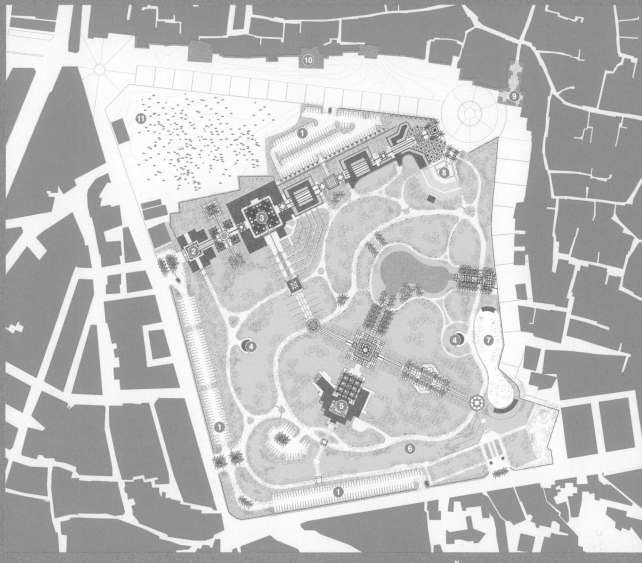

1	Parking	4	Cafeteria	7	Children's Play Area	10	Ayyubid Wall
2	Main Entrance	5	Restaurant	8	Amphitheatre	11	Existing Cemetery
3	Shopping Bazaar	6	Cave Area	9	Bab Qinessrine		

N ⊢————————————————⊣ 150 m

Project Scope / Objectives

Bab Qinessrine is an area of waste ground outside the Old City walls where AKTC is developing a Park to provide green space and to form a visitor circuit through the Old City. The Park is the core component of what is expected to become an urban regeneration project in the immediate area through a package of initiatives, including environmental rehabilitation and economic and social improvements, with additional benefits from private inward investment as a complement to the Park investment, and with public-sector investments on the periphery for roadways and other similar public infrastructure.

The Park is planned to feature a palm-lined walkway with water channels and fountains.

The Park's Master Plan design has been entrusted to the Cairo-based practice, Sites International, landscape architects for Azhar Park.

The Park design consists of two major zones with distinct design themes. The first zone occupies the northern area of the site alongside Bab Qinessrine Gate's approach road, consisting of a series of courtyard and low-scale retail modules arranged on both sides of a wide promenade punctuated with pools and fountains and lined with trees. Designed to accommodate large numbers of strollers and to provide diverse retail and food and beverage outlets, this zone will allow the Park to generate funds for its ongoing operations while screening the northern parking zone from the main park area.

The second and far larger Park zone consists of the sloping areas of the site, designed to provide areas for leisure along curvilinear paths and terraces. At the northern end an amphitheatre has been set into the slope at the eastern end of the main promenade, facing the historic city gate itself. The higher areas of the Park to the south will contain a small lake, a playground for children, a café and, at the highest point, a restaurant with indoor and outdoor seating for residents and tourists.

The Park design process has been accompanied by careful deliberation and planning with the Governorate of Aleppo regarding an appropriate future management system for the Park that will safeguard the quality and finish of the completed project. The Trust has entered into a 'Memorandum of Understanding' whereby the Park will be designed, built and then managed by the Trust for a period of time, allowing the management system to be put in place and operated in the best interest of park users, the city of Aleppo and neighbouring communities.

As the Park planning and design proceed, AKTC is in close coordination with the Aleppan authorities in the development of a series of proposals that aim at enhancing the quality of life in the adjacent communities. A socio-economic baseline survey has been undertaken to assess the present quality of life indicators and to identify the highest priority needs, and a community-based office has been set up. Consistent with other AKTC projects in inner city areas, the Park and socio-economic projects will be coordinated to provide a multiplicity of linkages and benefits across the project areas.

Above, a fountain in the midst of a square can be seen in the foreground of a view along the retail spine towards the Citadel of Aleppo and Bab Qinnesrine Gate.

Left, a view of the vacant land where the Park will be developed. The Citadel rises in the background.

CITADEL RESTORATION PROGRAMME
SYRIA

Citadel of Masyaf

MASYAF, SYRIA

Located in central western Syria, the town of Masyaf nestles on the eastern slope of the coastal mountains. The Citadel of Masyaf, which is built on a rocky promontory, is the result of several phases and is marked by considerable changes and destruction. The record of these changes is still recognizable in a few structures. The monument represents a unique cultural heritage for the quality of the architecture, the variety and quality of the materials and for the complexity of the historical stratifications. The Citadel rises at the eastern side of the Old City and is a landmark for the whole city. The site is one of the most famous monuments of the Islamic architecture of the coastal region. Furthermore, the Citadel can be the object of important archaeological investigations in the future.

The Aga Khan Trust for Culture (AKTC) signed a 'Memorandum of Understanding' with the Directorate General of Antiquities and Museums in Syria (DGAM) on 1 December 1999 to present support in the restoration of three citadels in Syria (Aleppo, Masyaf and Salah al-Din). Since that time a considerable amount of work has been completed in the Citadel of Masyaf through cooperation with the Antiquities department.

Most of the areas within the site were selected to become the focus of conservation efforts, with the intention that the DGAM would continue work elsewhere using methodologies and skills acquired during the joint project implementation. The work has been developed following international standards and methodology of conservation, restoration and rehabilitation. The choices made were the result of in-depth analyses of the monument's history, of its present physical and figurative state, and of its conservation status. Surveys were carried out with the analysis of materials and systems of decay.

The Citadel of Masyaf is a very dense complex containing a series of buildings and monuments with different historic elements and features, which called for a diversified approach and different forms of conservation and maintenance targeted to the specific requirements of each structure or category of structures.

The main structures are the barbican, the *hammam*, the stair and the main gateway; the ring wall and the towers; the south-western compound of the outer citadel; the tunnel, the cisterns and the store rooms; the eastern and western terraces; the donjon or inner castle; and the palace complex containing the Byzantine castle.

The facade of the Citadel of Masyaf, seen from the south, after several modern houses that had encroached on it have been removed.

Opposite page:
Above, an exploded axonometric plan showing the various levels and structures contained within the Citadel.
Below, masons are pictured working on the West Terrace.

Preceding pages:
The Castle of Salah al-Din is located on the western slope of the Syrian coastal mountains at an altitude of 400 to 460 metres. The lower town is on the right, the upper plateau on the left, and the remains of the Byzantine citadel can be seen above.

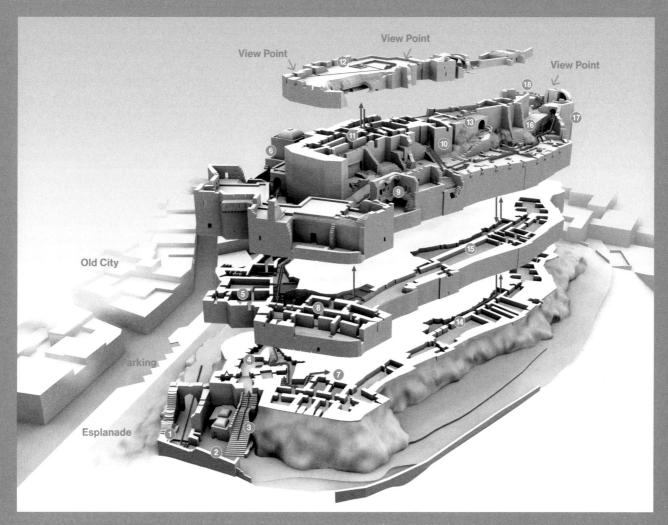

Old City

Parking

Esplanade

View Point

View Point

View Point

1 Barbican
2 *Hammam*
3 Stairway
4 Entrance Complex, lower level
5 Entrance Complex, upper level, visitor centre
6 Western Ottoman House – visitor centre
7 Southern Defensive Complex, lower level – tickets, information and bookshop
8 Southern Defensive Complex, upper level
9 Eastern Ottoman House
10 Stairway to Inner Castle-Palace
11 Inner Castle-Palace, lower level – northern and southern sections
12 Inner Castle-Palace, upper level
13 Quarter attributed to Sinan Rashid ad-Din
14 Eastern Front, lower level
15 Eastern Front, upper level
16 Tombs – hypogea from the Byzantine period
17 Room with distinctive plaster
18 Defensive Tower Terrace

Project Scope / Objectives

The scope of tasks included documentation, historic research and the definition of principles for the conservation of masonry. The project included the development of techniques for stabilization and structural reinforcement, and masonry conservation and major repairs. HCP was involved in the creation of tourism infrastructure and the access esplanade. Brochures and guidebooks for tourists were also created.

Right, east-west section of the Citadel, showing the outer and inner castle erected on the excavated promontory.

Opposite page:
The Citadel seen from the south-west with the town of Masyaf in the foreground.

1 Cistern
2 Outer Castle Eastern Front
3 Eastern Ottoman House
4 Entrance to the Palace
5 Inner Castle
6 Outer Castle Western Front
7 Western Ottoman House

⊢———————————⊣ 20 m

An access corridor in the Citadel is a 60-metre-long tunnel divided into sections separated by raised arches.

The project began in 2000 with the documentation work and the definition of the concept and principles of the preservation process. During the whole mission, detailed documentation was created, including topographical and architectural surveys of the six main levels of the Citadel. Plans of these levels and precise sections were drawn.

In 2001 the consolidation of the eastern wall was executed. As the structural base of the historic Citadel, the rocky promontory was also the object of periodic controls.

From 2001 to 2003 efforts concentrated on the core of the Citadel, and in particular on the western and eastern areas, which presented major structural issues. During this period, archaeological excavations were carried out.

From 2002 to 2004 the Trust completed the work on the upper levels. In the whole Citadel, drainage problems have been resolved by channelling water away from the walls' foundations towards the interior areas of the complex. Rain falls have been redefined to avoid concentration of groundwater near the walls to avoid aggravating the existing problems of erosion and the future occurrence of landslides: although both the ring walls and the walls existing within the Citadel have been repaired and often rebuilt with protective caps. The realization of the screeds on the terraces was executed according to traditional local techniques.

The preservation of the entrance complex, in and out of the portal, was undertaken during 2004 and 2005. Tasks were consolidation of the *hammam*, preservation of the barbican and the removal of the former modern stair access to the Citadel in favour of the rediscovered medieval access.

In 2006 and the beginning of 2007 the Trust concentrated its efforts on the development of visitor infrastructure: access, visitor centre, paths, signage and sanitation facilities. The Historic Cities Programme (HCP) has undertaken a review of the present Master Plan of the city of Masyaf. The project envisaged the improvement of the Citadel's urban context. In this framework, the immediate proximity of the Citadel was considered as an indivisible part of the historic site. The esplanade and the western terraces as well as the eastern terraces were created. Subsequently, brochures and a guidebook were published.

Background

BRIEF HISTORY OF PROJECT SITE
The town of Masyaf is located in the centre of the Syrian coastal mountains. Masyaf Citadel is one of the most intact medieval strongholds of the Syrian littoral. Built on a rocky promontory, most of the Citadel's extant structures date to the Ismaili occupation (12th and 13th centuries) when Masyaf was their state capital. A Byzantine structure that pre-dates the Citadel was included in the medieval fortress. In the Ottoman period some constructions were added. During the 20th century the Citadel was the subject of several consolidation campaigns, performed without any historical or architectural basis. Prior to HCP intervention the site was completely abandoned.

Challenges

PROJECT RISKS
The site analysis and definition of new structures and historical ruins represented a challenge, as did the effort of de-restoration (removing former substandard conservation and reinforcement works).

SITE CONDITIONS
Bombardments, erosion, human impact and long-term abandonment caused deterioration to the site. The western approach to the Citadel was blocked by a series of shabby informal apartment buildings.

INFRASTRUCTURE
The site lacked all electricity, water, rainwater and waste drainage infrastructure.

BUILDING CONDITIONS
The Citadel was in an advanced state of decay. Parts of the ring walls had collapsed.

Significant Issues and Impact

DATA COLLECTION/SURVEYS
AKTC carried out architectural, structural and topographical surveys of most of the site, documenting areas of intervention and detailing conditions before conservation or rehabilitation works.

MASTER PLANNING PROCESS
A general plan was defined for strategies related to emergency measures, drainage problems, visitor infrastructure and the phasing of interventions. The objective was to restore the Citadel and make it a catalyst for socio-economic development in the city, particularly through tourism. After its preservation, the Citadel was included within the 'National Plan' defined by the Ministry of Tourism. The number of visitors increased from less than 500 per year to more than 6000 in 2009.

PLANNING ISSUES
To develop visitor facilities, minimal but efficient infrastructure networks were planned and installed in co-operation with the Directorate General of Antiquities and Museums (DGAM). One of the major interventions was the development of tourist interpretation at the site. In addition to the tourist trail and signage, brochures and guidebooks were planned for availability in a new visitor centre. To enhance the appearance of the esplanade, and reproduce a view of the Citadel as it was in medieval times, the natural rock of the site was exposed and cleaned, and electrical networks were installed underground.

HISTORIC BUILDINGS/MONUMENTS CONSERVED
The Citadel and its immediate surroundings were the main conservation project.

NEW BUILDING FACILITIES
The Trust purchased 12 blocks of buildings blocking the western approach to the Citadel in 2003 and replaced them with an esplanade. Parking for tourist buses and cars was provided. A visitor centre and sanitation facilities were created, and a tourist route was defined and equipped with signage.

VOCATIONAL TRAINING/CAPACITY BUILDING
Accredited international and local experts conducted training sessions and programmes in up-to-date methodologies of documentation and conservation for the benefit of DGAM staff, contractors and craftsmen.

CONTRACTING METHODS
AKTC carried out most of the works with a team directly employed by the Trust in order to upgrade local restoration skills. Contractors were chosen for structural reinforcements of the ring walls, based on tender procedures after selected invitations.

NEW TECHNOLOGIES INTRODUCED
The monument's preservation entailed the revival of traditional building methods (such as lime-based mortar injection) that had disappeared during the last decades.

Partners

PUBLIC PARTNERS
Directorate General of Antiquities and Museums, Governorate of Hama, City Council of Masyaf Town.

Authoritative Framework

On 1 December 1999 AKTC signed a 'Memorandum of Understanding' with the Directorate General of Antiquities and Museums of Syria for providing support to the 'Restoration of Three Citadels in Syria'. One of these three sites was the Citadel of Masyaf. In 2001 the Trust signed a protocol with the Governorate of Hama and the City of Masyaf.

Castle of Salah al-Din

HAFFAH, SYRIA

The Castle rises amidst spectacular landscape and, together with the Crac des Chevaliers, was included in UNESCO's World Heritage List in 2006. Indeed, the site is one of the most famous monuments of Islamic architecture and one of the most visited places in Syria (around 100,000 visitors in 2008).

Its successive occupants were the Byzantines, the Franks, the Ayyubids and the Mamluks. The site is the result of numerous construction phases and the record of changes is still recognizable in most of the structures. The monument represents a unique cultural heritage for the quality of its military architecture, the variety and quality of the materials, and for the complexity of the historical stratifications, as well as for its environmental surroundings.

The Aga Khan Trust for Culture (AKTC) signed a 'Memorandum of Understanding' with the Directorate General of Antiquities and Museums in Syria (DGAM) on 1 December 1999 to provide support in the restoration of three citadels in Syria (Aleppo, Masyaf and Salah al-Din). Since that time a considerable amount of work has been completed with the cooperation of the Antiquities authorities.

The Castle of Salah al-Din is perched at an altitude of approximately 450 metres on a long rocky spur stretching from east to west and divided into two plateaux separated by a steep ridge. Only a number of historically or spatially coherent areas within the site were selected to become the focus of conservation efforts, with the intention that the DGAM would continue work elsewhere using methodologies and skills acquired during the joint project implementation. The work has been developed according to international standards and methodology of restoration and rehabilitation. The choices made were the result of in-depth analyses of the monument's history, of its present physical and figurative state, and of its conservation or rehabilitation status.

The Castle of Salah al-Din is a very large complex containing a series of buildings and monuments of different historical periods, which call for a diversified approach and different forms of conservation and maintenance targeted to the specific requirements of each structure or category of structures.

The main structures are the moat and the needle; the main gateway; the ring walls; the towers and the master tower; the Byzantine fortress and ramparts; the

This view of the Castle reveals its Frankish fortifications resting on top of cut bedrock, with the rectangular tower and the moat in the foreground.

Opposite page:
A guide shows visitors around the pillared hall constructed in the Islamic period.

■ Byzantine period 1		■ Frankish period 3	
■ Byzantine period 2		■ Frankish period 4	
■ Frankish period 1		■ Islamic period 1	
■ Frankish period 2		■ Islamic period 2	

1 Tower Gates	**5** Byzantine Palace	**9** Main Cistern	**12** Needle
2 Chapel	**6** Southern Gate to Lower Town	**10** Ayyubid Palace and	**13** Frankish Gate
3 Lower Western Town	**7** Industrial Sector	Islamic Complex	**14** Moat
4 Burj al-Banat	**8** Byzantine Fortress	**11** Byzantine Rampart	**15** Master Tower

N ⊢————————⊣ 100 m

Project Scope / Objectives

The scope of work included architectural, archaeo-logical and historical research, documentation and actual conservation of the Salah al-Din Palace. The implementation on site mainly concerned the conservation of the Islamic complex: the mosque, palace and *hammam*. Tourist infrastructure was also created.

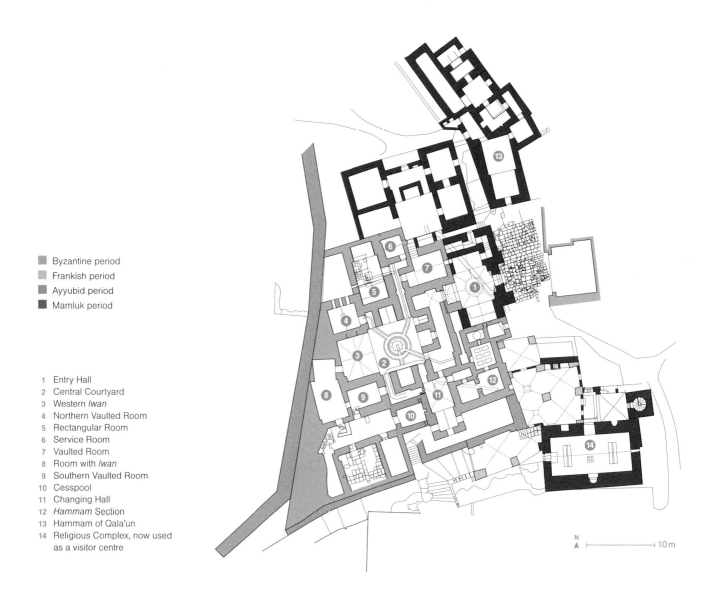

Byzantine period
Frankish period
Ayyubid period
Mamluk period

1 Entry Hall
2 Central Courtyard
3 Western *Iwan*
4 Northern Vaulted Room
5 Rectangular Room
6 Service Room
7 Vaulted Room
8 Room with *Iwan*
9 Southern Vaulted Room
10 Cesspool
11 Changing Hall
12 *Hammam* Section
13 Hammam of Qala'un
14 Religious Complex, now used
   as a visitor centre

N
A ⊢————————⊣ 10 m

This plan illustrates the historical chronology of the Ayyubid palace area on the upper plateau to the east of the Byzantine fortress.

Islamic complex (including the mosque, the palace and the public *hammam*); and the Lower Town, walls and towers and the two tower-gates.

During the years of the mission of the Historic Cities Programme (HCP), detailed surveys were carried out with the analysis of materials and systems of decay. An extensive programme of documentation, archaeological excavation, and historical and architectural analysis for the conservation and restoration work was carried out on the Islamic-era remains of the Castle, as well as the completion of tourism facilities.

The conservation work concentrated on the Islamic complex, and particularly on the mosque, the public *hammam* and the residential palace. The archaeological excavations, done in the palace to gain a better understanding of the complex, were led by a multidisciplinary team of Syrian and international specialists. The mosque and the adjacent building were rehabilitated as the visitor centre. Tourist paths and signage were executed in complete respect of the environmental topography of the site. The entrance tower was upgraded to offer visitors a suitable ticket and information space; the cafeteria was also upgraded; sanitation facilities were installed outside the limit of the fortifications; and brochures and a guidebook were published.

In terms of cultural site management, a maintenance programme includes the routine upkeep of the structures and periodic checks to ensure that all mechanical systems are in working order, as well as repairs to materials and components that are subject to predictable wear and tear.

Furthermore, the Castle is still the subject of archaeological investigations and historic research. The main areas of potential research concern firstly, an area east of the Islamic complex, the Byzantine rampart, which is partially under excavation. Some Ayyubid structures appear, and some excavations in this area could be of interest. Secondly, the DGAM has partially cleaned the lower part of the Castle. The need and effect of these excavations is evident for understanding the whole of the Lower Town. And thirdly the industrial sector and the area north of the Byzantine fortress where some excavations are needed for a better comprehension of the economic activities in the Castle.

The conservation work has been performed by local craftsmen. This choice seems successful, since, from the time of the HCP interventions, the DGAM in Syria, through its Department in Lattakia, is continuing this project with the restoration of certain Byzantine, Frankish and Islamic structures.

A bird's-eye view of the Castle showing its position on a long narrow ridge encompassed by a gorge on either side.

Background

BRIEF HISTORY OF PROJECT SITE
Standing against the striking backdrop of the Syrian coastal mountains, the Castle of Salah al-Din bears witness to more than 1000 years of history. The remains date to the Byzantine, Frankish, Ayyubid and Mamluk periods. These successive occupants did not destroy their predecessors' work, but instead strengthened existing structures and expanded the site to create the largest enclosed fortification in the Middle East. The only restoration of the site was performed by French architects in 1937 and 1940. A rare melange of architectural styles, the Castle, along with Crac des Chevaliers, was listed as a UNESCO World Heritage Site in 2006.

Challenges

PROJECT RISKS
Interventions needed to preserve the topography and vegetation that contribute to the site's evocative atmosphere.

SITE CONDITIONS
Prior to HCP interventions, the site had been long abandoned. Located in an area of heavy rainfall, the site was severely eroded and overgrown.

INFRASTRUCTURE
Electric cables and telephone lines were installed at the Castle entrance and remedial lighting was provided in some areas by the Directorate General of Antiquities and Museums (DGAM). Aside from these interventions, there was no infrastructure on site.

BUILDING CONDITIONS
Except for the main tower and parts of the fortifications, the structure had suffered from more than 60 years of abandonment. The first floor of the Ayyubid palace was no longer visible and the *hammam* was in ruins. Most roofs were not intact and water leakage affected most of the covered spaces.

Significant Issues and Impact

DATA COLLECTION/SURVEYS
Prior to the intervention of the Trust, site documentation consisted of several imprecise drawings. AKTC carried out architectural, structural and topographical surveys of the Islamic complex.

MASTER PLANNING PROCESS
A general plan for future interventions was based on strategies related to emergency measures, drainage problems, visitor infrastructure and phasing of the work.

PLANNING ISSUES
Improving tourist interpretation was a major concern. In addition to the design and execution of tourist trails and signage, a visitor centre was planned, including historical information panels, newly published brochures and guidebooks.

HISTORIC BUILDINGS/MONUMENTS CONSERVED
The conserved Islamic-era structures include the Castle mosque, its minaret and the adjacent room; two levels of the Ayyubid palace, with its private *hammam*; the public bath; the Burg al-Banat, rehabilitated into a cafeteria; and the entrance tower rehabilitated to serve as a ticket and information space.

NEW BUILDING FACILITIES
Sanitation facilities were built outside the fortification.

VOCATIONAL TRAINING/CAPACITY BUILDING
Accredited international and local experts employed by the AKTC conducted training sessions and programmes in up-to-date methodologies of documentation and conservation for the benefit of the DGAM and other local staff, contractors and craftsmen.

CONTRACTING METHODS
The bulk of the work was contracted. The choice of contractors was based on tender procedures after selected invitations. Miscellaneous maintenance works were executed by a team employed directly by the Trust.

Partners

PUBLIC PARTNERS
Directorate General of Antiquities and Museums, Governorate of Lattakia, Municipality of Haffeh.

Authoritative Framework

On 1 December 1999 the Aga Khan Trust for Culture signed a 'Memorandum of Understanding' with the Directorate General of Antiquities and Museums of Syria for providing support to the 'Restoration of Three Citadels in Syria'. One of these three sites was the Castle of Salah al-Din.

1 Darb al-Ahmar Social Projects   3 Darb al-Ahmar Monuments   5 Historic Wall   ■ Intervention area
2 Darb al-Ahmar Urban Regeneration   4 Azhar Park

N
200 m

FEATURED CASE STUDIES

DARB AL-AHMAR SOCIAL PROJECTS

DARB AL-AHMAR URBAN REGENERATION

DARB AL-AHMAR MONUMENTS

AZHAR PARK

HISTORIC WALL

Cairo Area Programme

Programme Scope/Objectives

In 1997 AKTC embarked on in the creation of a 30-hectare public Park in the Darb al-Ahmar district of Historic Cairo. The project also included the restoration of the 12th-century Historic Wall and the rehabilitation of monuments and landmark buildings in the area. These efforts are complemented by the 'Darb al-Ahmar Revitalization Project' aimed at improving the area's living conditions through integration of the built environment with social and economic interventions. Additionally, the Cairo portfolio includes the 'Urban Plaza Project' comprising a hotel, a multi-storey parking facility and a shopping area.

Preceding pages:

The central walkway in Azhar Park, Cairo, looking towards the Citadel of Cairo in the distance.

In the Old City of Cairo, the activities of the Aga Khan Trust for Culture (AKTC) started with the reconversion of a vast barren site (a hilly rubble-dump between the Fatimid city and the Mamluk cemetery) into a thirty-hectare urban Park with many visitor facilities. The Park has all of the geometric elements of traditional Islamic gardens and features soft-shaped hills and a small lake. A network of informal pathways surrounds the more formal garden areas and leads through all levels and corners of the site. The Park combines both widespread leisure areas inviting people to meet, to rest and to picnic on the ground, and more sophisticated facilities such as the Citadel View Restaurant on the hill and the Lakeside Café. The design of the Park provides the visitor with a dramatic and rich visual experience not available in any other area of Cairo.

Currently, Azhar Park receives more than two million visitors a year and has proven to be a catalyst for urban renewal in one of the world's most congested cities. Additionally, the Park manages to provide its visitors with an accommodating public space of quality that caters to different social and economic classes, while encouraging their integration. This has been achieved through tactful management and operation policies that offer the residents of Historic Cairo a reduced entry fee, while ensuring that the Park facilities provide quality services to different community classes and groups.

The Darb al-Ahmar neighbourhood, directly abutting the Park, is socially and physically depressed, but still features a lively and cohesive residential community. Over the past few decades, Darb al-Ahmar has gone through a spiral of decay affecting the living conditions of its inhabitants. This was primarily due to the decline in social status of the historic city since the early twentieth century because of the exodus of the local bourgeoisie into newer urban districts. Another reason behind this decline was the lack of a coherent urban management system that could deal effectively and appropriately with the particular problems and intricacies of the Historic City. Currently, several mosques, old palaces, historic houses and public open spaces have been, and are being, rehabilitated in an effort to make them accessible to the local community and visitors.

The most prominent of these are the sixteenth-century Khayrbek Mosque with the adjacent *sabil kuttab* and an attached eighteenth-century house, the fourteenth-century Alin Aq Palace, Umm al-Sultan Shabaan Mosque and Madrasa, Aslam Mosque and Aqsunqur Mosque (the Blue Mosque). These all

The Historic Cities Programme works to improve the lives of the residents of Darb al-Ahmar, a district close to Azhar Park. Above, engineers and planners study the Darb al-Ahmar Master Plan. A craftsman, below, works on the restoration of the decorative inlay of a door at the Programme's wood workshop.

represent significant assets of the Darb al-Ahmar community. Some of them are located adjacent to the Park. Many of these restored structures are reused for community purposes so as to enhance the identification and solidarity of residents with historic buildings and their district. In conjunction with physical upgrading, a wide range of ongoing socio-economic development initiatives have been implemented, beginning in the year 2000. The objective is to provide residents with new opportunities, including training, employment and micro-credits for small enterprises. Special programmes are targeting health issues, women's affairs and environmental problems. House owners and tenants are being provided with technical assistance, grants and micro-credits for upgrading their premises, and many local enterprises are now benefiting from the physical rehabilitation activities.

The uncovering of the formerly buried Historic Wall, with its enormous gates, towers, and interior chambers and galleries, is in itself one of the most important archaeological discoveries of the past decades relating to the Islamic period in Egypt. Over 1300 metres long, the Wall forms a distinctive third element of significance between the Park and Darb al-Ahmar, providing an interesting enclosure and backdrop for the Park, as well as a monument which can be visited. It physically separates the Park from Darb al-Ahmar and the Old City, but also acts as an attractive visual and functional connection, offering opportunities to visitors to enter the city from the Park, and vice versa. Over the centuries, the houses and monuments built against the Wall on the city side became an integral part of Cairo's urban and social history. Selective removal of encroaching elements was taken into consideration as part of the restoration process. Alongside this process, a valuable archaeological site was uncovered, bringing with it the development of a museum and visitor centre.

The 'Urban Plaza Development Project' is designed to be a mixed-use retail mall and commercial car park facility, situated on a site of approximately 17,900 square metres in the Old City of Cairo. The site is bounded on the east and south by Azhar Park, on the west by the old Historic Wall of Cairo, and on the north by al-Azhar Street. A landmark building for Cairo, it will create a new entrance to Azhar Park.

The minarets and domes of Cairo seen from Azhar Park: in the forefront, the dome of the Khayrbek Mosque complex, with the domes and minarets of Sultan Hassan and Rifa'ai mosques behind.

Azhar Park is situated in one of the most important parts of Cairo; the Citadel is seen to the left and the Historic Old City to the right.

Background

BRIEF HISTORY OF PROGRAMME AREA

Following the Fatimid conquest of Egypt in AD 969, the city of Cairo was founded to house the Fatimid court. Between 1087 and 1092, the city walls were expanded to incorporate an area to the south, now known as Darb al-Ahmar, located between the then future citadel and the old seat of power in the walled city. The wall defined the eastern edge of Darb al-Ahmar and the boundary between the urban area of the new elite and the dumping grounds for the city's rubbish. Over the course of centuries formidable mounds of debris accumulated, known as the al-Darassa Hills, dwarfing and eventually burying the city walls.

The early decades of the 20th century saw Darb al-Ahmar attempting to emulate the newer quarters of Cairo. New construction techniques, using reinforced concrete, began to replace traditional building materials, and 'modernist' urban design policies came into effect. The al-Darassa Hills remained uninhabited until the late 20th century. In the early 1990s, this site was selected by AKTC for the construction of Azhar Park, an idea that emerged in the 1980s following a seminar on the expansion of the city of Cairo organized by AKTC in 1984. Work began in 1997, following the construction of three major water reservoirs on the site by both the Government of Egypt and USAID.

Challenges

PROGRAMME RISKS

Income-generating activities such as Azhar Park and the Urban Plaza significantly contribute to the financial sustainability of the Cairo projects, but the institutional sustainability of these interventions represents a major challenge. The current capacity of both governmental and non-governmental agencies in the area requires intensive support to ensure the institutional sustainability of the project's approach.

SITE CONDITIONS

The Park's site represented a major challenge given the unstable nature of its soil and the fact that the Historic Wall was almost entirely buried beneath five centuries' worth of debris. Despite its central location, Darb al-Ahmar is not as densely populated as other areas of Cairo. It includes a significant number of monuments and low-rise traditional buildings connected by narrow streets and alleyways.

DEMOGRAPHICS

Between the mid 1970s and mid 1990s Darb al-Ahmar witnessed an almost 50% population decrease (from 146,000 to 78,000 inhabitants). The average household size in Darb al-Ahmar is five persons and 78% of the residents are tenants. More than 70% of the residents have been living in the area for more than 20 years. The bulk of the decrease occurred at the age of marriage, since members of the new generations preferred to seek better social and economic opportunities in other Cairo neighbourhoods. Due to the significant decrease of population, the area includes a number of empty plots and ruined buildings.

HOUSEHOLD ECONOMY

The economically active represent 30% of the population out of which 56% are involved in production-related occupations (small-scale industries and workshops), 28% in the services sector, 16% in the commerce sector and only 2% in professional occupations. In 2003 the annual average income per capita was US $207 (17 times lower than the average for Egypt as a whole).

STATUS OF HEALTH AND EDUCATION

On the household level, residents suffer from health problems mainly related to deteriorated living conditions such as inadequate infrastructure, increased dampness and lack of natural light and ventilation. On a more general level, Darb al-Ahmar lacks quality health services especially in the area of maternity and early childhood problems.

AVAILABILITY OF DRINKING WATER
AND PROPER SANITATION FACILITIES

Almost all houses in Darb al-Ahmar are connected to drinking water and sanitation services; quality, however, is an issue, especially regarding drinking water.

ENVIRONMENTAL CONCERNS

In Cairo, the per capita share of green space is meagre. Aside from environmental hazards related to the deteriorated condition of existing infrastructure, Darb al-Ahmar also lacks adequate solid waste management services.

INFRASTRUCTURE

While the Park's site included some recently added infrastructure mainly related to water reservoirs, the infrastructure in Darb al-Ahmar was inadequate after many years of neglect. Only in the past decade has the government paid some attention to upgrades. Consequently, the majority of households are now connected to infrastructure utilities but investments in water, sewage and electricity networks only impacted major streets. Cul-de-sacs and alleyways, where the majority of the population lives, still suffer from inadequate connections mostly implemented by residents.

Construction of Azhar Park begun; 'Al-Darb al-Ahmar Revitalization Project' (ADAARP): preliminary studies and design phase

Monuments restoration; ADAARP, Phase 1 begun

Extensive baseline survey undertaken in Darb al-Ahmar

Monuments restoration; 'Public-Private Partnership' agreement with Governorate of Cairo

Inauguration of Azhar Park; 'Urban Plaza Project'; ADAARP, Phase 2 begun

ADAARP, Phase 3 begun

1997   2000   2003   2004   2005   2010

ACCESS TO OPEN SPACE

The quality of public spaces has diminished, unless they are gated or exclusive to certain society groups. Open spaces in Darb al-Ahmar mostly consist of small nodes at road intersections or leftover spaces due to the demolition of older structures. These few open spaces, in addition to the existing street network, suffer from continuous deterioration, use of inappropriate finishing materials and interruption by vehicular movement. The possibility of providing a quality public space that caters for all social and economic classes and encourages their integration was a challenge for Azhar Park.

BUILDING CONDITIONS

The Park site included some minor public structures that were either removed or incorporated in the Park's overall design. Monuments and major public buildings in Darb al-Ahmar were in a state of decay due to the protracted absence of public investments. Moreover, existing housing stock suffered from severe deterioration owing to a lack of regular maintenance, complicated legal procedures, lack of technical know-how, unrealistic rent controls, low-income levels, multiple ownership and insecure tenure.

Significant Issues and Impact

MASTER PLANNING PROCESS

Darb al-Ahmar inherited a governmental Master Plan in 1973 that favoured major demolitions in the neighbourhood to introduce wide roads for vehicular traffic, especially along the eastern Historic Wall. If implemented, the results of this plan would have been catastrophic to the physical, social and economic fabric of the area. Realizing the implications of the plan, AKTC, along with its institutional partners, succeeded in replacing it with a more sensitive conservation programme ratified by the Cairo Governorate.

PLANNING ISSUES

While Azhar Park followed a formal planning approach with clear planning and design objectives, and hence clear implementation procedures, the adjacent neighbourhood projects followed an action planning approach to address urban planning issues adopting a more flexible process. The project worked on implementing these action plans using an integrated approach that encompasses restoration of key monuments and public buildings together with housing rehabilitation and the upgrading of infrastructure and public open spaces.

BASELINE STANDARDS

Along with various sector-based surveys and studies carried out since 1998, the project conducted a major baseline survey in 2003 covering the entire area of Darb al-Ahmar (13 *shiyakhat*, 100,000 inhabitants). The results were used as the base for a post-implementation survey carried out in 2008 in seven core *shiyakhat*, shedding light on the project's impact over this period of time.

SOCIO-ECONOMIC INITIATIVES

Since the project follows a multi-input integrated approach towards urban revitalization, socio-economic initiatives are a core element of the process. Besides the built environment programmes, AKTC works closely with other agencies (Aga Khan Foundation and Aga Khan Agency for Microfinance) on a wide range of social initiatives: health, education, support to civil society organizations, and environment; in addition to a range of economic initiatives including access to micro-credit, business development, vocational training and employment.

CONSERVATION ASPECTS

Restoration of key monuments in Darb al-Ahmar was an indispensible component of the project. During the course of the project a significant number of these buildings were restored including the eastern Historic Wall, the Madrasa of Umm al-Sultan Shabaan, Aslam Mosque, the Khayrbek complex, Alin Aq Palace, and the Tarabay al-Sharify complex in addition to a number of Ottoman and early 20th-century buildings. Restoration went hand-in-hand with programmes to raise the local community's awareness of the monuments' value, in addition to the training and capacity-building of local craftsmen in order to generate employment opportunities.

QUALITY OF LIFE

Azhar Park presented a rare opportunity to provide a major public space of quality to benefit Cairo's inhabitants. Since the mid 1990s, and following the project's inception, Darb al-Ahmar's population decline started to reverse. A 2009 post-implementation survey showed that literacy figures have slightly improved. Chest disease and allergies have decreased significantly between 2003 and 2009. Rheumatism and poor hearing also showed significant decreases. These improvements might be attributed to the housing interventions and their impact on the area's lifestyle, not to mention completion of construction activities at Azhar Park.

POST-IMPLEMENTATION PLANS

Both Azhar Park and the Urban Plaza projects are managed through long-term agreements with the Government of Egypt. Neighbourhood activities are currently in their third phase, during which the majority of the programmes and initiatives are meant to be phased out and handed over to the appropriate governmental and civil society organizations. Project sustainability is achieved financially through increasing support from Azhar Park's surplus revenues along with finance generated from other neighbourhood activities, such as the project's Darb al-Ahmar carpentry workshop.

Partners

PUBLIC PARTNERS

Governorate of Cairo, Supreme Council of Antiquities, Ministry of Awqaf Authority, Cairo Cleaning and Beautification Agency, General Authorization for Literacy and Adult Education, Ministry of Education, Ministry of Solidarity.

Authoritative Framework

Cooperation protocol agreements with Cairo Governorate, The Supreme Council of Antiquities and the Egyptian Awqaf Authority (Islamic Endowment). 'Al-Darb al-Ahmar Revitalization Project' (Phase 2) was implemented according to a tripartite agreement between AKTC, Cairo Governorate and the Egyptian Social Fund for Development.

Darb al-Ahmar Social Projects

CAIRO, EGYPT

Once construction activities for Azhar Park had commenced in earnest in the late 1990s, the Historic Cities Programme (HCP) began to focus on the development of Darb al-Ahmar, the impoverished neighbourhood adjacent to the future Park. Named after the historic street that passes through this area, today's Darb al-Ahmar is a vibrant but impoverished district that in no way resembles its rich past. Since the beginning of the twentieth century, this part of Historic Cairo saw a steady but continuous decline in living conditions. With the city expanding in all directions, offering improved standards of living to some, Darb al-Ahmar saw many of its wealthy residents replaced by people from poorer parts of Cairo, who had substantially lower incomes and lower education levels than those who had left. This shift in population led to rapid dilapidation of the built environment, as funding for maintenance of landmark buildings was no longer available. A virtual freeze on rent introduced by the government in the 1950s further accelerated the decline of Darb al-Ahmar. Many landlords saw no reason to finance the upkeep of buildings that had virtually no rental value and whose occupants could not be removed. With houses collapsing due to lack of maintenance, few employment opportunities and insufficient availability of utilities and municipal services, the area started to attract criminals and for some time even became the hub of the drug trade in Cairo. By March 2000, when HCP began its first activities, population levels had declined to 100,000 from an estimated 170,000 in 1972–77.

HCP's main objective for the development of Darb al-Ahmar is to improve the quality of life of the inhabitants in terms of their economy, housing conditions and health and education. In addition to this, HCP intends to preserve the social fabric by ensuring that the benefits of its activities will go to the actual population and not to newcomers with higher income levels. HCP realizes, however, that it has limited means at its disposal to counter gentrification.

The socio-economic development of Darb al-Ahmar started with a first phase that was initially designed for a three-year period (later extended by one more year) and that was chiefly co-funded by the Egyptian-Swiss Development Fund and the Ford Foundation. Activities that were identified as having the highest priority during this period were: improved housing; access to micro-credit; vocational

An art class is taking place at Darb Shouglan Community Centre.

Opposite page:
Above, children learn from a poster about recycling methods for the 'Solid Waste Management Project'.

Below, a sight test is given by a Health Programme optometrist.

Project Scope / Objectives

The goal of these projects was to improve the overall quality of life in Darb al-Ahmar. Socio-cultural and economic well-being were targeted through access to micro-credit, business development services, employment and vocational training, crafts development, education, health, environment, and capacity building for local government and civil society organizations.

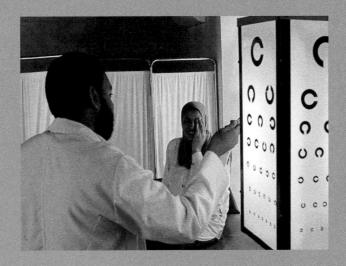

Above, residents are being interviewed during a baseline census survey in order to provide an accurate needs assessment not only of local inhabitants from a household perspective, but also of the needs of local entrepreneurs to assess their eligibility for micro-finance.

Below, a substantial number of beneficiaries, over the past ten years, have found financial security with the help of the vocational training programme. A young woman develops her skill at sewing to generate income.

training and employment; education; and, to a more limited extent, access to primary health care. Although largely successful during the initial four years, Phase 1 only had a limited reach in terms of its health activities and its micro-credit. Furthermore, most of the vocational training had been limited to the trades that were directly related to the building sector. With the experience gained during the first phase, a more accurate needs assessment was compiled through an extensive baseline survey, which was completed in late 2003. This survey not only looked at the needs of local inhabitants from a household perspective, but also took stock of the needs of local entrepreneurs as potential lenders from a micro-credit programme that, as of 2005, became a responsibility of the Aga Khan Agency for Microfinance (AKAM).

The outcome of the baseline survey of 2003 provided the inputs for a detailed implementation plan for Phase 2. Co-financed by the German Development Bank KfW, through the Egyptian Social Fund for Development, the Ford Foundation and a large number of other donors, Phase 2 started in January 2005 and continued until December 2009. A post-implementation survey of the same households that were first interviewed in late 2003, carried out by an independent external evaluator, provided HCP with a number of interesting before and after observations, showing the results and the outcome of some of the better and some of the less successful interventions.

The post-implementation survey consisted of a household survey and focus group meetings. The survey was conducted in seven core shiyakhat of Darb al-Ahmar (the entire district is made up of thirteen shiyakhat) during February 2009. The households surveyed in 2009 represent seventy-five per cent of those that were first surveyed in 2003 (the missing 25% having moved out and being replaced by others, often from within the district). In addition to this survey, two focus group discussions were held, one with men and another with women, covering relevant population groups. Although relatively small in size (the people surveyed in 2009 represent just under 2% of the population of the area) the fact that the same households are compared before and after the completion of Phase 2 makes this post-implementation survey relevant.

Housing Improvement

Since HCP started its housing improvement activities in 2000, eighty-four housing units – representing 218 individual apartments for 1100 people – have been completed as either newly built or completely renovated houses. Because families in the area lack cash, this work was carried out with a grant component that could rise as high as eighty per cent.

The 2009 survey found that over the preceding five years the average number of rooms per house had increased. This, however, was not due to an increase in living space, but because of more partitions within the existing space and hence higher levels of privacy within the household. Observations regarding crowding conditions and ventilation showed that de-crowding has improved. However, ventilation had worsened (there was an increase in percentage of non-ventilated windowless rooms), showing a need for more light wells and ventilation shafts.

People's perception of the market value of their house showed a remarkable increase. Estimates in 2003 ranged from EGP 10,000 to EGP 70,000 in 2003, whereas in 2009 they ranged from EGP 70,000 to EGP 250,000 and more.

From the focus group discussions, HCP learned that there is an influx of new residents coming into Darb al-Ahmar who occupy both old and new buildings, but with new leases; some of these new arrivals are originally from Darb al-Ahmar (married, moved out and now returning) and some from other popular districts of Cairo. This phenomenon

seems to be directly related to a perception of improvement in the district, namely the clearly visible rehabilitation of a number of houses and the creation of open spaces. *Shiyakhat* such as Batneyya, however, where little housing rehabilitation took place, seem to continue losing residents due to the dilapidated housing stock.

Household Economy

The average declared monthly household income doubled from EGP 497 in 2003 to EGP 983 in 2009. In 2003 more than seventy per cent of households earned between EGP 100 and EGP 600 per month, while in 2009 less than forty per cent fell into this category. Taking inflation into consideration, real gains in household income levels between 2003 and 2009 ranged from twenty per cent to twenty-five per cent. Evidence of increased household income levels comes from a noticeable reduction in expenditure on food as a percentage of the household budget. 2009 data showed that fifty-one per cent was spent on food items compared to fifty-six per cent in 2003. In all likelihood, food expenditure as a percentage of the household budget would have dropped well below the fifty per cent threshold (a key poverty indicator) had it not been for the exceptionally high inflation of prices for food items. The cost of food increased by twenty-five per cent in 2008 when many subsidies were removed.

Employment

More than 4300 people have been assisted with finding employment through the programme since 2000, either by finding (new) employment or through job referrals. Not

Computer literacy is taught to young people at the Community Centre and art classes are offered in the evening through the education programme.

surprisingly, most of the respondents in the household survey reported knowing the 'Employment Programme' (second to 'Housing', where only 19% reported not knowing the programme). As a result of HCP's interventions, the percentage of economically active individuals increased from thirty per cent in 2003 to thirty-four per cent in 2009. Of this thirty-four per cent, nearly three quarters (78%) were employees (generally employed by other family members) whereas twenty-two per cent were self-employed (that is, they own their own business, or they work in the family business with no wages). Comparisons with 2003 show that there is a decrease in the percentage of those who work for family members without wages. This change can in part be contributed to the substantial number of beneficiaries who, over the past ten years, found employment with the help of the programme's employment unit.

Education

The 2009 study reports a decrease in the levels of illiteracy among those surveyed (a 5.5% drop in illiteracy for men and a 2.5% drop for women). HCP's literacy classes since the survey have continued at the same level and illiteracy levels are therefore expected to drop even further. School drop-out rates, a measurement of success of HCP's engagement with parents of school-going children who are at risk of leaving school prematurely, went down by 3.5 per cent during the course of Phase 2. However, the success was nearly entirely due to more girls completing primary school (drop-out rates were down from 16% in 2003 to 13% in 2009). Boys' drop-out rates, unfortunately, remained critical with no measurable changes between 2003 and 2009.

Health

Following the creation of a new health-care centre located close to Khayrbek Mosque in Darb al-Ahmar Street and following a review of the principal health development activities (which resulted in a programme change whereby future focus would be on mother and child health care), the health programme saw a dramatic improvement in its outreach to the community during the second phase. More than three thousand children received a health check-up and a large number of counselling sessions were held for teenagers and women on subjects ranging from 'Care for the Elderly' and 'Care for Working Children' to issues such as 'Female Genital Mutilation' and 'Domestic Violence'.

Quality of Life

Disputes among neighbours in the past twelve months, an indicator for local perceptions of changes in the quality of life, showed a remarkable drop amongst those polled (from 18% in 2003 to just 5% in 2009). This reflects positive community participation potential for the future. In direct relation to the observed reduction in the numbers of conflicts, perhaps, comes a measurable increase in the desire to continue living in the same locality. Willingness to stay in Darb al-Ahmar was already high in 2003 (89% wished to stay) and has increased during the course of the second phase, now reaching ninety-three per cent. During focus group discussions where residents revealed general appreciation of the revitalization efforts by the project, housing rehabilitation and open-space development were in particular mentioned as key points.

A health-care centre was set up adjacent to Khayrbek Mosque and the health programme saw a dramatic increase in its outreach to the local population.

Background

BRIEF HISTORY OF PROJECT SITE
The Darb al-Ahmar district, together with the adjacent Khan al-Khalili district, comprises the core of Historic Cairo and hosts the highest concentration of Islamic monuments in the world. The easternmost part of Darb al-Ahmar borders the Historic Wall built by Salah al-Din during the second half of the 12th century. The area prospered until the beginning of the 20th century. It fell into disrepair as Cairo expanded rapidly and wealthy residents chose to move to the city's outskirts leaving poorer migrants to occupy their houses. A virtual freeze on rents from the 1950s onwards, alongside hereditary lease agreements, diminished incentives on behalf of local landlords to keep up their properties. Consequently, living conditions deteriorated rapidly, a process that continued and seemed irreversible until the creation of Azhar Park at the start of the new millennium.

Challenges

PROJECT RISKS
The main risk was the potential lack of sufficient local capital to rehabilitate a significant number of houses. In addition, nearly all the houses had complex, multiple ownership status. Interventions could not proceed without properly identifying legal owners, and wherever possible obtaining financial contributions from those who would stand to benefit. Darb al-Ahmar's limited open spaces also required rehabilitation. Future maintenance of this open space will be a major challenge.

SITE CONDITIONS
Sites for housing improvement generally suffered from poor accessibility, complicating the construction process. The poor status of solid waste collection has been an ongoing problem in the area. Many initiatives were started in the past, sometimes leading to temporary improvement, but those cannot succeed unless there is support at the district government level too. The general tendency, however, has been towards a lack of sustained preparedness by the responsible agencies to collect solid waste. Local civil society organizations have so far failed to successfully pressure government to improve waste collection services.

STATUS OF HEALTH AND EDUCATION
Health surveys revealed that on the household level, poor eyesight is the most common ailment with an average 42% of the population suffering from it. Rheumatism was ranked second with an overall average of 36% in 2003, followed by poor hearing with 13%. Darb al-Ahmar generally lacks quality health services especially in the area of maternity and early childhood problems. Childhood development is of concern along with development of children's life skills.

INFRASTRUCTURE
Drinking water and waste water infrastructure was upgraded in the 1960s, but the quality of the work was poor. Gas-related utilities were also poor or non-existent.

Significant Issues and Impact

DATA COLLECTION/SURVEYS
An extensive socio-economic baseline survey was conducted in 2003, covering health status and household income and expenditure. At later stages of the project new information was added. A post-implementation survey, carried out in 2009 at the conclusion of Phase 2, covered the same households that were first surveyed in 2003. In 2010, at the start of Phase 3, a new baseline survey for the area was conducted.

HISTORIC BUILDINGS/MONUMENTS CONSERVED
Discussions with the Supreme Council of Antiquities resulted in the adoption of building regulations that would safeguard the built environment of this historic part of Cairo. External sources of funding were needed and found in order to help co-finance the rebuilding of almost 90 traditional housing units in the area. These now stand as a model for urban rehabilitation.

COMMUNITY INVOLVEMENT
AKTC teamed up with local civil society organizations to ensure that there is sufficient local ownership to maintain the newly created open spaces in good condition, through the creation of socio-cultural events for the benefit of users. Following the completion of Phase 3 in 2013, most activities with an open-ended commitment, such as health and education, will be transferred to local entities with whom HCP is already collaborating.

Other AKDN agencies will remain active in the provision of micro-credit and small- and medium- enterprise development.

VOCATIONAL TRAINING/CAPACITY BUILDING
During the course of Phase 2, a number of new initiatives were added to the vocational training programme with the aim of reaching more women. Administrative training has subsequently attracted substantially more women than men. The 2010 baseline survey served as a benchmark for the Canadian International Development Agency funded 'Cairo Economic Livelihoods Programme', which focuses on vocational training and employment.

Partners

PUBLIC PARTNERS
Governorate of Cairo.

Donors

Egyptian-Swiss Development Fund (Phase 1), Social Fund for Development (Phases 2 and 3), Canadian International Development Agency (Phases 2 and 3), United Nations Development Programme, World Monuments Fund, Ford Foundation, Daimler Chrysler (Egypt), Flora Family Foundation, Danny Kaye and Sylvia Fine Kaye Foundation, The American University in Cairo, Mubarak Kohl Initiative, Industrial Modernization Centre, Azhar Park, Caritas (Egypt).

Authoritative Framework

Overall agreement with the Cairo Governorate for the development of the Darb al-Ahmar district and specific tripartite agreements with Cairo Governorate, Egyptian Social Fund for Development and AKTC for partial financing of project activities during Phases 2 and 3.

Darb al-Ahmar Urban Regeneration

CAIRO, EGYPT

Despite its central location, valuable cultural assets, strong community ties and active community of artisans, Darb al-Ahmar, a historic inner-city district of 100,000 residents, is one of Egypt's most distressed neighbourhoods. Over the past decades the area has been suffering from social, economic, cultural and environmental deterioration resulting in general urban decline that has led to the gradual loss of irreplaceable social, economic and cultural assets. The immediate causes of this decline can be grouped in two major categories. First, socio-economic causes including low incomes and lack of housing finance mechanisms, together with a weak level of community mobilization, sense of ownership and participation. And second, institutional causes including a lack of governmental interest or awareness of heritage and urban conservation concepts; complicated legal procedures, planning constraints and outdated plans; and limited access to appropriate technical support and lack of technical know-how and conservation standards.

These obstacles primarily stem from different social and institutional factors. The social factors include the decline in social status of the historic city since the early twentieth century due to the exodus of the local bourgeoisie into newer urban districts. The institutional factors include the lack of a coherent urban management system that could deal effectively and appropriately with the particular problems and the intricacies of the historic city. In turn, social and institutional factors have lead to this rampant physical decay of Darb al-Ahmar over the past decades.

The situation was aggravated due to the absence of public funding for the improvement of infrastructure, services and social facilities on the one hand, and the weak level of private investments on the other. In addition, Darb al-Ahmar inherited a 1973 Master Plan that was in flagrant contradiction with recognized urban conservation practices. According to this plan, major highways were supposed to penetrate Darb al-Ahmar. This plan, if implemented, would have led to the demolition of significant parts of Darb al-Ahmar's urban fabric.

Several attempts have been made in the past to reverse the spiral of decay in different parts of Historic Cairo. As far as individual monuments were concerned, most of these projects have succeeded. However, attempts at large-scale area

This 2002 view of Sharia Abdullah al-Guweiny is typical of the terrible state of much of the building stock in Darb al-Ahmar.

Opposite page:
Above, Darb Shouglan Community Centre, a focal point of many of the district's activities, links up Darb al-Ahmar with Azhar Park and the Historic Wall.

Below, housing repair and reconstruction provides employment opportunities for the local population.

Project Scope / Objectives

This project includes rehabilitation of existing housing, the upgrading of public open space and infrastructure, as well as support for neighbourhood master and urban planning initiatives.

The area's revitalization has included Aslam Square, seen in 2009 before and after intervention. The square now hosts many public events and the shops facing on to it have undergone rehabilitation.

conservation covering whole districts such as Darb al-Ahmar never went beyond the paper stage, since some of these attempts did not consider enough the intricacies of the physical and socio-economic realities that caused this decline in the first place.

In order to reverse this decline, the Aga Khan Trust for Culture (AKTC) along with its different partners, has been working in Darb al-Ahmar for more than a decade, initiating the 'Darb al-Ahmar Revitalization Project' (ADAARP) with the overall objective of initiating a series of activities aimed at bringing long-lasting improvements in the socio-economic status and living conditions of the Darb al-Ahmar community. The project's strategy for complementary local development aims at upgrading Darb al-Ahmar's physical assets on the one hand, and social and economic development of the local community on the other, as two complementary goals to achieve total development of the district.

This occurs through increased public and private investments, incremental change and strengthening of the available socio-economic capital. However, this process remains incomplete without the capacity building of local stakeholders to achieve long-term sustainability. This situation calls for a long-term step-by-step regeneration process carefully interweaving planning, rehabilitation and conservation activities with socio-economic initiatives. Accordingly, the ADAARP encompasses the rehabilitation of important monuments and landmark buildings in Darb al-Ahmar, together with extensive social and economic development programmes, including apprenticeship, micro-credit, health care and housing rehabilitation.

Since its inception, the ADAARP was not committed to rigid blueprints and results fixed in advance, but offered a flexible framework that would be continuously confirmed or revised by the feedback received from the field. Rather than relying on preconceived, top-down strategies and implementation schemes, it developed the project substance by working from the bottom up. Through this process, the ADAARP has been able to gradually shift revitalization attempts from the physical restoration of some old buildings towards a viable concept of integrated urban conservation.

The ADAARP primarily focused on two major initial tasks. Firstly it took the time to understand the area, getting to know different stakeholders, and assessing local community needs. Secondly it carried out pilot socio-economic and physical initiatives to build trust and partnerships. Based on the success of different pilot initiatives, lessons learned have been used to design comprehensive programmes and intervention packages aiming at long-term sustainability of the project activities. Once successful, these

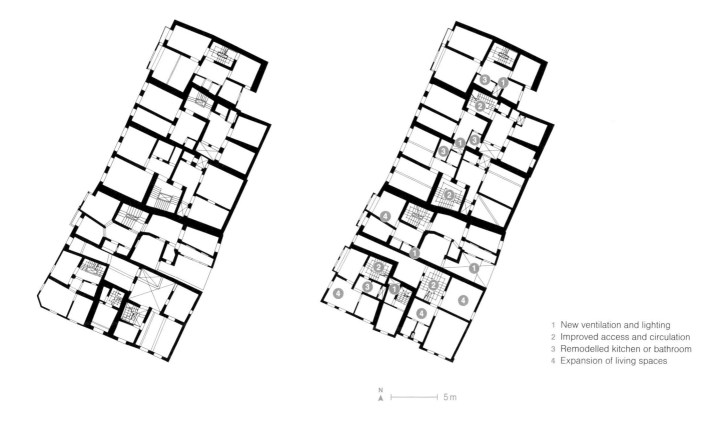

1 New ventilation and lighting
2 Improved access and circulation
3 Remodelled kitchen or bathroom
4 Expansion of living spaces

N ⊢————⊣ 5 m

different programmes were used to forge, together with different stakeholders, viable development frameworks and plans. These successes encouraged other partners to join the project and helped stimulate local investments in the area.

In practical terms, the ADAARP has been able to resolve some of the complicated legal procedures, planning constraints and outdated plans through: working with different authorities to change the demolition plans in favour of rehabilitastion; coordination of a transparent decision-making process involving different stakeholders; and legal mediation between tenants and owners.

The project has also been able to address lack of technical know-how and standards for rehabilitation of traditional structures through development – with local craftsmen – of a body of knowledge on cost effective and appropriate rehabilitation techniques; in addition to dissemination of this knowledge through technical manuals and training activities. On the other hand the ADAARP has been able to address economic issues such as low incomes and lack of housing finance through the introduction of a housing finance mechanism offering grants and loans.

Civil society issues have also been addressed by means of: community-based planning through participatory design with different community groups; promoting models of leadership through policies rewarding collective communal efforts; and promoting gender equality through sensitive design and planning measures catering for different groups, especially women.

In plans of typical housing on Darb Shouglan, before and after intervention, residents provided input on modifications to internal spaces that focused on expanding room volumes, improving air quality, and installing private bathroom and kitchen facilities where, previously, families had shared.

The street facade of Aslam Mosque and its adjoining square in 2000 (above) and in 2009 (below), after their restoration and rehabilitation.

This wide scope of interrelated activities could not be implemented without the active participation of the community and its individual members. The housing rehabilitation programme was an opportunity to demonstrate the latent potentials of public-private partnerships. Following the implementation of the first demonstration projects, a competitive situation was created among the owners and tenants who increased their own financial participation to reach up to fifty per cent of total rehabilitation costs. Meanwhile, a total of 320 apartment units have been restored. And due to its innovative and integrated approach towards addressing housing rehabilitation problems in historic areas, the Darb al-Ahmar housing rehabilitation programme was selected by UN-HABITAT in 2008 as a 'Best Practice' for improving the living environment.

These efforts were also complemented by the construction and rehabilitation of public buildings. These buildings have been turned from underused ruins or empty shells to vibrant nodes of community activities. The adaptive reuse of such buildings provided the area with public services that were much needed by the local residents. Indeed, this was an opportunity to rely on local craftsmanship and human resources to provide apprenticeship activities, eventually leading to sustainable job opportunities. The purpose of these interventions was not limited to physical rehabilitation or direct economic benefits, but also extended to restoring the community's self-esteem and confidence. This was possible when the community members, as well as other stakeholders, soon came to realize that the area's latent resources, if tactfully identified and properly utilized, can become valuable community assets, spearheading the area's overall socio-economic and physical development.

ADAARP efforts also extended to the public realm where major public spaces and corridors linking Azhar Park and the area's major attractions were upgraded. Through the open space and infrastructure programme it was possible to improve the existing utilities' networks, directly impacting the residents' public health and living conditions. Enhanced public space treatments and designs were developed and employed, in participation with different community groups, in order to provide quality public spaces for the residents as well as the area's visitors. As a result, the area started to regain its economic vitality and has become an attraction for local investments in terms of housing activities and new business opportunities.

In order to provide an overarching, more formal framework to these grassroots rehabilitation efforts, a conservation plan for Darb al-Ahmar was developed by the ADAARP along with its partners. The objective was to revise and replace the existing 1973 Master Plan with its disastrous proposals. As a result of continuous cooperative efforts, a new plan was developed and ratified by the Cairo Governorate in 2005, laying the institutional foundations for a more sensitive urban rehabilitation process in Darb al-Ahmar.

For more than a decade the endeavour of the ADAARP was not free of obstacles. Indeed, it was full of challenges at different levels. If it has proven anything, the ADAARP experience has shown that positive change in underprivileged urban areas is possible. It is possible if a long-term vision is in place, flexible operational frameworks engaging different stakeholders on various levels are employed, and, finally, if local communities are trusted to lead that change.

Background

BRIEF HISTORY OF PROJECT SITE
Darb al-Ahmar is a densely populated district in the heart of historic Cairo with a high concentration of Islamic monuments. Despite its valuable cultural assets, strong community ties and an active community of artisans, Darb al-Ahmar is one of Cairo's most distressed neighborhoods. Over the past decades the area has suffered from social, economic, cultural and environmental deterioration.

Challenges

PROJECT RISKS
Although the project contributed to the rehabilitation of existing housing, infrastructure and public open spaces, the area still suffers from the ongoing demolition of traditional buildings in the absence of clear conservation policies. The project is working to encourage private investments in the area, while guiding the revitalization process through appropriate urban conservation planning and implementation mechanisms.

SITE CONDITIONS
Darb al-Ahmar includes a significant number of monuments and low-rise traditional buildings linked by narrow streets and alleyways, as well as a number of empty plots and ruined buildings. The street network and its few public open spaces (mostly nodes at road intersections or plots where a building was demolished) suffer from continuous deterioration, use of inappropriate finishing materials and interruption by vehicular movement.

AVAILABILITY OF DRINKING WATER
AND PROPER SANITATION FACILITIES
Many houses have poor natural light and ventilation and lack dedicated kitchen spaces and private toilets. Most water connections are made of lead, a highly toxic material.

INFRASTRUCTURE
Over the past decade, the government invested in infrastructure upgrades in water, sewage and electricity networks on major streets. Cul-de-sacs and alleyways, where the majority of the population lives, still have inadequate connections mostly installed by residents. Substantial stretches of road, pavement and open space were in need of leveling and repaving. Water leakage undermines the structural safety of residential buildings, especially traditional structures.

BUILDING CONDITIONS
Lack of regular maintenance and technical know-how, complicated legal procedures, unrealistic rent controls, low-income levels, multiple ownership and insecure tenure have all contributed to the severe deterioration of the existing housing stock. Traditional residential buildings as well as newly built structures have fallen into disrepair due to a lack of municipal follow-up on construction activities.

Significant Issues and Impact

DATA COLLECTION/SURVEYS
Physical surveys have been carried out since the programme's start and form the basis of an extensive GIS database concerning Darb al-Ahmar.

MASTER PLANNING PROCESS
The main Master Plan for the area, dating to 1973, was withdrawn upon the agreement reached to create Azhar Park. Certain elements of this plan, however, have periodically come to the fore, particularly with regards to the proposed widening of roads to encourage a smoother flow of vehicular traffic in the area. The Darb al-Ahmar Planning Unit, created by the project during the course of the second phase, prepared a plan for land use, application of appropriate building guidelines and traffic regulation. This plan was partially approved at a district level and now serves as a guideline for future developmental activities.

PLANNING ISSUES
The 'Housing Rehabilitation Programme' was designed to reverse the overall decline in the built environment while improving living conditions in both residential and workshop spaces. The project assessed the infrastructure conditions in various locations in order to replace inadequate utilities networks with upgraded, environmentally safe materials. Through the 'Open Space and Infrastructure Upgrading Programme' comprehensive technical specifications for streetscape treatment were developed to fit with the area's traditional context. These were implemented in strategically located public spaces, including Darb Shoughlan and Aslam Square.

COMMUNITY INVOLVEMENT/PROGRAMME
The project follows a multi-input integrated approach towards urban revitalization, and community-based socio-economic initiatives are a core element of the process. Besides the built environment programmes, AKTC works closely with other agencies (Aga Khan Foundation and Aga Khan Agency for Microfinance) on a wide range of initiatives impacting health, education and support to civil society organizations, and environment.

VOCATIONAL TRAINING/CAPACITY BUILDING
The project's economic initiatives included providing access to micro-credit, business development, vocational training and employment. The built environment project focused on generating training and employment opportunities through the implementation of conservation and construction activities.

Partners

COMMUNITY PARTNERS
Tenants and property owners, community-based organizations and partners (Al-Asheera Mohamadeya Association, Darb al-Ahmar Club, Darb al-Ahmar Khadamat Association, Hedaya Islameya Association, Abou El Fadl Association, Wasat Association).

Donors

Canadian International Development Agency, Caritas (Egypt), Daimler Chrysler (Egypt), Danny and Sylvia Fine Kaye Foundation, Egyptian Construction Federation, Egyptian-Swiss Development Fund, Embassy of the Federal Republic of Germany, Ford Foundation, GTZ (Deutsche Gesellschaft für Technische Zusammenarbeit), Global Environment Fund/United Nations Development Programme, Goethe Institute, Integrated Care Society, Egypt Industrial Training Council, Industrial Modernization Centre, Ministry of Economic Affairs for the State of Baden-Wurttemberg (Germany), KFW Entwicklungsbank, Microsoft (Egypt), Mubarak Kohl Initiative, Near East Foundation – Centre for Development Services.

Authoritative Framework

Cooperation protocol agreements with Cairo Governorate, The Supreme Council of Antiquities and the Egyptian Awqaf Authority (Islamic Endowment). 'Al-Darb al-Ahmar Revitalization Project' (Phase 2) was implemented according to a tripartite agreement between AKTC, Cairo Governorate and the Social Fund for Development.

The restored 13th-century Alin Aq Palace, used as a residence in the 16th century by Amir Khayrbek.

Darb al-Ahmar Monuments

CAIRO, EGYPT

In spite of its inscription as a World Heritage Site in 1979, Historic Cairo was not given enough attention and individual buildings were suffering neglect, serious deteriorations and lack of maintenance. During the early phases of the design of Azhar Park, new light was projected on the adjacent neighbourhood of Darb al-Ahmar, as the Park hills provide views of a number of magnificent heritage edifices. With its medieval structures, with the domes and minarets amid the dense urban fabric, the Darb al-Ahmar district invites visitors of the Park to come and explore the jewels of Islamic art and architecture.

The conservation projects of the Aga Khan Trust for Culture (AKTC) in Darb al-Ahmar started with two minarets in the vicinity of Azhar Park, that of Umm al-Sultan Shaaban Mosque (1368–69) and that of Khayrbek Mosque (1502–20). Both minarets had lost their upper parts as a result of the devastating 1884 earthquake. Collapses and reconstructions of minarets were not unknown to the history of Cairo. Despite attempts to reconstruct them in 1941, the minarets of Umm al-Sultan Shaaban and of Khayrbek mosques waited until 2003 to recover their integrity, when AKTC, on the basis of historic documentation, started with the Supreme Council of Antiquities in Egypt not only to restore them to their original shape but also to restore and revive the skills and the craftsmanship of artisans whose crafts were, and still are, in danger of being lost.

The technical challenges required multidisciplinary inputs from foreign and local consultants, historians, conservators and archaeologists in order to study Mamluk architecture, especially minarets, and develop adequate designs. These activities included regular conservation activities, such as documentation, condition assessment, fine conservation, architectural and structural conservation, presentation and publication.

The successful reconstruction of the minarets signalled the potential for social change brought by conservation and was followed by the complete conservation of the Umm al-Sultan Shaaban Madrasa and Mosque while the Khayrbek complex was restored and conserved. After restoration was completed in 2006, Umm al-Sultan Shaaban Mosque was returned to its original function and is currently being used as a mosque for the community. The *madrasa* spaces, neglected and empty before the conservation project, also provided an excellent

Conservators clean a wooden frame from the mausoleum of Aslam Mosque.

Opposite page:
Above, a view of Khayrbek Mosque from the Historic Wall.

Below, restoration work is being undertaken on the upper roundel in the mausoleum of Aslam Mosque.

Project Scope / Objectives

The scope of these projects included documentation and condition surveys, structural stabilization, and architectural and fine conservation and restoration. This was coupled with archaeological excavations and surrounding landscape work where necessary, along with the installation of lighting and sound systems and the design and construction of new ablution areas. Training was provided for local craftsmen and conservators in the course of the process and the restored mosques were finally returned for use by the community.

The 14th-century Umm al-Sultan Shaaban Mosque was restored by the Historic Cities Programme. The minaret had lost its upper part as a result of the devastating 1884 earthquake. It was returned to its original shape on the basis of historic documentation.

Opposite page:
Conservation and restoration work has continued at the Khayrbek Mosque complex with work on Alin Aq Palace in the foreground, a ruined structure to be reused as a museum.

reuse option for community-based activities. Agreements between AKTC and the Supreme Council of Antiquities were signed in order to reuse these edifices and hence bring life to them and revive their functional integrity, paving the way for many other organizations to follow this example. The reuse integrates the 'monuments' into their context and offers a variety of possible functions in the building that encourages local groups to use them and also to take care of their maintenance. As restoration work could not be complete without looking after the environmental needs of residents, conservation of individual monuments was closely followed by infrastructure and urban upgrading of its context.

In a secondary stage, the success of AKTC's conservation activities attracted donors, such as the World Monuments Fund, and the American Research Center in Egypt through a grant from the United States Agency for International Development, to partner with AKTC for new projects in the Darb al-Ahmar district, such as the Tarabay al-Sharify Mausoleum (1503), Aslam Mosque (1348) and Aqsunqur Mosque (also known as the Blue Mosque, 1345–1652).

To date, the impact of the conservation of the majority of historic landmarks in Darb-al-Ahmar has to be measured as an integral part of AKTC's regeneration plan including other physical and social interventions. Impacts can be listed as follows and have:
· reversed decline of monuments' condition. Projects have ensured the long-term structural stability of the edifices, conserving their authenticity and reinstating their architectural integrity by addressing the problems stemming from decades of neglect;

A drawing of the elevation of the
Tarabay al-Sharify complex (left),
seen under scaffolding and
undergoing conservation and
cleaning in 2006 (right).

· established a technical reference of quality in the field of conservation and were the cradle of future local heritage specialists;
· improved environmental and social conditions of the neighbouring community;
· monuments play an important role both for their historic and artistic value as well as for their symbolic, spiritual, and community importance. Conservation can only become sustainable if the social and economic fabric is being simultaneously revitalized and if secondary physical assets, forming the bulk of the urban fabric, are being rehabilitated, together with a provision of basic social services;
· created an economic stimulus for the local market by job creation, local construction suppliers and training opportunities, not only improving income levels but raising awareness towards heritage preservation and introducing new conservation methods in the field. This has also created a critical mass of change in the perception that both residents and visitors have of the area;
· and created visitor circuits along connecting streets between important tourist attractions in Cairo such as the Citadel, the Bab Zuwayla area and Azhar Park.

Above, the wooden *minbar* and the
interior of Khayrbek Mosque complex have
undergone thorough restoration.

Below, a view of the interior of Aqsunqur
Mosque (known as the Blue Mosque) during
restoration in 2009.

Overleaf:
An interior view of Aslam Mosque
after restoration.

KHAYRBEK COMPLEX

Background

BRIEF HISTORY OF PROJECT SITE
Amir Khayer Bek, a former governor of Aleppo under the last Mamluk sultan al-Ghuri, was appointed as the first Ottoman governor of Cairo following the Ottoman conquest of Egypt in 1517. Khayrbek Mosque, a religious and funerary complex, was built between 1502 and 1520 adjacent to Khayer Bek's residence, the Alin Aq Palace (13th–14th century). The *sabil* (public water source) of Janim al-Hamzawy (1532) was erected nearby, as were two Ottoman houses (17th century). In 1884, an earthquake caused serious damage to the top of the Khayrbek Mosque minaret, leading to the collapse of its pavilion. In 2002, in coordination with the Supreme Council of Antiquities (SCA), AKTC started reconstruction of the upper part of the minaret and a conservation project involving the entire complex and adjacent structures.

Challenges

PROJECT RISKS
The project targeted a variety of buildings dating from different periods, involving a wide range of materials, techniques and interventions. The reconstruction of the upper part of the Khayrbek Mosque minaret was a major concern, as it is one of the few extant minarets with an upper pavilion made of timber.

SITE CONDITIONS
The Khayrbek complex site covers more than 8000 m² and is located on a major route between the Citadel and Bab Zuwayla. The site is adjacent to a community sports club that caused some damage and trespass on the premises.

INFRASTRUCTURE
None of the Khayrbek complex buildings had adequate electrical and lighting systems. The Ottoman houses had no water supply, drainage or toilet facilities.

BUILDING CONDITIONS
The various buildings on the site suffered from neglect and had fallen into a state of decay. The Ottoman houses were occupied by squatters. Historically, the Mosque was never used as a place of worship due to an inaccurate *qibla* orientation and hence was rarely visited. Alin Aq Palace was in ruins.

Significant Issues and Impact

DATA COLLECTION/SURVEYS
Historic photographs and drawings dating from the 1880s were collected before the project started. Architectural surveys were performed using a combination of topographic gridding and rectified photography. The project was methodically documented throughout the construction phases. A set of as-built drawings and photographs was handed over to the authorities upon project completion.

HISTORIC BUILDINGS/MONUMENTS CONSERVED
The conservation project targeted Khayrbek Mosque and Mausoleum, Alin Aq Palace, the *sabil* of Janim al-Hamzawy (1532) and two Ottoman houses. The houses were equipped with toilet and plumbing facilities and all buildings provided with electricity and lighting fixtures.

VOCATIONAL TRAINING/CAPACITY BUILDING
This project was among the first AKTC conservation projects in Egypt. Local and foreign experts were consulted in order to provide the adequate and necessary information and training to the team involved. 120 local residents and craftsmen were trained throughout the project's duration.

CONTRACTING METHODS
A contractor was hired for the reconstruction of the minaret; all other architectural and fine conservation activities were carried out with direct labour recruited and supervised by AKTC professional staff.

NEW TECHNOLOGIES INTRODUCED
The minaret's base structural damage was addressed using steel anchors acting as tie beams, a technique that required the expertise of a specialized contractor.

RELEVANT CODES/STANDARDS ADOPTED
The conservation project followed all the international conservation charters and guidelines. For other aspects, the Egyptian Code for Construction was adopted.

Partners

PUBLIC PARTNERS
Supreme Council of Antiquities.

Donors

World Monuments Fund, American Research Center in Egypt.

Authoritative Framework

The Supreme Council of Antiquities and Aga Khan Cultural Services-Egypt (2001–10), World Monuments Fund and the Aga Khan Trust for Culture (2001–03), 'Reuse Agreement' (The Supreme Council of Antiquities and AKCS-E; 2004–14).

TARABAY COMPLEX

Background

BRIEF HISTORY OF THE PROJECT SITE
The project site lies on the southern side of Azhar Park, just outside the Historic Wall. The buildings on site include the mausoleum and *sabil* of Tarabay as well as the *ribat* of Azdumur. Tarabay al-Sharify was purchased as a slave by Mamluk sultan Qaytbay, and subsequently freed and appointed *amir* in the late 15th century. Azdumur was also purchased by Qaytbay, and appointed to a number of governmental positions. He built his tomb on the northern side of the mausoleum of Tarabay. There is no documentation regarding the relationship between Tarabay and Azdumur to explain why their mausoleums were constructed in such proximity.

Challenges

PROJECT RISKS
The *sabil* was structurally in a very dangerous condition and shored up for a number of years before the conservation project began.

SITE CONDITIONS
The cluster of monuments is located in the cemetery of Bab al-Wazir, relatively distant from public passage. Consequently, the area and the monuments were neglected for a number of years.

BUILDING CONDITIONS
All the buildings of this cluster of monuments were in a very poor state due to either serious structural problems or neglect. Despite splendid architecture and decoration, they were unappreciated and inaccessible to visitors.

Significant Issues and Impact

PLANNING ISSUES
Excavation works around the monuments produced a large recessed open space showcasing the Tarabay mausoleum. Located at the future south entrance to Azhar Park, this was designed as a resting place for visitors, equipped with greenery and benches. A retaining wall around the cluster of monuments and the landscaping of the lower level (at the monuments' base) were likewise planned and constructed.

HISTORIC BUILDINGS/MONUMENTS CONSERVED
Conserving the cluster of monuments of Tarabay Mausoleum, Azdumur Madrasa and Tarabay Sabil and excavating the exterior archaeological remains was the project's aim. The process of documenting, dismantling and reconstructing three sides of the *sabil's* structure challenged the project architects and craftsmen, illustrating the mastery of the medieval workers who first assembled the *sabil*.

VOCATIONAL TRAINING/CAPACITY BUILDING
The team working on the Tarabay conservation project was previously trained by AKTC. This project offered the opportunity to deepen acquired skills.

CONTRACTING METHODS
All architectural and fine conservation works were carried out with direct labour recruited and supervised by AKTC professional staff. The retaining walls were designed by a specialized consultant and implemented by an external contractor.

RELEVANT CODES/STANDARDS ADOPTED
The conservation project followed all the international conservation charters and guidelines. For other aspects, including hardscapes, landscapes and new construction, the Egyptian Code for Construction was adopted.

Partners

PUBLIC PARTNERS
Supreme Council of Antiquities.

Donors

World Monuments Fund, American Research Center in Egypt.

Authoritative Framework

The Supreme Council of Antiquities and Aga Khan Cultural Services-Egypt (2006–09), World Monuments Fund and the Aga Khan Trust for Culture (2006–09).

AQSUNQUR MOSQUE

Background

BRIEF HISTORY OF PROJECT SITE
Aqsunqur Mosque was built in 1347 by Amir Aqsunqur, a son-in-law of Sultan al-Nasir Muhammad, adjacent to the mausoleum of al-Kujuk (1341). In 1652, the Ottoman *amir* Ibrahim Agha Mustahfazan initiated a restoration campaign of the Mosque that had fallen into decay and redecorated the sanctuary with the Iznik tiles that have given the Mosque its modern name, the 'Blue Mosque'. The Comité de Conservation des Monuments de l'Art Arabe performed a number of interventions in the late 19th to early 20th century, the most important being the reconstruction of the upper part of the minaret.

Challenges

PROJECT RISKS
In 1992, a powerful earthquake struck Cairo, structurally damaging a number of monuments. The Blue Mosque was closed and heavy shoring put in place. The AKTC project aims at restoring the structural stability of the Mosque and reopening it to the public.

SITE CONDITIONS
Aqsunqur Mosque is located on Bab al-Wazir Street, between the Citadel and Bab Zuwayla, on the same street as other AKTC projects such as the Khayrbek complex and Umm al-Sultan Shaaban Mosque and Madrasa. The Mosque's history and architecture make it an attractive destination for visitors, but it is located on a narrow, busy street, lacking an open public space as buffer zone.

ENVIRONMENTAL CONCERNS
High-pollution levels from traffic, sand and dust affect the Mosque and the entire area.

INFRASTRUCTURE
The interior of the Mosque had no electrical systems and fixtures. The water supply and drainage of the ablution area were in very poor condition. Toilets and cleaning areas did not meet hygiene standards and sanitation was not properly designed.

BUILDING CONDITIONS
Aside from earthquake-related structural issues, the Mosque has suffered damage from rising groundwater, the loss of material, especially the blue Iznik tiles, and the accumulation of crusted grime on the facades and interior.

Significant Issues and Impact

DATA COLLECTION/SURVEYS
Historic photographs and drawings dating from the 1880s were collected before the project began. Architectural surveys were performed using a combination of topographic gridding and rectified photography. The project was methodically documented throughout the construction phases. A set of as-built drawings and photographs will be handed over to the authorities upon project completion.

PLANNING ISSUES
Egypt's Supreme Council for Antiquities transferred a piece of land adjacent to the Mosque to the AKTC project, indicating that it was the original ablution area. As no structures existed on it, a new ablution area was designed and built by AKTC. Reconstructing the ablution facilities not only served the Mosque, but raised community health standards by providing an accessible public toilet block. The adjacent land was used instead to create a public open space with sitting areas. It serves as a buffer zone between the Mosque and the bustling street and restored the monument's status as an important community gathering point. Upgrades for all electricity and plumbing facilities were planned and incorporated. The Mosque sound system was also upgraded.

HISTORIC BUILDINGS/MONUMENTS CONSERVED
Conserving the historic Aqsunqur Mosque involved restoring its use as a place of prayer and a community focal point, but also as a valuable historic monument open for visitation.

VOCATIONAL TRAINING/CAPACITY BUILDING
The implementation team working on the Aqsunqur Mosque conservation project was trained earlier by AKTC on other conservation projects. The Aqsunqur project offered fresh challenges and a new field of training and capacity building for 80 craftsmen and conservation technicians.

RELEVANT CODES/STANDARDS ADOPTED
The conservation project followed all the international conservation charters and guidelines. For other aspects, the Egyptian Code for Construction was adopted.

Partners

PUBLIC PARTNERS
Supreme Council of Antiquities.

Donors

World Monuments Fund, American Research Center in Egypt.

Authoritative Framework

The Supreme Council of Antiquities and Aga Khan Cultural Services-Egypt (2001–10), World Monuments Fund and the Aga Khan Trust for Culture (2001–03), 'Reuse Agreement' (The Supreme Council of Antiquities and AKCS-E; 2004–14).

UMM AL-SULTAN SHAABAN COMPLEX

Background

BRIEF HISTORY OF PROJECT SITE
The Mamluk sultan Sha'ban built the complex for his mother Khwand Baraka in 1368. It comprises a mosque, two *madrasas* (religious schools), two mausoleums, a *sabil*, a *kuttab* and a water trough for animals. In 1884 the upper part of its minaret collapsed due to an earthquake and, based on historic references and proposals by the Comité de Conservation des Monuments de l'Art Arabe, has been reconstructed by AKTC.

Challenges

PROJECT RISKS
The decision to design and reconstruct the upper part of the minaret was a major work that required coordination with local authorities and a number of specialized consultants. Despite the various challenges encountered, the minaret was reconstructed accommodating the historic requirements and international technical specifications.

DEMOGRAPHICS
Darb al-Ahmar is one of Cairo's most densely populated areas. At the start of the project, most households had significantly low income levels and limited access to education and health services. Conversion of the Umm al-Sultan Shaaban *madrasa's* under-utilized spaces into an education centre was part of a reuse agreement with the site's owner, returning this building component to its original function.

INFRASTRUCTURE
The infrastructure was in bad condition or not available. Also the surrounding environment of the Mosque posed a number of complications; it was necessary to shift underground and above-ground utilities away from the building.

BUILDING CONDITIONS
As with most of Historic Cairo today, the Darb al-Ahmar community around the complex is affected by serious environmental hazards, air contamination from traffic and dust, leaking infrastructure and absence of public open spaces. Within this environment the Mosque of Umm al-Sultan Shaaban was a functioning and active community mosque. Its adjacent rooms were used for a girls' school prior to 1992. However, the building suffered from neglect and degradation.

Significant Issues and Impact

DATA COLLECTION/SURVEYS

Historic photographs and drawings dating from the 1880s were collected before the project started. Project documentation was methodologically carried out during the entire project. Architectural surveys were performed using a combination of topographic gridding and rectified photography. A complete set of existing and post-restoration architectural drawings was produced. All was handed over to the authorities upon project completion.

HISTORIC BUILDINGS/MONUMENTS CONSERVED

Conservation of the entire monument of the Umm al-Sultan Shaaban complex was the main objective of the project, which ensured the installation of proper lighting for all spaces, new toilets, drainage and water supply for the *madrasa* too.

NEW BUILDING FACILITIES

The Mosque was supplied with a new ablution area designed and constructed during the project. Public open spaces were created with sitting areas to act as a buffer zone between the Mosque and the bustling street.

VOCATIONAL TRAINING/CAPACITY BUILDING

This project was one of AKTC's first conservation projects in Egypt. Local and foreign experts were consulted to provide the adequate and necessary information for conservation work. Local residents and craftsmen, numbering more than 120, were employed and trained throughout the duration of the project

CONTRACTING METHODS

A contractor was hired for the architectural works during the first two phases of the project; the last phase was implemented with direct labour recruited and supervised by AKTC's professional conservation staff.

NEW TECHNOLOGIES INTRODUCED

The reconstruction of the minaret was a challenging engineering work that required the reintroduction of traditional crafts, but also modern structural techniques to guarantee the stability of the minaret.

RELEVANT CODES/STANDARDS ADOPTED

The conservation project followed all international conservation charters and guidelines. For other aspects, the Egyptian Code for Construction was adopted.

Partners

PUBLIC PARTNERS

Supreme Council of Antiquities.

Donors

World Monuments Fund, American Research Center in Egypt.

Authoritative Framework

The Supreme Council of Antiquities and Aga Khan Cultural Services-Egypt (2001–10), World Monuments Fund and the Aga Khan Trust for Culture (2001–03), 'Reuse Agreement' (The Supreme Council of Antiquities and AKCS-E; 2004–14).

ASLAM MOSQUE

Background

BRIEF HISTORY OF PROJECT SITE

Located in the Darb al-Ahmar district adjacent to Bab al-Mahruq Gate, Aslam Mosque was built in 1344–45 by Amir Aslam al-Baha'I (known as al-Silahdar 'the sword-bearer'). Aslam al-Silahdar was a Mamluk prince (*amir*) in the court of al-Sultan al-Nasir Muhammad, who was one of the most prolific patrons of architecture in the Mamluk period (1250–1517). The Mosque comprises a prayer hall, the *amir's* mausoleum, a number of rooms and an ablution area. The Comité de Conservation des Monuments de l'Art Arabe carried out a number of interventions in the late 19th to early 20th century.

Challenges

SITE CONDITIONS

The square around Aslam Mosque, one of the few in dense Historic Cairo, is an important node in Darb al-Ahmar as it lies on the route between Bab Zuwayla and Azhar Park. Like most of Cairo, the Mosque site suffers from a combination of pollution from traffic and dust, as well as leaking sewage and water infrastructure.

INFRASTRUCTURE

Electrical cables and fixtures in the Mosque interior were substandard and haphazardly installed, diminishing both the function and overall appearance and authenticity of the building. The water supply and drainage of the ablution area were likewise in very poor condition.

BUILDING CONDITIONS

Aslam Mosque has been in constant use since its 14th-century construction and remains an important mosque for the local community. Over time, it has suffered from overall and continuous degradation of its authentic fabric. The western facade and a number of interior areas were structurally unsound.

Significant Issues and Impact

DATA COLLECTION/SURVEYS

Historic photographs and drawings dating from the 1880s were collected before the project began. Architectural surveys were performed using a combination of topographic gridding and rectified photography. The project was methodically documented throughout the construction phases. A set of as-built drawings and photographs will be handed over to the authorities upon project completion.

PLANNING ISSUES

Structural and architectural interventions were required to stabilize the Mosque. The project plan also included an important component of infrastructure improvement; all electrical and sound systems were re-placed and made more compatible with the historic nature of the fabric. The derelict ablutions area was totally replaced by a construction reusing some of the early 20th-century

elements. Reconstructing the ablution facility has raised health standards for those using the Mosque and has created a public toilet block accessible to the neighbouring community. The square around Aslam Mosque was upgraded by AKTC in the year following completion of the Mosque's conservation. Creating a public open space with sitting areas as a buffer zone between the Mosque and the bustling street has restored the Mosque's status as a community gathering point.

HISTORIC BUILDINGS/MONUMENTS CONSERVED

The Aslam Mosque conservation project aimed to make its religious use compatible with the building fabric while ensuring the protection of the Mosque's authentic material and construction. In addition, the plaza in front of the Mosque was re-paved, landscaped and closed to vehicular traffic in order to protect the monument and create a public open space.

COMMUNITY INVOLVEMENT/PROGRAMME

A number of meetings were held with neighbourhood residents to show and discuss the conservation work being carried out.

VOCATIONAL TRAINING/CAPACITY BUILDING

The implementation team working on the Aslam al-Silahdar conservation project had been trained during previous conservation projects. The Aslam Mosque project ensured continuous *in situ* training of 40 local craftsmen and conservation technicians. Neighbourhood craftsmen were involved in producing lighting fixtures for the building.

CONTRACTING METHODS

All architectural and fine conservation works have been carried out with labour directly recruited and supervised by AKTC professional staff.

RELEVANT CODES/STANDARDS ADOPTED

The conservation project followed all the international conservation charters and guidelines. For other aspects, the Egyptian Code for Construction was adopted.

Partners

PUBLIC PARTNERS

Supreme Council of Antiquities.

Donors

World Monuments Fund, American Research Center in Egypt.

Authoritative Framework

The Supreme Council of Antiquities and Aga Khan Cultural Services-Egypt (2001–10), World Monuments Fund and the Aga Khan Trust for Culture (2001–03), 'Reuse Agreement' (The Supreme Council of Antiquities and AKCS-E; 2004–14).

Azhar Park

CAIRO, EGYPT

Reconciling conservation and development is a prerequisite for achieving improvements in the quality of life in environmentally and culturally sensitive places. It calls for the introduction of appropriate new functions such as the reuse of historic structures, improvement of services, urban regeneration of public open spaces, community supported rehabilitation of historic housing districts and the creation of parks.

Successful parks inspire residents, provide joy to viewers, and foster civil society in the important realm of leisure and connection to nature and one's environment. They become the settings for families to come together, novels, films and festivities, and are often the containers for memories of a society.

The involvement of the Aga Khan Trust for Culture (AKTC) in Egypt began with the Aga Khan's decision to donate a park to the citizens of Cairo, in 1984. Soon thereafter, the thirty-hectare site on al-Darassa was selected, because of its enormous potential as a 'lung' at the very centre of the historic Old City.

The site is surrounded by the most significant historic districts of Islamic Cairo. To the west are the Fatimid city and its extension, Darb al-Ahmar, with their wealth of mosques, *madrasas* and mausolea, signalled by a long line of minarets. To the south are the Sultan Hassan Mosque and its surroundings, as well as the Ayyubid Citadel. And to the east is the Mamluk "City of the Dead". The hilly topography of the site, formed by debris accumulated over centuries, now provides elevated viewpoints dominating the city and offers a spectacular 360° panorama over the townscape of Historic Cairo.

Following a major programme of debris removal and master grading involving the excavation and off-site disposal of more than one million cubic metres of fill, and the creation of specialized plant nurseries to identify the best plants and trees for the soil, terrain and climate, the experience of the site has been radically changed. The design makes maximum and skilful use of the site's location, elevated topography and unique vistas overlooking Historic Cairo. Transformed from hills of rubble, Azhar Park is a natural, organic landscaped area with an array of amenities next to a dense, urban community and medieval monuments.

The Park is marked by walkways, pools, hills, informal picnic spaces, formal gardens and amenities. Its vegetation varies from dry, succulent plants on the

The Citadel View Restaurant provides a dramatic view over the Park, with the Citadel of Cairo in the distance.

Opposite page:
Above, the view shows the Park's main spine, looking towards the Citadel.

Below, the site of the future Park in 1992, before work commenced, looking south down the same view.

Project Scope / Objectives

The aim was the master planning and landscape design for the environmental rehabilitation of a 30-hectare site and its transformation into a significant public, green space in the centre of Cairo that could act as an economic catalyst for the adjacent neighbourhood. The scope of tasks included environmental and geotechnical works, grading, landscape architecture (soft- and hard-scaped areas), horticulture, infrastructure engineering, architectural services for Park amenities, including two restaurants, entry gates, an amphitheatre, a lake and formal gardens, as well as the conservation of the Historic Wall and gates along the edge of the Park.

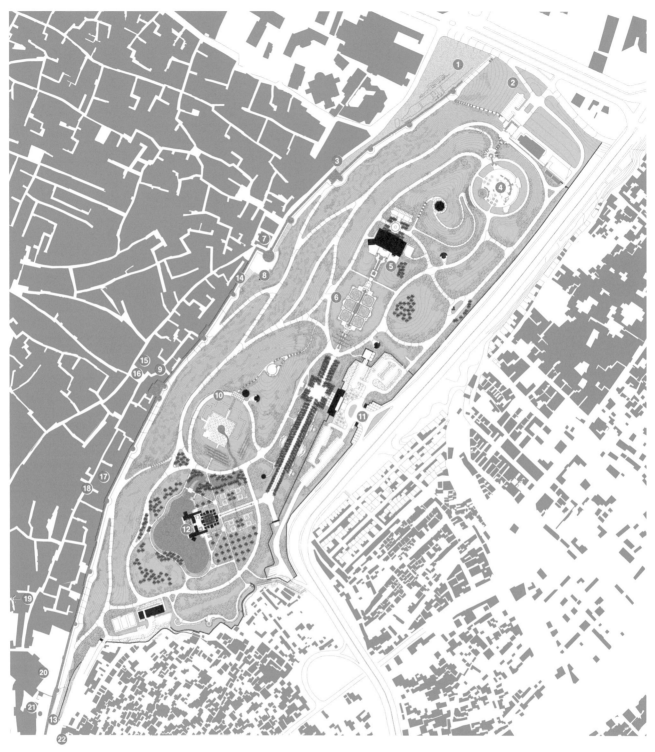

1 Archaeological Exhibition
2 Proposed Urban Plaza
3 Bab al-Barqiyya, Historic Wall gate
4 Children's Playground
5 Citadel View Restaurant
6 Formal Gardens
7 Burg al-Mahruq, Historic Wall
   fortress tower

8 Amphitheatre at Burg al-Mahruq
9 Bab al-Mahruq, Historic Wall gate
   and community acces gate
10 Hilltop Trianon Café
11 Main Entrance
12 Lakeside Café
13 Bab al-Wazir, community access gate

Other related HCP projects
14 Atfet Assad
15 Aslam Mosque
16 Aslam Square
17 Darb Shoughlan School
18 Darb Shoughlan Housing
19 Umm al-Sultan Shaaban Complex

20 Aqsunqur Mosque
21 Khayrbek Complex
22 Tarabay Complex

N
▲ |———————————| 150 m

Phasing 1984 → 2010

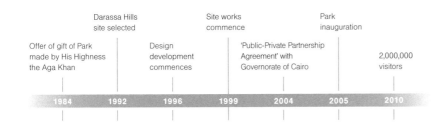

	Darassa Hills site selected		Site works commence		Park inauguration	
Offer of gift of Park made by His Highness the Aga Khan		Design development commences		'Public-Private Partnership Agreement' with Governorate of Cairo		2,000,000 visitors
1984	1992	1996	1999	2004	2005	2010

western slopes to lush, grassy meadows with shade trees, to formal gardens and, finally, to *bustan*-like orchard spaces. The variety of species, particularly native Egyptian plants, establishes a new benchmark for park spaces in the region. At Azhar Park, historical models of Islamic gardens are evoked in the form of symmetrical layout, inner and outer zones, the defining medium of pools and fountains, and important axes.

The Park is held together by a formal axis or spine that itself is tied together along its entire length by a water channel providing an additional and traditional theme from Islamic gardens. Water fountains and pools are dispersed and lead, ultimately, to the freer form of the lake in the south meadow. Gardens and pavilions in the classical Islamic tradition, surrounded by geometrically planted orchards, enhance the arrival point on the edge of the lake. The central pathway, accompanying alleyways and series of formal gardens are anchored at each end by the Citadel View Restaurant and Lakeside Café, which act as internal landmarks. A network of informal pathways surrounds the more formal areas and leads through all levels and corners of the site.

The terrain in the western half of the Park consists predominantly of steep and continuous slopes, running from the summits to the foot of the uncovered and restored Historic Wall. By means of extensive excavation along the Historic Wall, the park topography was brought in cascading slopes down to a new promenade, which forms a principal walkway at the base of the Wall and western slopes, interconnected to all parts of the Park.

Left, an aerial view of 2000 shows the site after debris removal and master grading.

Right, by 2006 the Park has become a much-needed "green lung" for overcrowded Cairo.

313

The design of the Citadel View Restaurant (above) is inspired by Fatimid archways, whereas the design of the Lakeside Café (below) is more abstract in its interpretation of Islamic architecture.

The western hillside is cloaked with flowering and succulent plants with luxuriant tones. Views from the many vantage points along the west, across these slopes and the Historic Wall to Old Cairo, beyond, with its rich constellation of monuments and minarets, offers a walk in an open-air museum, where the impressive history of Cairo unfolds with each step.

Significant time and attention was devoted to exploring the potential for a sound, creative and interpretative relationship between the architectural design treatment of key architectural features in the Park – in particular, the Citadel View Restaurant, the Lakeside Café and various plazas – and the architecture of Historic Cairo.

Due to size and centrality, Azhar Park fulfils a vital function in expanding park and green space available to the public in Greater Cairo, one of the densest cities in the world with a population that stood close to nineteen million in 2009. Operated under a 'Public-Private Partnership Agreement' between AKTC and the Governorate of Cairo, surpluses from Park revenue fund social and economic projects in the neighbouring Darb al-Ahmar district.

With over two million visitors in 2009 Azhar Park has proven to be self-sustainable and a driver and catalyst for a whole range of associated urban regeneration projects in its surroundings. It has become a case study for a variety of development challenges, ranging from environmental rehabilitation to cultural restoration and has become a model of development that can be replicated in many other settings, and in particular in the historic cities of the Islamic world.

Background

BRIEF HISTORY OF PROJECT SITE

The al-Darrasa site had been situated for centuries just outside the boundaries of Historic Old Cairo (the original city during the Fatimid and Ayyubid eras), marked by the Historic Walls of these periods. As Cairo grew, the Park site was used as a point for tipping debris and rubble from the Old City, arising from normal urban growth and earthquakes. In more recent times, the Governorate of Cairo had used the grounds for horse stables and then construction equipment, which were cleared to make way for three municipal water reservoirs and distribution pipeline network (by USAID) and the future Park proposed by AKTC. AKTC and USAID reached special agreements with the General Organization of Greater Cairo Water Supplies (GOGCWS) for the interface between the Park and the water reservoir systems.

Challenges

PROJECT RISKS

A project of this complexity requires coordination with government partners. Azhar Park presented a new model of cultural development both for AKTC and for the Government of Egypt and necessitated the need for legal agreements and approvals with regard to public partners and the GOGCWS for the design and installation of a park on this site; a legal and technical agreement with the Supreme Council of Antiquities for the restoration of the Historic Wall; and coordination with the Governorate of Cairo to determine the site's eastern boundaries. Additionally, there was a large geotechnical risk with respect to the unstable and poorly consolidated soils and extreme slopes which required regrading and special subsurface drainage systems.

SITE CONDITIONS

The site soils were highly unstable due to the lack of compaction of the man-made fills. The Park design and landscaping had to accommodate and address steep slopes, highly saline soil and ongoing encroachment of the site on the south by the Bab al-Wazir Cemetery.

DEMOGRAPHICS

The population of Greater Cairo at the time of the Park's planning (17 million) and lack of sufficient park space in Cairo indicated an extremely high level of visitation, especially on weekends and feast days. The project needed to be open to the largest number of people possible while safeguarding the quality of the plants and hardscape. The ticketing rates needed to ensure that the Park would be self-sustainable, yet would not exclude any income group.

ENVIRONMENTAL CONCERNS

The greening of the site presented a significant horticultural challenge due to soil conditions and the need to irrigate such a large site, areas of which are steeply sloping. The project necessitated the establishment of an off-site nursery in which, over several years, plants, trees and ground cover appropriate to the site conditions and climate were propagated.

INFRASTRUCTURE

The site required more than 1000 cubic metres of water daily for irrigation purposes; a 7600-square-metre man-made lake was provided to serve as a safety reservoir as well as a Park amenity. The practice of high levels of visitation of parks in Cairo at night called for a comprehensive lighting system. Irrigated green spaces required subsurface drainage and collection systems.

BUILDING CONDITIONS

Due to the poor geotechnical conditions, there was a need for specially prepared sub-bases for hardscape surfaces, liners for irrigated zones and piling support for all substantial buildings.

Significant Issues and Impact

DATA COLLECTION/SURVEYS

Site surveys originating from aerial and terrestrial surveys were digitalized; numerous geotechnical surveys and soil tests were carried out with Cairo University and foreign partners; research on existing parks in Cairo was undertaken with the assistance of Shawki Associates (Egypt).

MASTER PLANNING PROCESS

A project this size required careful review of public access (pedestrian and vehicular), visitation and circulation studies, park facility programme development, infrastructure load projections, feasibility planning, and construction logistical analysis.

PLANNING ISSUES

Gates and special areas were subjected to detailed planning, including pedestrian access and circulation, presentation circuits, rehabilitation of houses encroaching on the Historic Wall, promenades on the ramparts and at the base of the Wall and rehabilitation of interior galleries and passages.

HISTORIC BUILDINGS/MONUMENTS CONSERVED

As a corollary to this project, the excavation, documentation, conservation and restoration of the adjacent, 1500-metre Historic Wall was carried out by an AKTC/AKCS-E team in coordination with the Supreme Council of Antiquities.

NEW BUILDING FACILITIES

Azhar Park was designed by Sites International (Egypt). The entry gate and Citadel View Restaurant was designed by Rami el-Dahan and Soheir Farid Architects (Egypt). The Lakeside Café was designed by Serge Santelli Architect (France).

COMMUNITY INVOLVEMENT/PROGRAMME

The Park project was closely coordinated by AKTC/AKCS-E with the two related HCP projects under the Area Development umbrella: the conservation of the Historic Wall and Darb al-Ahmar socio-economic projects. The entire Area Development Project was the subject of careful coordinated planning and the sharing of technical knowledge and resources.

VOCATIONAL TRAINING/CAPACITY BUILDING

In the construction phase of the Park, training and employment of surveyors and site labour was sourced from the adjacent community wherever feasible. A certain amount of the wood furniture was made in the Darb al-Ahmar carpentry workshop. During operations, the Park has employed a large number of nearby community residents in its operations division.

RELEVANT CODES/STANDARDS ADOPTED

Master grading and surveying, done by trade contractors, was internally supervised and coordinated by a project management team. Site work, landscaping and construction have followed Egyptian building codes. Conservation of the Historic Wall was completed in accordance with international charters.

LESSONS LEARNED

The project was pioneering in terms of testing and identifying solutions for: the greening of sharply inclined and unstable slopes; irrigation systems with below-surface clay and membrane liners and drainage collection; the development of special controlled fill sub-bases for hardscapes; the propagation and transplantation of large areas of ground cover, plants and trees; a sophisticated blending of a derelict site with a historic district in terms of access, views and compatible architecture; and the development of a detailed operational plan which would ensure the Park's sustainability. Azhar Park has become a precursor to many subsequent projects in HCP's parks portfolio. It offers lessons in planning, design, feasibility studies, linkage to adjacent community development initiatives and operations under a 'Public-Private Partnership' arrangement, and now serves as a model for other HCP projects in their conception.

Partners

PUBLIC PARTNERS

Governorate of Cairo.

Authoritative Framework

A protocol agreement between the Governorate of Cairo and AKTC was signed in 1990. A 'Public-Private Partnership Agreement' between the Governorate of Cairo and AKTC for the management and operation of Azhar Park was signed in July 2007.

Historic Wall

CAIRO, EGYPT

The historic urban Wall is the south-eastern segment of Cairo's Ayyubid fortifications, which were partially exposed during the works to create the new Azhar Park. The Wall measures over 1500 metres in length, running north from Bab al-Wazir to al-Azhar Street, and forms the boundary between the Darb al-Ahmar district of Historic Cairo and the new Park. It is the longest and best-preserved portion of Cairo's old fortifications. Following preliminary investigations, the Aga Khan Trust for Culture (AKTC) began restoration works in 2000. Most of the work along the side facing the Park was completed in 2008.

Built in the twelfth and thirteenth centuries by Salah al-Din and his successors, this portion of the city wall was Cairo's eastern boundary for centuries. Over time, its role changed: although it continued to be a defining element for the city, it long ago ceased to be a defensive structure. This shift in function meant that the city gradually spread to and into the very edge of the Wall, following an accretive process common to historic cities everywhere. From the fifteenth century onwards, the area just outside the Wall began to be used as a dumping ground and the Wall gradually disappeared under the debris, where, in fact, it remained protected from the ravages of time and weather.

Today, following the interventions to create the Park, the outer face of the Historic Wall is once again exposed to view and to the elements, while, on the city side, private development pressures as well as institutional requirements raise complex urban development issues. The interventions considered not only the preservation of the Wall, but also how best to intervene in the surrounding urban context. Thus, comprehensive restoration, planning and design policies were established with regard to the monument itself, as well as the residential fabric abutting the Wall, the historic gates and the pedestrian promenade along the western edge of the new Park.

History

Construction of the Historic Wall was begun in 1176 by Salah al-Din, a Kurd of the Ayyubid clan who came to Cairo from Syria and overthrew the Fatimid caliphate in 1171. Salah al-Din's idea of a single wall surrounding the entire city of Cairo would prove a long-lasting legacy. The new fortifications encircled

A new paved promenade is now located along the Historic Wall inside the Park.

Opposite page:
Above, the Historic Wall acts as both the perimeter of the Park and an interface with the Darb al-Ahmar neighbourhood.

Below, the most prominent tower of the Historic Wall, Burg al-Mahruq, was still buried in debris in 1994. Its excavation was a painstaking archaeological process (see p. 321 for the final result).

Project Scope / Objectives

Documentation and the development of presentation designs and operational plans were carried out, as were archaeological excavation, shoring and stabilization, cleaning, reconstruction of core walls, stone repair, stone replacement, re-pointing, construction of retaining walls, and the construction of metal stairs, gates and parapets. Finally, electrical services were installed.

Left, the fortifications included advanced defensive techniques such as arrow slits.

Right, restored houses have been integrated into the historic preservation of Bab al-Mahruq.

Opposite page:
A plan of Bab al-Mahruq in its context (above) and in section (below).

within a single system the Citadel and the Fatimid city, as well as the pre-Fatimid settlements of Fustat, al-Askar and al-Qata'i. The new city walls were built entirely of stone and made use of new advanced defensive techniques imported from Syria, with bent entrances and arrow slits reaching to the floor.

The east Wall was built as part of the new fortification and seems to have remained important for two centuries after its construction. Soon after, as the threat posed by crusader armies and other invaders declined, so did the importance of maintaining the defensive walls. On the eastern side, urban expansion virtually stopped. Already during the late Mamluk and early Ottoman periods, although the walls continued to mark the limits of the Old City, the area outside the fortifications became a dumping ground, a practice that continued unabated during the following centuries.

The maps drawn at the time of the French occupation, around 1800, in fact show that buildings in Darb al-Ahmar were generally built right up to the edge of the city. During the rest of the nineteenth century an increasing number of travellers came to Egypt, who sketched and photographed what they saw. A series of panoramas taken by French photographer Pascal Sebah in 1880 provides one of the most valuable visual documents of the eastern Historic Wall, showing that much of the original stonework, including the crenellations, still existed at that time.

In 1882 the government established the Comité de Conservation des Monuments de l'Art Arabe to preserve Egypt's Islamic and Christian architectural heritage. Although the Comité repaired the city walls from time to time during the first half of the twentieth century, it was not until 1950 that they undertook a major campaign along the eastern Historic Wall. This consisted of the reconstruction of two towers along with extensive replacement of the missing facing stonework in several areas of the flank wall. For the next fifty years no further repairs or restoration were undertaken.

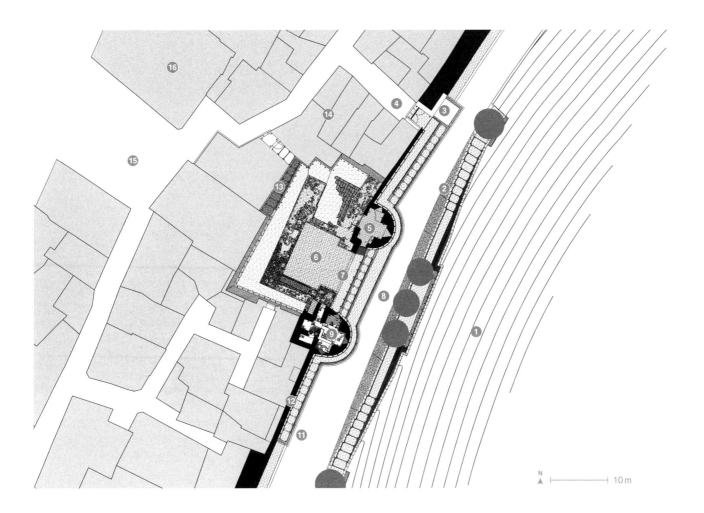

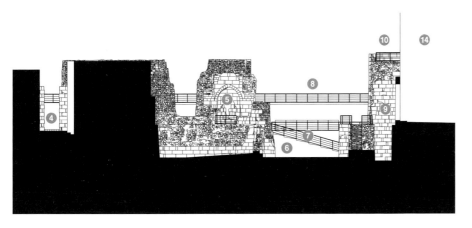

1 Azhar Park
2 Stepped Ramp and Walkway
  between Community and Park
3 Park Ticket Office
4 Community Street, access to
  and from the Park
5 North Fortress Tower, viewing
  area with new access stairs
6 Ruins of Bab al-Mahruq Exhibit
7 Ramp from Intermediate Area to Ruins
8 Historic Wall Promenade
9 South Fortress Tower, exhibits
  with new access stairs
10 South Fortress Tower, viewing platform
11 Ramp from Historic Wall
   Promenade to Intermediate Area
12 Historic Wall
13 Service Entrance
14 Surrounding Housing, rehabilitated
15 Aslam Square, public space renewal
16 Aslam Mosque, restored monument

Above, an archaeologist working on top of Tower 5, excavating the remains of Ottoman houses built later on top of the Wall.

Below, a view south along the Wall from Tower 10, showing a defensive tower under scaffolding.

The interior of Burg al-Mahruq, which has now become a space for exhibitions, after its restoration.

The Historic Wall remained, as it had been for centuries, the eastern boundary of the densely built up Darb al-Ahmar district of Historic Cairo. The continued dumping of rubbish meant that the mounds of debris, now known as the Darassa Hills, had buried the outer face of the Wall all the way up to the level of the crenellations. It was only after AKTC began moving earth for the future Azhar Park that the accumulated debris was removed. The regrading brought to light not only the buried section of the Wall known through early photographs and historic maps, but also the northern section, unrecorded even on Napoleon's map of 1798, and probably buried since Mamluk times.

The Survey

The first step in the conservation process was a comprehensive study of the Wall's physical condition followed by a detailed assessment of each part of the monument that would be subject to intervention. The general study documented the Wall's overall condition, including an analysis of the masonry and identification of areas of significant deterioration, distinguishing between the loss of facing stone and total loss of the Wall. It also documented the presence and extent of previous repairs. The subsequent detailed condition survey provided a fuller quantitative analysis, complemented with a qualitative assessment of the causes and effects of deterioration. Severity of loss, for example, was classified according to the extent and depth, as well as to whether the process was still active or inactive. In addition, samples were taken for laboratory testing to ascertain the exact nature of the materials and their conditions and problems.

Together, the field survey, graphic documentation and laboratory work yielded a comprehensive record of the construction of the Wall and its present state of conservation, as well as the diagnostic tools needed to formulate an intervention programme. Recommended measures included archaeological investigation, emergency stabilization, masonry treatment (including cleaning, removal of salt and biological growth, grouting, consolidation of deteriorating stone and selective stone replacement), as well as limited reconstruction where needed to maintain the structural stability or visual continuity of the Wall. The resulting policies and guidelines for masonry intervention were designed to achieve maximum retention of the original historic fabric while ensuring the visual and functional continuity of the Wall as an urban element.

Approach and Methodology of Intervention

The restoration works started in 2000 with the launching of pilot interventions on limited sections of the Historic Wall gradually extended to increasingly greater portions of the monument. The principles underlying the interventions can be summarized as follows: firstly, to research and document all evidence, including physical, archival and historical information, before, during and after intervention; secondly, to respect the cumulative age-value of the structure, by recognizing the stratification of human activity, displaying the passage of time and embodying different materials and techniques, as well as changing cultural beliefs and values; thirdly, to safeguard authenticity as a cultural value associated with the original actions of the making or remaking of an object or site, recognized as the embodiment of authorship or the record of a time and place; and fourthly, to avoid harm to the monument, either by minimizing physical interference to re-establish structural and aesthetic legibility and meaning, or by intervening in ways that will allow other options and further treatment in the future.

These tenets are rooted in internationally recognized and accepted standards of conservation, namely the 'International Charter for the Conservation and Restoration of Monuments and Sites' of 1964 (the Venice Charter). It builds on the fundamental principles set out in the Athens Charter (1931) with the added emphasis on the importance of context, the discouragement of reconstruction except in cases of anastylosis (reassembling of preserved fragments), and the integration of modern scientific technology where appropriate and useful.

In line with these general principles, the intervention guidelines applied by the AKTC team to the conservation of the Historic Wall expressed, whenever possible, preference for retention or compatible repair of original fabric over reconstruction. The recommendations for intervention on the surrounding urban fabric advocated respect for the changes accrued over time, in order to preserve the integrity, scale and significance of the Wall in its current configuration and context. Ultimately, the proposed interventions promoted continuity rather than transformation. The long-term goal is to integrate and harmonize the remnants of a valuable past with present realities and future uses in ways that are compatible and sustainable.

The following conservation treatments were carried out between 2000 and 2008 at the Historic Wall: stone replacement, masonry cleaning, epoxy injection and reattachment, repointing, plaster reattachment, core injection, and the application of artificial patinas. All interventions were thoroughly documented. Selected replacement materials were physically and chemically compatible with the original fabric and clearly distinguishable upon close examination.

The Wall as a Culural Resource and Visitor Destination

Conservation of the original wall structure and preservation of the living city fabric around the Historic Wall are seen as the best antidotes against further decay on the one hand, and destructive commercialization on the other. The actions to ensure that the Historic Wall maintains its original significance and that it be properly reintegrated into its contemporary context included: firstly, creating pedestrian circulation along the western side of the Park and access through the former city gates (Bab al-Mahruq, Bab al-Barqiyya and Bab al-Wazir) to enhance the perception of the Historic Wall as a dynamic edge and meeting point, rather than as a barrier between the community and the Park; secondly, establishing didactic programmes, exhibits and an overall interpretive scheme to enhance appreciation of the Wall as an important urban feature of Historic Cairo, to explain its changing role in the development of the city and to introduce visitors to the life of the Darb al-Ahmar community; thirdly, introducing educational and training activities that are relevant to promoting a deeper understanding of the cultural heritage among visitors and residents and the development of capacity through enrichment of local skills and abilities to preserve and protect Historic Cairo; and fourthly, ensuring the future management and long-term sustainability of the Wall through the establishment of permanent repair and maintenance programmes and the monitoring of future changes and transformations.

The shift in perceiving the Historic Wall as an abstract, isolated monument to its reinvention as part of a larger urban programme can turn this obsolete structure, buried for centuries and removed from the city's mainstream development, into a cultural asset and vital component of the rehabilitation of Historic Cairo. The challenge ahead lies in safeguarding the remains and true significance of the Historic Wall, while shaping its new role in the years to come.

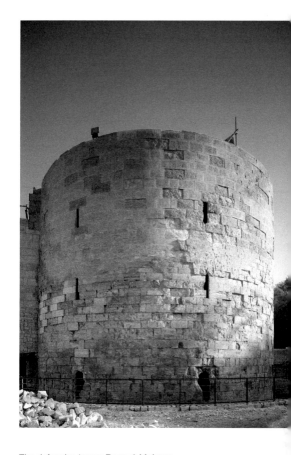

The defensive tower, Burg al-Mahruq, now seen unearthed and conserved (see page 317 for a view of the same site before intervention).

The restored Darb Shoughlan Community Centre, formerly a school, is integrated into its historic surrounds. Once a barrier, the Wall has become a catalyst for regeneration.

Phasing 1999 → 2010

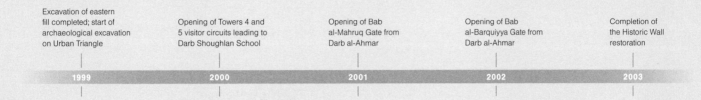

Excavation of eastern fill completed; start of archaeological excavation on Urban Triangle	Opening of Towers 4 and 5 visitor circuits leading to Darb Shoughlan School	Opening of Bab al-Mahruq Gate from Darb al-Ahmar	Opening of Bab al-Barquiyya Gate from Darb al-Ahmar	Completion of the Historic Wall restoration
1999	**2000**	**2001**	**2002**	**2003**

Background

BRIEF HISTORY OF PROJECT SITE
The eastern portion of the Historic Wall is part of the city wall of Cairo built by Salah al-Din in the later part of the 12th century to contain the Fatimid city and its suburbs, as well as the pre-Fatimid city of Fustat, within a single fortification system. In the following centuries, the area outside the eastern wall became a dumping ground, rising to a height of some 30 metres and eventually burying the fortifications under the debris. The accumulated rubbish formed a major barrier to modern urban expansion and contributed to preserving the Historic Wall to this day. Following the completion of Azhar Park, approximately 1500 metres of Wall were exposed, from Bab al-Wazir to al-Azhar Street, forming the boundary between the Darb al-Ahmar district and the Park. A comprehensive restoration programme began in 2000.

Challenges

SITE CONDITIONS
The poor state of conservation and unstable conditions of some portions of the Historic Wall required extensive shoring. Also housing encroachments against the walls, as well as inside and on top of the one-time fortifications, posed an additional challenge and greatly complicated restoration work.

INFRASTRUCTURE
New water and sewer connections had to be established for the houses abutting the Wall to avoid infiltration of water and rising damp. New concealed electrical connections had to be established to light the ramparts and interior galleries of the restored monument.

BUILDING CONDITIONS
The recording of the Wall's general conditions (Level 1) distinguished between total loss (core and facing stones), partial loss (facing stones and parts of the core walls), loss of facing stones, structural instability, presence of earlier repairs, basal erosion, and loss of paving along the ramparts. The detailed survey (Level 2) recorded the conditions of the individual stones and distinguished cases of surface erosion, and the presence of black crust or carbon soot, cracking, de-lamination,

detachment, disaggregation, displacement, flaking, loss and the presence of salts and metal stains. In addition, housing encroachments were classified by type and included houses built: along the back face of the Wall; over part of the rampart; within the interior galleries; and to replace, in part or in full, entire sections of the Wall.

Significant Issues and Impact

DATA COLLECTION/SURVEYS
The documentation prepared before the interventions included architectural, archaeological and condition surveys. In addition, laboratory analyses on existing mortars and stones were carried out throughout the restoration work to identify best matches and compatible materials.

MASTER PLANNING PROCESS
These defined the general programme and priorities of intervention for the entire Wall and led to the preparation of area plans, descriptions of works, operational schedules and budgets.

PLANNING ISSUES
Gates and special areas were subjected to detailed planning, including pedestrian access and circulation, presentation circuits, rehabilitation of houses encroaching on the Wall, promenades on the ramparts and at the base of the Wall and rehabilitation of interior galleries and passages.

VOCATIONAL TRAINING/CAPACITY BUILDING
In order to disseminate and reinforce local expertise in architectural conservation, the Historic Wall restoration served as a training ground for the development of skills among Egyptian professionals and craftsmen. On-the-job training activities included the cutting, dressing and tooling of stones, preparation and use of mortars and renders, stone masonry repair and cleaning, and stone masonry construction.

CONTRACTING METHODS
With the exception of a limited number of subcontracts for electrical works, all restoration activities were carried out with direct labour recruited by AKTC, often from the resident community, and supervised by the project's professional staff.

RELEVANT CODES/STANDARDS ADOPTED
All conservation work was undertaken in accordance with the relevant international charters and in keeping with Egyptian antiquities laws and procedures. The formulation of standards and operational guidelines drew on documented examples of similar types of interventions carried out elsewhere in the region.

LESSONS LEARNED
Techniques and guidelines for the treatment, repair and replacement of limestone in traditional construction, as well as the characterization and matching of traditional mortars, were thoroughly investigated and tested during the course of the project. This work provides lessons which can be applied to similar AKTC/HCP projects carried out in the surrounding region and elsewhere.

Partners

PUBLIC PARTNERS
Governorate of Cairo, Supreme Council of Antiquities.

Authoritative Framework

'Memorandum of Understanding' between the Supreme Council of Antiquities and the Aga Khan Trust for Culture covering the restoration of the Historic Wall and other monuments in Darb al-Ahmar.

KHOROG
TAJIKISTAN

Khorog City Master Plan

KHOROG, TAJIKISTAN

The city of Khorog is the administrative centre of the Gorno-Badakhshan autonomous region and the second largest city in Tajikistan. The city suffers from the lack of a land-use plan and is in need of a clearly defined city development plan. In 2007 AKTC prepared a 'Development Control Report' that outlined the development history of Khorog and characterized the hazardous and isolated mountain environment that severely restricts safe land supply and makes servicing a challenge. The report recognized a general lack of local planning methodology and human resource capacity to guide Khorog in the many needed areas of urban services reform, and recommended more orderly controlled growth as a goal with a minimum of disruption to cultural and community norms.

In mid 2009 a planning team was engaged to develop a Master Plan in coordination with the local and national government authorities and with AKDN agencies operating in the city. The planning team proposed a phased pattern of modest growth synchronized with services, sensitive to impacts on individuals while recognizing the need for affordability. Khorog is located in a seismically hazardous corridor, thus there is a need to review future design while allowing time for the construction industry to mature. Approval processes that raise safety standards in this context become all the more paramount.

The Master Plan proposes a set of guidelines and recommendations to address the future growth of the city by defining development patterns that allow the city to expand in a controlled manner while meeting the needs of its citizens. The AKTC commissioned planning team is currently completing a development model that focuses on defining guidelines on city planning and building codes; understanding and guiding the spatial city patterns over the next twenty years; and identifying key areas of intervention, infrastructure requirements and opportunistic areas of economic improvement.

The Master Plan goes into further detail, identifying city-wide impact recommendations that include improving city infrastructure; updating building codes; emphasizing energy efficiency and earthquake-proof building design; developing a life-safety strategy in the event of a natural disaster; increasing the city's self-sufficiency in food needs through community green spaces; and creating an institutional city building and planning unit and properly trained staff.

The town of Khorog is situated on the Gunt River, 2100 metres above sea level in the heart of the Pamir Mountains near the border with Afghanistan.

Opposite page:
Above, the axonometric view is a detail from the Khorog Master Plan.

Below, a view of the Park's contiguity with the river.

Preceding pages:
Children enjoying the Park equipment amongst the poplar trees that are changing colour with the autumn.

1 Hospital Entry Square Improvements
2 Main Building of Existing Hospital
3 Future Mixed-Use Building
4 Path Improvements
5 Proposed Sculpture Garden
6 Public Square Improvements
7 Facade Improvements to Existing Pump Building
8 Proposed Park and Children's Play Area
9 Pedestrian Bridge Improvements

Project Scope/Objectives

To stem the tide of unregulated, inefficient urban sprawl in Khorog, AKTC is developing a Strategic Master Plan with the aim of sharing best practices on city planning ideas and methodologies with the Government of Tajikistan. The programme seeks to establish a set of design and planning principles that will serve as the foundation for collaborative efforts, and to provide technical services for planning. Work on building and land-control design and management, which recognize the vulnerable nature of the region and the limits of sustainable growth, is also underway.

Proposed

1 Four-Storey Mixed-Use Buildings, lining street edge
2 Landmark Buildings, to punctuate important intersections
3 Preservation of Traditional Settlement Areas
4 Four- to Six-Storey Residential Buildings
5 Theatre District Housing
6 New Pedestrian Bridge
7 River-Edge Improvements
8 Cultural Square
9 River-Edge Library
10 Row-House Typology, along river edge

Existing

11 Food Market
12 School
13 Jamatkhana
14 Khorog City Park
15 Theatre
16 Khorog University

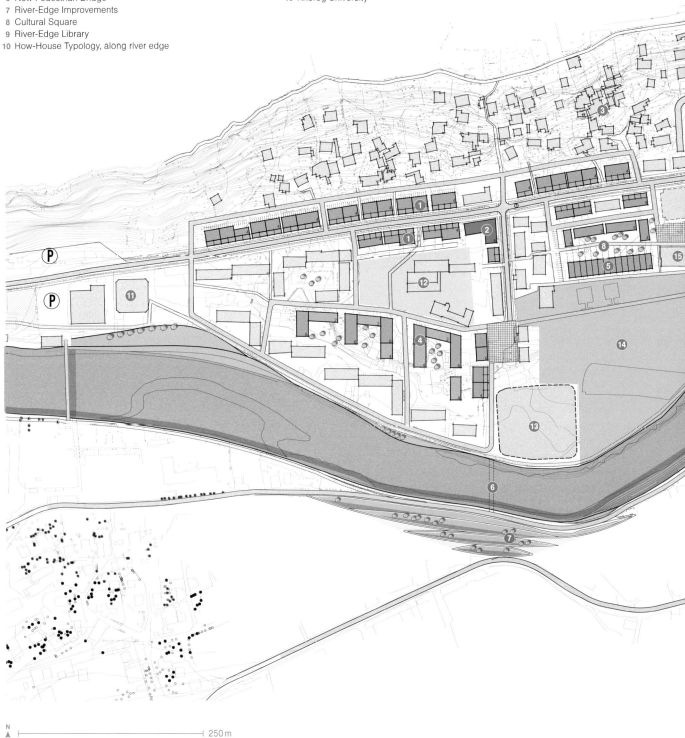

N
▲ ├──────────────────────┤ 250 m

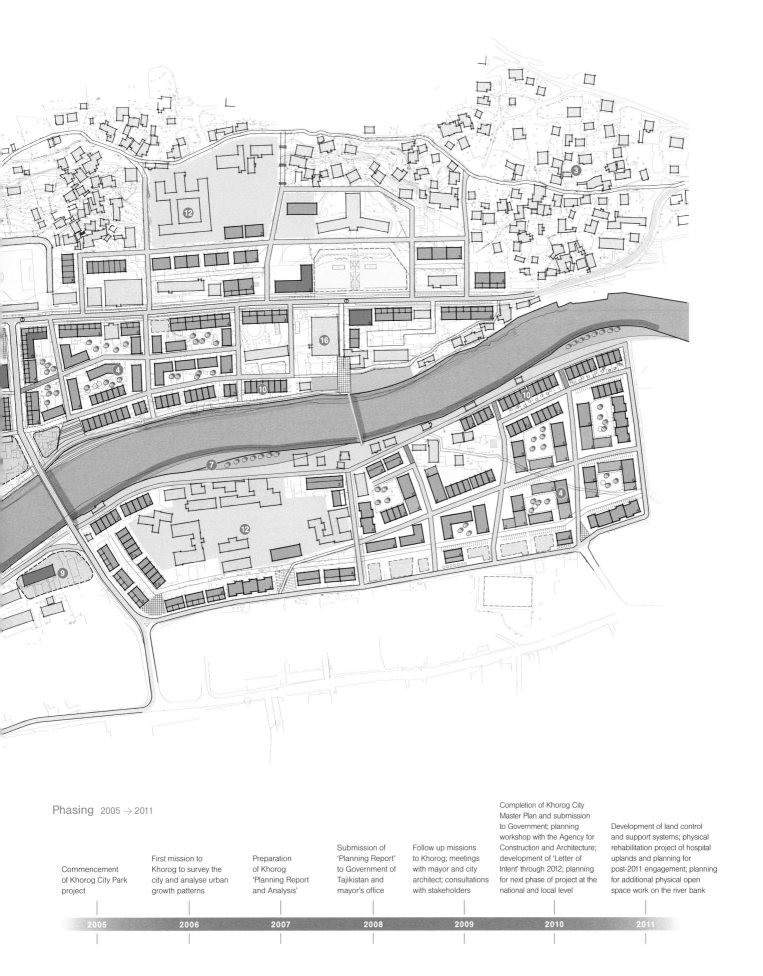

Phasing 2005 → 2011

Commencement
of Khorog City Park
project

First mission to
Khorog to survey the
city and analyse urban
growth patterns

Preparation
of Khorog
'Planning Report
and Analysis'

Submission of
'Planning Report'
to Government of
Tajikistan and
mayor's office

Follow up missions
to Khorog; meetings
with mayor and city
architect; consultations
with stakeholders

Completion of Khorog City
Master Plan and submission
to Government; planning
workshop with the Agency for
Construction and Architecture;
development of 'Letter of
Intent' through 2012; planning
for next phase of project at the
national and local level

Development of land control
and support systems; physical
rehabilitation project of hospital
uplands and planning for
post-2011 engagement; planning
for additional physical open
space work on the river bank

2005	2006	2007	2008	2009	2010	2011

Khorog City Park

KHOROG, TAJIKISTAN

The town of Khorog is the capital of the Gorno-Badakhshan autonomous region in Tajikistan and it is situated in the heart of the Pamir Mountains near the border with Afghanistan. Khorog is a remote settlement and out of necessity must cultivate self-sufficiency. Its dedicated recreational areas are few but vital to the lives of the inhabitants as spaces to socialize and places to play.

The Park site, comprising a run-down open space on the riverfront, is roughly in the city centre of Khorog and is nested on an alluvial plain only a few hundred metres wide, caught between the steep and barren mountain range of the Pamirs and a bend in the Gunt River. The site was gifted to His Highness the Aga Khan on the occasion of the fortieth anniversary of his Imamat, and since 2005 has been the focus of a rehabilitation project designed to offer visitors a high-standard public park with amenities.

Between June and August 2004 the Aga Khan Trust for Culture (AKTC) initiated an exercise of extensive consultation with the population of Khorog, with the aim of assessing what would be core functions and essential features of an upgraded park. The resulting six-hectare Khorog Park is a place to reflect, relax and enjoy nature in the company of friends and family. At its commencement, the project presented an opportunity to provide an enhanced park facility for the entire city; a lively green place and civic space for all of its citizens; recreational facilities for families and children; and the means to integrate the urban green space into the city network.

Construction of the Park commenced in spring 2005. Work on the Park by AKTC included the enhancement of the already well-wooded area; a programme of levelling works, topsoil enhancement, fertilizing and irrigation; the sowing of lawns; planting of appropriate plants and flowers, which were raised in an on-site nursery; and the restoration of stone channels used for irrigation in the summer. The first phase of Park construction was completed in 2007 and involved approximately ninety local workers. Work on the Park's main features – the pond, the restaurant, tea-house and open-air theatre – was completed in 2009.

The design inspiration for the Park came as a direct response to the dramatic climate and landscape of the region and the common need for a public garden

People stroll along the main paved spine looking towards the north-western entrance to the Park. The Pamir Mountains can be seen in the background.

Opposite page:
Workmen are laying out stone paving in a special zig-zag pattern. Where possible, all of the designs, as well as the materials, are local.

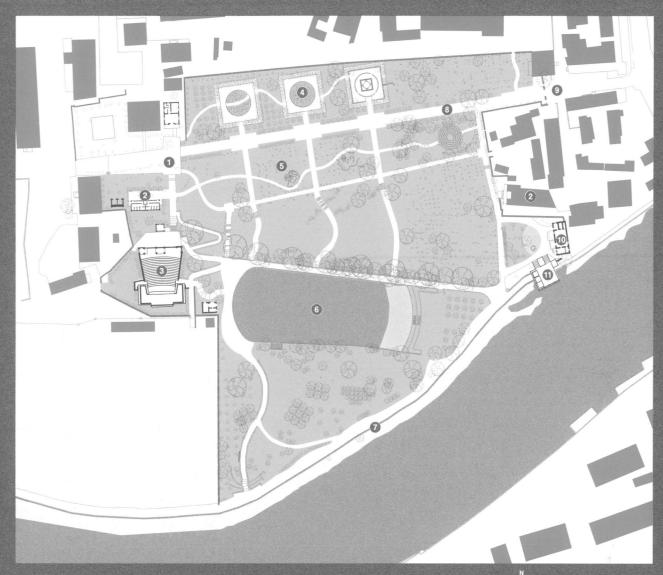

1 North-West Entrance   4 Formal Gardens   7 River Promenade   10 Restaurant / Internet Café
2 Toilets   5 Children's Play Area   8 Main Axial Path   11 Chai Khana (tea-house)
3 Open-Air Theatre   6 Swimming Pool and Ice-Skating Rink   9 North-East Entrance

N   150 m

Project Scope / Objectives

The development of Khorog City Park contributes a significant public green space to the city. It was gifted to His Highness the Aga Khan on the occasion of the 40th anniversary of his Imamat, and, since 2003, it has been the focus of a rehabilitation project designed to offer visitors the possibility to reflect, relax and enjoy nature. Income generated by a newly built tea-house, café and open-air theatre aim to support the ongoing Park operations.

Left, steps lead down from a main pathway.
Adjacent to the path is a play area.

Right, children swim and sun themselves
at the swimming pool ('The Pond'), which
functions as an ice-skating rink in winter.

Opposite page:
A view of the waterfront walk along the
Gunt River in Khorog City Park with the
Pamir Mountains behind.

for both refuge and recreation. The design intent was to preserve the best of what existed and then work creatively with the ordinary – stone, water, flowers and shade trees – in an extraordinary way.

The Park, containing facilities such as a restaurant and tea-house and an open-air theatre, along with such other attractions as a children's playground and stone labyrinth, encourages visitors to explore further. It is central to Khorog's riverine urban form and incorporates an old meander as a water feature: in summer a pool for swimming and reflections, in winter an ice rink. It has been designed with the convenience of users in mind, with extensive lighting and benches, and a public toilet block.

Magnificent mature avenues and groves of Pamir poplar, natural rock outcrops and even historic gravity irrigation canals were integrated into the design and protected during construction. The long, harsh winters make spring and its accompanying blossom of flowering trees, crab apples and cherries an emotional event. Although short, the summer growing season is special to the inhabitants, who nurture and love flowers. The Park has three formal flower gardens designed as discreet and peaceful chambers with generous seating. They, in turn, link with formal and informal paths for strolling through the woods and glades of the Park.

The stone-paved riverside promenade, an important pedestrian corridor, is enhanced by a revetment of the river embankment and, with the addition of stairs and river wall, presents a platform from where the stunning natural landscape of the area can be appreciated. The use of stone is a major feature of the Park, particularly in the extensive rehabilitation and extension of pathways, often paved in striking herringbone patterns. The path of the main spine, panoramic pathway, riverside promenade, the wall of the ponds, fountains, stairways and features in the garden chambers are also built using stone, often involving exquisite detailing.

In the evening, restrained lighting offers a more urban dimension to the Park experience. The enthusiastic response of the local population and visitors has been very encouraging and should ensure Khorog City Park's future. The development of Khorog City Park and its surrounding urban environment contributes a significant public green space to the city and has become an integral part of the circulation through the city. Its revival represents a substantial step towards the revitalization of Khorog as a whole.

Background

BRIEF HISTORY OF PROJECT SITE

The site was part of the Gunt River flood plain including an elbow of redundant meander, now a pond. It has many mature trees, especially the distinctive Pamir poplar. It survived as an area of open space on the banks of the river within the very centre of the city's urban development. When still part of the former USSR, the area was developed as a civic park, with some formal pathways, flower beds and statuary. The riverbank, subject to erosion, was formalized. It was a conduit for two major cross-town thoroughfares, a pedestrian link below and parallel to the main road, and a riverside walkway on top of failing bank revetments. Overused and under-maintained, the park fell into disrepair and ad hoc animal grazing, erosion and encroachment continued. Moves to restore and upgrade the site began, leading to the opening of the new multi-purpose Park.

Challenges

PROJECT RISKS

The river adjacent to the Park has a fearsome summer flow, due to melt water from glaciers upstream, where strong currents can carry large boulders and batter obstacles. Careful survey of the riverbed and banks, flow rate and volumes, were useful to scientifically inform the engineering design specifications for new revetments. Khorog's remoteness made importing materials difficult and so local sourcing was paramount.

SITE CONDITIONS

The extreme mountain and valley topography, combined with the flood plain of the river, severely limited available land for both urban and open spaces. Long winters with deep snow and frozen ground require the seasonal coordination of works. In addition, the area is prone to earthquakes.

ENVIRONMENTAL CONCERNS

Potential riverbank erosion, pollution of the river during construction and the protection of site vegetation were all ongoing environment issues during the roll out of this project.

BUILDING CONDITIONS

Seasonal extremes required tight and rapid programming of works and shift working. Incomplete site works were protected during winter close downs. Local materials, namely stone, were used throughout the Park for pavings, structures and buildings. Specific attention was given to frost proofing of construction details and incorporating structural elements in buildings to offset earthquake damage. Most of the plant material was sourced from either the local State Botanical Garden or neighbouring farms in order to ensure its hardiness, suitability, ease of transport and to support local suppliers.

Significant Issues and Impact

DATA COLLECTION/SURVEYS

The documentation prepared before the interventions included an evaluation of all site features, rocky outcrops, specimen trees, boundary condition, offsite views, adjacent development proposals and river dynamics, including a visual assessment of the riverbank opposite the Park. Prototypes of construction materials and details were produced early on in the planning process to inform design and define acceptable levels of workmanship.

MASTER PLANNING PROCESS

The master planning process defined the general programme and priorities of intervention and framed the character of a unique Tajik City Park. This led to the preparation of area plans, descriptions of works, operational standards and budgets. The plan was tailored to its context within the heart of the city. In form and function it was designed to interact with adjacent land uses, be they planned *jamatkhana*, residential, commercial or city pedestrian linkages.

INFRASTRUCTURE

New lines for water, sewage and electrical reticulation were installed to service proposed Park facilities. New bore holes and an irrigation ring main were installed to serve the new Park's planting and provide a clean source of water for the central pond. Several existing buildings were rehabilitated or transformed for new relevant purposes, namely Park administration and maintenance, ablution facilities, open-air theatre, and tea-house and restaurant precinct. Few construction resources were available *in situ*, but creative use of stone and local plants enhanced the project implementation.

COMMUNITY INVOLVEMENT/PROGRAMME

School children participated in Park clean-ups in non-construction areas during the upgrade and even the army contributed to general site clearance works.

VOCATIONAL TRAINING/CAPACITY BUILDING

Stone masonry, general construction, landscape earthworks and horticulture were all fields of capacity development in the execution of this project.

Partners

PUBLIC PARTNERS

City of Khorog, Gorno-Badakhshan Autonomous Oblast.

ACKNOWLEDGMENTS

Publication Acknowledgments

The Aga Khan Trust for Culture would like to acknowledge the teams and individuals who have made this publication on the Historic Cities Programme a captivating story and a fulfilling project of its own. Some of these individuals planned the publication, some contributed essays, and others contributed to the case studies, which, alone, represent many person-years of dedication and labour.

AKTC GENEVA

Luis Monreal, General Manager
Shiraz Allibhai, Assistant to the General Manager
Nicholas Bulloch, Director Finance
William O'Reilly, Librarian

AKTC'S HISTORIC CITIES PROGRAMME (HCP)

Cameron Rashti, Director
Jurjen van der Tas, Deputy Director
Jeff Allen, Project Planner/Communications Consultant
Christophe Bouleau, Conservation Officer
Roberto Fabbro, Project Manager
Martin Ovenden, Parks and Historic Sites Manager
Robert Pilbeam, Architectural Technical Coordinator
Karim Rahemtulla, Special Projects Manager
Ibai Rigby, Project Coordinator
Francesco Siravo, Senior Programme Officer
Anthony Steel, Master Stone Conservator

AKTC'S SERVICE COMPANIES/ PROJECT OFFICES

Saiffulah Baig, Deputy CEO, Aga Khan Cultural Services (Pakistan)

Salman Beg, CEO, Aga Khan Cultural Services (Pakistan)
Sherif Erian, CEO, Aga Khan Cultural Services (Egypt)
Ali Esmaiel, CEO, Aga Khan Cultural Services (Syria)
Masood Khan, Technical Director, Aga Khan Cultural Services (Pakistan)
Ajmal Maiwandi, CEO, Aga Khan Cultural Services (Afghanistan)
Ratish Nanda, Project Director, AKTC India Office

The teams of in-house professionals and consultants working under the direction of the above individuals have prepared painstakingly detailed drawings and accounts of the projects presented and have had first-hand knowledge of the projects during planning and implementation. Input received from Thierry Grandin and Zeina Hirbli (Syria), Dina Bakhoum (Egypt) and Anthony Wain (South Africa) is additionally cited.

AKTC WOULD LIKE TO ACKNOWLEDGE THE CONTRIBUTION OF PRIOR MEMBERS OF ITS STAFF, INCLUDING

Stefano Bianca, Director, HCP, 1992–2006
Amin Bapoo, CEO, AKCS (Zanzibar) 2005–2007
Stephen Battle, Project Officer, HCP, 1998–2008
Karel Bos, CEO, AKTC (Afghanistan) 2002–2003
Mohamed el Mikawi, CEO, AKCS (Egypt) 2002–2008
Osama Hambazaza, CEO, AKCS (Egypt) 1997–2002
Shehin Hirani, COO, AKCS (Zanzibar), 1998–2003
Essa Khan, CEO, AKCS (Pakistan) 1992–2002

Jolyon Leslie, CEO, AKTC (Afghanistan) 2004–2009

AKDN RESIDENT REPRESENTATIVES

The Trust would also like to thank collectively the AKDN Resident Representatives in countries in which HCP initiatives are situated:
Aziz Bhaloo, Kenya
Amin Kurji, Tanzania/Zanzibar
Ali Mawji, Afghanistan
Munir Merali, Tajikistan
Ferid Nandjee, Mali
Mohamed Seifou, Syria

HCP PROJECT TECHNICAL TEAMS AND MAIN CONSULTANTS

AKTC and the Historic Cities Programme wish they could list individually the many specialist consultants, staff, contractors and suppliers who have contributed to the realization of the projects presented in this publication. Many such individuals or firms are acknowledged in existing AKTC publications and brochures on specific countries or initiatives. The work in this publication should make manifest the fact that the regeneration of historic cities and sites is a collaborative effort, spanning significant periods of time and relying on a very wide base of involvement by public and private sectors. The Historic Cities Programme would like to acknowledge and thank all those who have been associated with its initiatives, past and present.

PUBLICATION PRODUCTION ACKNOWLEDGMENTS

This publication benefited from a true collaboration between Prestel publisher's art department and a number of individuals under AKTC's direction who interacted with project teams, photographers, the editor and essay and case study authors, to achieve the fine balance required for a publication which combines cultural, socio-economic and urban and architectural concerns.

The Trust would like to thank, in particular, the publishing team:

Curt Holtz, Editor (Prestel)

Harriet Graham, Copy-Editor (Prestel)

Carsten Wolff, Thomas Rott and Lilly Zeiler (Fine German Design), Graphic Designers.

Working closely with Prestel on AKTC's behalf, Jeff Allen and Shiraz Allibhai oversaw the publication and coordinated the graphics, text and case study materials across the project offices and with consultants; Ibai Rigby, Elisa Trapani and Rob Pilbeam provided enhancement and standardization of architectural drawings across case studies; William O'Reilly developed the captions for the publication.

PHOTOGRAPHY

A publication on a range of sites and communities as dispersed as those featured in this publication could not succeed without a parallel set of high-resolution, professional photography to complete the story. The photographs displayed in this publication come from a wide array of sources, some more historic and some recent.

In 2009 and 2010, Christian Richters, one of the foremost architectural photographers in the world, was commissioned to photograph all the sites that were intended to be included in the case studies.

ILLUSTRATIONS

The underlying architectural drawings throughout this publication derive from years of dedicated effort by in-house professionals and consultants working on the individual projects. The case study materials, in the first instance, were prepared by the AKTC project teams and were supplemented as noted by a team in the main office. In all known instances, these drawings represent original and field-based surveys and designs originating from AKTC's initiatives on the sites in question and thus represent a major investment of time and care. These drawings present an important set of assets that the Trust is pleased to add to the intellectual capital of the already impressive heritage of these sites.

The editor wishes to thank Shiraz Allibhai and Jeff Allen for their very significant contributions to this book.

For further information about the programmes and projects of the Aga Khan Trust for Culture and the Aga Khan Development Network, please consult www.akdn.org.

Photo and Illustration Credits

IMPRINT

© Prestel Verlag, Munich · London · New York
and the Aga Khan Trust for Culture, Geneva, 2011

All images and drawings (with the exception of those on pp. Cover, 12, 13, 25, 166-167) are copyright of the Aga Khan Trust for Culture.

Front Cover: A sweeping view over the lush, green garden around Humayun's Tomb, with the city of Delhi in the background. The garden was restored by AKTC in 2002–03, while the Tomb is under restoration and will be completed in 2012.

Frontispiece: View of the restored Khayrbek complex in Darb al-Ahmar, Cairo.

Prestel Verlag, Munich
A member of Verlagsgruppe Random House GmbH

Prestel Verlag
Neumarkter Strasse 28
81673 Munich
Tel. +49 (0) 89 4136 - 0
Fax +49 (0) 89 4136 - 2335

Prestel Publishing Ltd.
4 Bloomsbury Place
London WC1A 2QA
Tel. +44 (0) 20 7323 - 5004
Fax +44 (0) 20 7636 - 8004

Prestel Publishing
900 Broadway, Suite 603
New York, NY 10003
Tel. +1 (212) 995 - 2720
Fax +1 (212) 995 - 2733

www.prestel.com

Library of Congress Control Number: 2010926504

The British Library Cataloguing-in-Publication Data:
a catalogue record for this book is available from the British Library;
Deutsche Nationalbibliothek holds a record of this publication in
the Deutsche Nationalbibliografie; detailed bibliographical data can be
found under: http://dnb.d-nb.de.

Prestel books are available worldwide. Please contact your nearest
bookseller or one of the above addresses for information concerning
your local distributor.

Editorial direction: Curt Holtz
Copy-editing: Harriet Graham, Turin
Design and layout: FINE GERMAN DESIGN, Frankfurt
Carsten Wolff, Thomas Rott, Nicole Lange, Lilly Zeiler
Production: Nele Krüger
Art direction: Cilly Klotz
Photolithography: Reproline mediateam, Munich
Printing and binding: Firmengruppe APPL, aprinta druck, Wemding

Verlagsgruppe Random House FSC-DEU-0100
The FSC-certified paper LuxoSamt has been
supplied by Sappi, Biberist, Switzerland.

ISBN 978-3-7913-4406-5